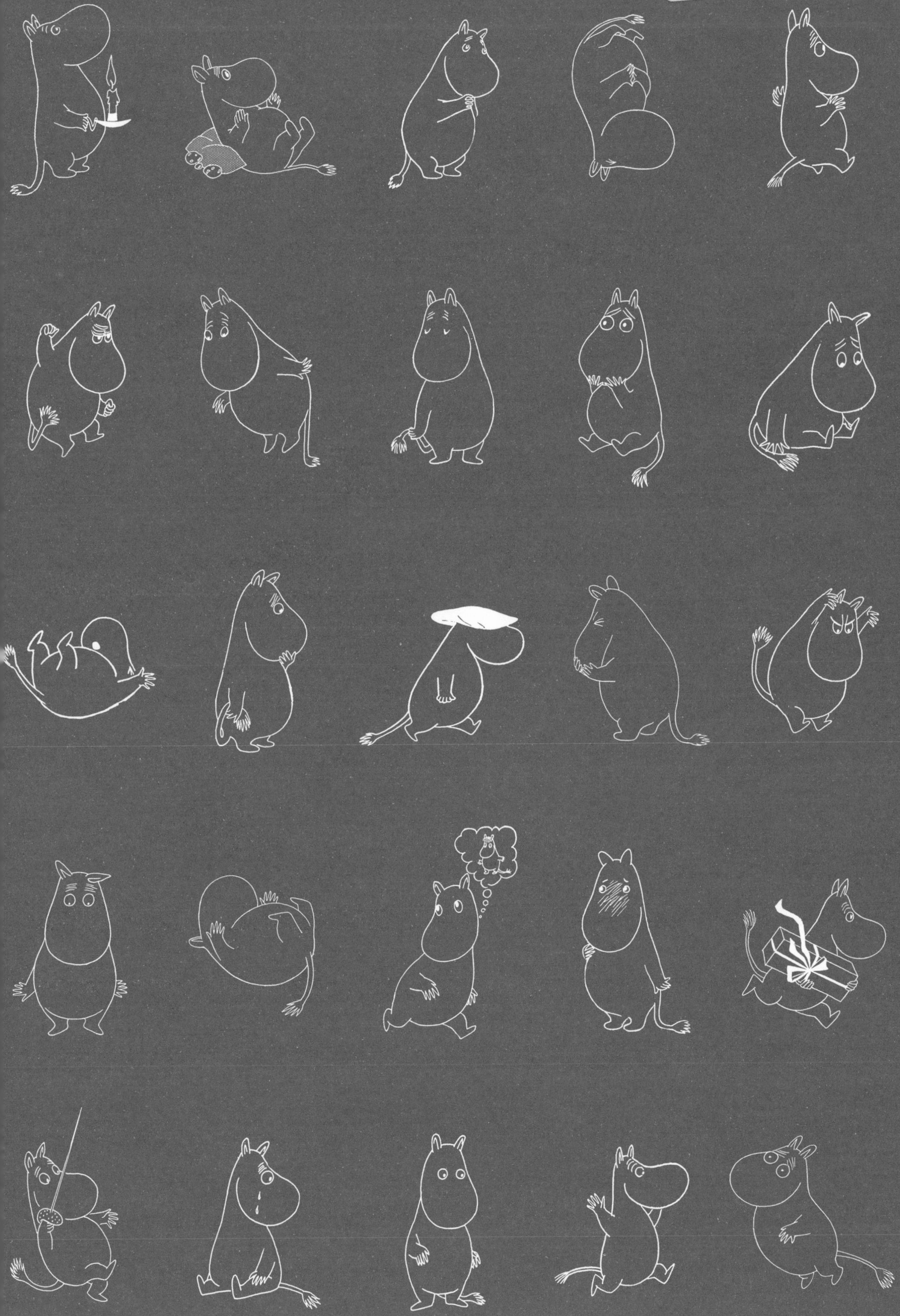

THE COMPLETE TOVE JANSSON

MOOMIN

COMIC STRIP

Drawn & Quarterly

MONTRÉAL

Also available in the *Moomin* series:
Moomin: The Complete Tove Jansson Comic Strip books 1–5
Moomin: The Complete Lars Jansson Comic Strip books 6–10
Moomin Deluxe: Volume One
Moomin Deluxe: Volume Two
The Book About Moomin, Mymble and Little My
Who Will Comfort Toffle?
The Moomins and the Great Flood
The Dangerous Journey: A Tale of Moomin Valley
Moomin's Winter Follies
Moominvalley Turns Jungle
Moomin Falls in Love
Moomin Builds a House
Moomin and the Comet
Moomin and the Sea
Moomin's Desert Island
Moomin and the Golden Tail
Moomin on the Riviera
Moomin and the Martians
Moomin and the Brigands
Moomin Begins a New Life
Moomin and Family Life
Club Life in Moominvalley
Moominmamma's Maid
Moomin Winter

drawnandquarterly.com

Moomin Book Two: The Complete Tove Jansson Comic Strip by Tove Jansson
ISBN 978-1-89729-919-7
First edition: September 2007; Second printing: January 2008; Third printing: October 2008; Fourth printing: September 2011; Fifth printing: February 2013; Sixth printing: May 2015; Seventh printing: June 2021.
Printed in China
10 9 8 7

Cataloguing data available from Library and Archives Canada

Published in the USA by Drawn & Quarterly,
a client publisher of
Farrar, Straus & Giroux

Published in Canada by Drawn & Quarterly,
a client publisher of
Raincoast Books

Published in the United Kingdom by Drawn & Quarterly,
a client publisher of
Publishers Group UK

MOOMIN

VOLUME TWO

5. Moomin's Winter Follies

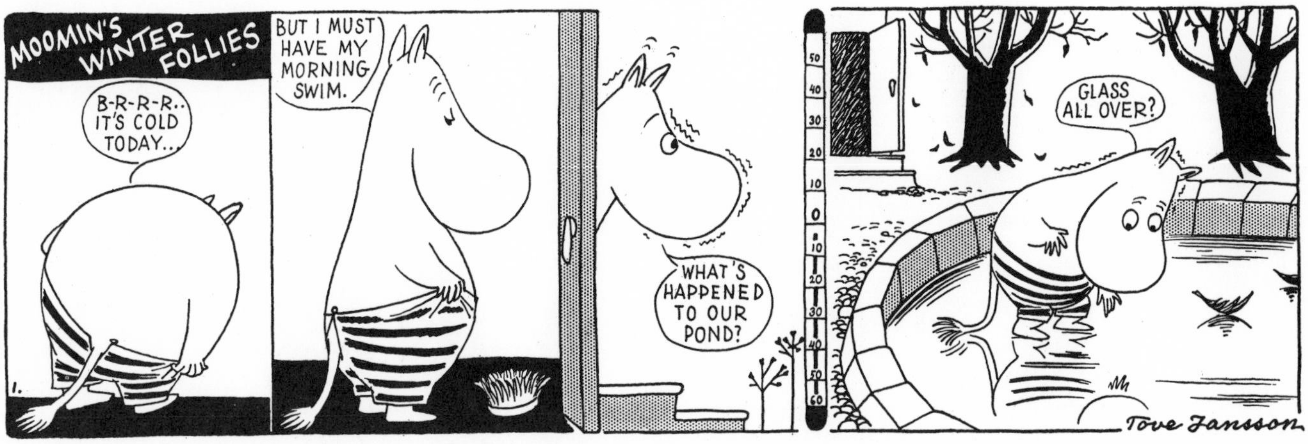
MOOMIN'S WINTER FOLLIES
B-R-R-R.. IT'S COLD TODAY..
BUT I MUST HAVE MY MORNING SWIM.
WHAT'S HAPPENED TO OUR POND?
GLASS ALL OVER?
Tove Jansson

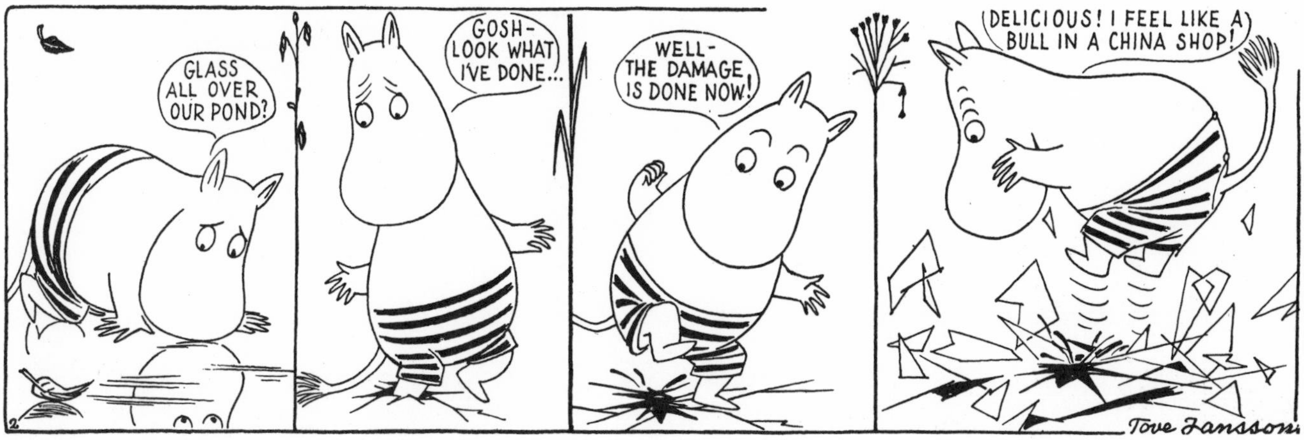
GLASS ALL OVER OUR POND?
GOSH- LOOK WHAT I'VE DONE...
WELL- THE DAMAGE IS DONE NOW!
DELICIOUS! I FEEL LIKE A BULL IN A CHINA SHOP!
Tove Jansson

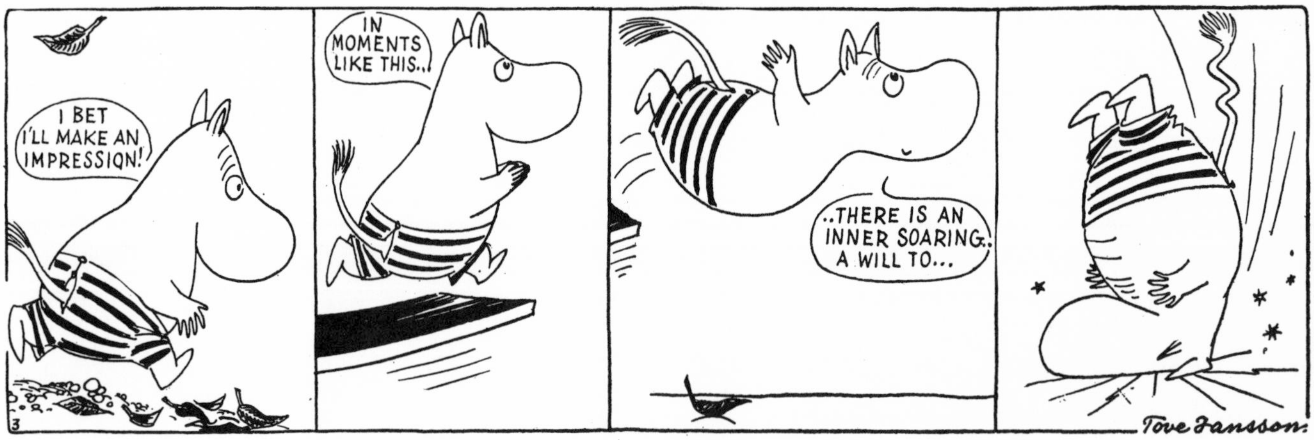
3
I BET I'LL MAKE AN IMPRESSION!
IN MOMENTS LIKE THIS..
..THERE IS AN INNER SOARING.. A WILL TO...
Tove Jansson

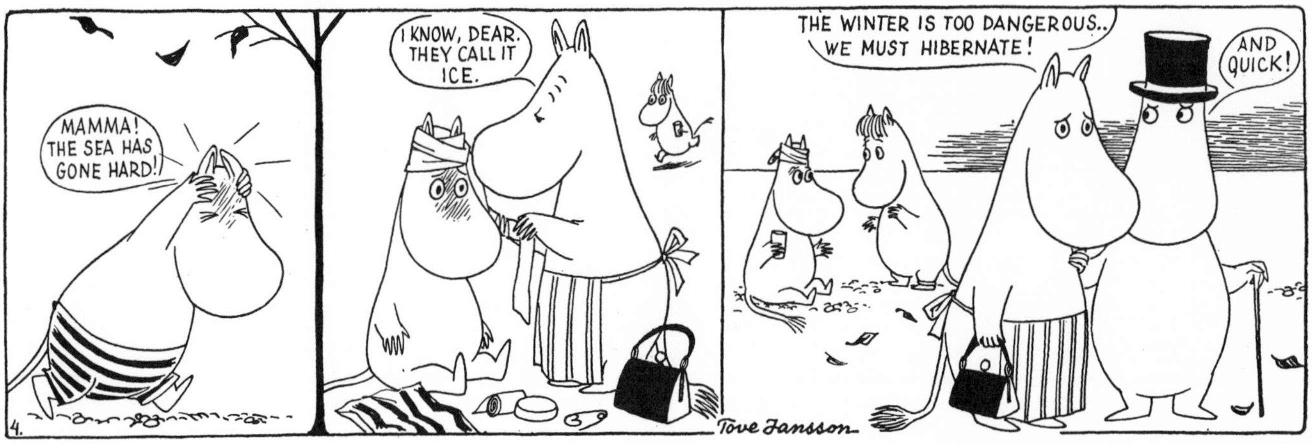
4.
MAMMA! THE SEA HAS GONE HARD!
I KNOW, DEAR. THEY CALL IT ICE.
THE WINTER IS TOO DANGEROUS.. WE MUST HIBERNATE!
AND QUICK!
Tove Jansson

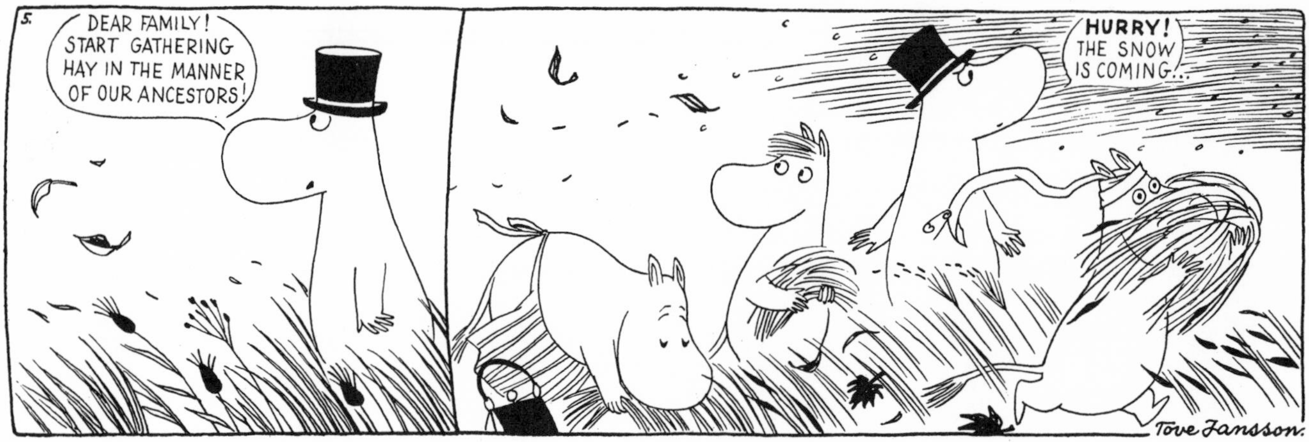
5.
DEAR FAMILY! START GATHERING HAY IN THE MANNER OF OUR ANCESTORS!
HURRY! THE SNOW IS COMING...
Tove Jansson

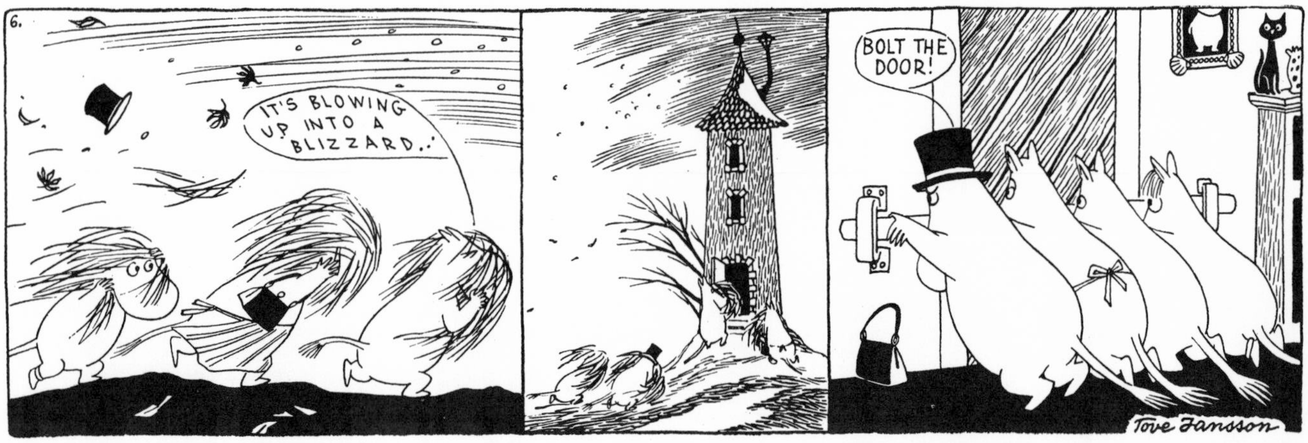
6.
IT'S BLOWING UP INTO A BLIZZARD..
BOLT THE DOOR!
Tove Jansson

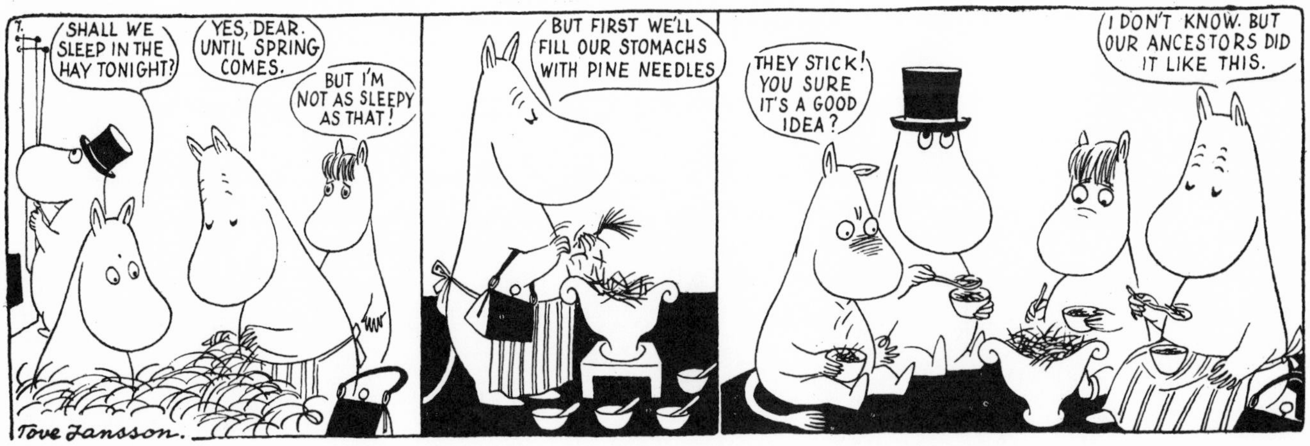
7.
SHALL WE SLEEP IN THE HAY TONIGHT?
YES, DEAR. UNTIL SPRING COMES.
BUT I'M NOT AS SLEEPY AS THAT!
BUT FIRST WE'LL FILL OUR STOMACHS WITH PINE NEEDLES
THEY STICK! YOU SURE IT'S A GOOD IDEA?
I DON'T KNOW. BUT OUR ANCESTORS DID IT LIKE THIS.
Tove Jansson.

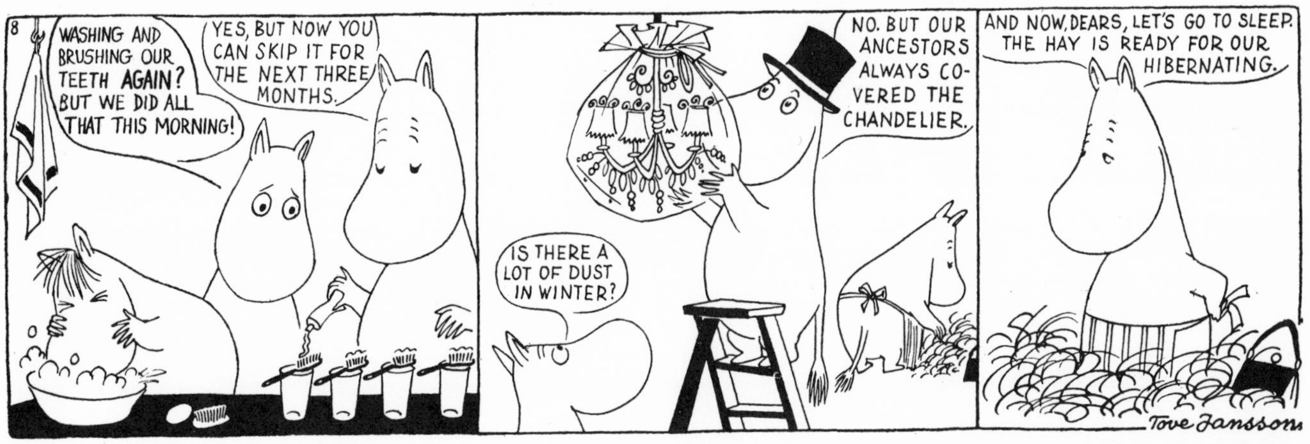
8
WASHING AND BRUSHING OUR TEETH AGAIN? BUT WE DID ALL THAT THIS MORNING!
YES, BUT NOW YOU CAN SKIP IT FOR THE NEXT THREE MONTHS.
IS THERE A LOT OF DUST IN WINTER?
NO. BUT OUR ANCESTORS ALWAYS COVERED THE CHANDELIER.
AND NOW, DEARS, LET'S GO TO SLEEP. THE HAY IS READY FOR OUR HIBERNATING.
Tove Jansson.

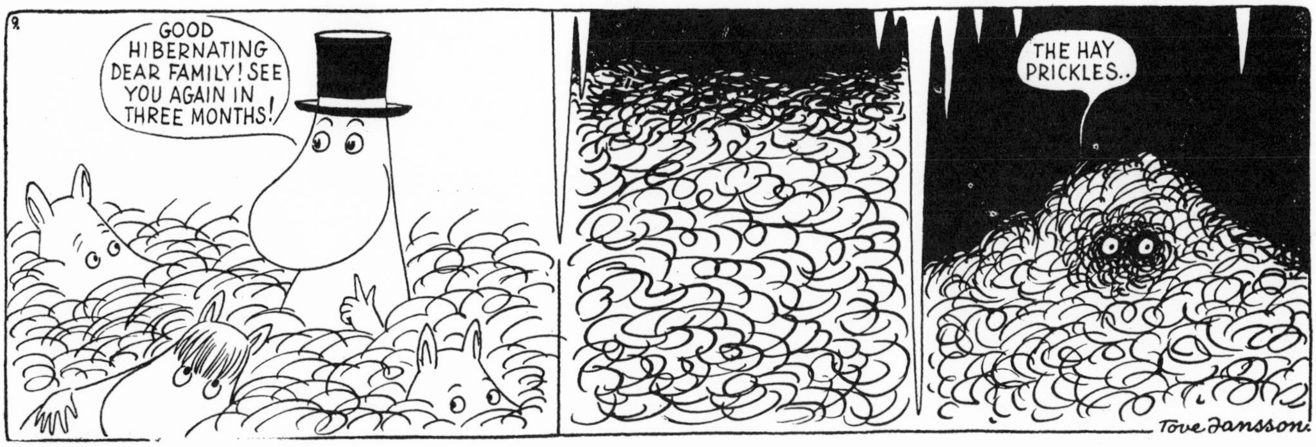
9.
GOOD HIBERNATING DEAR FAMILY! SEE YOU AGAIN IN THREE MONTHS!
THE HAY PRICKLES..
Tove Jansson.

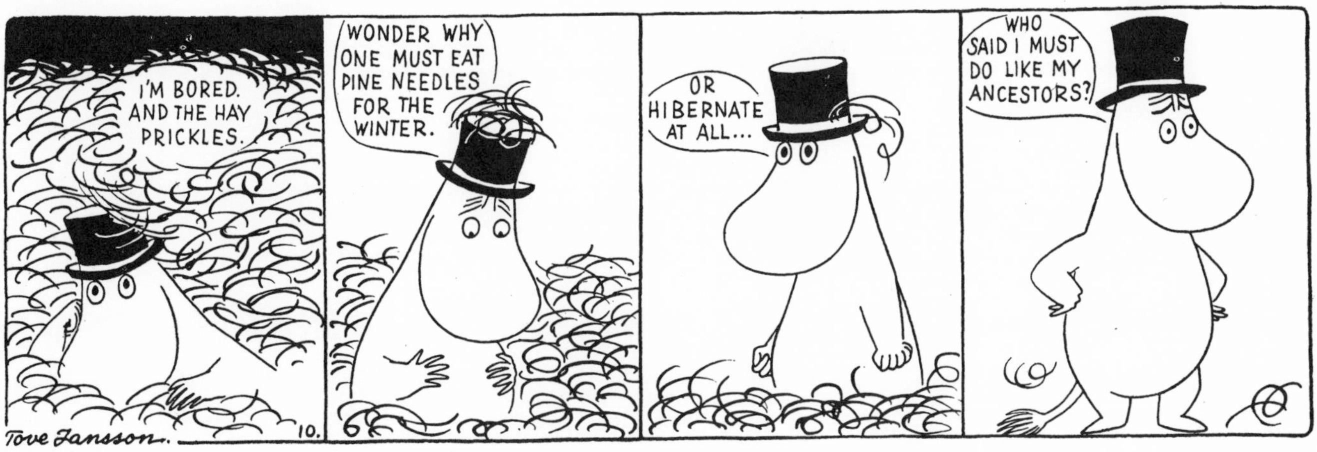
I'M BORED. AND THE HAY PRICKLES.
WONDER WHY ONE MUST EAT PINE NEEDLES FOR THE WINTER.
OR HIBERNATE AT ALL...
WHO SAID I MUST DO LIKE MY ANCESTORS?
Tove Jansson.
10.

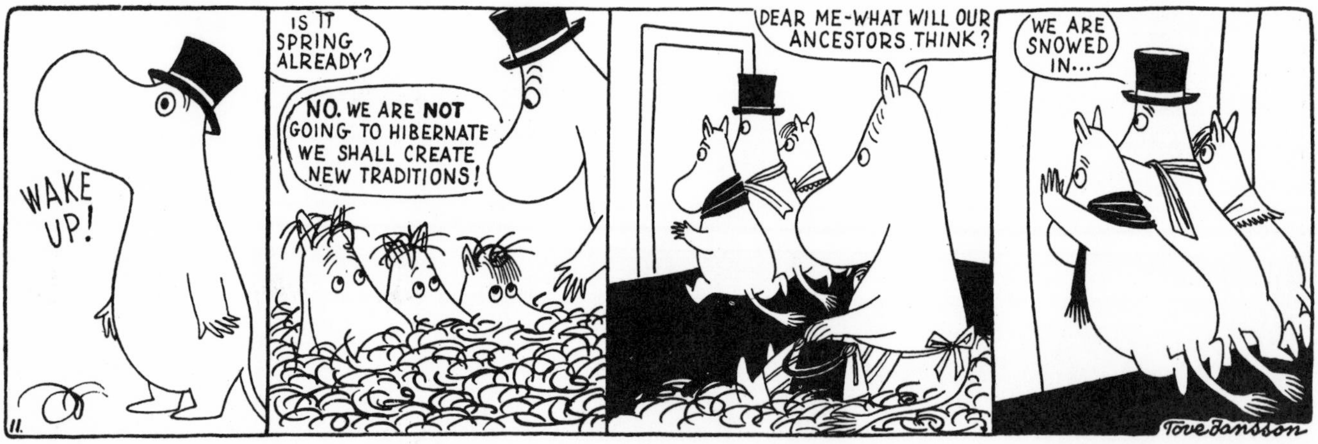
11.
WAKE UP!
IS IT SPRING ALREADY?
NO. WE ARE NOT GOING TO HIBERNATE WE SHALL CREATE NEW TRADITIONS!
DEAR ME-WHAT WILL OUR ANCESTORS THINK?
WE ARE SNOWED IN...
Tove Jansson

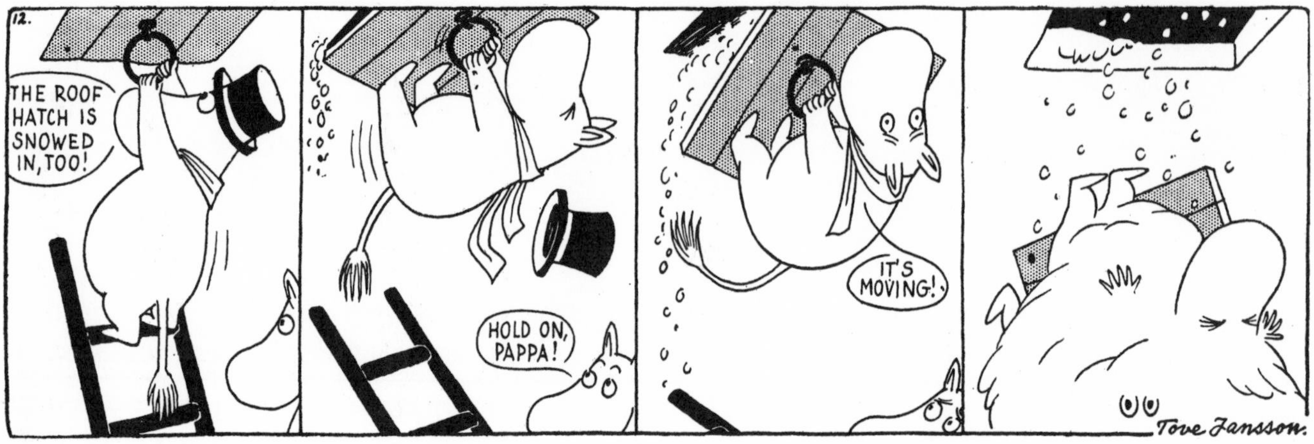
12.
THE ROOF HATCH IS SNOWED IN, TOO!
HOLD ON, PAPPA!
IT'S MOVING!
Tove Jansson.

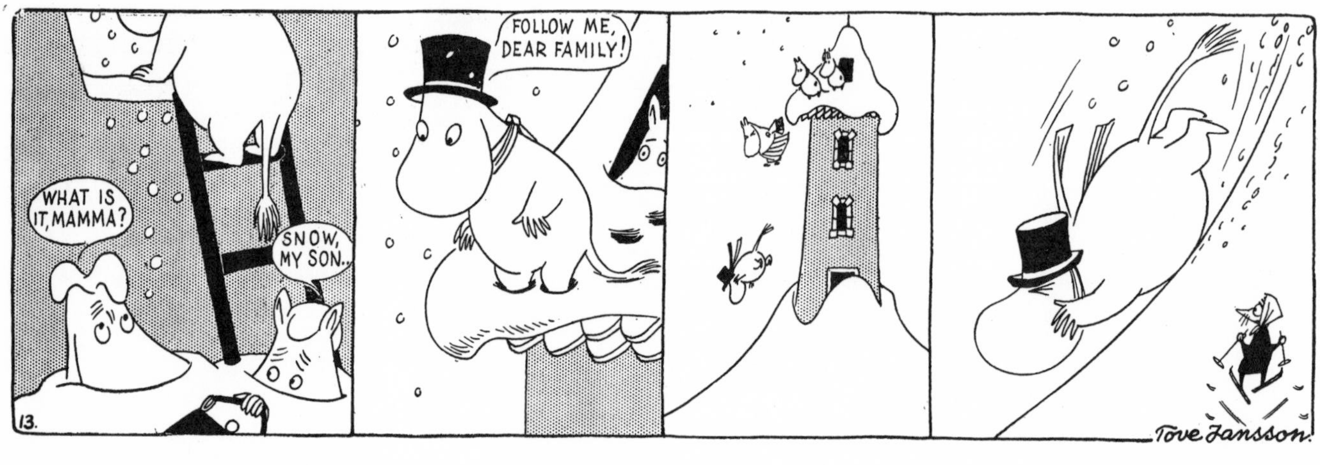
13.
WHAT IS IT, MAMMA?
SNOW, MY SON..
FOLLOW ME, DEAR FAMILY!
Tove Jansson.

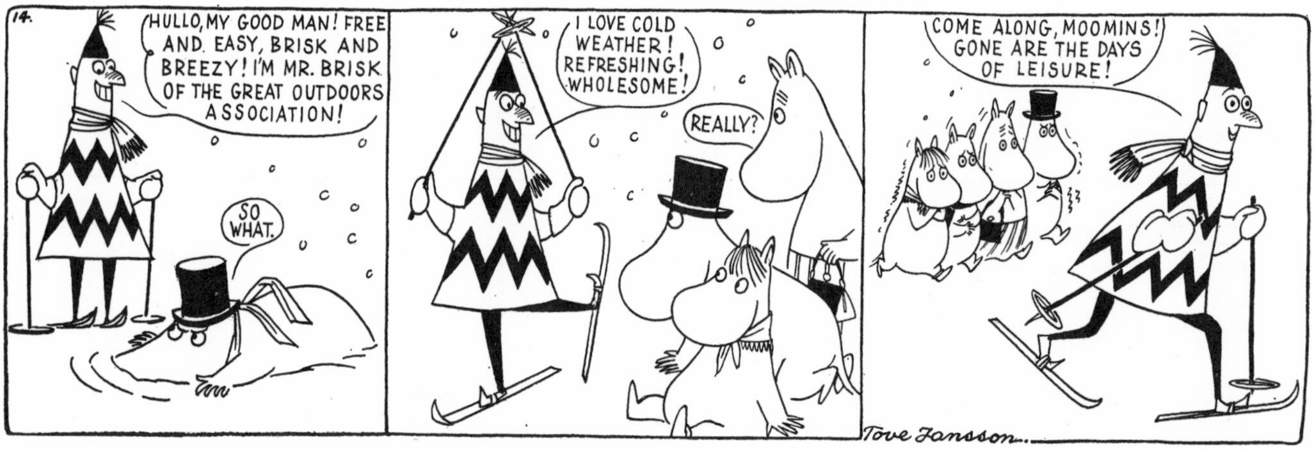
14.
HULLO, MY GOOD MAN! FREE AND. EASY, BRISK AND BREEZY! I'M MR. BRISK OF THE GREAT OUTDOORS ASSOCIATION!
SO WHAT.
I LOVE COLD WEATHER! REFRESHING! WHOLESOME!
REALLY?
COME ALONG, MOOMINS! GONE ARE THE DAYS OF LEISURE!
Tove Jansson..

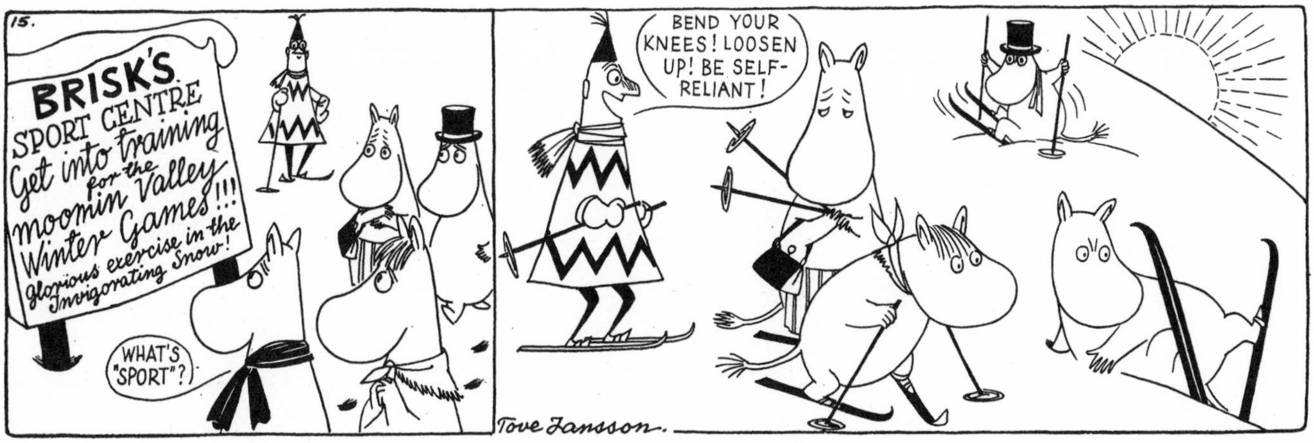
15.
BRISK'S SPORT CENTRE
Get into training for the moomin Valley Winter Games!!!
Glorious exercise in the Invigorating Snow!
WHAT'S "SPORT"?
BEND YOUR KNEES! LOOSEN UP! BE SELF-RELIANT!
Tove Jansson.

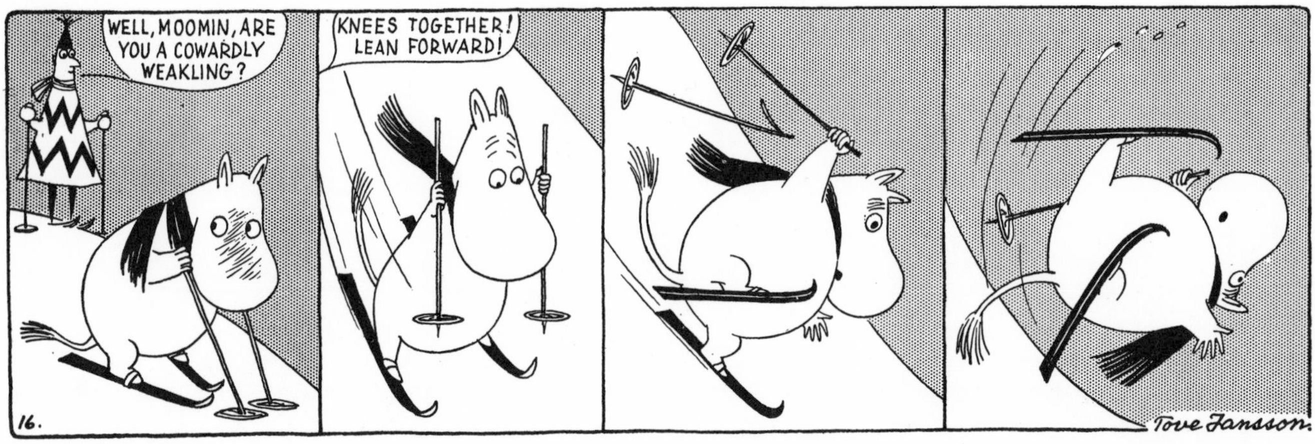
WELL, MOOMIN, ARE YOU A COWARDLY WEAKLING?
16.
KNEES TOGETHER! LEAN FORWARD!
Tove Jansson.

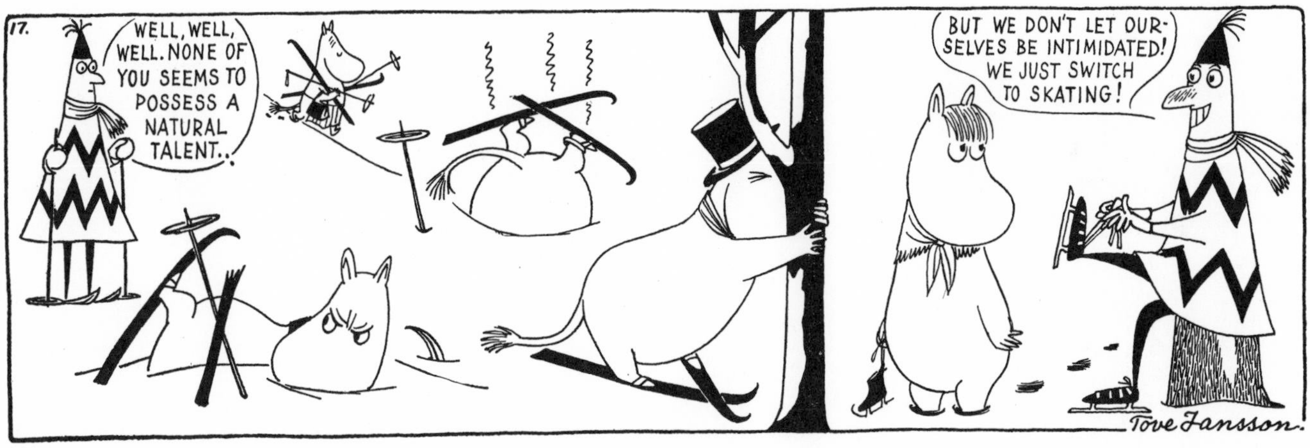
17.
WELL, WELL, WELL. NONE OF YOU SEEMS TO POSSESS A NATURAL TALENT..
BUT WE DON'T LET OURSELVES BE INTIMIDATED! WE JUST SWITCH TO SKATING!
Tove Jansson.

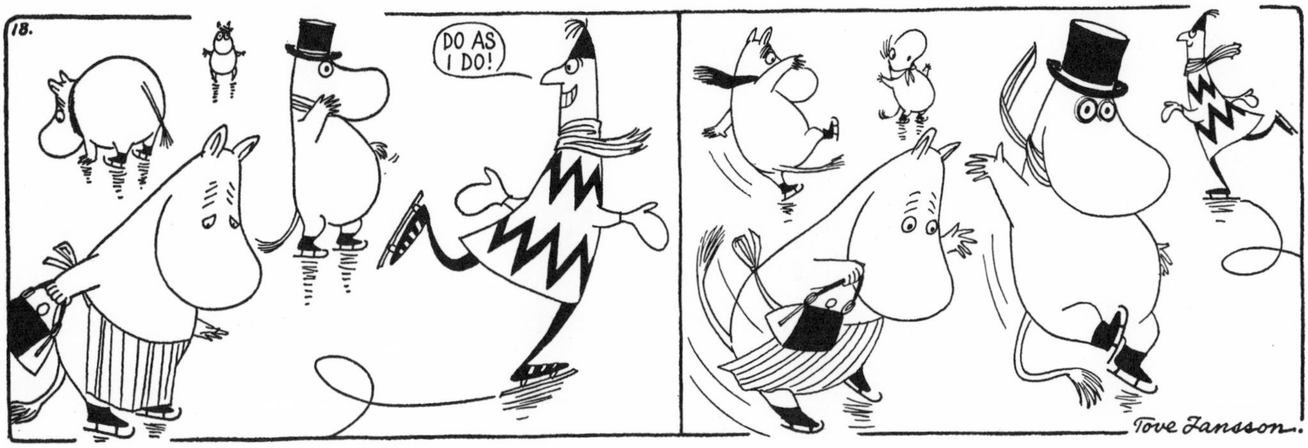
18.
DO AS I DO!
Tove Jansson.

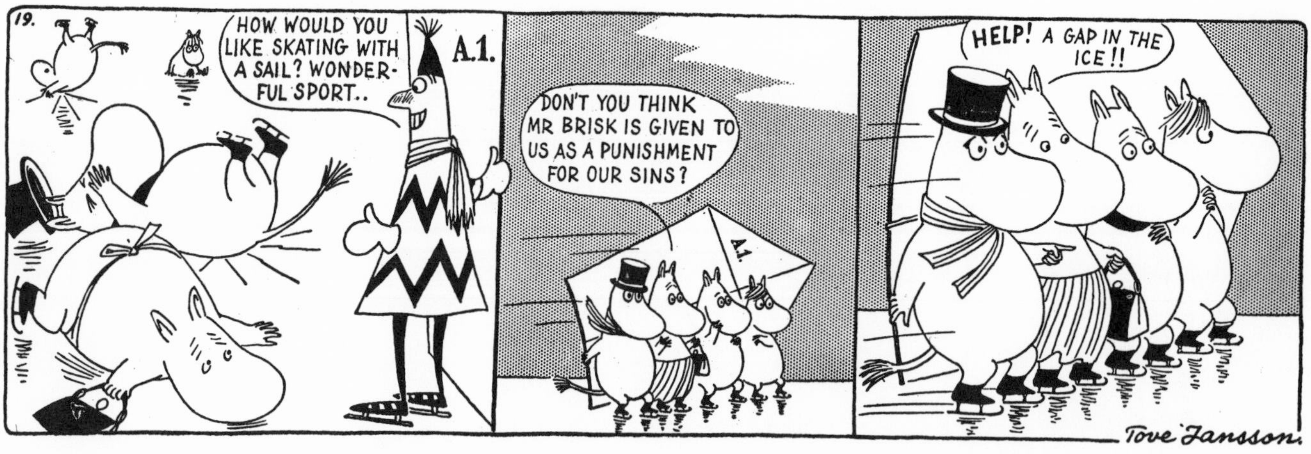
19.
HOW WOULD YOU LIKE SKATING WITH A SAIL? WONDERFUL SPORT..
A.1.
DON'T YOU THINK MR BRISK IS GIVEN TO US AS A PUNISHMENT FOR OUR SINS?
HELP! A GAP IN THE ICE!!
Tove Jansson

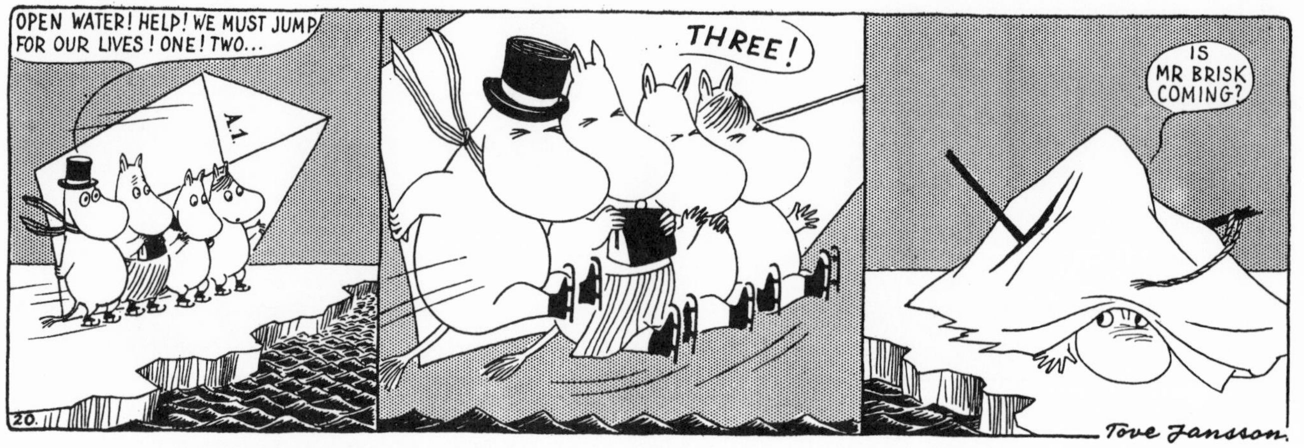
OPEN WATER! HELP! WE MUST JUMP FOR OUR LIVES! ONE! TWO...
...THREE!
IS MR BRISK COMING?
20.
Tove Jansson

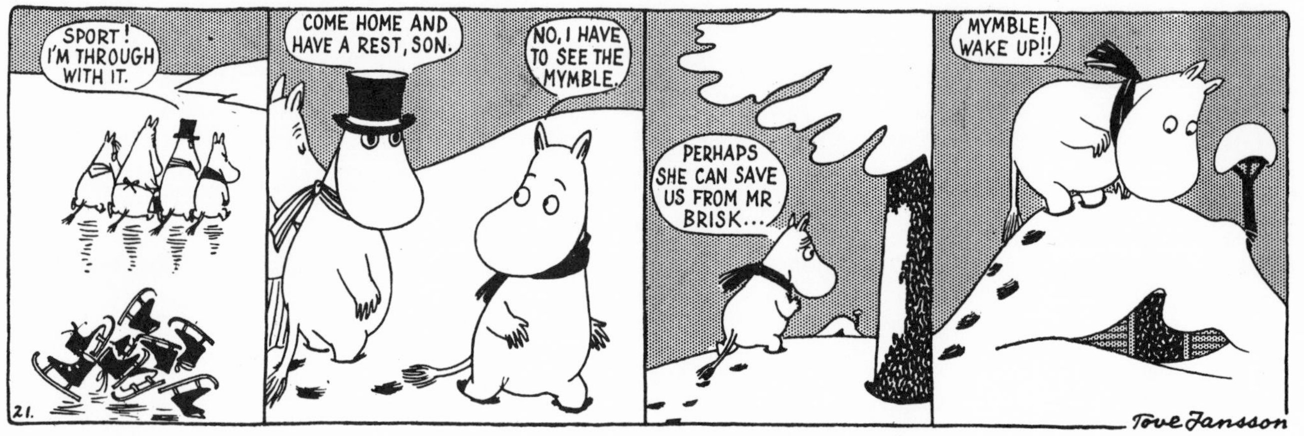
SPORT! I'M THROUGH WITH IT.
21.
COME HOME AND HAVE A REST, SON.
NO, I HAVE TO SEE THE MYMBLE.
PERHAPS SHE CAN SAVE US FROM MR BRISK...
MYMBLE! WAKE UP!!
Tove Jansson

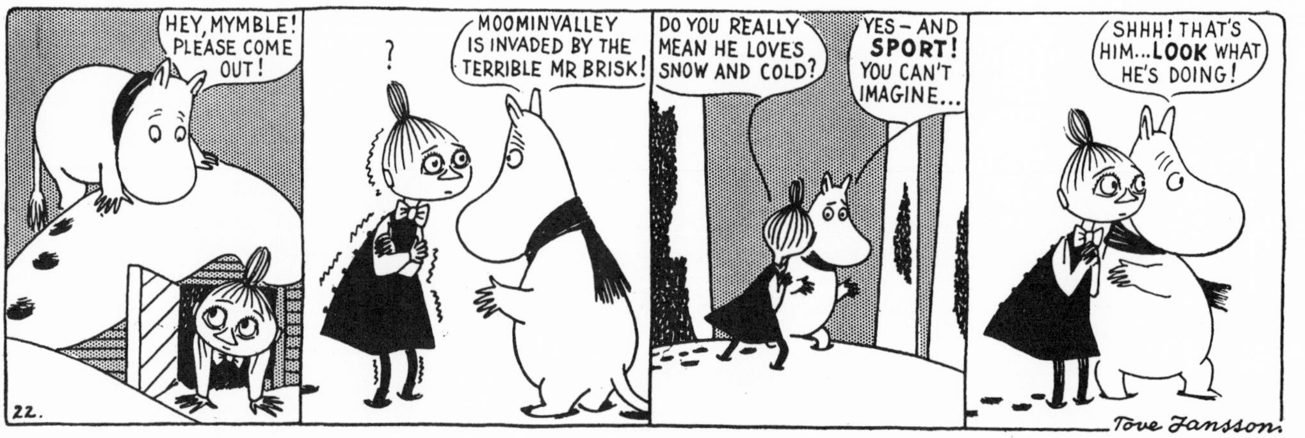
HEY, MYMBLE! PLEASE COME OUT!
22.
?
MOOMINVALLEY IS INVADED BY THE TERRIBLE MR BRISK!
DO YOU REALLY MEAN HE LOVES SNOW AND COLD?
YES – AND SPORT! YOU CAN'T IMAGINE...
SHHH! THAT'S HIM...LOOK WHAT HE'S DOING!
Tove Jansson

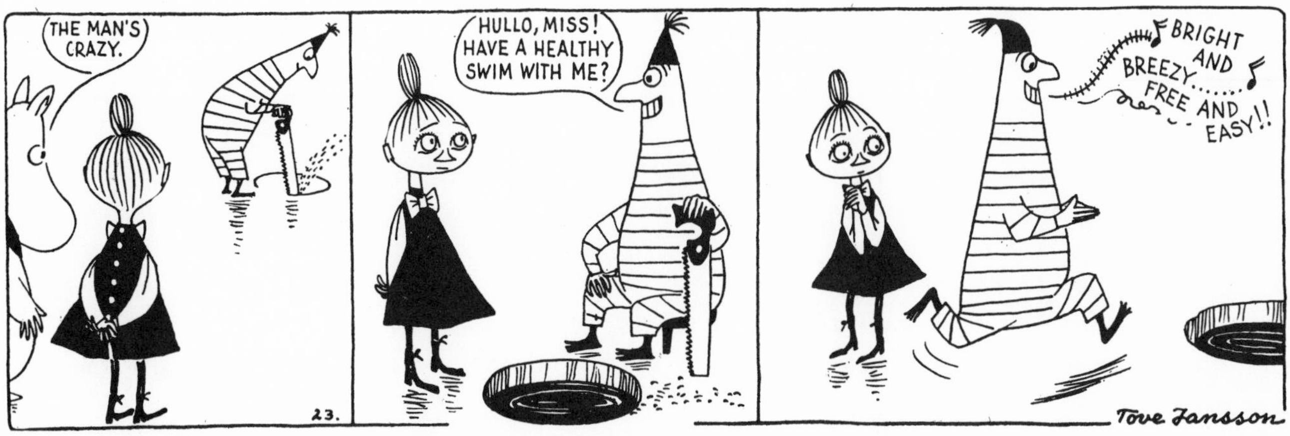
THE MAN'S CRAZY.
23.
HULLO, MISS! HAVE A HEALTHY SWIM WITH ME?
BRIGHT AND BREEZY...... FREE AND EASY!!
Tove Jansson

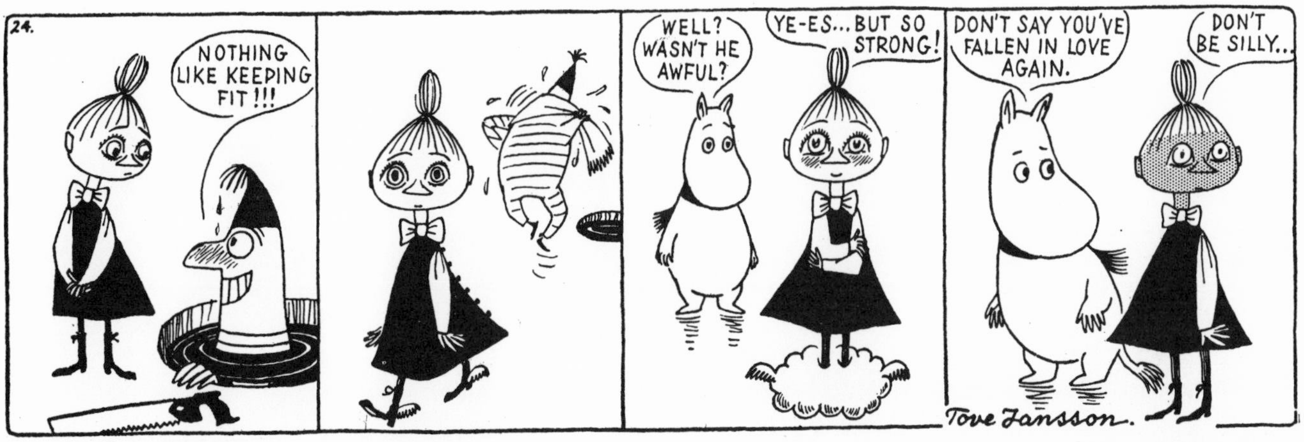
24.
NOTHING LIKE KEEPING FIT!!!
WELL? WASN'T HE AWFUL?
YE-ES... BUT SO STRONG!
DON'T SAY YOU'VE FALLEN IN LOVE AGAIN.
DON'T BE SILLY...
Tove Jansson.

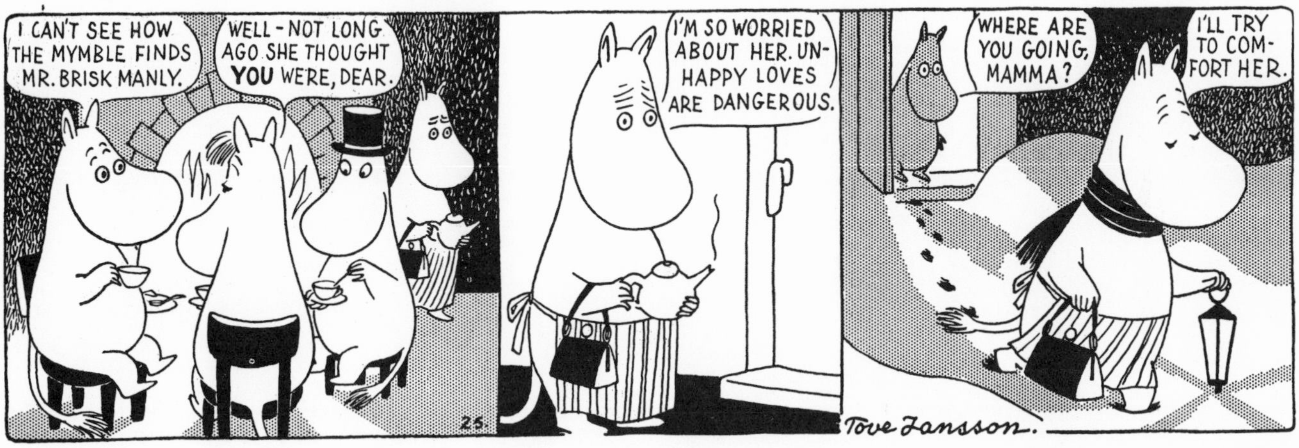
I CAN'T SEE HOW THE MYMBLE FINDS MR. BRISK MANLY.
WELL - NOT LONG AGO SHE THOUGHT **YOU** WERE, DEAR.
25.
I'M SO WORRIED ABOUT HER. UNHAPPY LOVES ARE DANGEROUS.
WHERE ARE YOU GOING, MAMMA?
I'LL TRY TO COMFORT HER.
Tove Jansson.

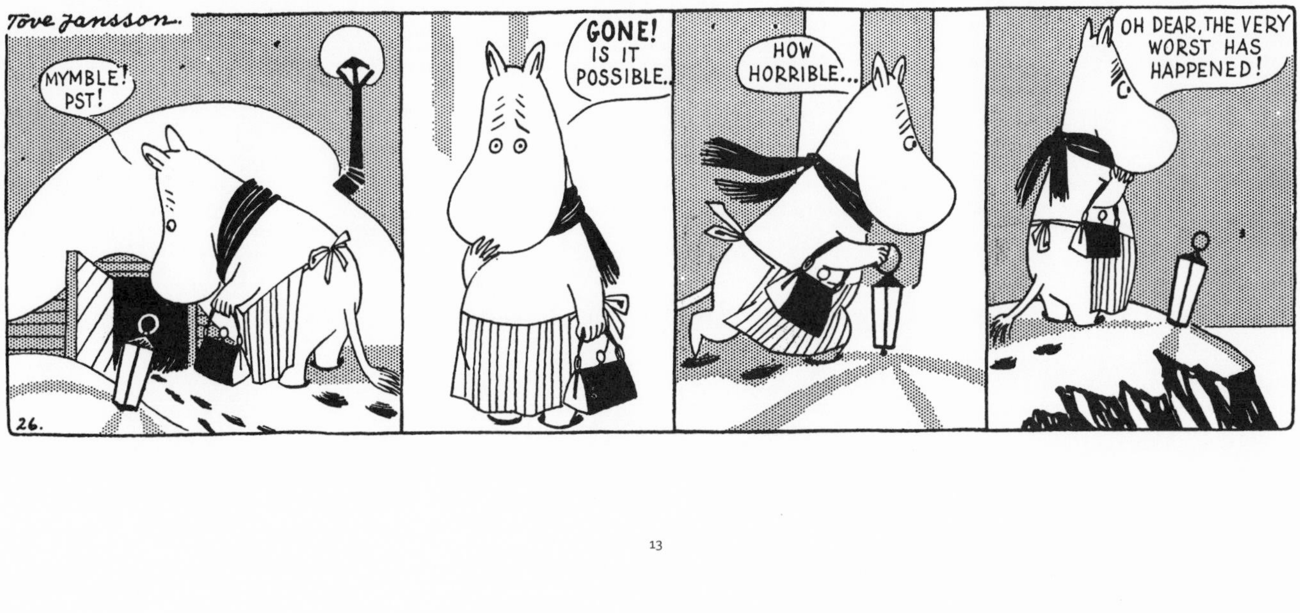
Tove Jansson.
MYMBLE! PST!
26.
GONE! IS IT POSSIBLE.
HOW HORRIBLE...
OH DEAR, THE VERY WORST HAS HAPPENED!

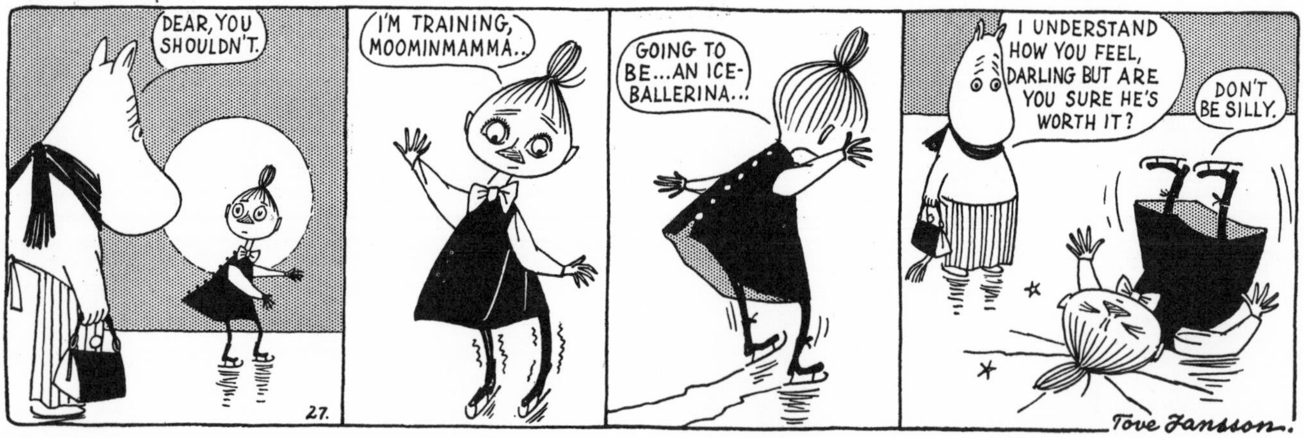
DEAR, YOU SHOULDN'T.
27.
I'M TRAINING, MOOMINMAMMA..
GOING TO BE...AN ICE-BALLERINA...
I UNDERSTAND HOW YOU FEEL, DARLING BUT ARE YOU SURE HE'S WORTH IT?
DON'T BE SILLY.
Tove Jansson.

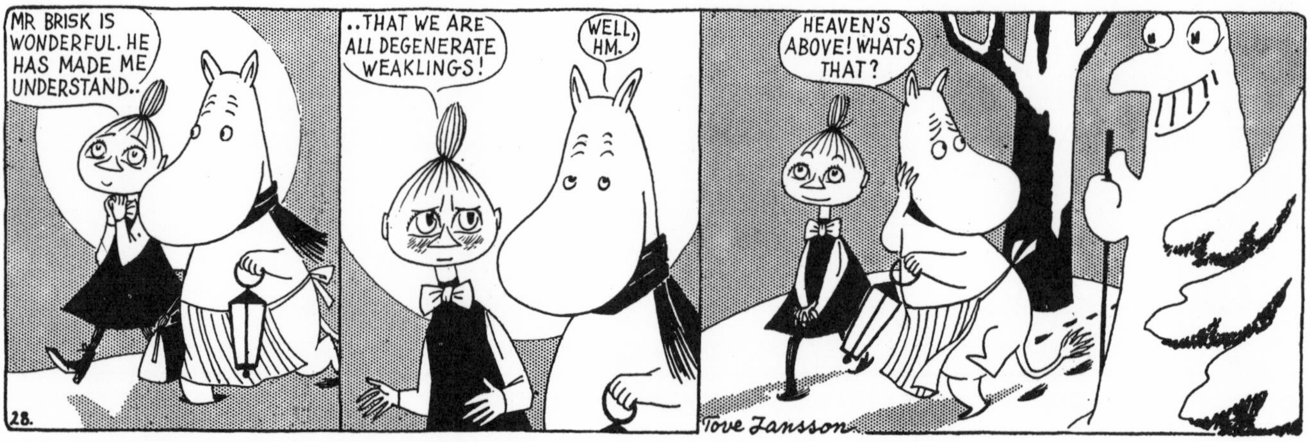
MR BRISK IS WONDERFUL. HE HAS MADE ME UNDERSTAND..
28.
..THAT WE ARE ALL DEGENERATE WEAKLINGS!
WELL, HM.
HEAVEN'S ABOVE! WHAT'S THAT?
Tove Jansson

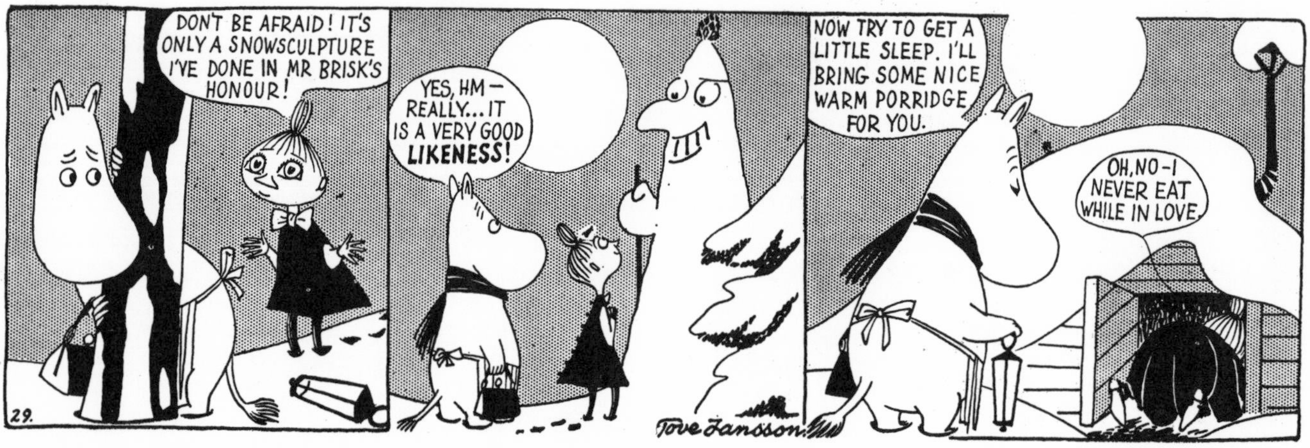
DON'T BE AFRAID! IT'S ONLY A SNOWSCULPTURE I'VE DONE IN MR BRISK'S HONOUR!
29.
YES, HM— REALLY...IT IS A VERY GOOD **LIKENESS**!
Tove Jansson
NOW TRY TO GET A LITTLE SLEEP. I'LL BRING SOME NICE WARM PORRIDGE FOR YOU.
OH, NO-I NEVER EAT WHILE IN LOVE.

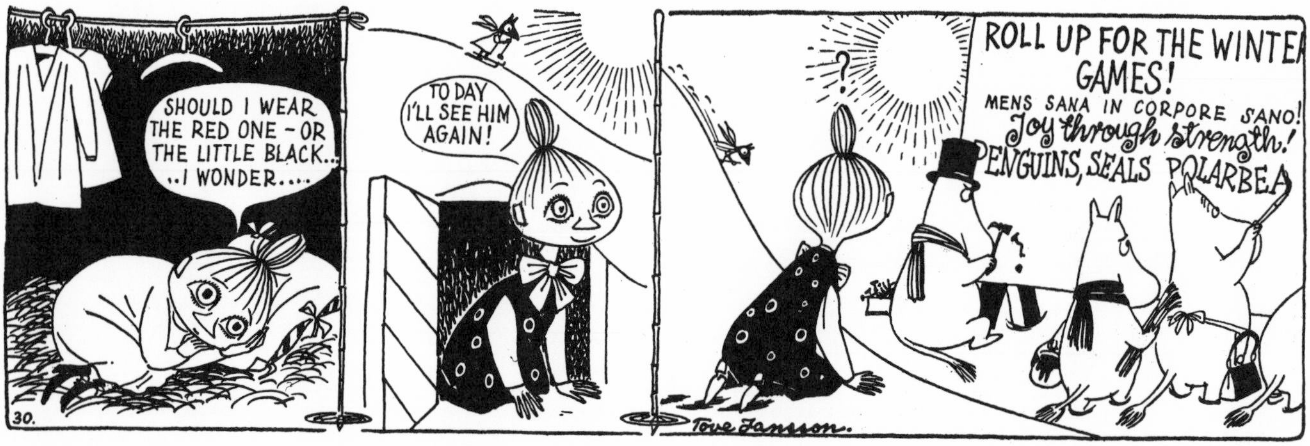
SHOULD I WEAR THE RED ONE - OR THE LITTLE BLACK... ..I WONDER....
30.
TO DAY I'LL SEE HIM AGAIN!
Tove Jansson.
?
ROLL UP FOR THE WINTE
GAMES!
MENS SANA IN CORPORE SANO!
Joy through strength!
PENGUINS, SEALS POLARBEA

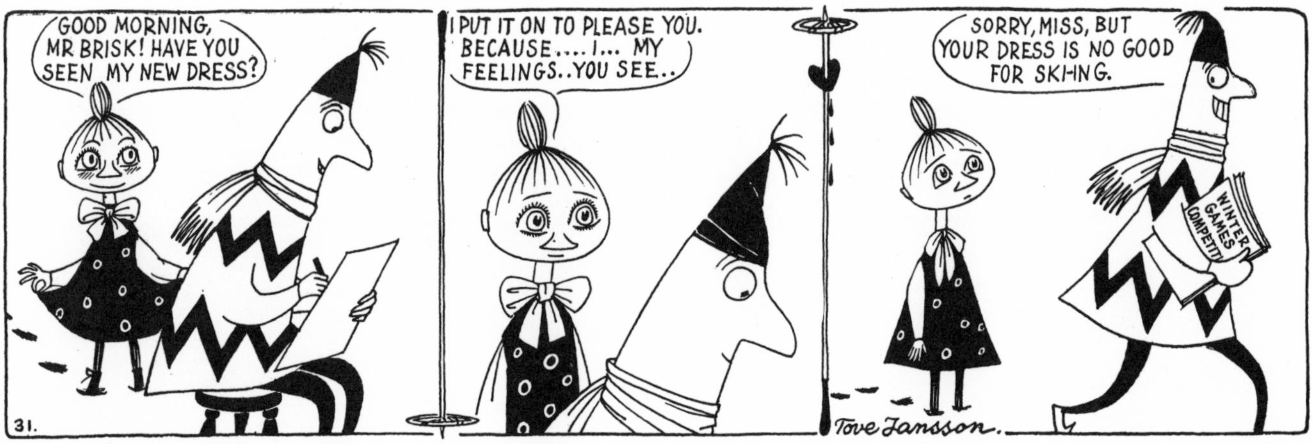
GOOD MORNING, MR BRISK! HAVE YOU SEEN MY NEW DRESS?
I PUT IT ON TO PLEASE YOU. BECAUSE.... I... MY FEELINGS..YOU SEE..
SORRY, MISS, BUT YOUR DRESS IS NO GOOD FOR SKI-ING.
WINTER GAMES COMPETITI
31.
Tove Jansson.

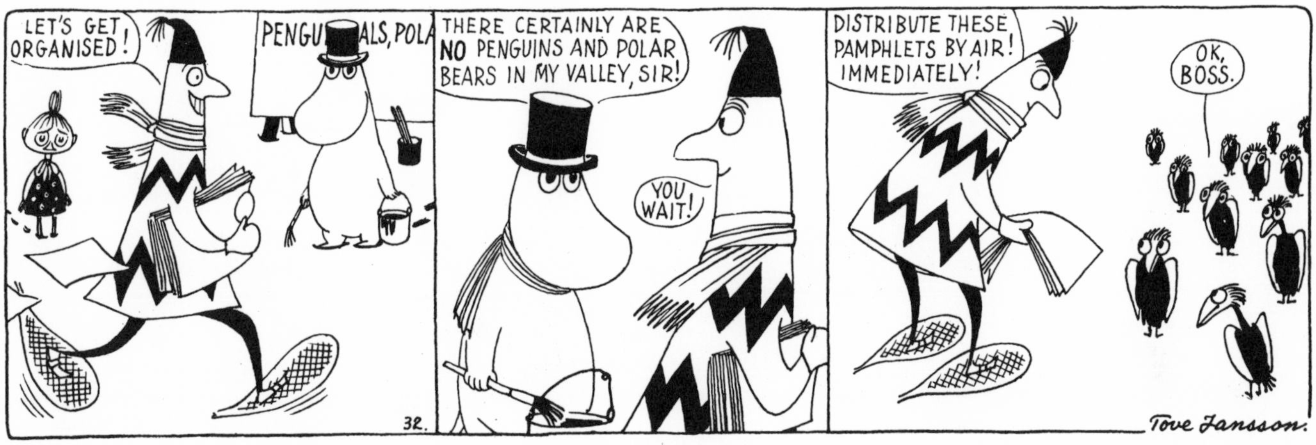
LET'S GET ORGANISED!
PENGU ALS, POLA
THERE CERTAINLY ARE **NO** PENGUINS AND POLAR BEARS IN MY VALLEY, SIR!
YOU WAIT!
32.
DISTRIBUTE THESE PAMPHLETS BY AIR! IMMEDIATELY!
OK, BOSS.
Tove Jansson.

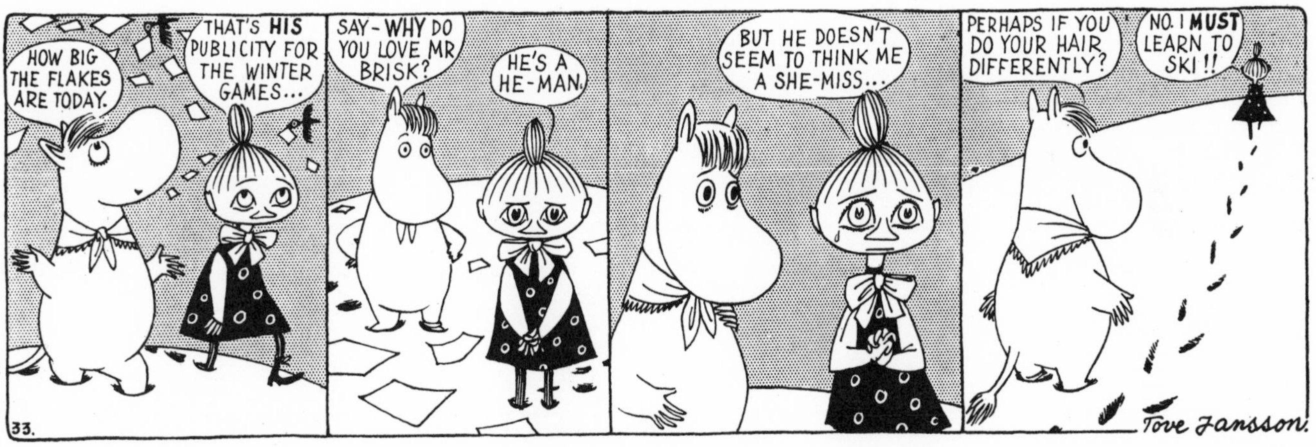
HOW BIG THE FLAKES ARE TODAY.
THAT'S **HIS** PUBLICITY FOR THE WINTER GAMES...
33.
SAY - **WHY** DO YOU LOVE MR BRISK?
HE'S A HE-MAN.
BUT HE DOESN'T SEEM TO THINK ME A SHE-MISS...
PERHAPS IF YOU DO YOUR HAIR DIFFERENTLY?
NO. I **MUST** LEARN TO SKI!!
Tove Jansson.

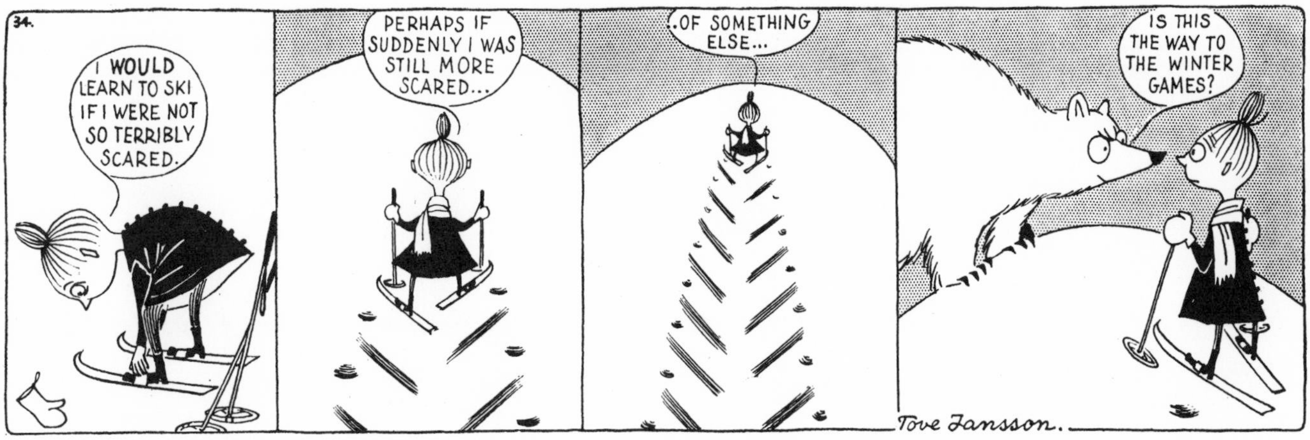
34.
I **WOULD** LEARN TO SKI IF I WERE NOT SO TERRIBLY SCARED.
PERHAPS IF SUDDENLY I WAS STILL MORE SCARED...
.OF SOMETHING ELSE...
IS THIS THE WAY TO THE WINTER GAMES?
Tove Jansson.

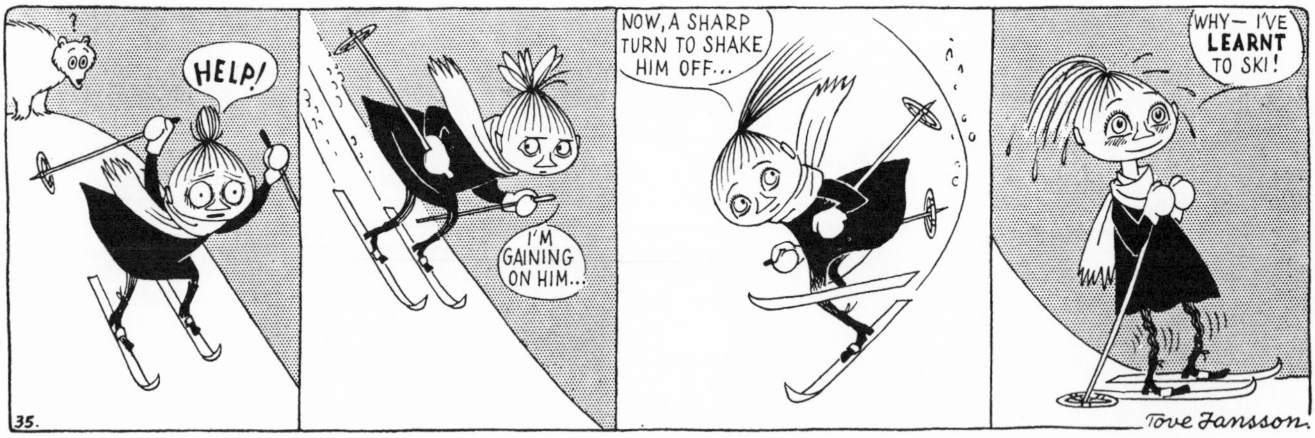
35.
?
HELP!
I'M GAINING ON HIM...
NOW, A SHARP TURN TO SHAKE HIM OFF...
WHY— I'VE **LEARNT** TO SKI!
Tove Jansson

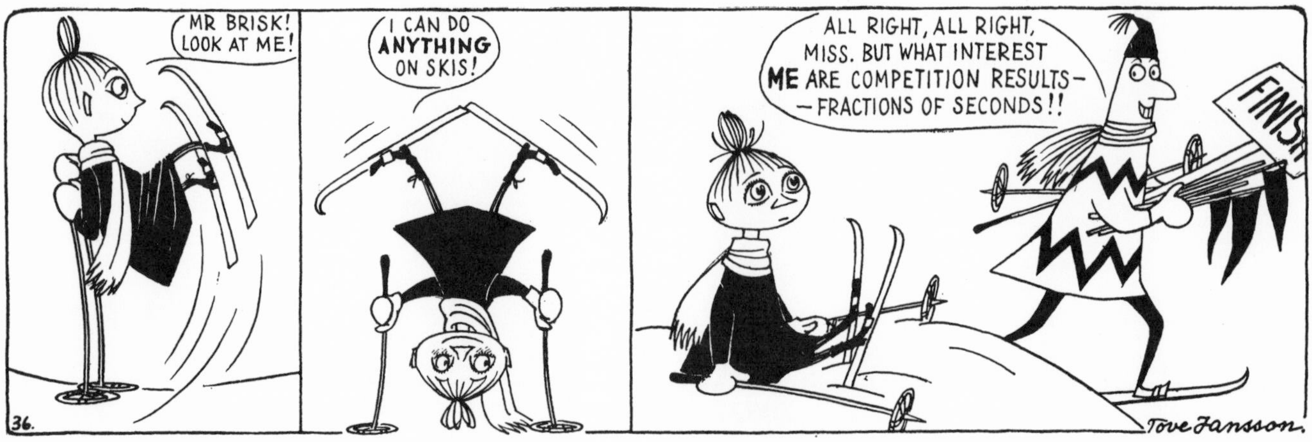
36.
MR BRISK! LOOK AT ME!
I CAN DO **ANYTHING** ON SKIS!
ALL RIGHT, ALL RIGHT, MISS. BUT WHAT INTEREST **ME** ARE COMPETITION RESULTS— —FRACTIONS OF SECONDS!!
FINISH
Tove Jansson

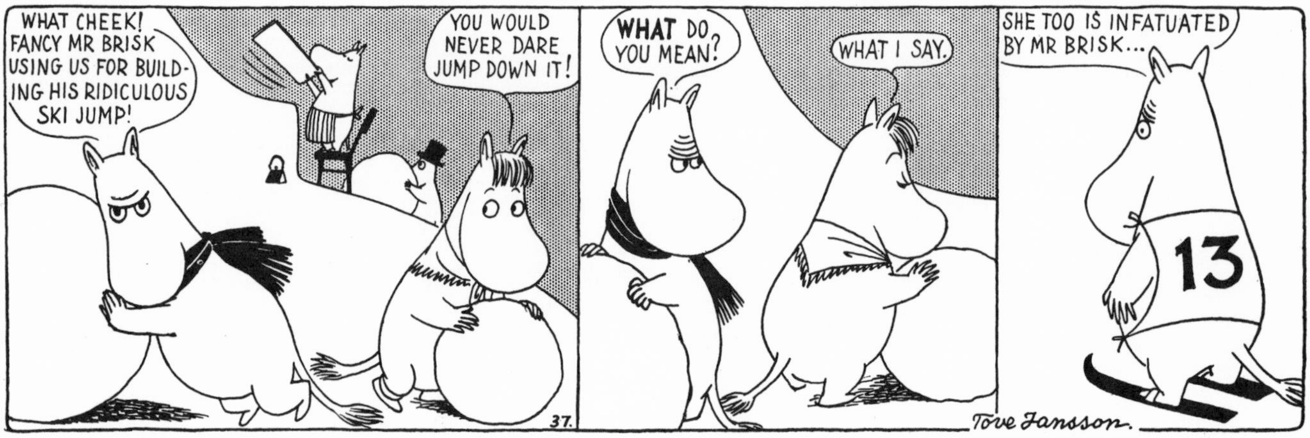
WHAT CHEEK! FANCY MR BRISK USING US FOR BUILDING HIS RIDICULOUS SKI JUMP!
YOU WOULD NEVER DARE JUMP DOWN IT!
37.
WHAT DO YOU MEAN?
WHAT I SAY.
SHE TOO IS INFATUATED BY MR BRISK...
13
Tove Jansson

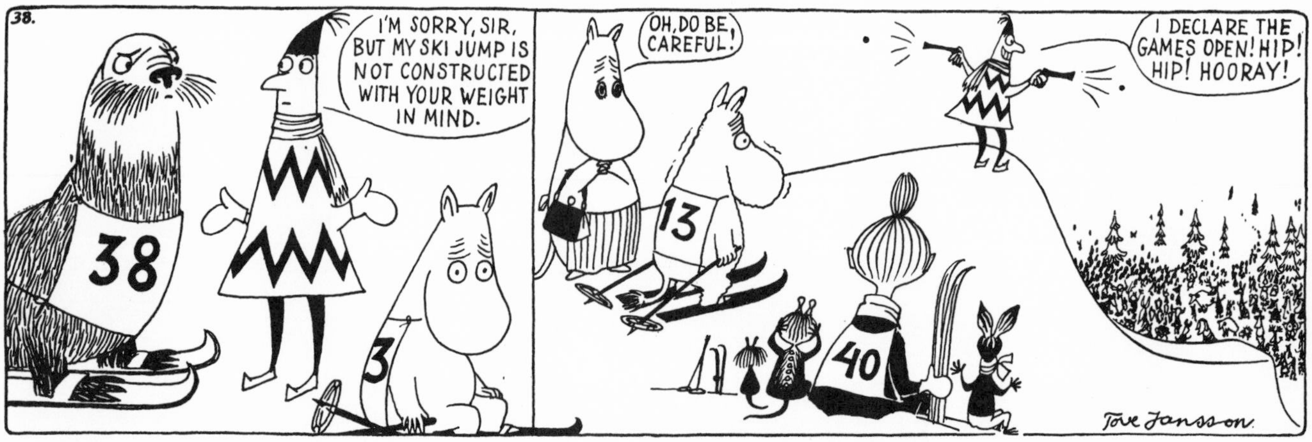
38.
38
I'M SORRY, SIR, BUT MY SKI JUMP IS NOT CONSTRUCTED WITH YOUR WEIGHT IN MIND.
3
OH, DO BE CAREFUL!
13
I DECLARE THE GAMES OPEN! HIP! HIP! HOORAY!
40
Tove Jansson

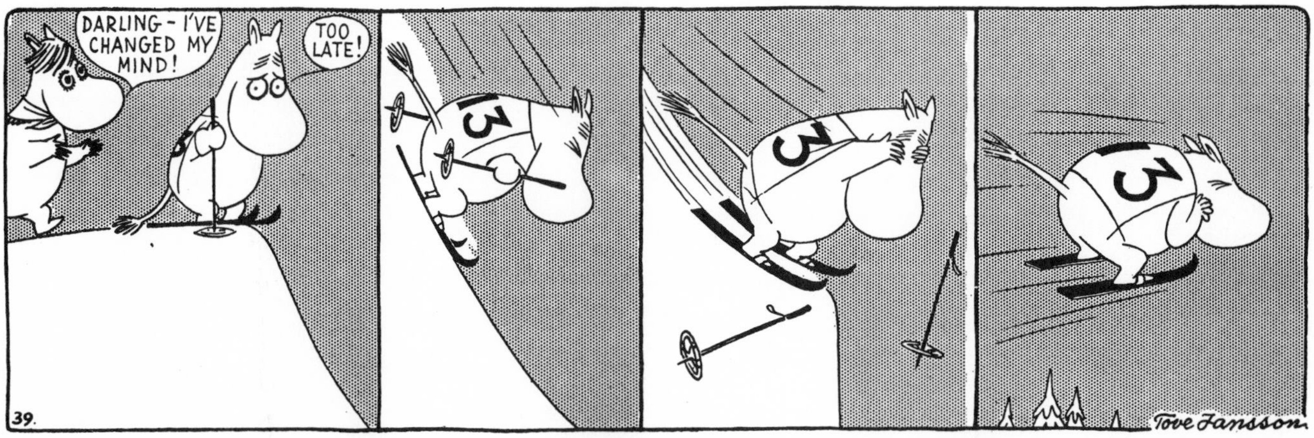
39.
DARLING - I'VE CHANGED MY MIND!
TOO LATE!
13
Tove Jansson

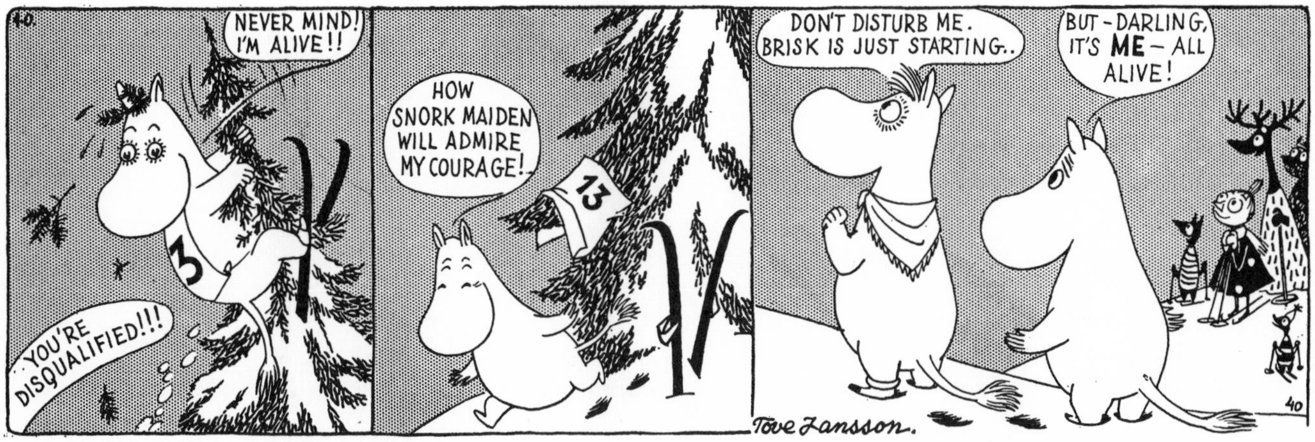
40.
NEVER MIND! I'M ALIVE!!
YOU'RE DISQUALIFIED!!!
HOW SNORK MAIDEN WILL ADMIRE MY COURAGE!
13
DON'T DISTURB ME. BRISK IS JUST STARTING..
BUT - DARLING, IT'S **ME** - ALL ALIVE!
Tove Jansson.

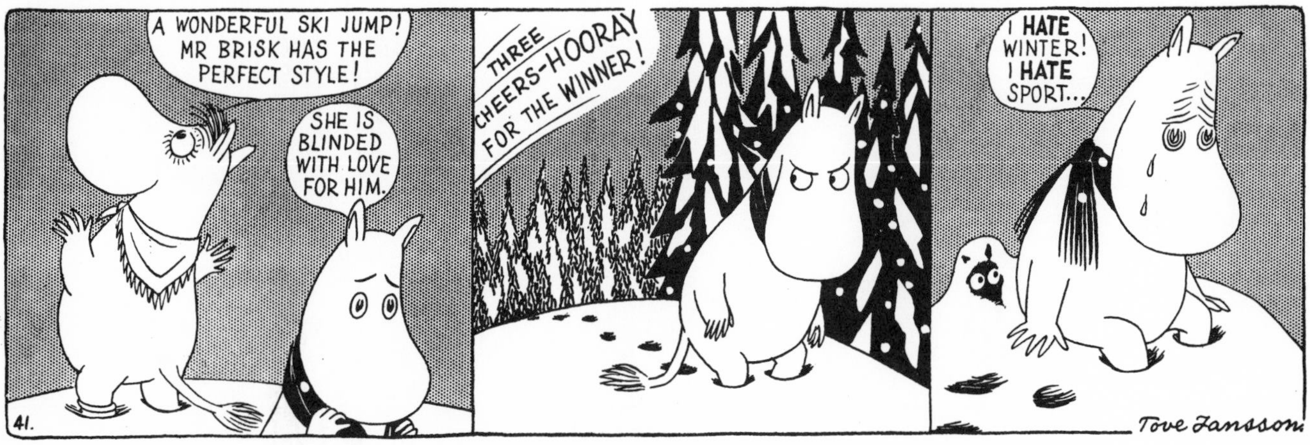
41.
A WONDERFUL SKI JUMP! MR BRISK HAS THE PERFECT STYLE!
SHE IS BLINDED WITH LOVE FOR HIM.
THREE CHEERS-HOORAY FOR THE WINNER!
I **HATE** WINTER! I **HATE** SPORT...
Tove Jansson

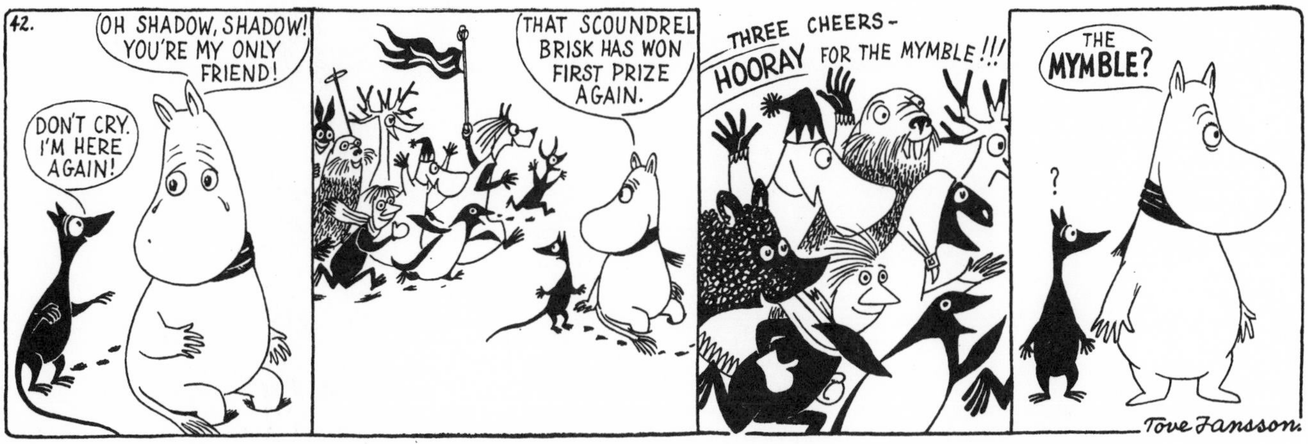
42.
OH SHADOW, SHADOW! YOU'RE MY ONLY FRIEND!
DON'T CRY. I'M HERE AGAIN!
THAT SCOUNDREL BRISK HAS WON FIRST PRIZE AGAIN.
THREE CHEERS - HOORAY FOR THE MYMBLE!!!
?
THE **MYMBLE**?
Tove Jansson.

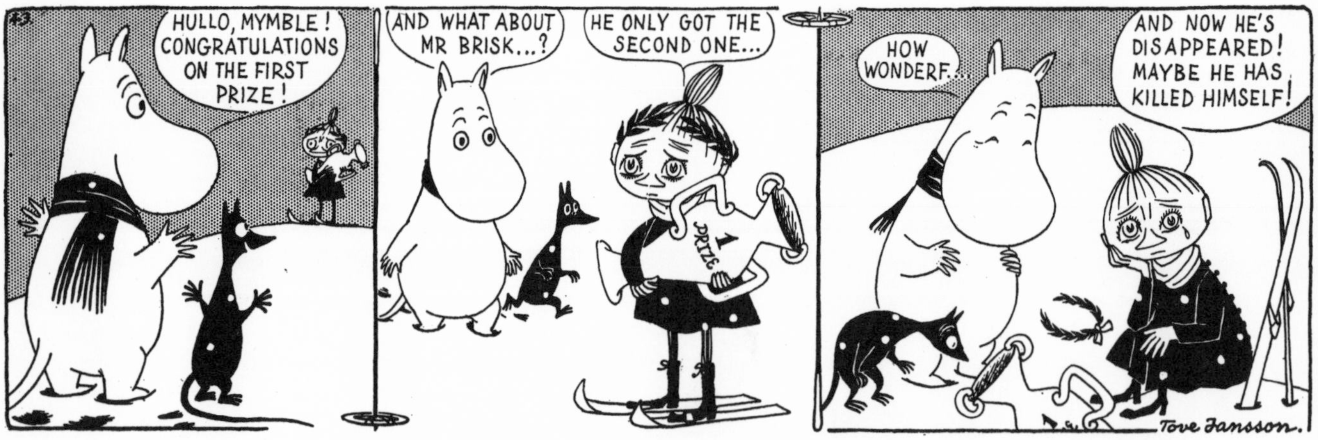
43.
HULLO, MYMBLE! CONGRATULATIONS ON THE FIRST PRIZE!
AND WHAT ABOUT MR BRISK...?
HE ONLY GOT THE SECOND ONE...
HOW WONDERF....
AND NOW HE'S DISAPPEARED! MAYBE HE HAS KILLED HIMSELF!
Tove Jansson.

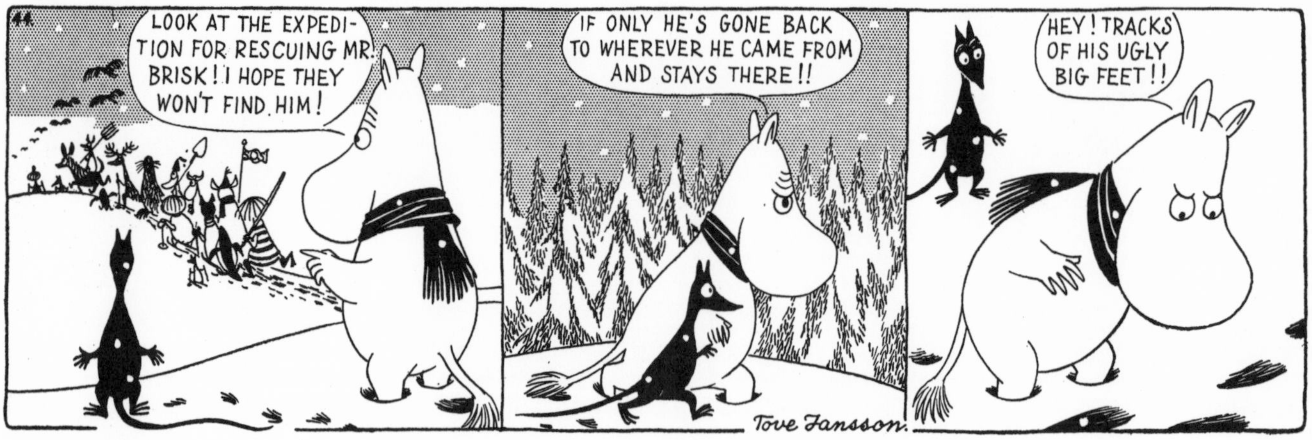
44.
LOOK AT THE EXPEDITION FOR RESCUING MR BRISK! I HOPE THEY WON'T FIND HIM!
IF ONLY HE'S GONE BACK TO WHEREVER HE CAME FROM AND STAYS THERE!!
HEY! TRACKS OF HIS UGLY BIG FEET!!
Tove Jansson.

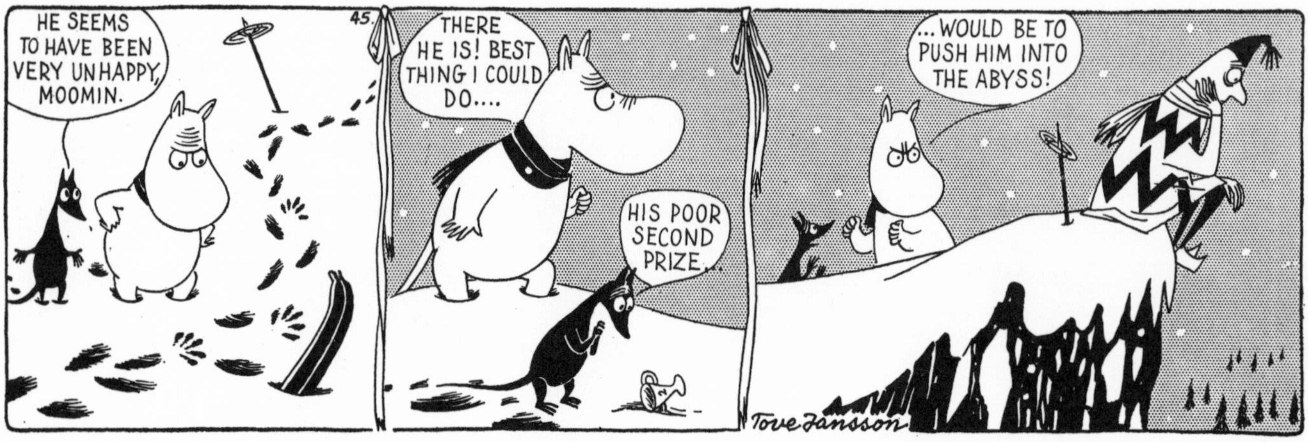
HE SEEMS TO HAVE BEEN VERY UNHAPPY, MOOMIN.
45.
THERE HE IS! BEST THING I COULD DO....
HIS POOR SECOND PRIZE...
...WOULD BE TO PUSH HIM INTO THE ABYSS!
Tove Jansson

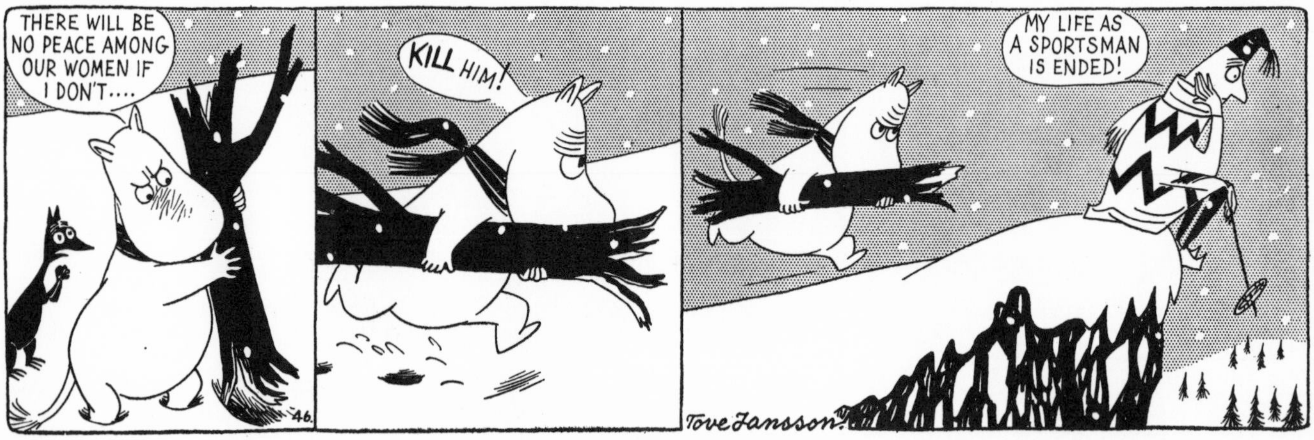
THERE WILL BE NO PEACE AMONG OUR WOMEN IF I DON'T....
46.
KILL HIM!
MY LIFE AS A SPORTSMAN IS ENDED!
Tove Jansson.

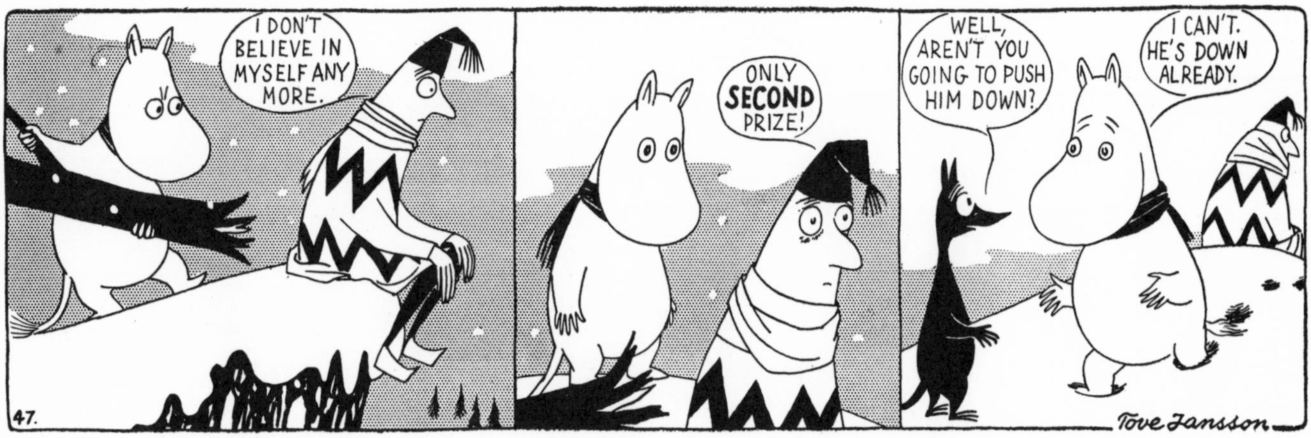
I DON'T BELIEVE IN MYSELF ANY MORE.
ONLY SECOND PRIZE!
WELL, AREN'T YOU GOING TO PUSH HIM DOWN?
I CAN'T. HE'S DOWN ALREADY.
47.
Tove Jansson

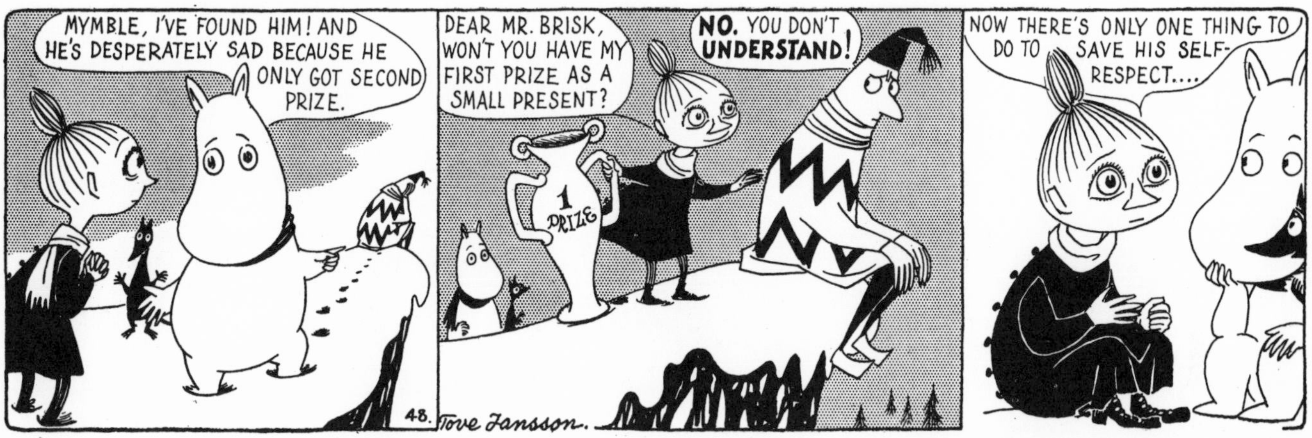
MYMBLE, I'VE FOUND HIM! AND HE'S DESPERATELY SAD BECAUSE HE ONLY GOT SECOND PRIZE.
DEAR MR. BRISK, WON'T YOU HAVE MY FIRST PRIZE AS A SMALL PRESENT?
1 PRIZE
NO. YOU DON'T UNDERSTAND!
48.
Tove Jansson
NOW THERE'S ONLY ONE THING TO DO TO SAVE HIS SELF-RESPECT....

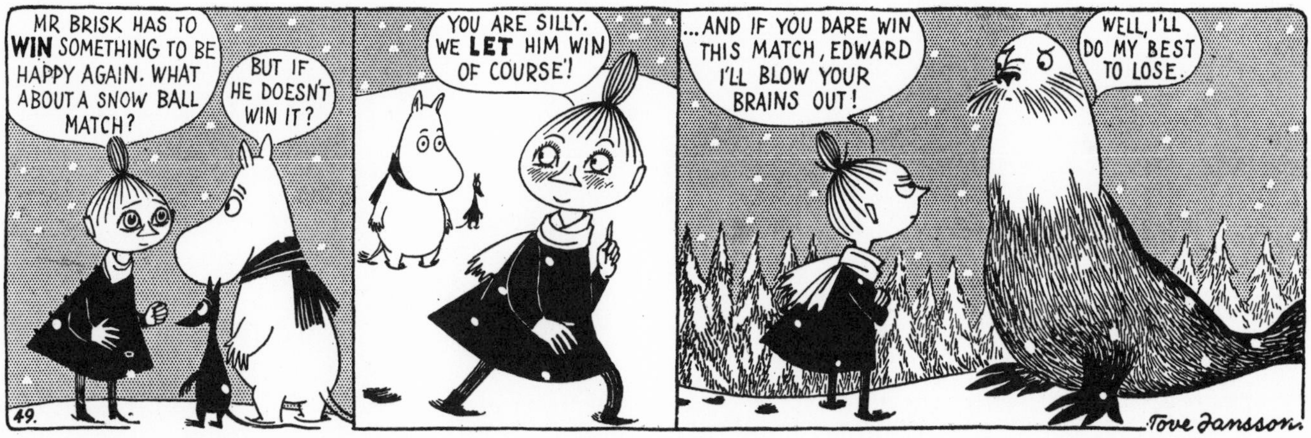
MR BRISK HAS TO WIN SOMETHING TO BE HAPPY AGAIN. WHAT ABOUT A SNOW BALL MATCH?
BUT IF HE DOESN'T WIN IT?
YOU ARE SILLY. WE LET HIM WIN OF COURSE!
...AND IF YOU DARE WIN THIS MATCH, EDWARD I'LL BLOW YOUR BRAINS OUT!
WELL, I'LL DO MY BEST TO LOSE.
49.
Tove Jansson

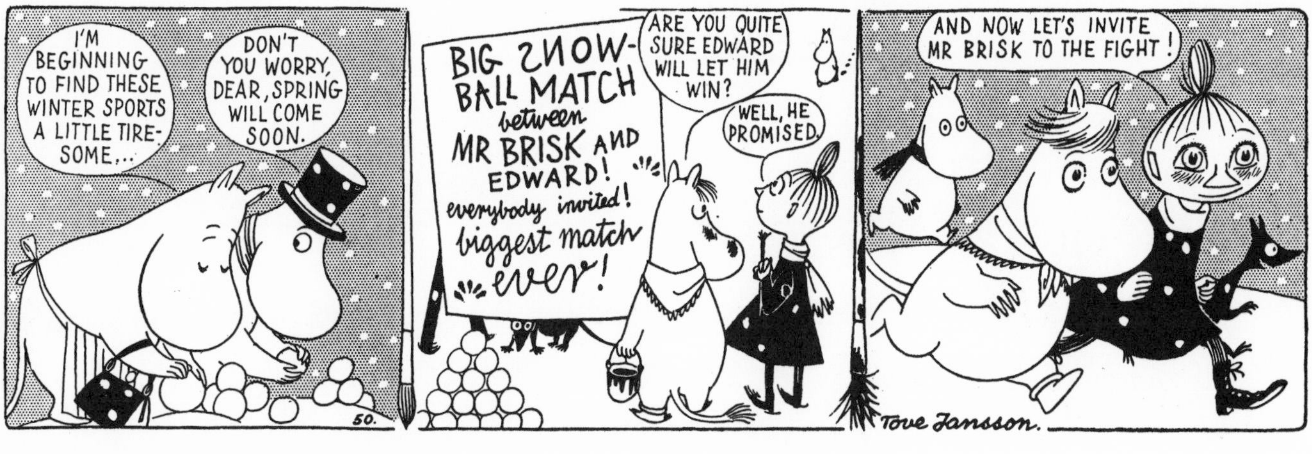
I'M BEGINNING TO FIND THESE WINTER SPORTS A LITTLE TIRE-SOME,..
DON'T YOU WORRY, DEAR, SPRING WILL COME SOON.
50.
BIG SNOW-BALL MATCH between MR BRISK AND EDWARD! everybody invited! biggest match ever!
ARE YOU QUITE SURE EDWARD WILL LET HIM WIN?
WELL, HE PROMISED.
AND NOW LET'S INVITE MR BRISK TO THE FIGHT!
Tove Jansson

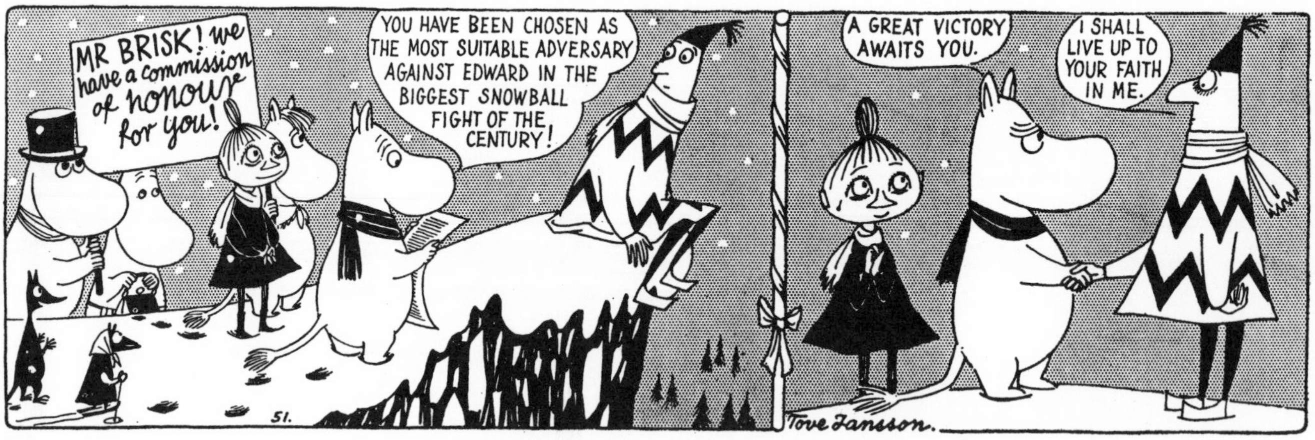
MR BRISK! we have a commission of honour for you!
YOU HAVE BEEN CHOSEN AS THE MOST SUITABLE ADVERSARY AGAINST EDWARD IN THE BIGGEST SNOWBALL FIGHT OF THE CENTURY!
51.
A GREAT VICTORY AWAITS YOU.
I SHALL LIVE UP TO YOUR FAITH IN ME.
Tove Jansson.

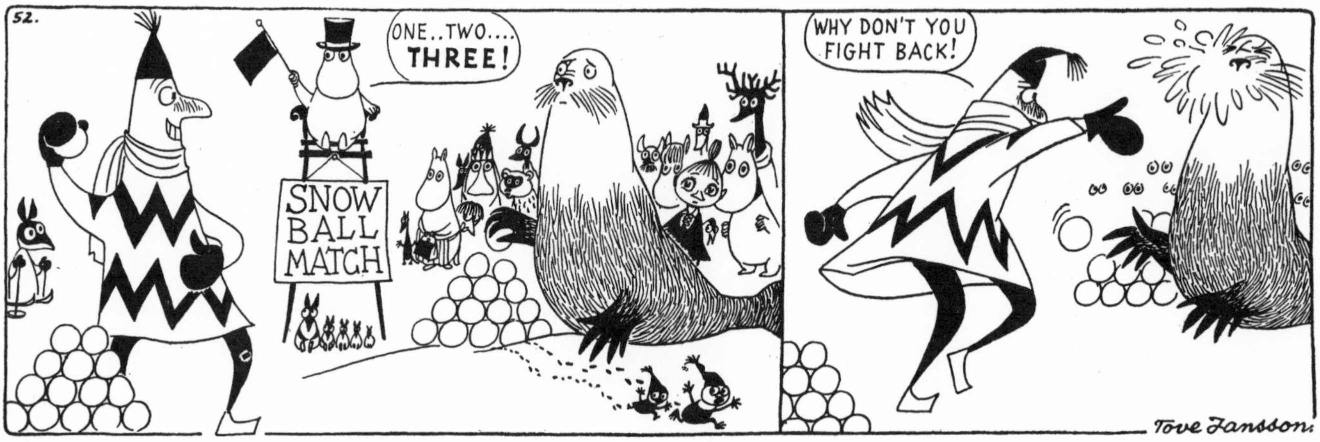
52.
SNOW BALL MATCH
ONE..TWO.... THREE!
WHY DON'T YOU FIGHT BACK!
Tove Jansson.

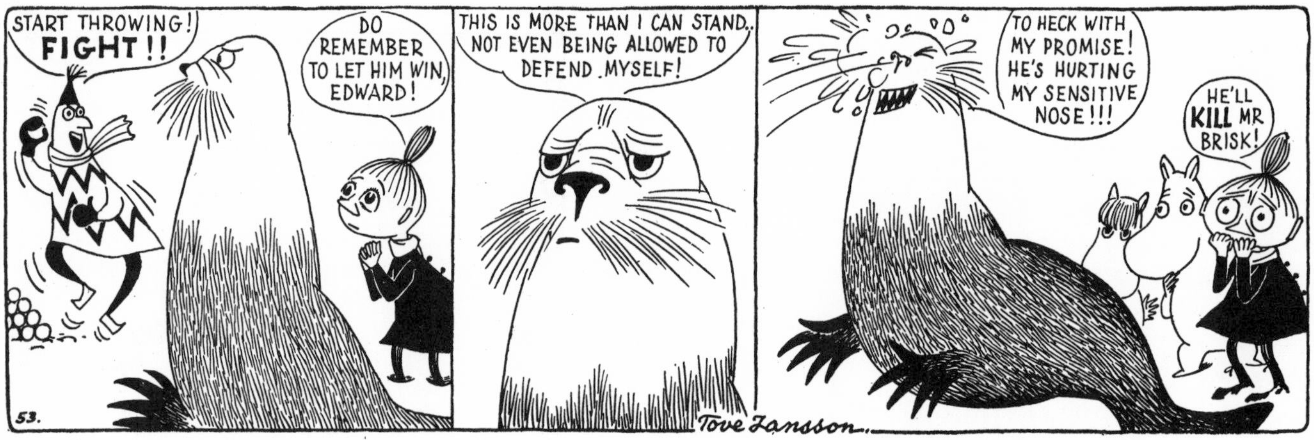
START THROWING! FIGHT!!
DO REMEMBER TO LET HIM WIN, EDWARD!
53.
THIS IS MORE THAN I CAN STAND.. NOT EVEN BEING ALLOWED TO DEFEND MYSELF!
Tove Jansson.
TO HECK WITH MY PROMISE! HE'S HURTING MY SENSITIVE NOSE!!!
HE'LL KILL MR BRISK!

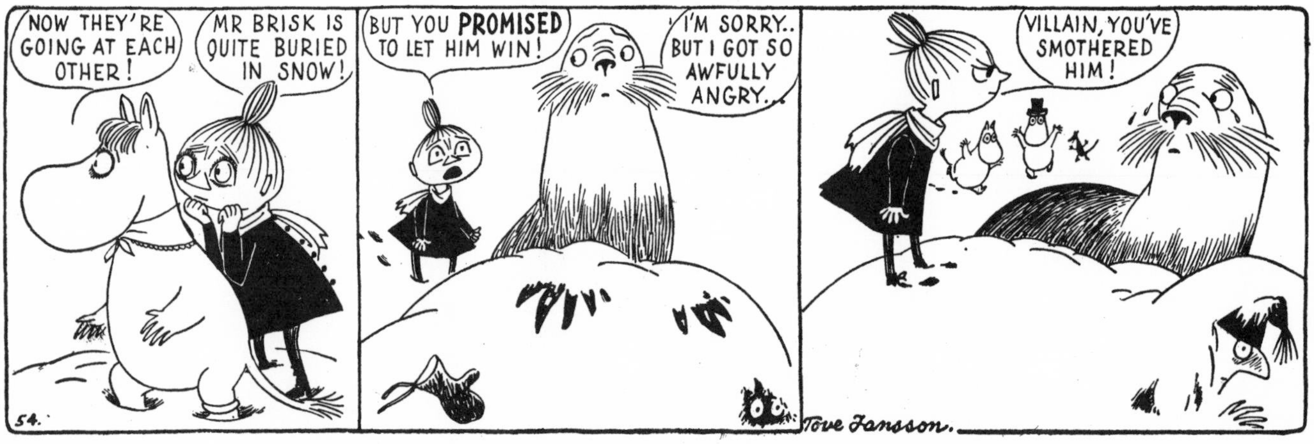
NOW THEY'RE GOING AT EACH OTHER!
MR BRISK IS QUITE BURIED IN SNOW!
54.
BUT YOU PROMISED TO LET HIM WIN!
I'M SORRY.. BUT I GOT SO AWFULLY ANGRY...
Tove Jansson.
VILLAIN, YOU'VE SMOTHERED HIM!

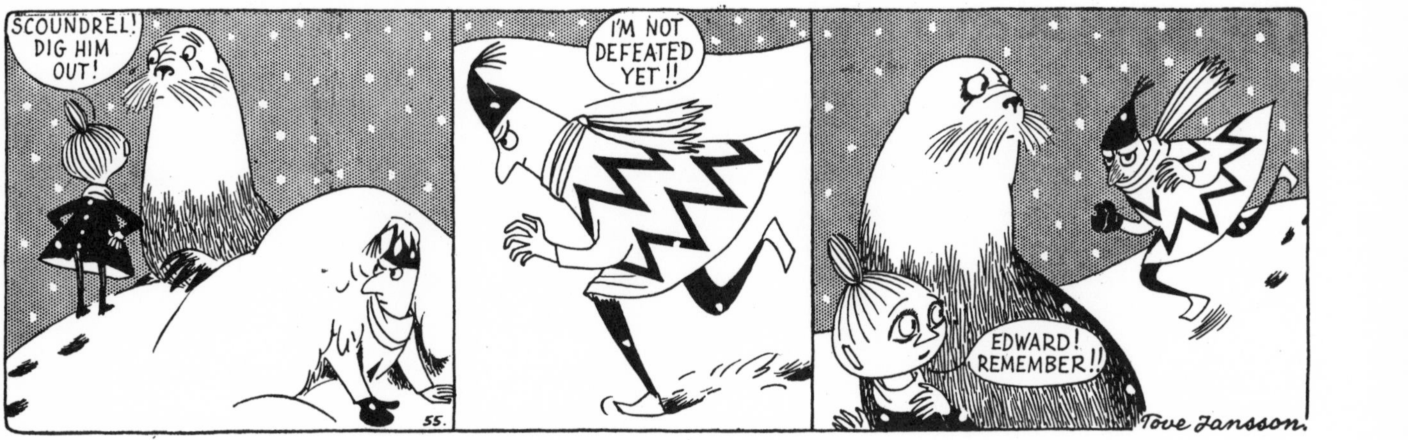
SCOUNDREL! DIG HIM OUT!
55.
I'M NOT DEFEATED YET!!
EDWARD! REMEMBER!!
Tove Jansson.

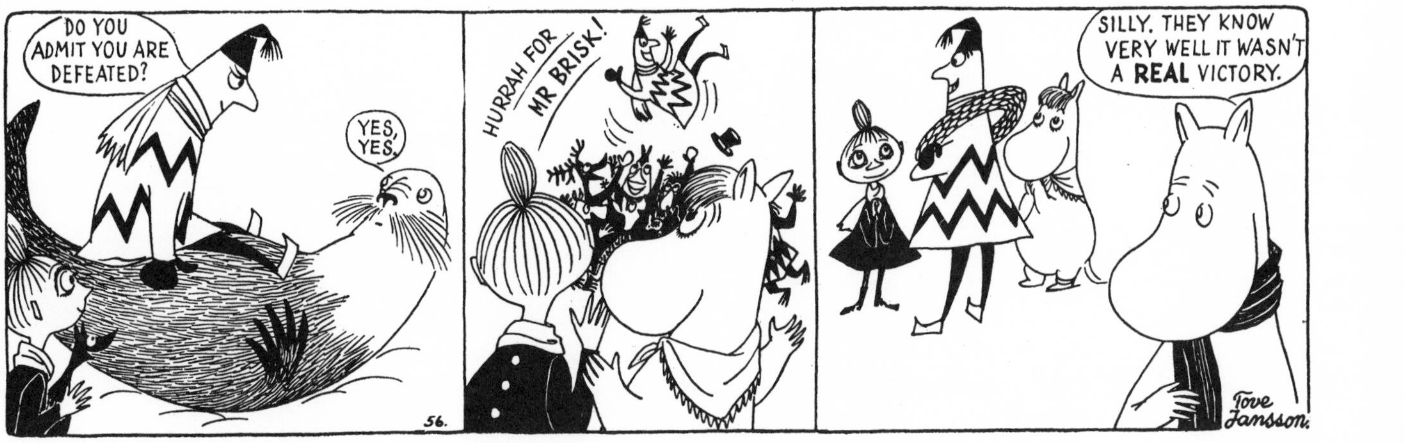
DO YOU ADMIT YOU ARE DEFEATED?
YES, YES.
56.
HURRAH FOR MR BRISK!
SILLY. THEY KNOW VERY WELL IT WASN'T A **REAL** VICTORY.
Tove Jansson.

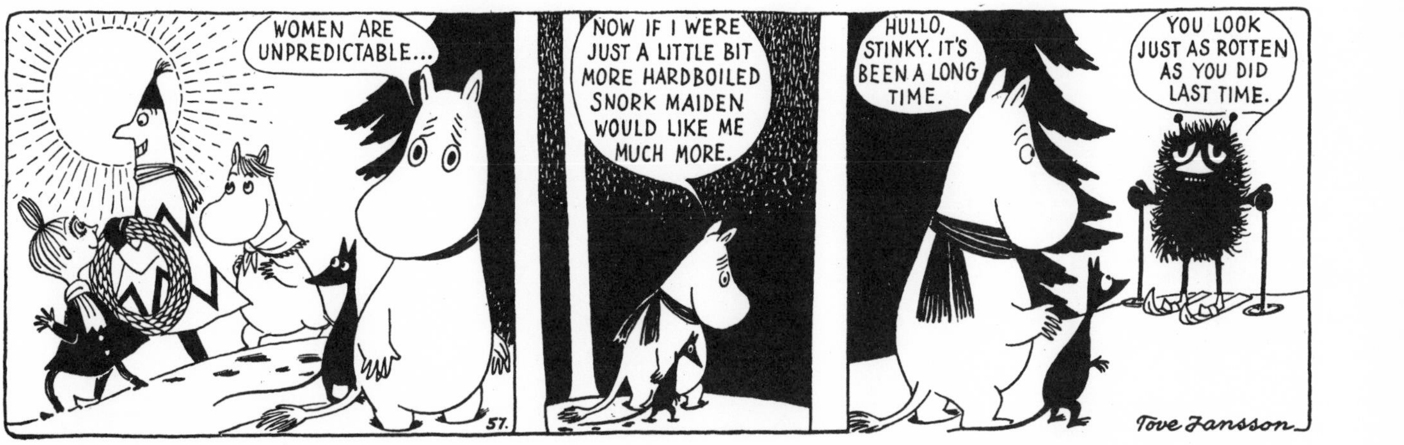
WOMEN ARE UNPREDICTABLE...
57.
NOW IF I WERE JUST A LITTLE BIT MORE HARDBOILED SNORK MAIDEN WOULD LIKE ME MUCH MORE.
HULLO, STINKY. IT'S BEEN A LONG TIME.
YOU LOOK JUST AS ROTTEN AS YOU DID LAST TIME.
Tove Jansson

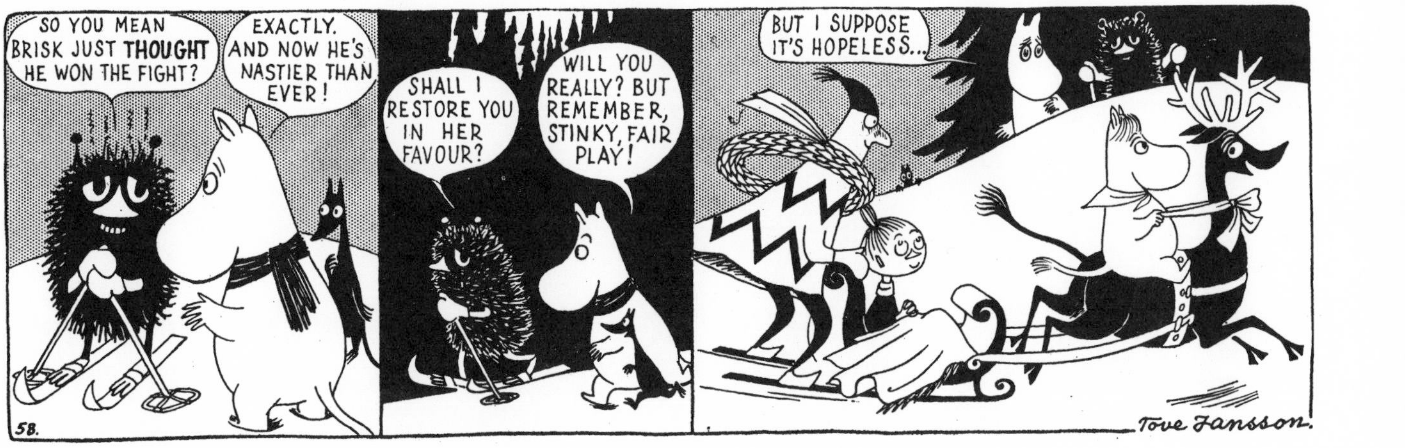
SO YOU MEAN BRISK JUST **THOUGHT** HE WON THE FIGHT?
EXACTLY. AND NOW HE'S NASTIER THAN EVER!
58.
SHALL I RESTORE YOU IN HER FAVOUR?
WILL YOU REALLY? BUT REMEMBER, STINKY, FAIR PLAY!
BUT I SUPPOSE IT'S HOPELESS...
Tove Jansson.

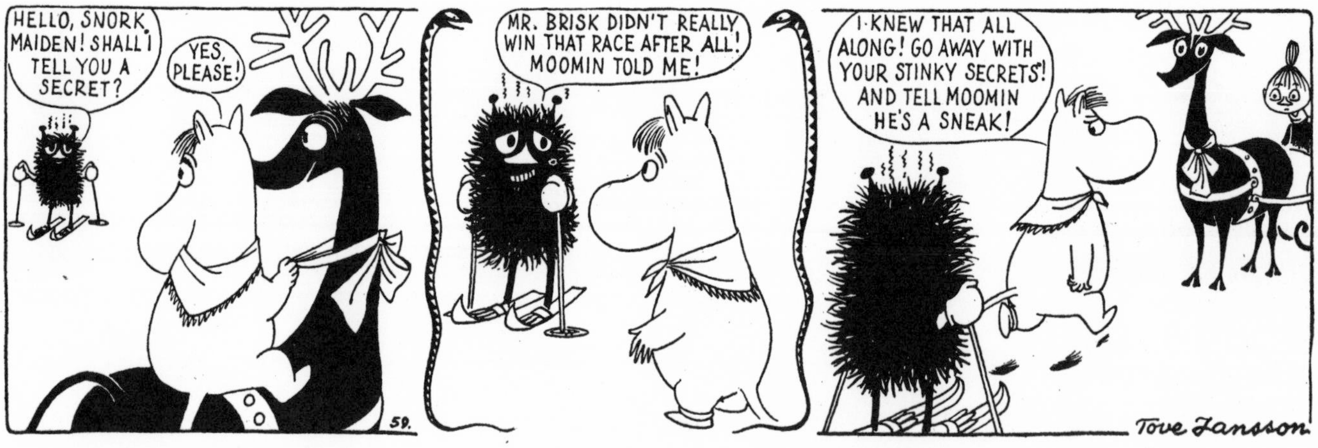
HELLO, SNORK MAIDEN! SHALL I TELL YOU A SECRET?
YES, PLEASE!
59.
MR. BRISK DIDN'T REALLY WIN THAT RACE AFTER ALL! MOOMIN TOLD ME!
I KNEW THAT ALL ALONG! GO AWAY WITH YOUR STINKY SECRETS! AND TELL MOOMIN HE'S A SNEAK!
Tove Jansson.

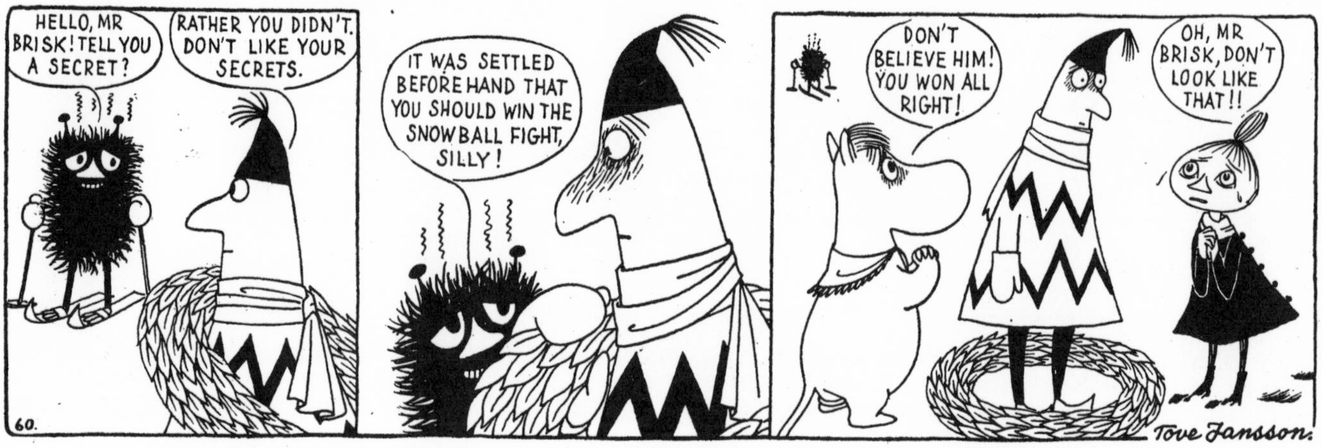
HELLO, MR BRISK! TELL YOU A SECRET?
RATHER YOU DIDN'T. DON'T LIKE YOUR SECRETS.
60.
IT WAS SETTLED BEFOREHAND THAT YOU SHOULD WIN THE SNOWBALL FIGHT, SILLY!
DON'T BELIEVE HIM! YOU WON ALL RIGHT!
OH, MR BRISK, DON'T LOOK LIKE THAT!!
Tove Jansson.

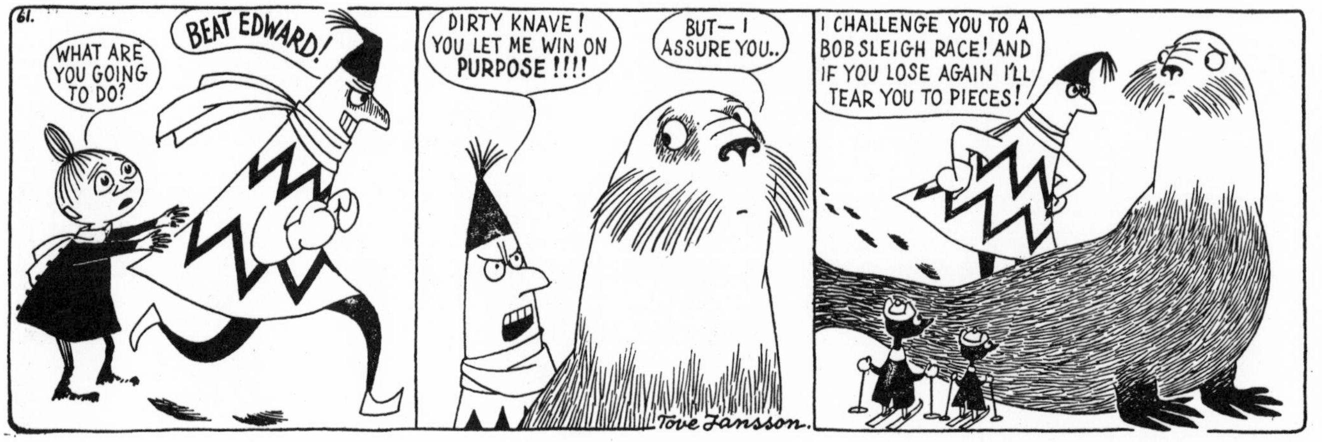
61.
WHAT ARE YOU GOING TO DO?
BEAT EDWARD!
DIRTY KNAVE! YOU LET ME WIN ON PURPOSE!!!!
BUT— I ASSURE YOU..
Tove Jansson.
I CHALLENGE YOU TO A BOBSLEIGH RACE! AND IF YOU LOSE AGAIN I'LL TEAR YOU TO PIECES!

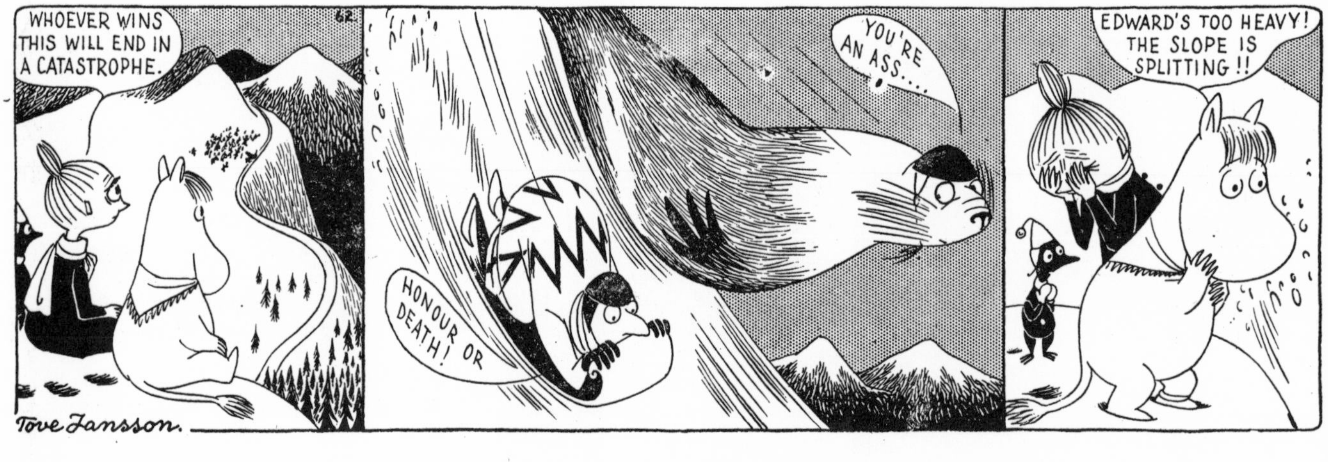
WHOEVER WINS THIS WILL END IN A CATASTROPHE.
62.
Tove Jansson.
YOU'RE AN ASS....
HONOUR OR DEATH!
EDWARD'S TOO HEAVY! THE SLOPE IS SPLITTING!!

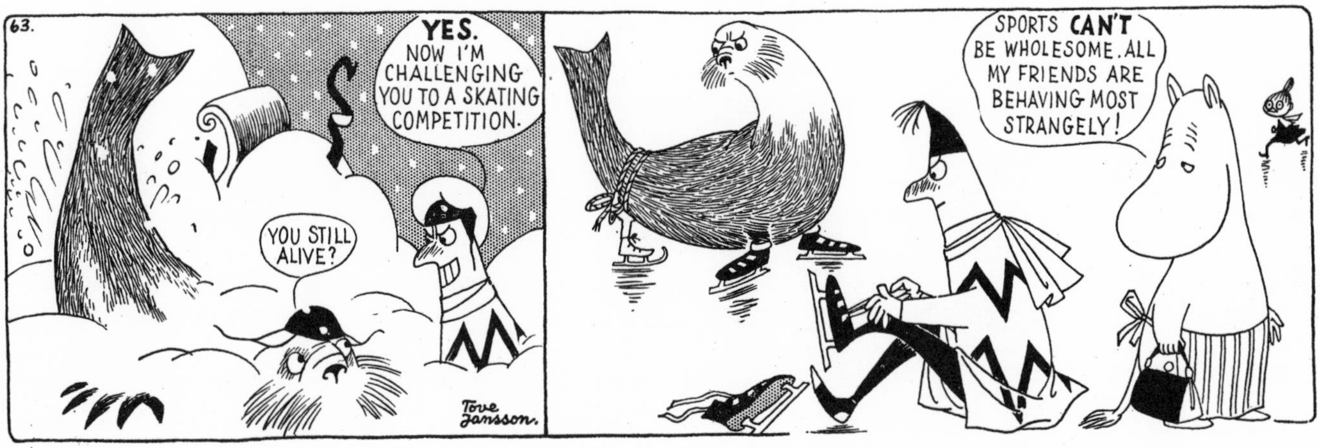
63.
YES. NOW I'M CHALLENGING YOU TO A SKATING COMPETITION.
YOU STILL ALIVE?
Tove Jansson.
SPORTS CAN'T BE WHOLESOME. ALL MY FRIENDS ARE BEHAVING MOST STRANGELY!

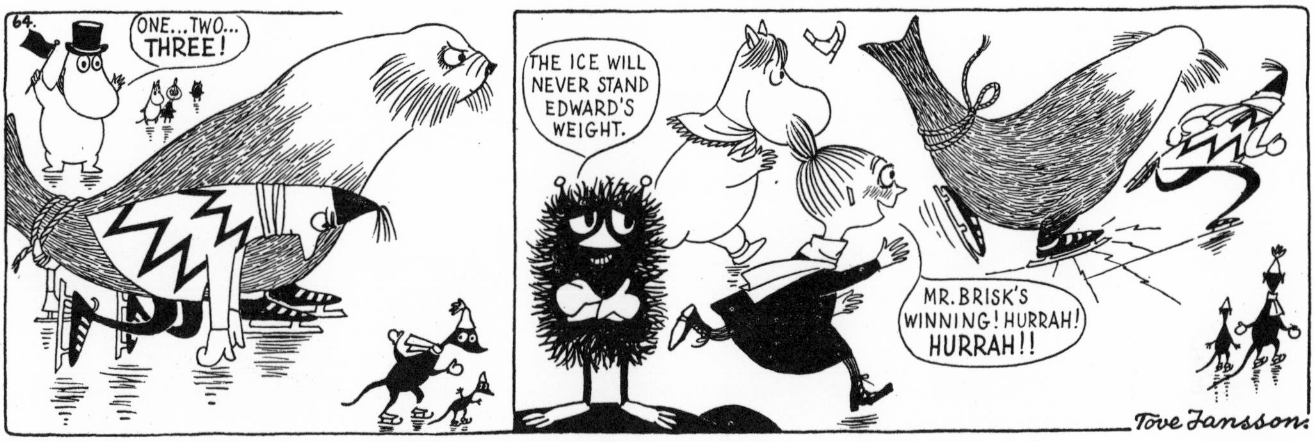
64.
ONE...TWO... THREE!
THE ICE WILL NEVER STAND EDWARD'S WEIGHT.
MR. BRISK'S WINNING! HURRAH! HURRAH!!
Tove Jansson.

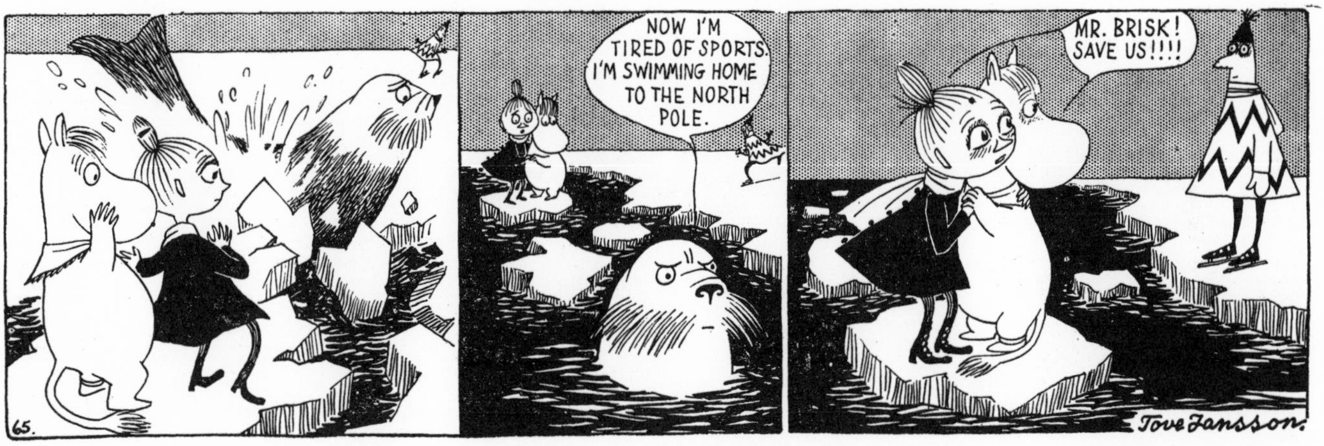
65.
NOW I'M TIRED OF SPORTS. I'M SWIMMING HOME TO THE NORTH POLE.
MR. BRISK! SAVE US!!!!
Tove Jansson.

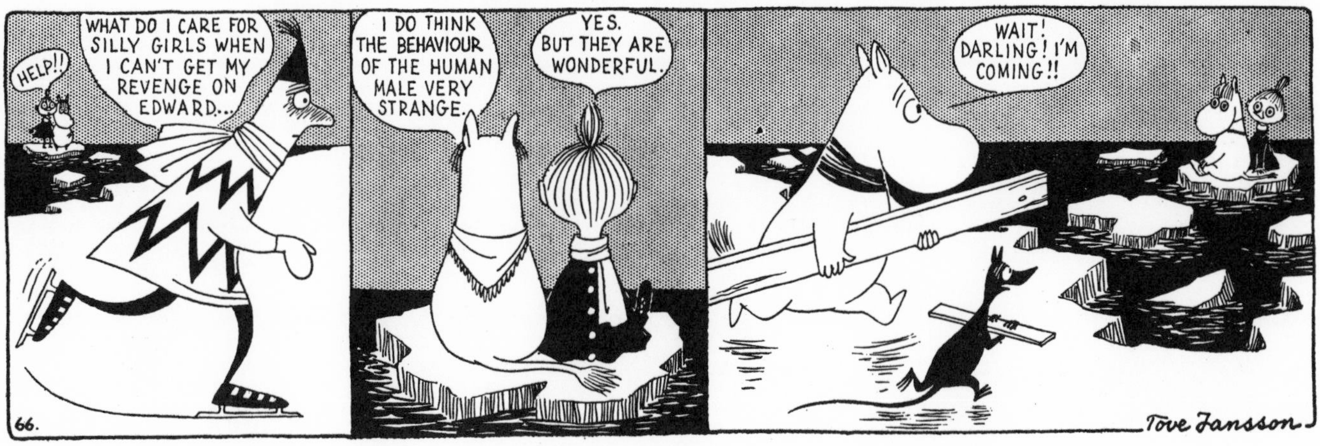
66.
HELP!!
WHAT DO I CARE FOR SILLY GIRLS WHEN I CAN'T GET MY REVENGE ON EDWARD...
I DO THINK THE BEHAVIOUR OF THE HUMAN MALE VERY STRANGE.
YES. BUT THEY ARE WONDERFUL.
WAIT! DARLING! I'M COMING!!
Tove Jansson

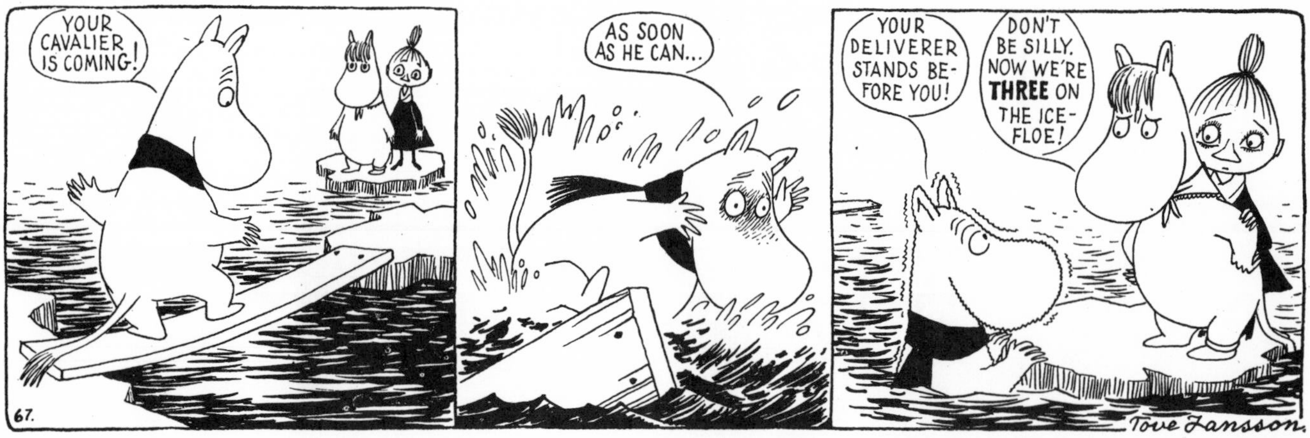
67.
YOUR CAVALIER IS COMING!
AS SOON AS HE CAN...
YOUR DELIVERER STANDS BEFORE YOU!
DON'T BE SILLY. NOW WE'RE **THREE** ON THE ICE-FLOE!
Tove Jansson.

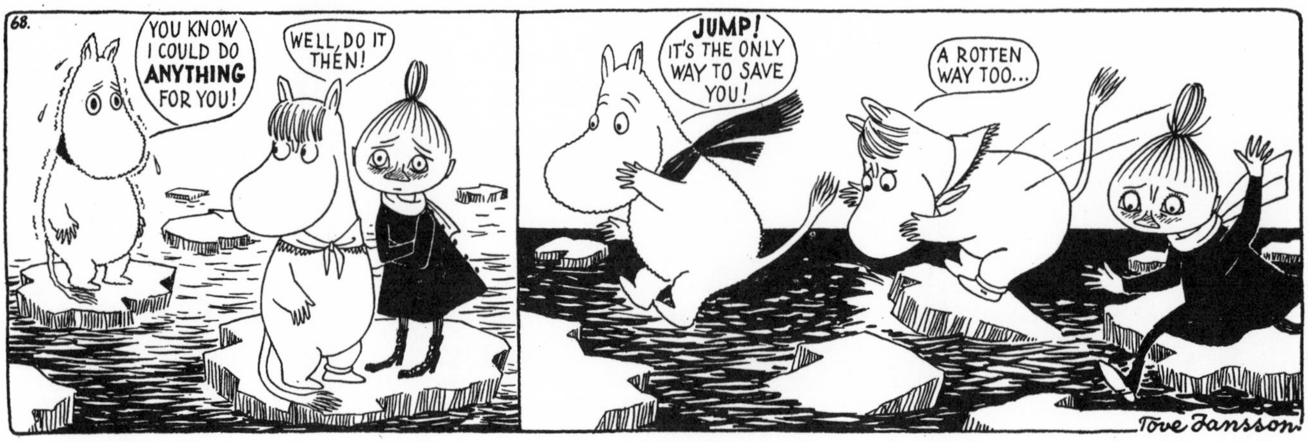
68.
YOU KNOW I COULD DO **ANYTHING** FOR YOU!
WELL, DO IT THEN!
JUMP! IT'S THE ONLY WAY TO SAVE YOU!
A ROTTEN WAY TOO...
Tove Jansson.

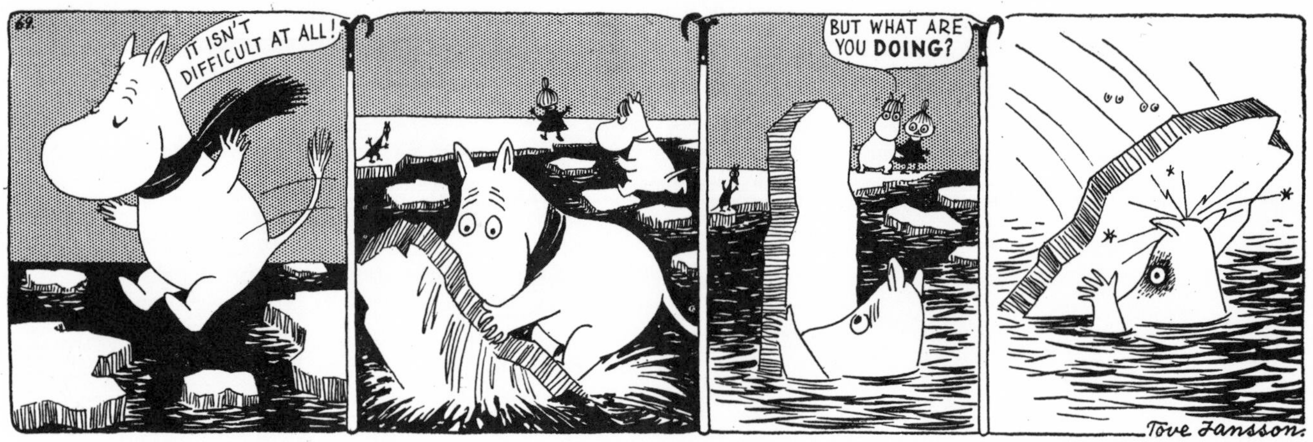
69.
IT ISN'T DIFFICULT AT ALL!
BUT WHAT ARE YOU **DOING?**
Tove Jansson.

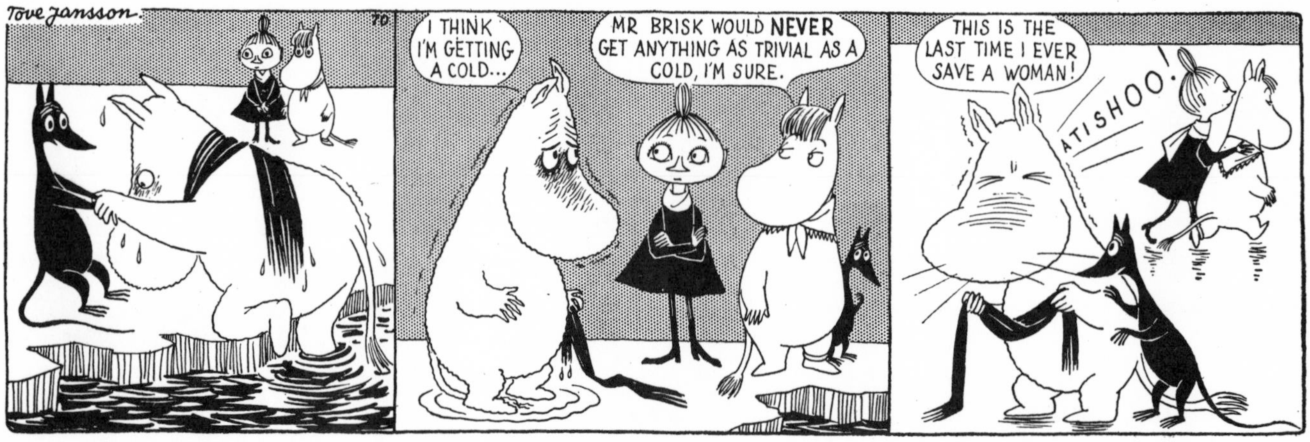
Tove Jansson.
70.
I THINK I'M GETTING A COLD...
MR BRISK WOULD **NEVER** GET ANYTHING AS TRIVIAL AS A COLD, I'M SURE.
THIS IS THE LAST TIME I EVER SAVE A WOMAN!
ATISHOO!

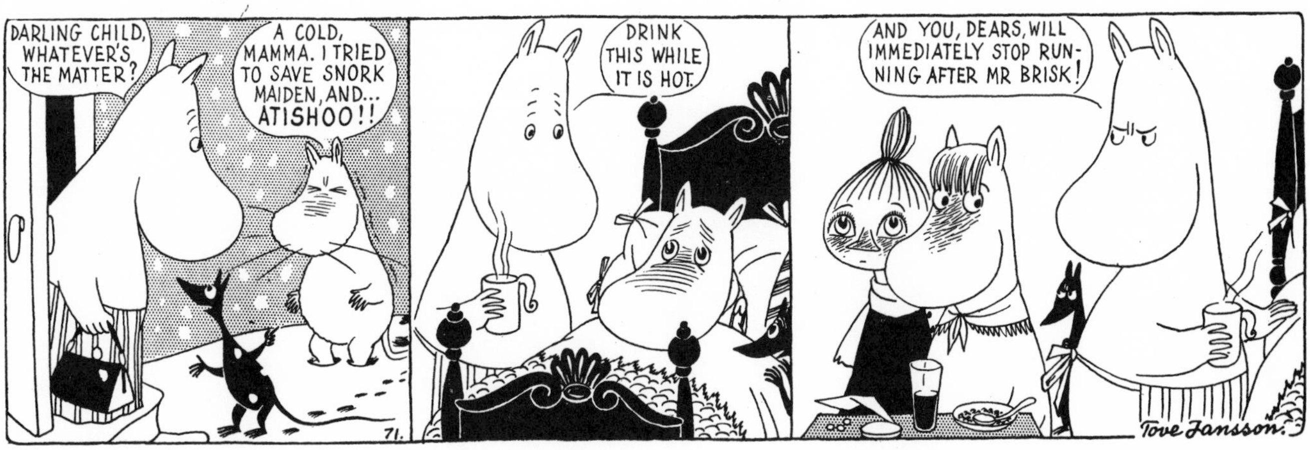
DARLING CHILD, WHATEVER'S THE MATTER?
A COLD, MAMMA. I TRIED TO SAVE SNORK MAIDEN, AND... ATISHOO!!
DRINK THIS WHILE IT IS HOT.
AND YOU, DEARS, WILL IMMEDIATELY STOP RUNNING AFTER MR BRISK!
Tove Jansson.

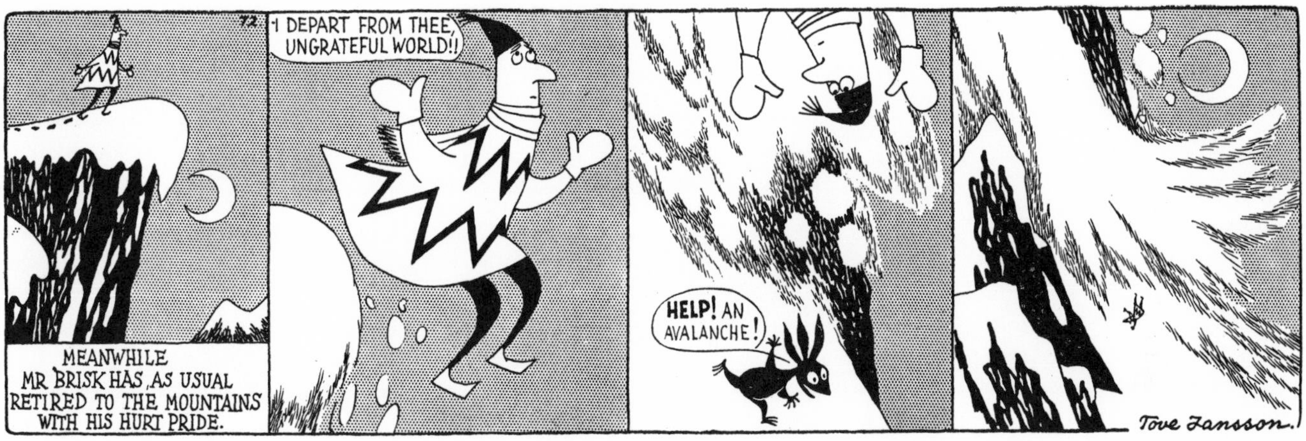
MEANWHILE MR BRISK HAS, AS USUAL RETIRED TO THE MOUNTAINS WITH HIS HURT PRIDE.
I DEPART FROM THEE, UNGRATEFUL WORLD!!
HELP! AN AVALANCHE!
Tove Jansson.

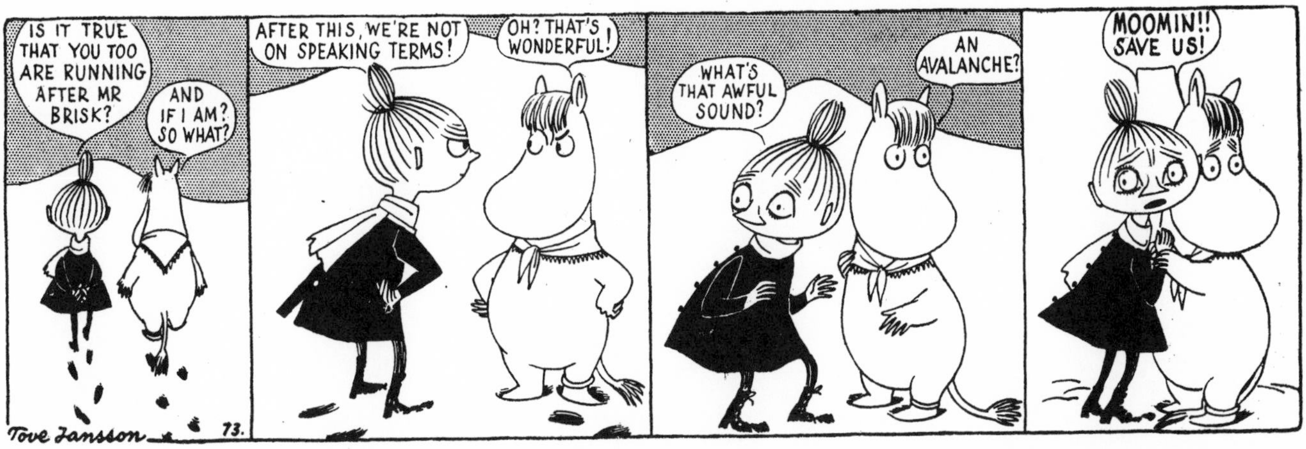
IS IT TRUE THAT YOU TOO ARE RUNNING AFTER MR BRISK?
AND IF I AM? SO WHAT?
Tove Jansson
AFTER THIS, WE'RE NOT ON SPEAKING TERMS!
OH? THAT'S WONDERFUL!
WHAT'S THAT AWFUL SOUND?
AN AVALANCHE?
MOOMIN!! SAVE US!

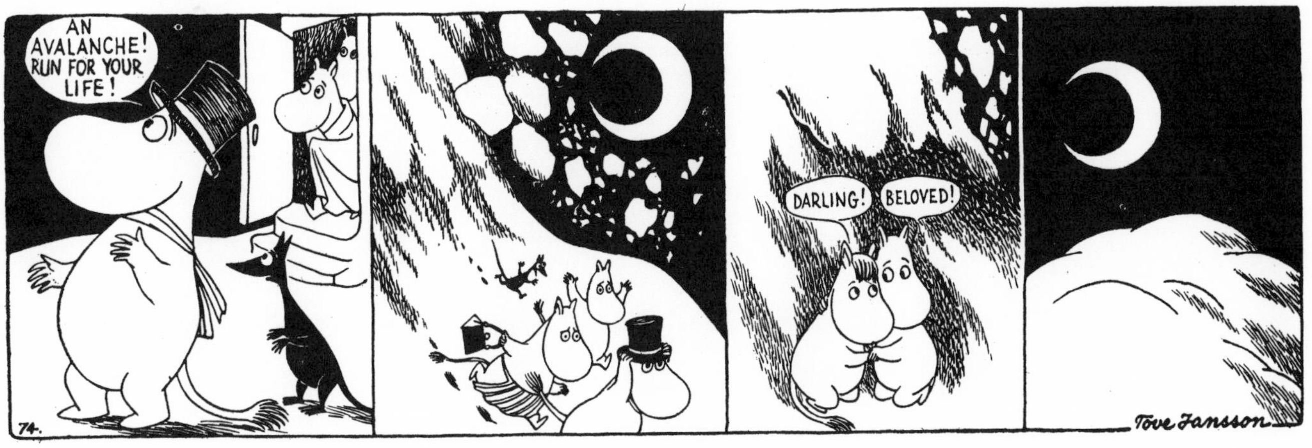
AN AVALANCHE! RUN FOR YOUR LIFE!
DARLING!
BELOVED!
Tove Jansson

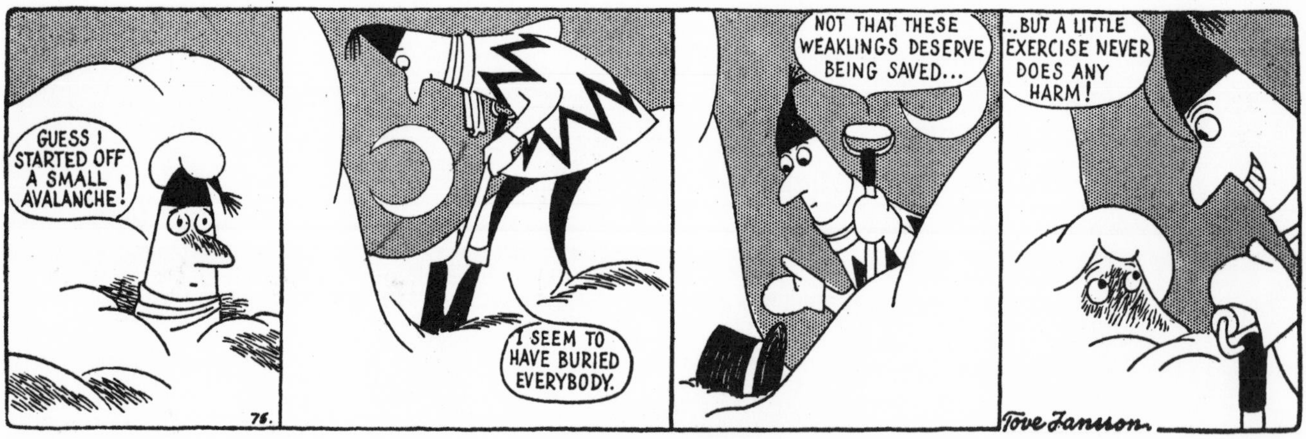
GUESS I STARTED OFF A SMALL AVALANCHE!
I SEEM TO HAVE BURIED EVERYBODY.
NOT THAT THESE WEAKLINGS DESERVE BEING SAVED...
...BUT A LITTLE EXERCISE NEVER DOES ANY HARM!
75.
Tove Jansson

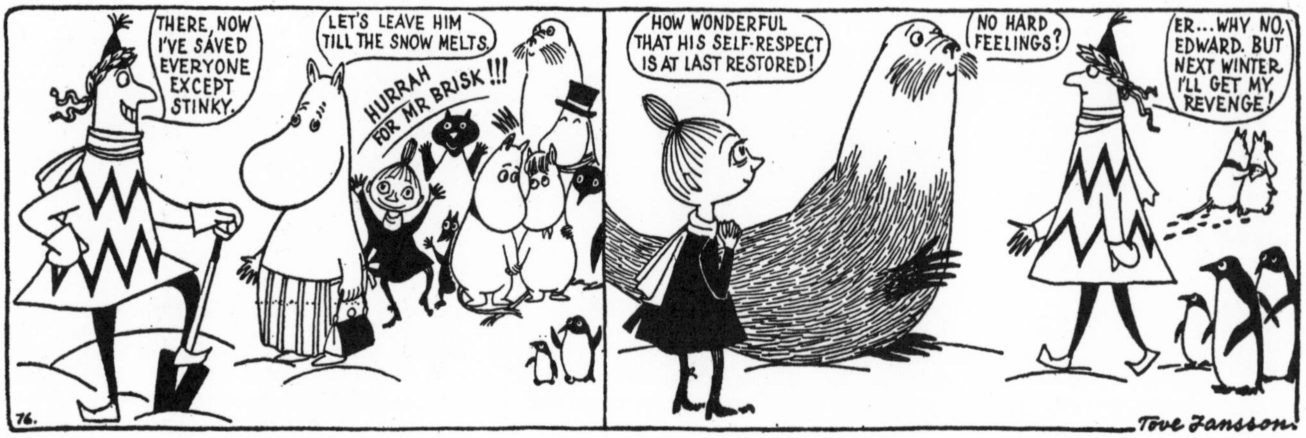
THERE, NOW I'VE SAVED EVERYONE EXCEPT STINKY.
LET'S LEAVE HIM TILL THE SNOW MELTS.
HURRAH FOR MR BRISK !!!
HOW WONDERFUL THAT HIS SELF-RESPECT IS AT LAST RESTORED!
NO HARD FEELINGS?
ER...WHY NO, EDWARD. BUT NEXT WINTER I'LL GET MY REVENGE!
76.
Tove Jansson

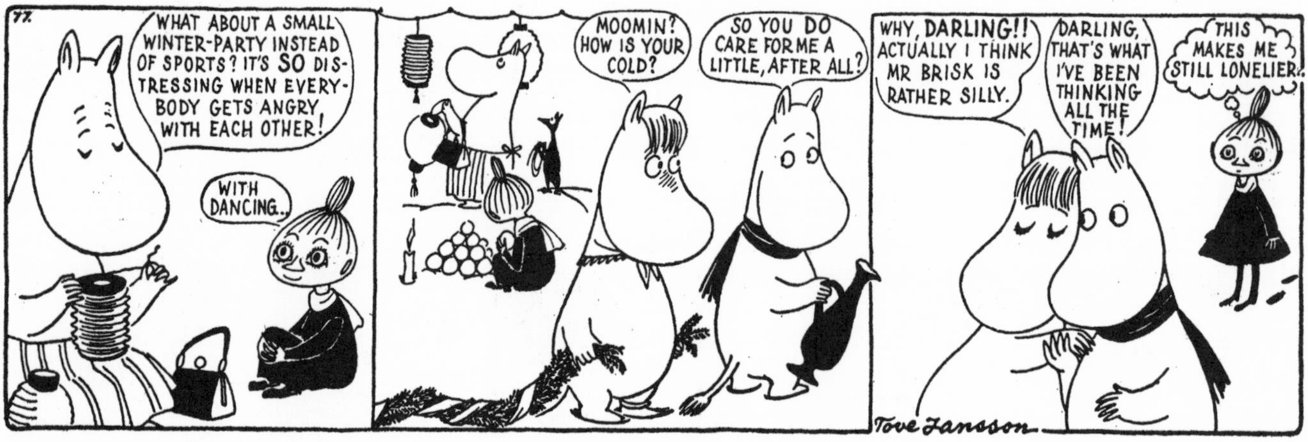
77.
WHAT ABOUT A SMALL WINTER-PARTY INSTEAD OF SPORTS? IT'S SO DISTRESSING WHEN EVERYBODY GETS ANGRY WITH EACH OTHER!
WITH DANCING..
MOOMIN? HOW IS YOUR COLD?
SO YOU DO CARE FOR ME A LITTLE, AFTER ALL?
WHY, DARLING!! ACTUALLY I THINK MR BRISK IS RATHER SILLY.
DARLING, THAT'S WHAT I'VE BEEN THINKING ALL THE TIME!
THIS MAKES ME STILL LONELIER.
Tove Jansson

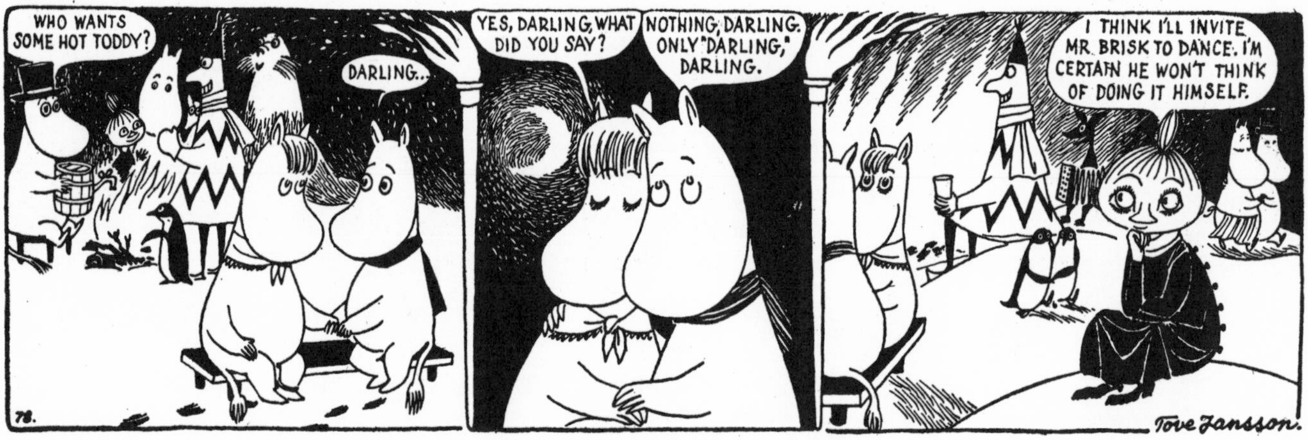
WHO WANTS SOME HOT TODDY?
DARLING...
YES, DARLING, WHAT DID YOU SAY?
NOTHING, DARLING. ONLY "DARLING," DARLING.
I THINK I'LL INVITE MR. BRISK TO DANCE. I'M CERTAIN HE WON'T THINK OF DOING IT HIMSELF.
78.
Tove Jansson

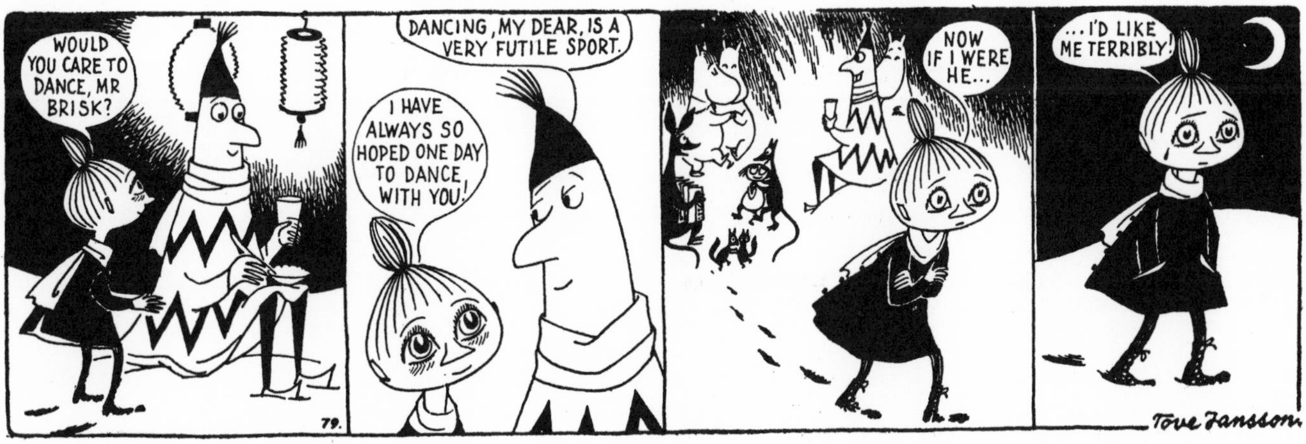
WOULD YOU CARE TO DANCE, MR BRISK?
79.
DANCING, MY DEAR, IS A VERY FUTILE SPORT.
I HAVE ALWAYS SO HOPED ONE DAY TO DANCE WITH YOU!
NOW IF I WERE HE...
...I'D LIKE ME TERRIBLY!
Tove Jansson.

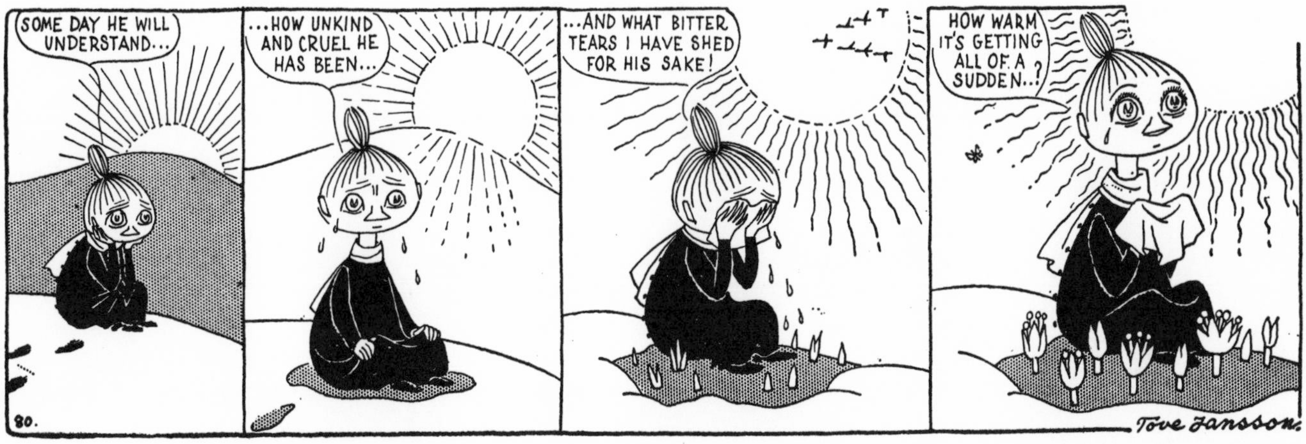
SOME DAY HE WILL UNDERSTAND...
80.
...HOW UNKIND AND CRUEL HE HAS BEEN...
...AND WHAT BITTER TEARS I HAVE SHED FOR HIS SAKE!
HOW WARM IT'S GETTING ALL OF A SUDDEN..?
Tove Jansson.

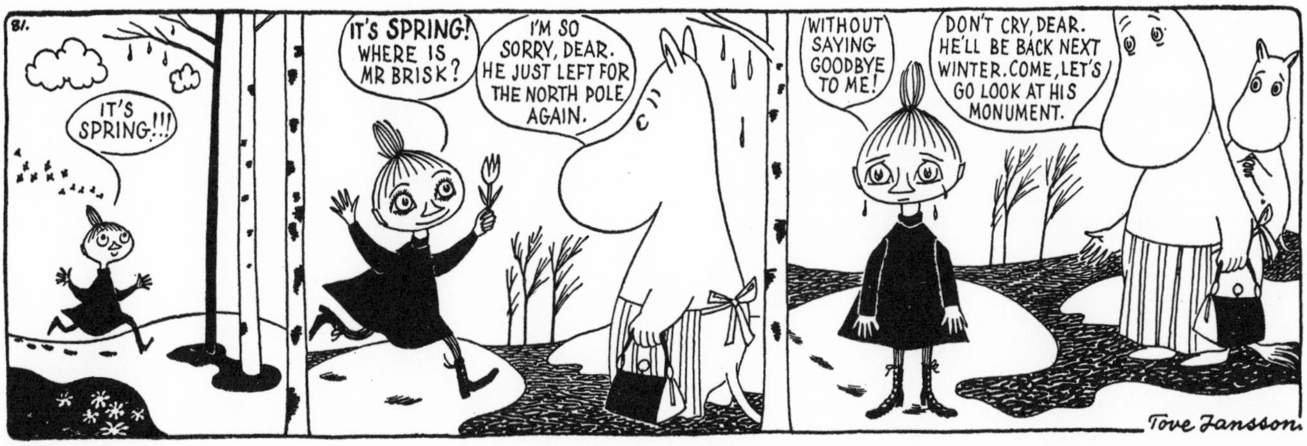
81.
IT'S SPRING!!!
IT'S SPRING! WHERE IS MR BRISK?
I'M SO SORRY, DEAR. HE JUST LEFT FOR THE NORTH POLE AGAIN.
WITHOUT SAYING GOODBYE TO ME!
DON'T CRY, DEAR. HE'LL BE BACK NEXT WINTER. COME, LET'S GO LOOK AT HIS MONUMENT.
Tove Jansson.

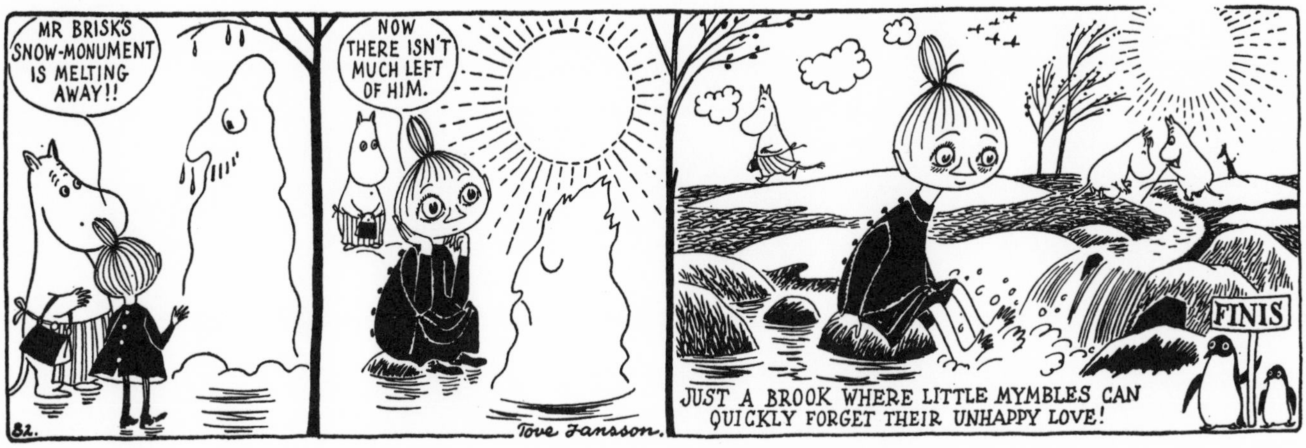
MR BRISK'S SNOW-MONUMENT IS MELTING AWAY!!
82.
NOW THERE ISN'T MUCH LEFT OF HIM.
Tove Jansson.
FINIS
JUST A BROOK WHERE LITTLE MYMBLES CAN QUICKLY FORGET THEIR UNHAPPY LOVE!

6. Moomin Mamma's Maid

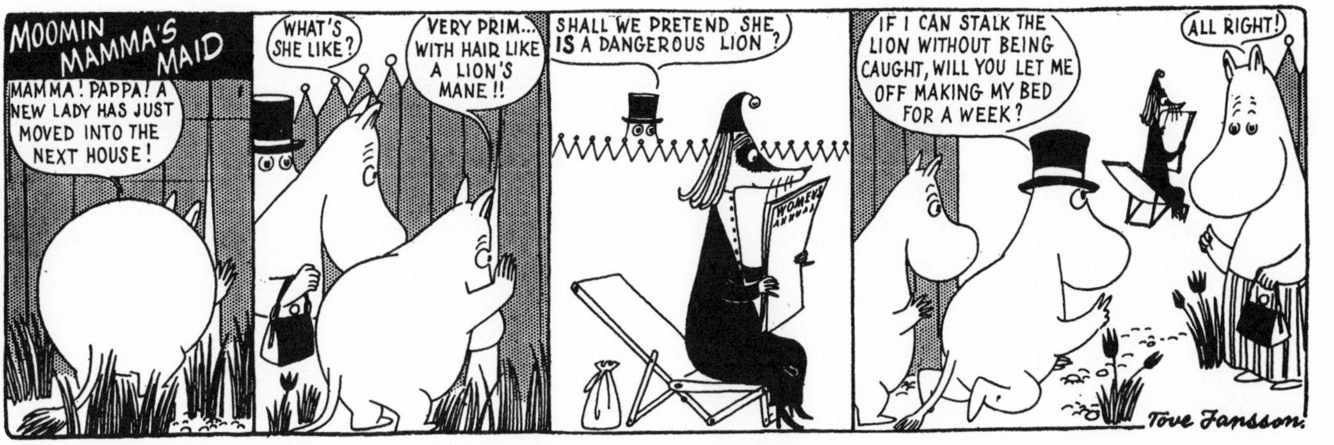

MOOMIN MAMMA'S MAID
MAMMA! PAPPA! A NEW LADY HAS JUST MOVED INTO THE NEXT HOUSE!
WHAT'S SHE LIKE?
VERY PRIM... WITH HAIR LIKE A LION'S MANE!!
SHALL WE PRETEND SHE IS A DANGEROUS LION?
WOMEN'S ANNUAL
IF I CAN STALK THE LION WITHOUT BEING CAUGHT, WILL YOU LET ME OFF MAKING MY BED FOR A WEEK?
ALL RIGHT!
Tove Jansson.

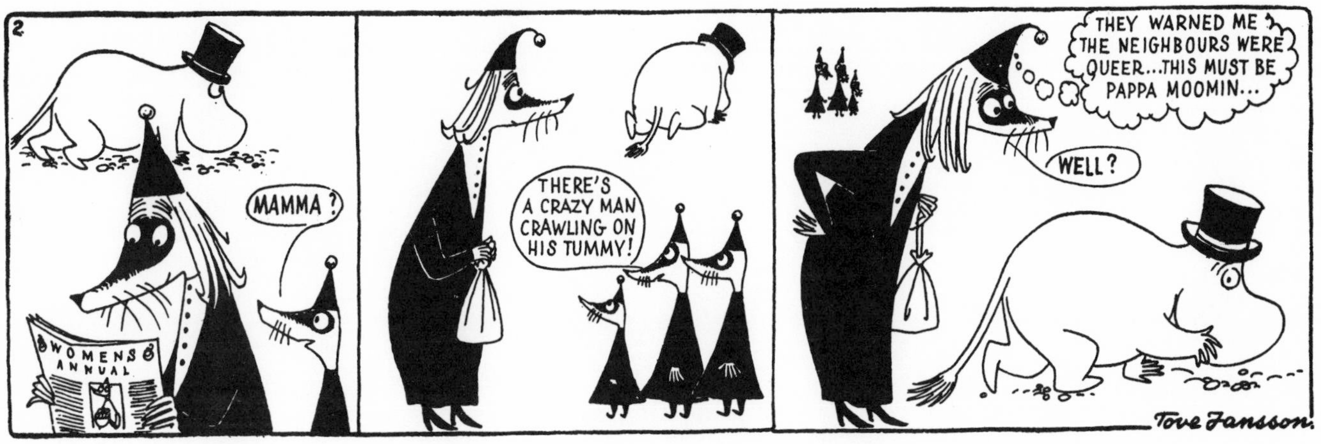

2
WOMENS ANNUAL
MAMMA?
THERE'S A CRAZY MAN CRAWLING ON HIS TUMMY!
THEY WARNED ME THE NEIGHBOURS WERE QUEER...THIS MUST BE PAPPA MOOMIN...
WELL?
Tove Jansson.

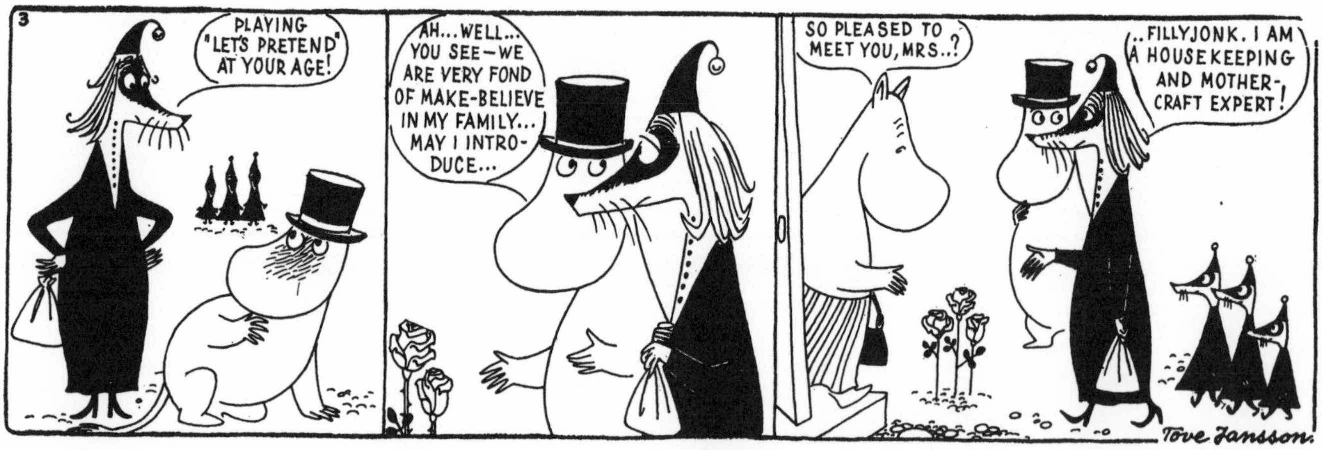
3
PLAYING "LET'S PRETEND" AT YOUR AGE!
AH...WELL... YOU SEE—WE ARE VERY FOND OF MAKE-BELIEVE IN MY FAMILY... MAY I INTRODUCE...
SO PLEASED TO MEET YOU, MRS..?
..FILLYJONK. I AM A HOUSEKEEPING AND MOTHER-CRAFT EXPERT!
Tove Jansson.

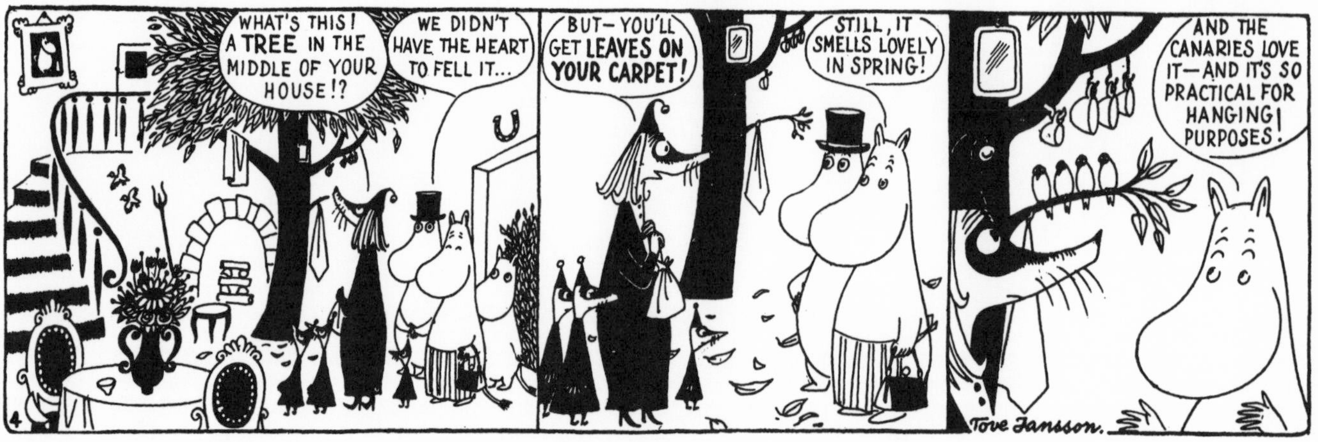
4
WHAT'S THIS! A TREE IN THE MIDDLE OF YOUR HOUSE!?
WE DIDN'T HAVE THE HEART TO FELL IT...
BUT—YOU'LL GET LEAVES ON YOUR CARPET!
STILL, IT SMELLS LOVELY IN SPRING!
AND THE CANARIES LOVE IT—AND IT'S SO PRACTICAL FOR HANGING PURPOSES!
Tove Jansson.

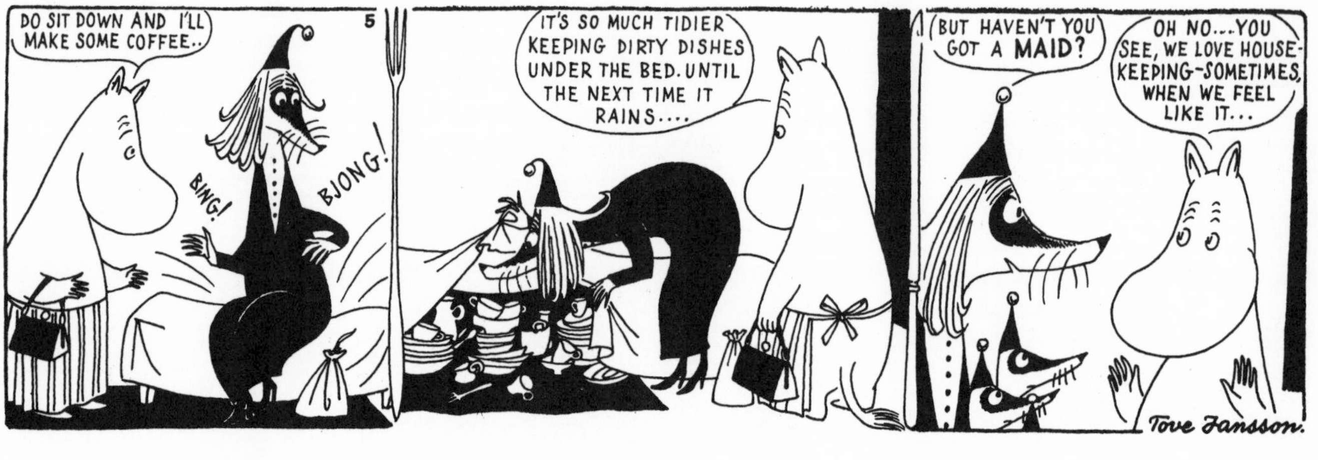
5
DO SIT DOWN AND I'LL MAKE SOME COFFEE..
BING!
BJONG!
IT'S SO MUCH TIDIER KEEPING DIRTY DISHES UNDER THE BED. UNTIL THE NEXT TIME IT RAINS....
BUT HAVEN'T YOU GOT A MAID?
OH NO...YOU SEE, WE LOVE HOUSE-KEEPING—SOMETIMES, WHEN WE FEEL LIKE IT...
Tove Jansson.

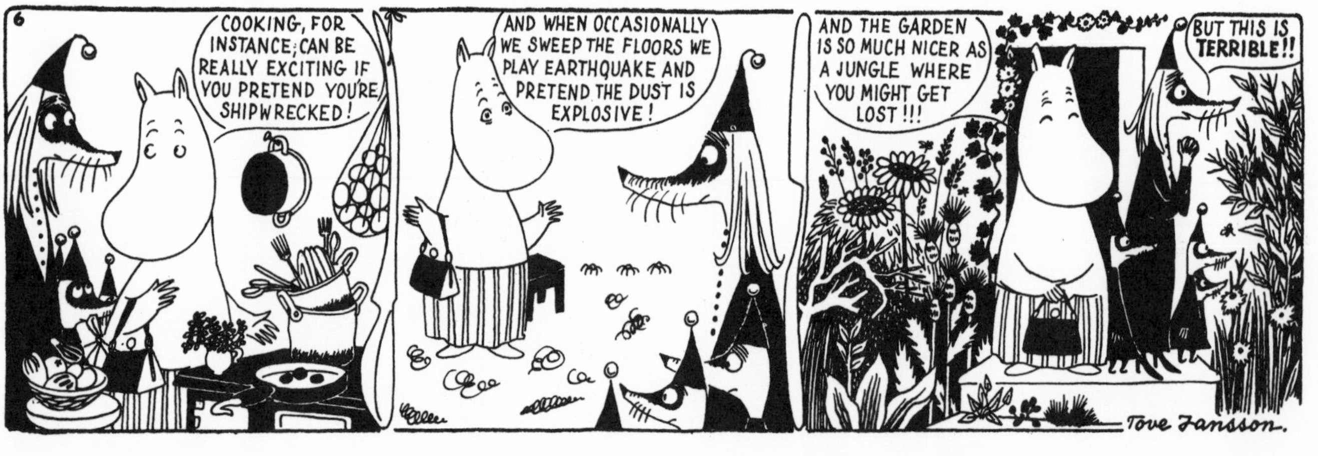
6
COOKING, FOR INSTANCE, CAN BE REALLY EXCITING IF YOU PRETEND YOU'RE SHIPWRECKED!
AND WHEN OCCASIONALLY WE SWEEP THE FLOORS WE PLAY EARTHQUAKE AND PRETEND THE DUST IS EXPLOSIVE!
AND THE GARDEN IS SO MUCH NICER AS A JUNGLE WHERE YOU MIGHT GET LOST!!!
BUT THIS IS TERRIBLE!!
Tove Jansson.

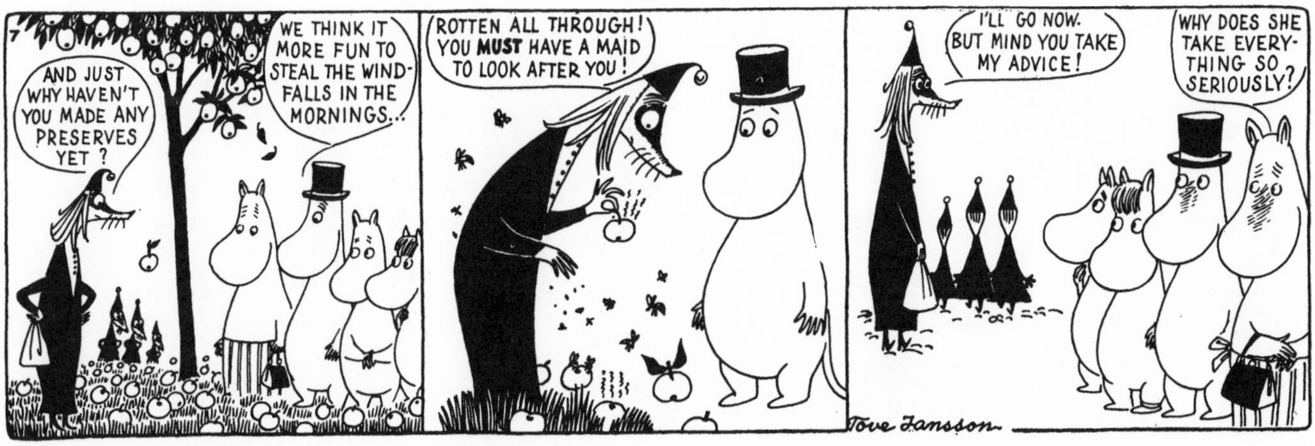
7
AND JUST WHY HAVEN'T YOU MADE ANY PRESERVES YET ?
WE THINK IT MORE FUN TO STEAL THE WINDFALLS IN THE MORNINGS...
ROTTEN ALL THROUGH! YOU **MUST** HAVE A MAID TO LOOK AFTER YOU!
I'LL GO NOW. BUT MIND YOU TAKE MY ADVICE!
WHY DOES SHE TAKE EVERYTHING SO SERIOUSLY?
Tove Jansson

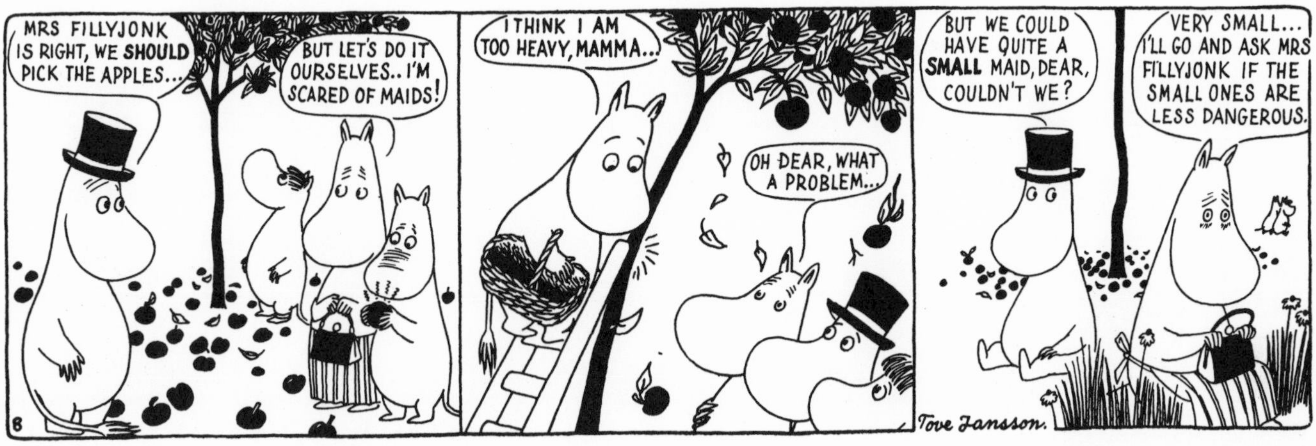
MRS FILLYJONK IS RIGHT, WE **SHOULD** PICK THE APPLES...
BUT LET'S DO IT OURSELVES.. I'M SCARED OF MAIDS!
I THINK I AM TOO HEAVY, **MAMMA**...
OH DEAR, WHAT A PROBLEM...
BUT WE COULD HAVE QUITE A **SMALL** MAID, DEAR, COULDN'T WE?
VERY SMALL... I'LL GO AND ASK MRS FILLYJONK IF THE SMALL ONES ARE LESS DANGEROUS.
8
Tove Jansson.

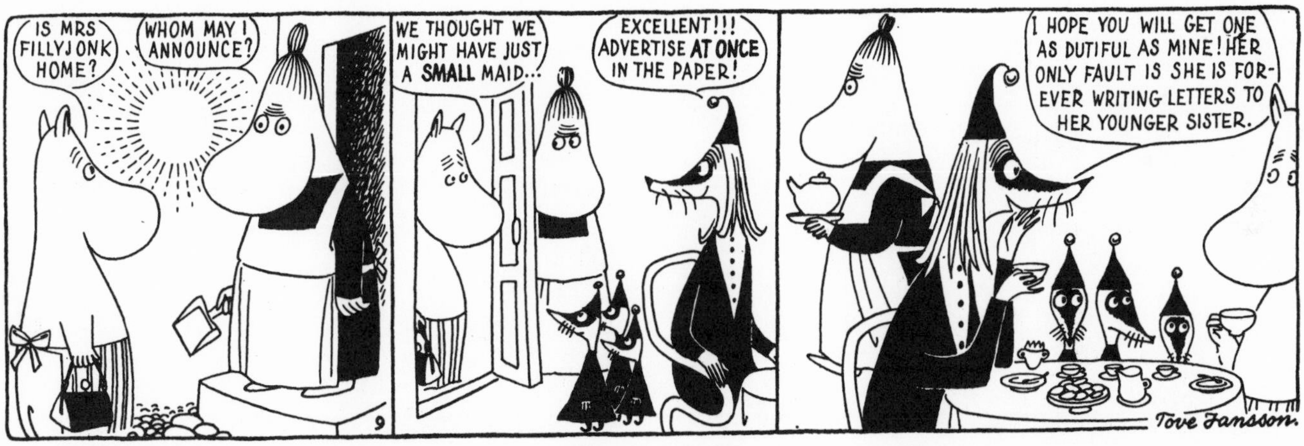
IS MRS FILLYJONK HOME?
WHOM MAY I ANNOUNCE?
9
WE THOUGHT WE MIGHT HAVE JUST A **SMALL** MAID...
EXCELLENT!!! ADVERTISE **AT ONCE** IN THE PAPER!
I HOPE YOU WILL GET ONE AS DUTIFUL AS MINE! HER ONLY FAULT IS SHE IS FOREVER WRITING LETTERS TO HER YOUNGER SISTER.
Tove Jansson.

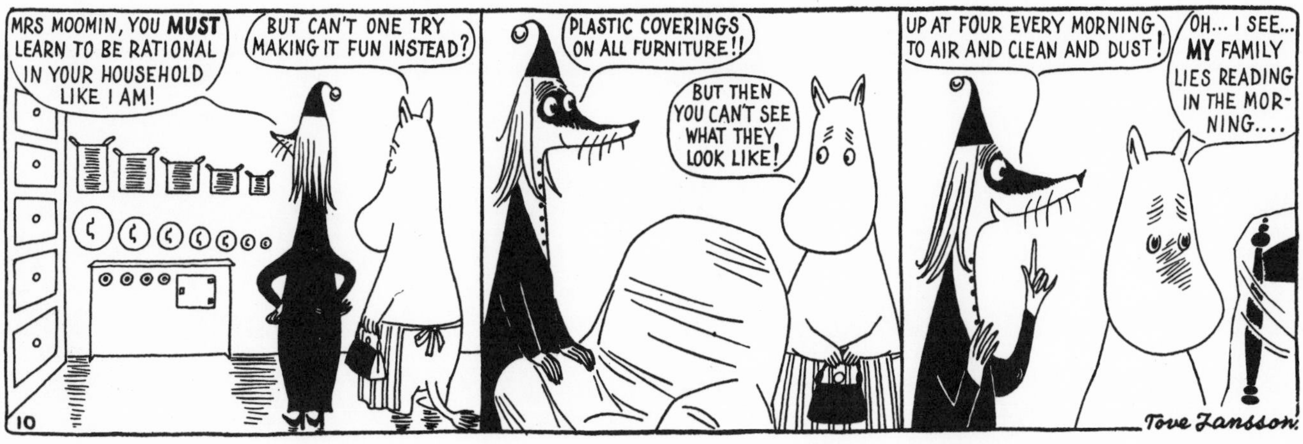
MRS MOOMIN, YOU **MUST** LEARN TO BE RATIONAL IN YOUR HOUSEHOLD LIKE I AM!
BUT CAN'T ONE TRY MAKING IT FUN INSTEAD?
10
PLASTIC COVERINGS ON ALL FURNITURE!!
BUT THEN YOU CAN'T SEE WHAT THEY LOOK LIKE!
UP AT FOUR EVERY MORNING TO AIR AND CLEAN AND DUST!
OH... I SEE... **MY** FAMILY LIES READING IN THE MORNING....
Tove Jansson.

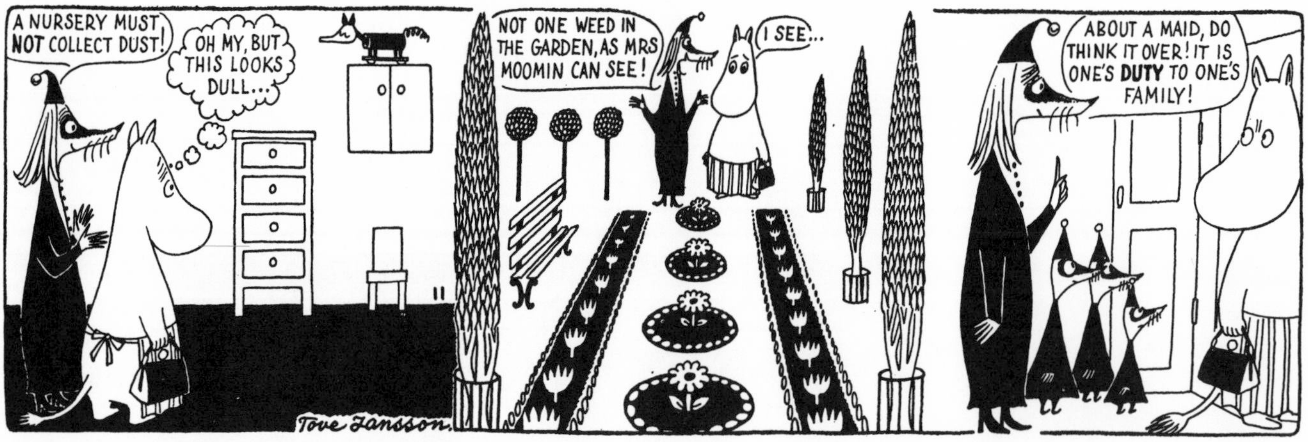
A NURSERY MUST NOT COLLECT DUST!
OH MY, BUT THIS LOOKS DULL...
11
NOT ONE WEED IN THE GARDEN, AS MRS MOOMIN CAN SEE!
I SEE...
ABOUT A MAID, DO THINK IT OVER! IT IS ONE'S DUTY TO ONE'S FAMILY!
Tove Jansson.

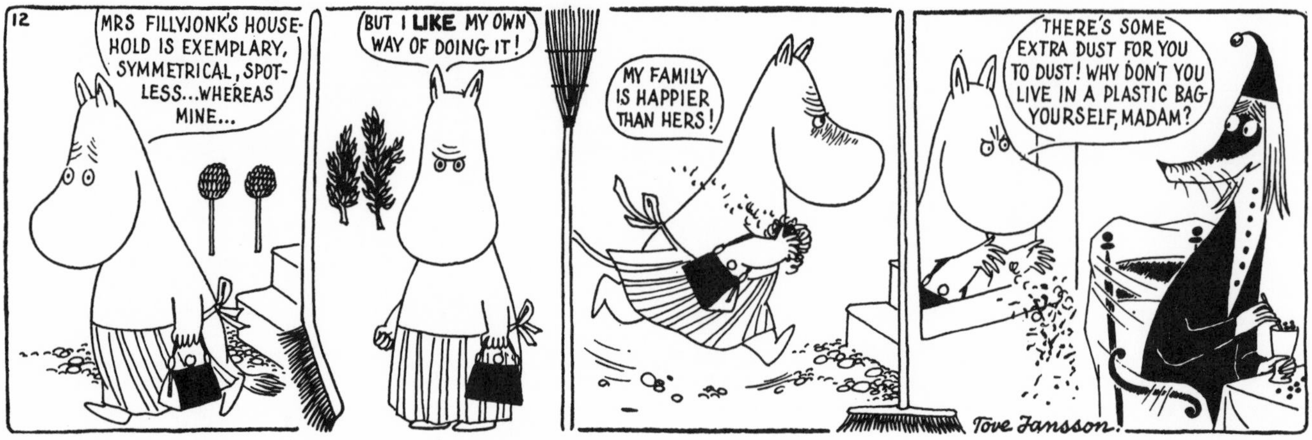
12
MRS FILLYJONK'S HOUSEHOLD IS EXEMPLARY, SYMMETRICAL, SPOTLESS...WHEREAS MINE...
BUT I LIKE MY OWN WAY OF DOING IT!
MY FAMILY IS HAPPIER THAN HERS!
THERE'S SOME EXTRA DUST FOR YOU TO DUST! WHY DON'T YOU LIVE IN A PLASTIC BAG YOURSELF, MADAM?
Tove Jansson.

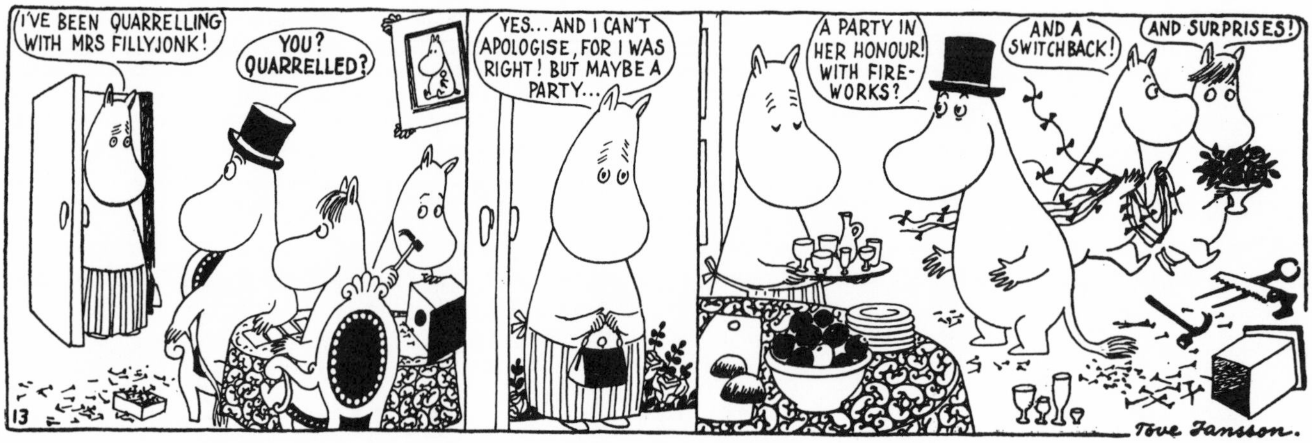
I'VE BEEN QUARRELLING WITH MRS FILLYJONK!
YOU? QUARRELLED?
13
YES... AND I CAN'T APOLOGISE, FOR I WAS RIGHT! BUT MAYBE A PARTY...
A PARTY IN HER HONOUR! WITH FIRE-WORKS?
AND A SWITCHBACK!
AND SURPRISES!
Tove Jansson.

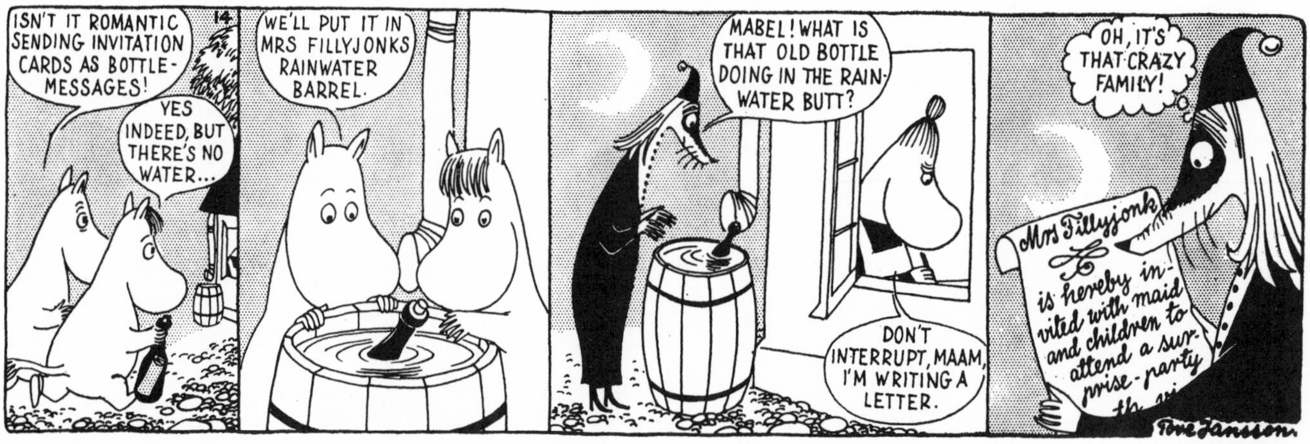
ISN'T IT ROMANTIC SENDING INVITATION CARDS AS BOTTLE-MESSAGES!
14
YES INDEED, BUT THERE'S NO WATER...
WE'LL PUT IT IN MRS FILLYJONKS RAINWATER BARREL.
MABEL! WHAT IS THAT OLD BOTTLE DOING IN THE RAIN-WATER BUTT?
DON'T INTERRUPT, MAAM, I'M WRITING A LETTER.
OH, IT'S THAT CRAZY FAMILY!
Mrs Fillyjonk
is hereby invited with maid and children to attend a surprise-party
Tove Jansson.

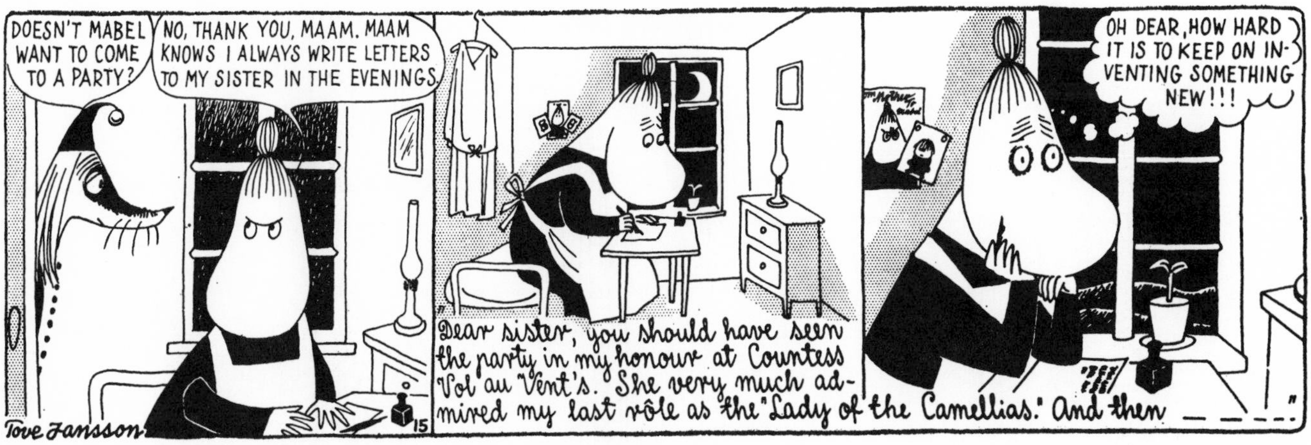
DOESN'T MABEL WANT TO COME TO A PARTY?
NO, THANK YOU, MAAM. MAAM KNOWS I ALWAYS WRITE LETTERS TO MY SISTER IN THE EVENINGS.
"Dear sister, you should have seen the party in my honour at Countess Vol au Vent's. She very much admired my last rôle as the "Lady of the Camellias." And then ————"
OH DEAR, HOW HARD IT IS TO KEEP ON INVENTING SOMETHING NEW!!!
Tove Jansson
15

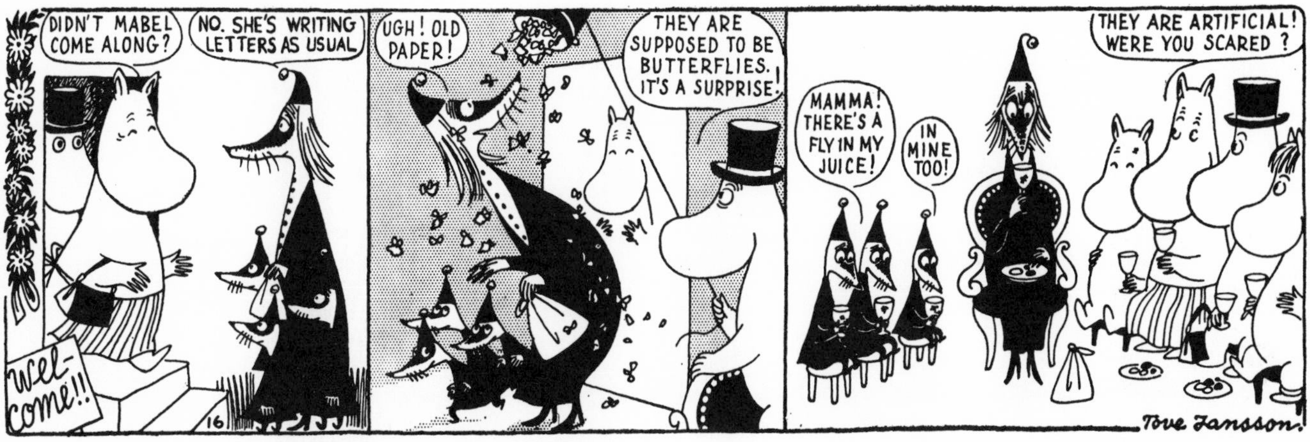
DIDN'T MABEL COME ALONG?
NO. SHE'S WRITING LETTERS AS USUAL.
WEL-COME!!!
16
UGH! OLD PAPER!
THEY ARE SUPPOSED TO BE BUTTERFLIES. IT'S A SURPRISE!
MAMMA! THERE'S A FLY IN MY JUICE!
IN MINE TOO!
THEY ARE ARTIFICIAL! WERE YOU SCARED?
Tove Jansson

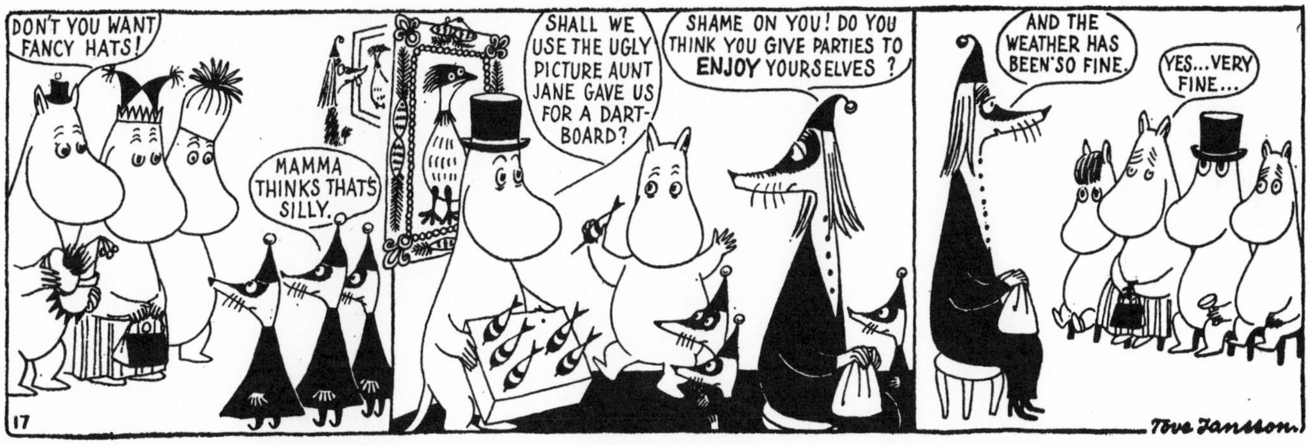
DON'T YOU WANT FANCY HATS!
MAMMA THINKS THAT'S SILLY.
17
SHALL WE USE THE UGLY PICTURE AUNT JANE GAVE US FOR A DART-BOARD?
SHAME ON YOU! DO YOU THINK YOU GIVE PARTIES TO ENJOY YOURSELVES?
AND THE WEATHER HAS BEEN SO FINE.
YES... VERY FINE...
Tove Jansson

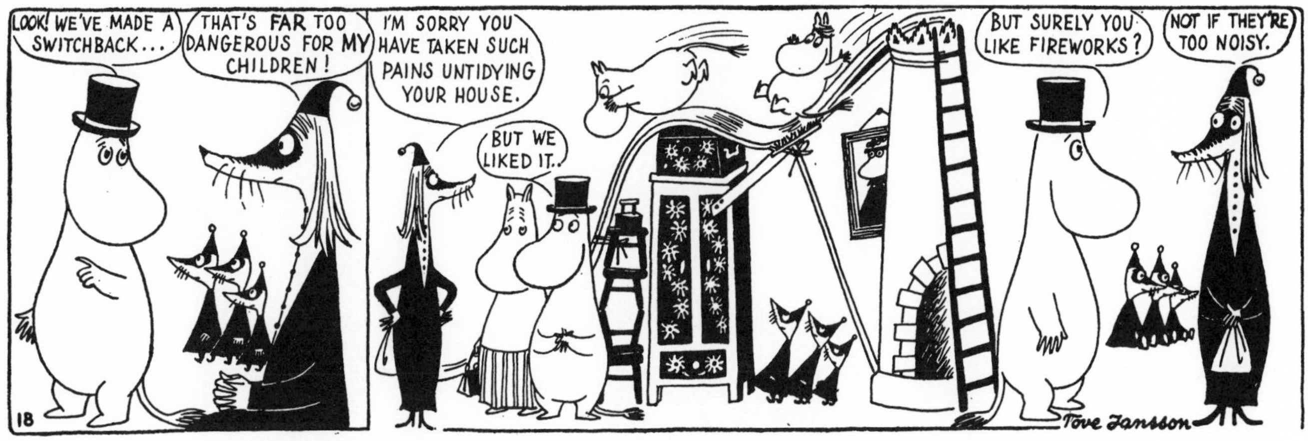
LOOK! WE'VE MADE A SWITCHBACK...
THAT'S FAR TOO DANGEROUS FOR MY CHILDREN!
18
I'M SORRY YOU HAVE TAKEN SUCH PAINS UNTIDYING YOUR HOUSE.
BUT WE LIKED IT.
BUT SURELY YOU LIKE FIREWORKS?
NOT IF THEY'RE TOO NOISY.
Tove Jansson

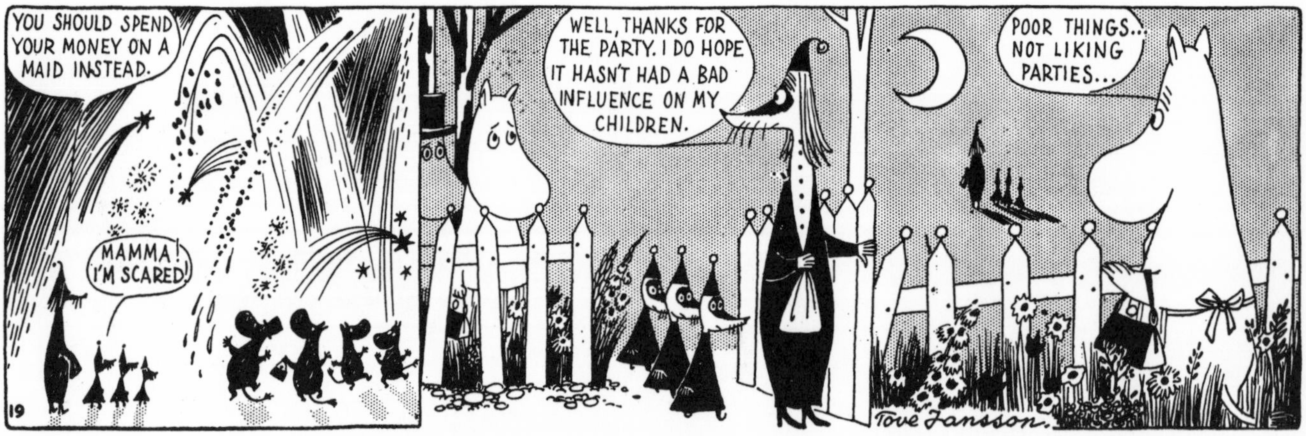
YOU SHOULD SPEND YOUR MONEY ON A MAID INSTEAD.
MAMMA! I'M SCARED!
19
WELL, THANKS FOR THE PARTY. I DO HOPE IT HASN'T HAD A BAD INFLUENCE ON MY CHILDREN.
POOR THINGS... NOT LIKING PARTIES...
Tove Jansson.

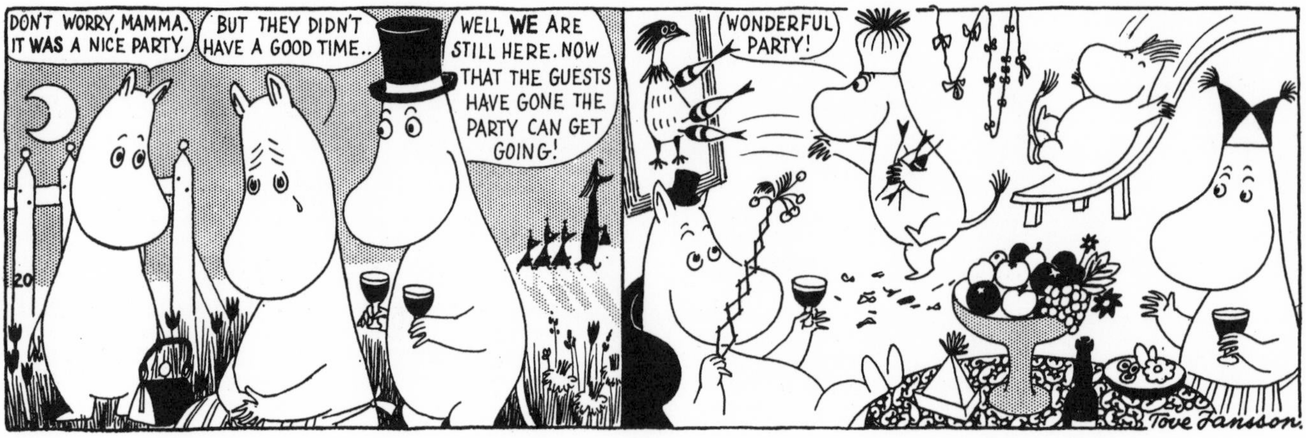
DON'T WORRY, MAMMA. IT WAS A NICE PARTY.
BUT THEY DIDN'T HAVE A GOOD TIME..
WELL, WE ARE STILL HERE. NOW THAT THE GUESTS HAVE GONE THE PARTY CAN GET GOING!
20
WONDERFUL PARTY!
Tove Jansson.

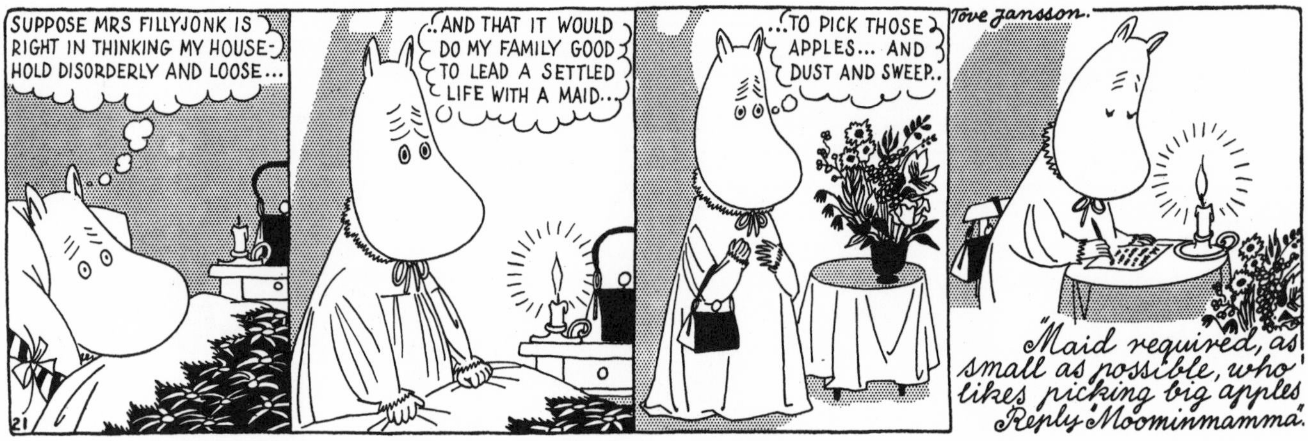
SUPPOSE MRS FILLYJONK IS RIGHT IN THINKING MY HOUSEHOLD DISORDERLY AND LOOSE...
21
..AND THAT IT WOULD DO MY FAMILY GOOD TO LEAD A SETTLED LIFE WITH A MAID...
...TO PICK THOSE APPLES... AND DUST AND SWEEP..
Tove Jansson.
"Maid required, as small as possible, who likes picking big apples Reply 'Moominmamma'.

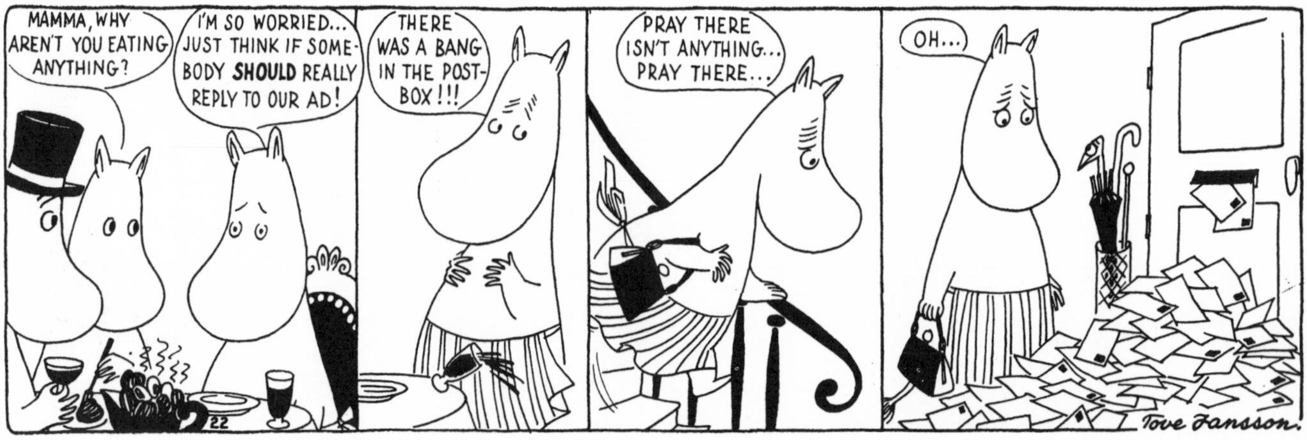
MAMMA, WHY AREN'T YOU EATING ANYTHING?
I'M SO WORRIED... JUST THINK IF SOMEBODY SHOULD REALLY REPLY TO OUR AD!
22
THERE WAS A BANG IN THE POST-BOX!!!
PRAY THERE ISN'T ANYTHING... PRAY THERE...
OH...
Tove Jansson.

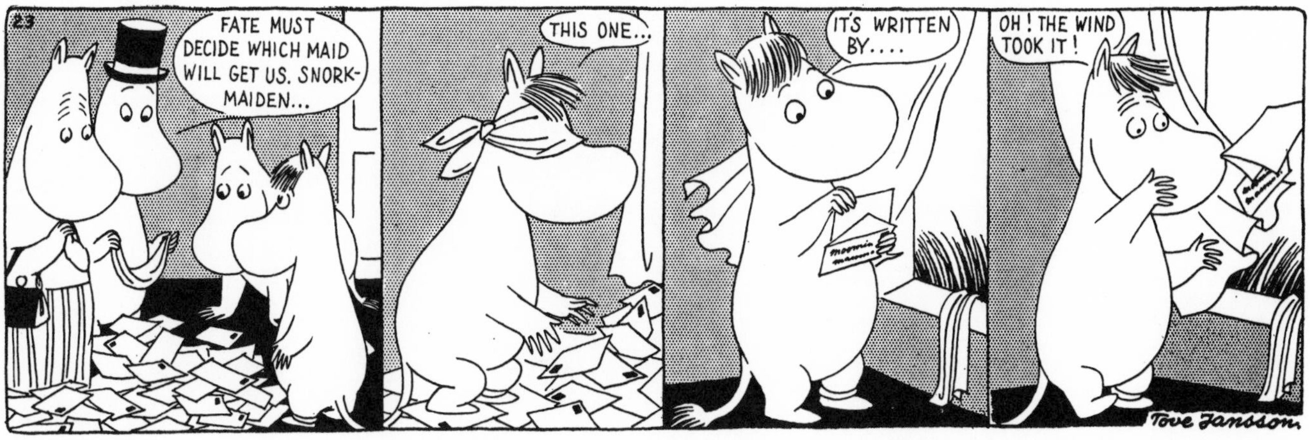
23
FATE MUST DECIDE WHICH MAID WILL GET US. SNORK-MAIDEN...
THIS ONE...
IT'S WRITTEN BY....
OH! THE WIND TOOK IT!
Tove Jansson

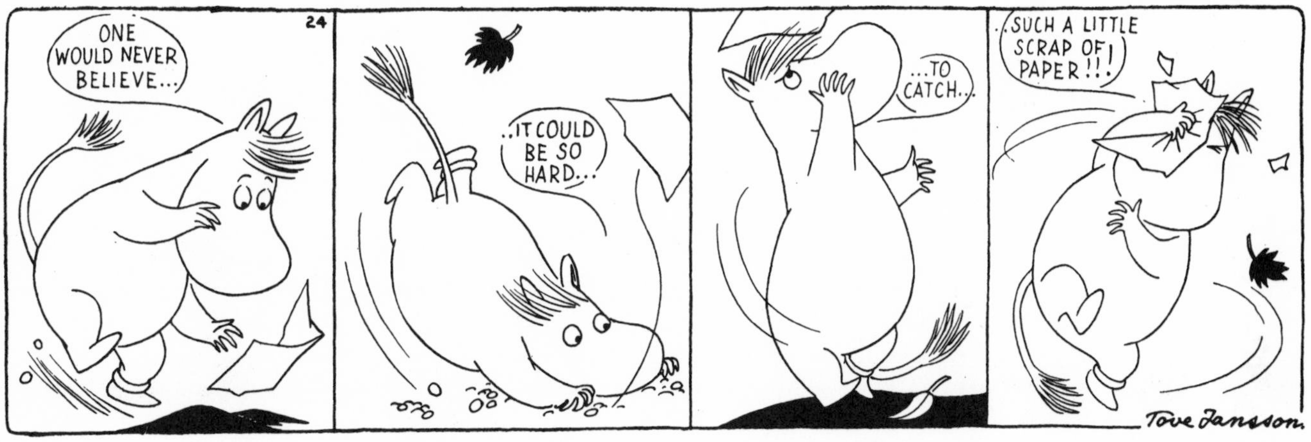
24
ONE WOULD NEVER BELIEVE...
..IT COULD BE SO HARD...
...TO CATCH...
..SUCH A LITTLE SCRAP OF PAPER!!!
Tove Jansson

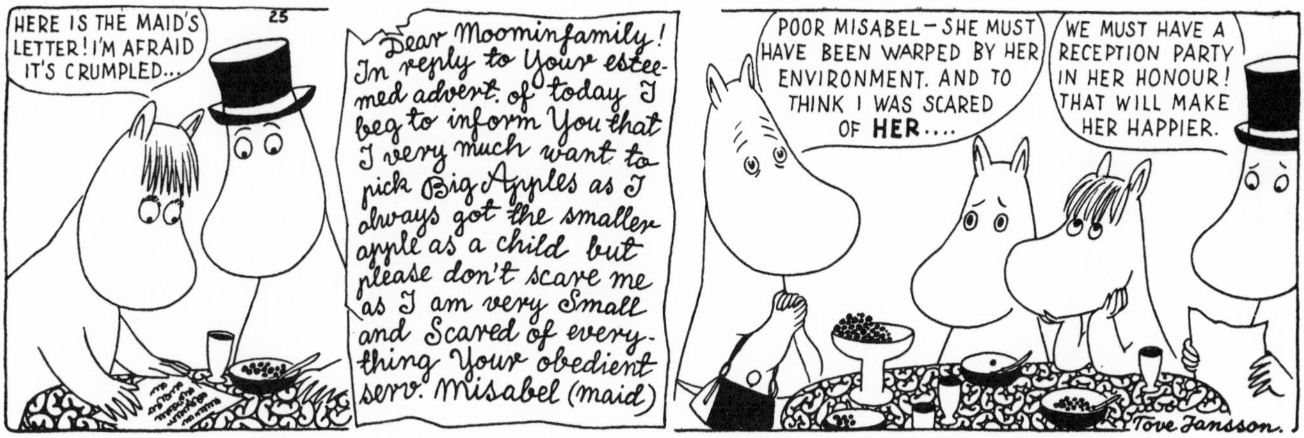
25
HERE IS THE MAID'S LETTER! I'M AFRAID IT'S CRUMPLED...
Dear Moominfamily! In reply to Your esteemed advert. of today I beg to inform You that I very much want to pick Big Apples as I always got the smaller apple as a child but please don't scare me as I am very Small and Scared of everything Your obedient serv. Misabel (maid)
POOR MISABEL – SHE MUST HAVE BEEN WARPED BY HER ENVIRONMENT. AND TO THINK I WAS SCARED OF HER....
WE MUST HAVE A RECEPTION PARTY IN HER HONOUR! THAT WILL MAKE HER HAPPIER.
Tove Jansson.

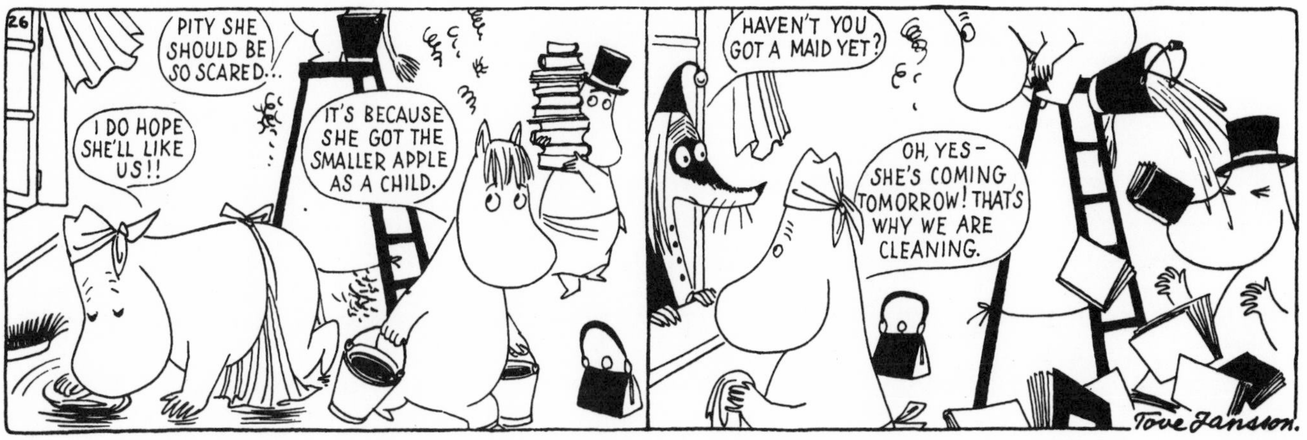
26
PITY SHE SHOULD BE SO SCARED...
I DO HOPE SHE'LL LIKE US!!
IT'S BECAUSE SHE GOT THE SMALLER APPLE AS A CHILD.
HAVEN'T YOU GOT A MAID YET?
OH, YES – SHE'S COMING TOMORROW! THAT'S WHY WE ARE CLEANING.
Tove Jansson.

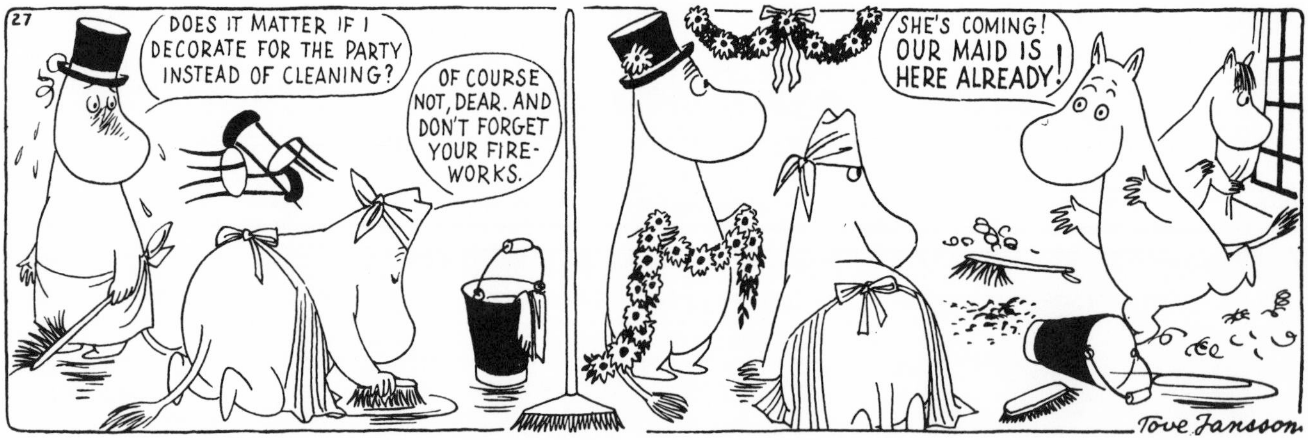
27
DOES IT MATTER IF I DECORATE FOR THE PARTY INSTEAD OF CLEANING?
OF COURSE NOT, DEAR. AND DON'T FORGET YOUR FIRE-WORKS.
SHE'S COMING! OUR MAID IS HERE ALREADY!
Tove Jansson

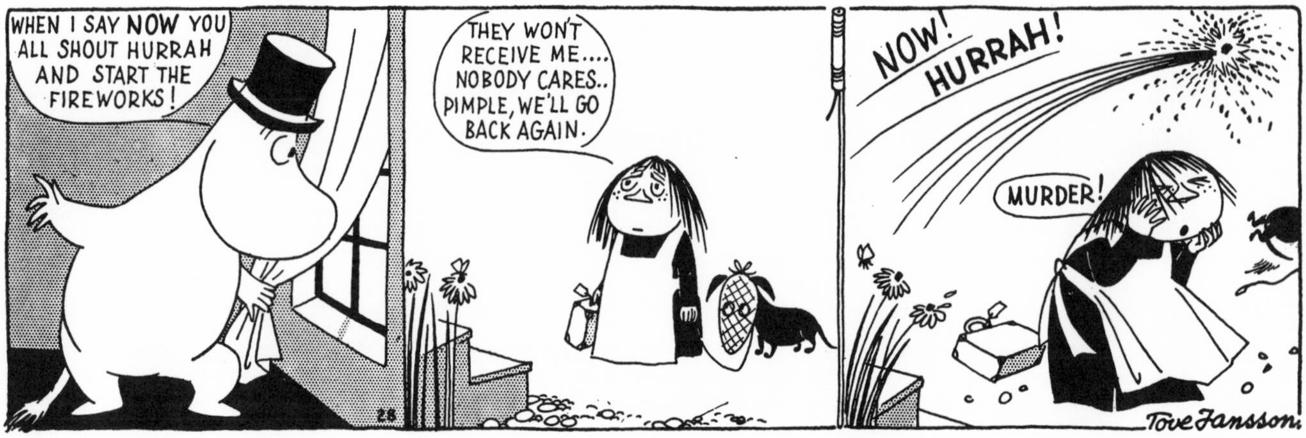
WHEN I SAY NOW YOU ALL SHOUT HURRAH AND START THE FIREWORKS!
28
THEY WON'T RECEIVE ME.... NOBODY CARES.. PIMPLE, WE'LL GO BACK AGAIN.
NOW!
HURRAH!
MURDER!
Tove Jansson

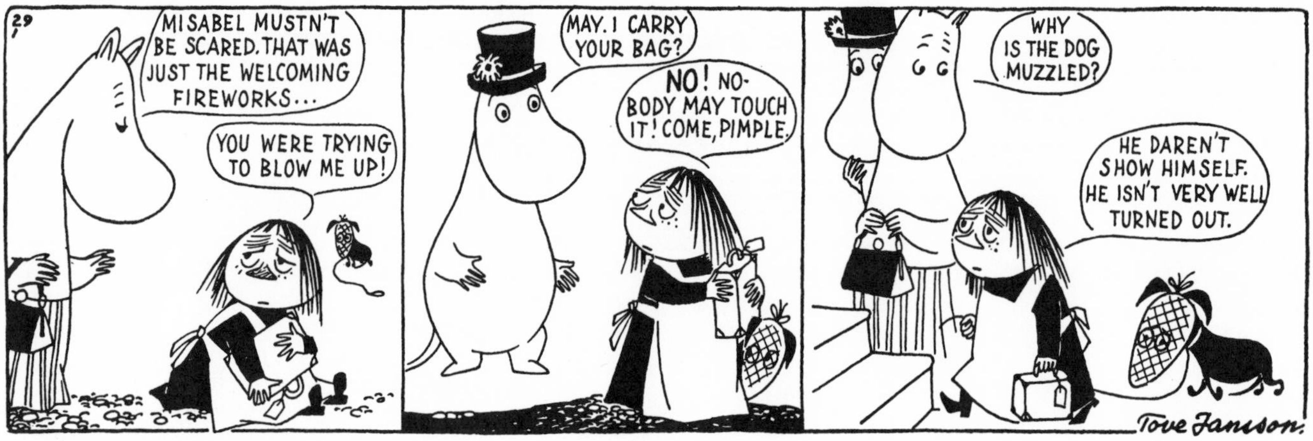
29
MISABEL MUSTN'T BE SCARED. THAT WAS JUST THE WELCOMING FIREWORKS...
YOU WERE TRYING TO BLOW ME UP!
MAY. I CARRY YOUR BAG?
NO! NO-BODY MAY TOUCH IT! COME, PIMPLE.
WHY IS THE DOG MUZZLED?
HE DAREN'T SHOW HIMSELF. HE ISN'T VERY WELL TURNED OUT.
Tove Jansson

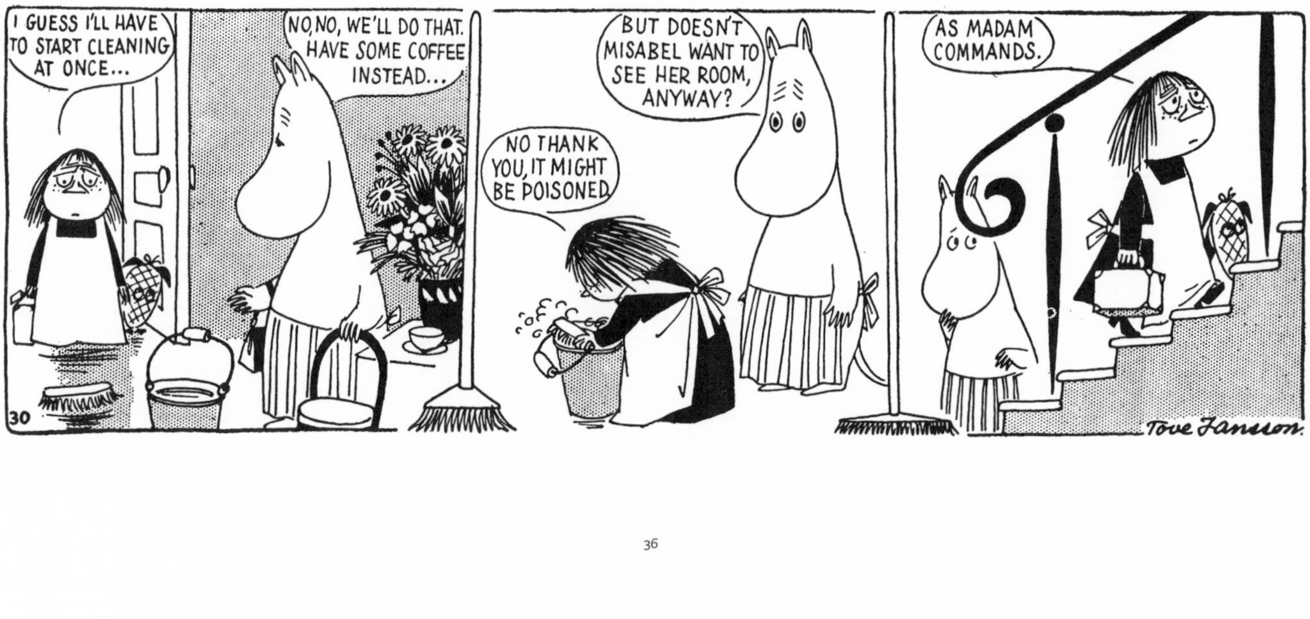
I GUESS I'LL HAVE TO START CLEANING AT ONCE...
NO, NO, WE'LL DO THAT. HAVE SOME COFFEE INSTEAD...
30
BUT DOESN'T MISABEL WANT TO SEE HER ROOM, ANYWAY?
NO THANK YOU, IT MIGHT BE POISONED.
AS MADAM COMMANDS.
Tove Jansson

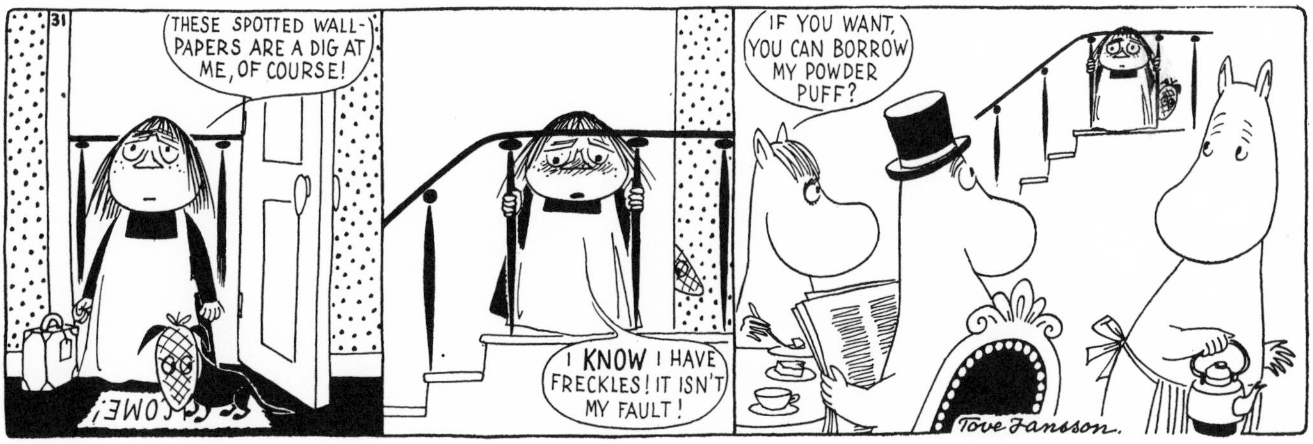
31
THESE SPOTTED WALLPAPERS ARE A DIG AT ME, OF COURSE!
I KNOW I HAVE FRECKLES! IT ISN'T MY FAULT!
IF YOU WANT, YOU CAN BORROW MY POWDER PUFF?
Tove Jansson.

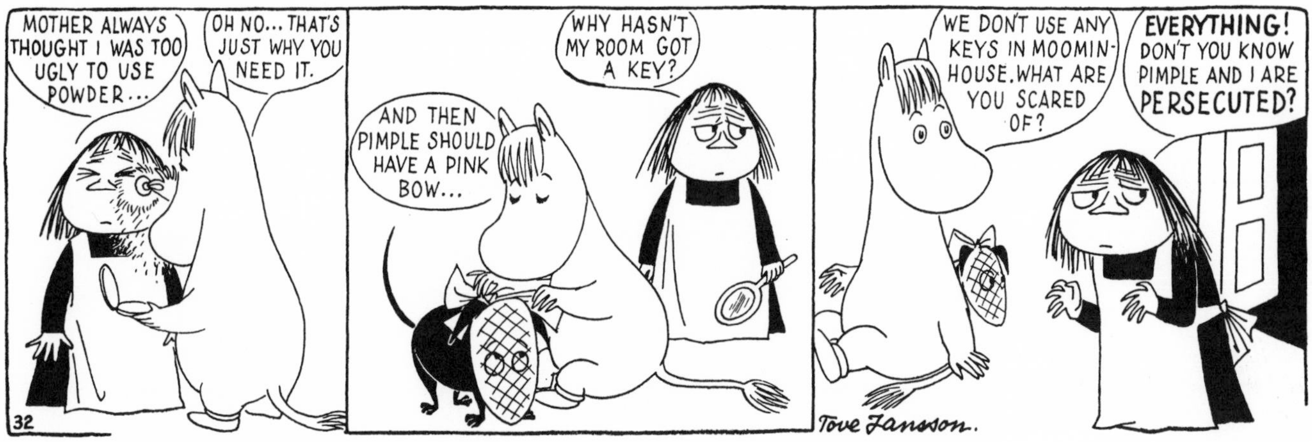
MOTHER ALWAYS THOUGHT I WAS TOO UGLY TO USE POWDER...
OH NO... THAT'S JUST WHY YOU NEED IT.
32
WHY HASN'T MY ROOM GOT A KEY?
AND THEN PIMPLE SHOULD HAVE A PINK BOW...
WE DON'T USE ANY KEYS IN MOOMINHOUSE. WHAT ARE YOU SCARED OF?
EVERYTHING! DON'T YOU KNOW PIMPLE AND I ARE PERSECUTED?
Tove Jansson.

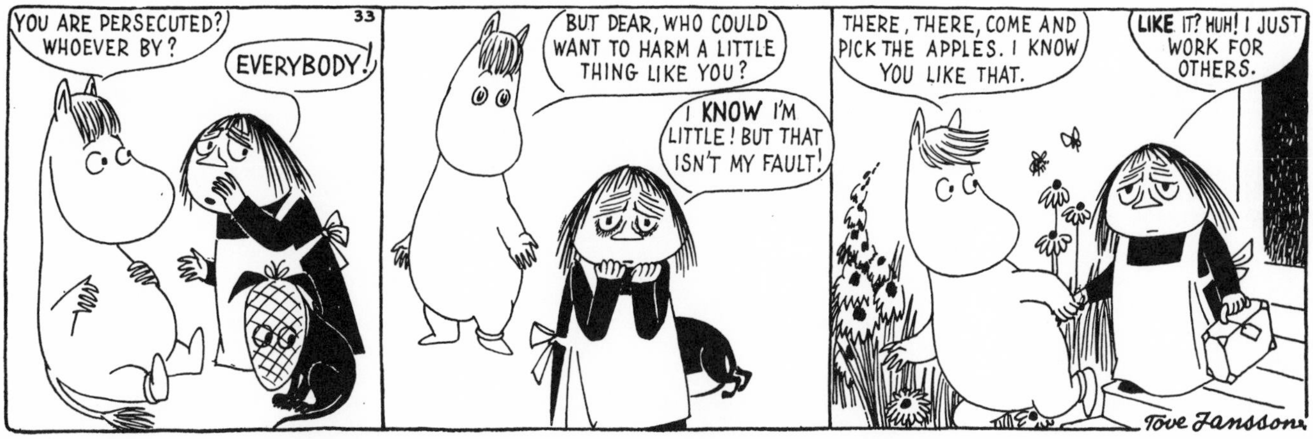
YOU ARE PERSECUTED? WHOEVER BY?
33
EVERYBODY!
BUT DEAR, WHO COULD WANT TO HARM A LITTLE THING LIKE YOU?
I KNOW I'M LITTLE! BUT THAT ISN'T MY FAULT!
THERE, THERE, COME AND PICK THE APPLES. I KNOW YOU LIKE THAT.
LIKE IT? HUH! I JUST WORK FOR OTHERS.
Tove Jansson.

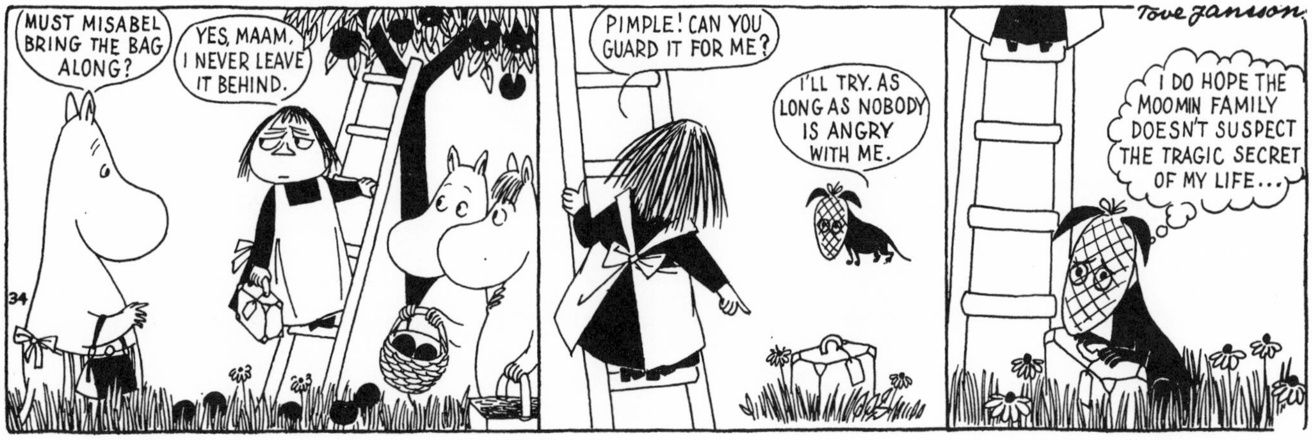
MUST MISABEL BRING THE BAG ALONG?
YES, MAAM, I NEVER LEAVE IT BEHIND.
34
PIMPLE! CAN YOU GUARD IT FOR ME?
I'LL TRY. AS LONG AS NOBODY IS ANGRY WITH ME.
Tove Jansson.
I DO HOPE THE MOOMIN FAMILY DOESN'T SUSPECT THE TRAGIC SECRET OF MY LIFE...

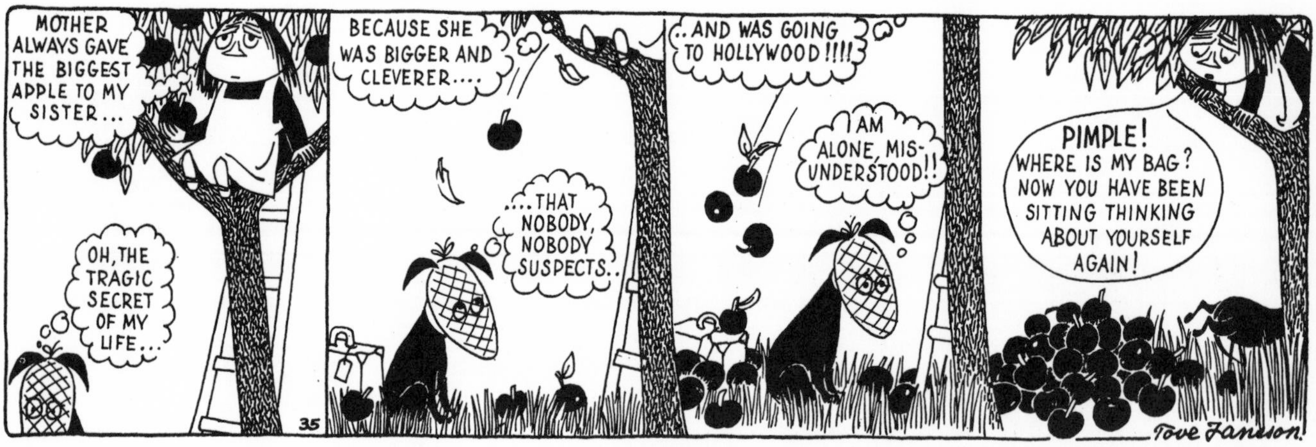
MOTHER ALWAYS GAVE THE BIGGEST APPLE TO MY SISTER...
OH, THE TRAGIC SECRET OF MY LIFE...
35
BECAUSE SHE WAS BIGGER AND CLEVERER....
....THAT NOBODY, NOBODY SUSPECTS...
..AND WAS GOING TO HOLLYWOOD!!!!
I AM ALONE, MISUNDERSTOOD!!
PIMPLE! WHERE IS MY BAG? NOW YOU HAVE BEEN SITTING THINKING ABOUT YOURSELF AGAIN!
Tove Jansson

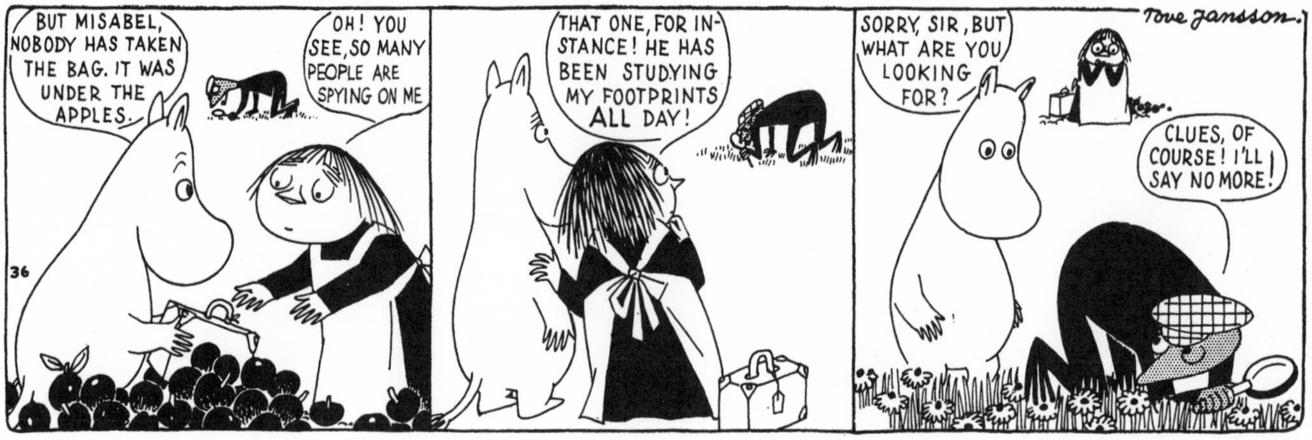
BUT MISABEL, NOBODY HAS TAKEN THE BAG. IT WAS UNDER THE APPLES.
OH! YOU SEE, SO MANY PEOPLE ARE SPYING ON ME
36
THAT ONE, FOR INSTANCE! HE HAS BEEN STUDYING MY FOOTPRINTS ALL DAY!
SORRY, SIR, BUT WHAT ARE YOU LOOKING FOR?
CLUES, OF COURSE! I'LL SAY NO MORE!
Tove Jansson

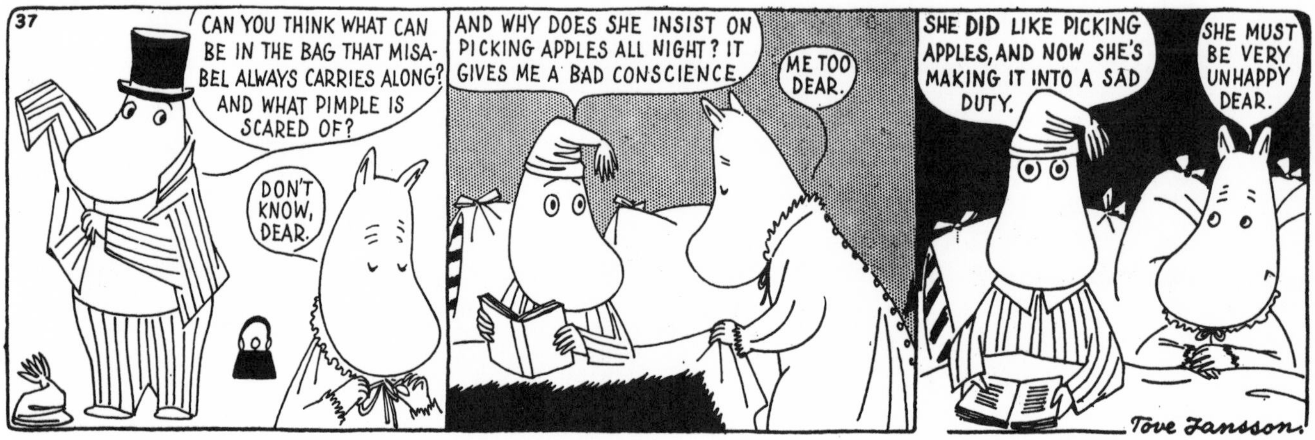
37
CAN YOU THINK WHAT CAN BE IN THE BAG THAT MISABEL ALWAYS CARRIES ALONG? AND WHAT PIMPLE IS SCARED OF?
DON'T KNOW, DEAR.
AND WHY DOES SHE INSIST ON PICKING APPLES ALL NIGHT? IT GIVES ME A BAD CONSCIENCE.
ME TOO DEAR.
SHE DID LIKE PICKING APPLES, AND NOW SHE'S MAKING IT INTO A SAD DUTY.
SHE MUST BE VERY UNHAPPY DEAR.
Tove Jansson

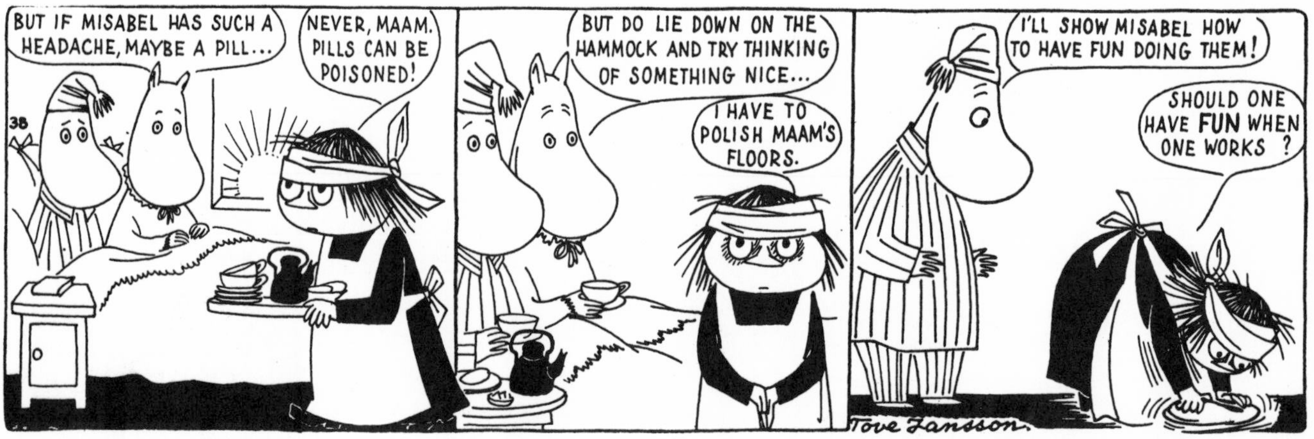
BUT IF MISABEL HAS SUCH A HEADACHE, MAYBE A PILL...
NEVER, MAAM. PILLS CAN BE POISONED!
38
BUT DO LIE DOWN ON THE HAMMOCK AND TRY THINKING OF SOMETHING NICE...
I HAVE TO POLISH MAAM'S FLOORS.
I'LL SHOW MISABEL HOW TO HAVE FUN DOING THEM!
SHOULD ONE HAVE FUN WHEN ONE WORKS?
Tove Jansson

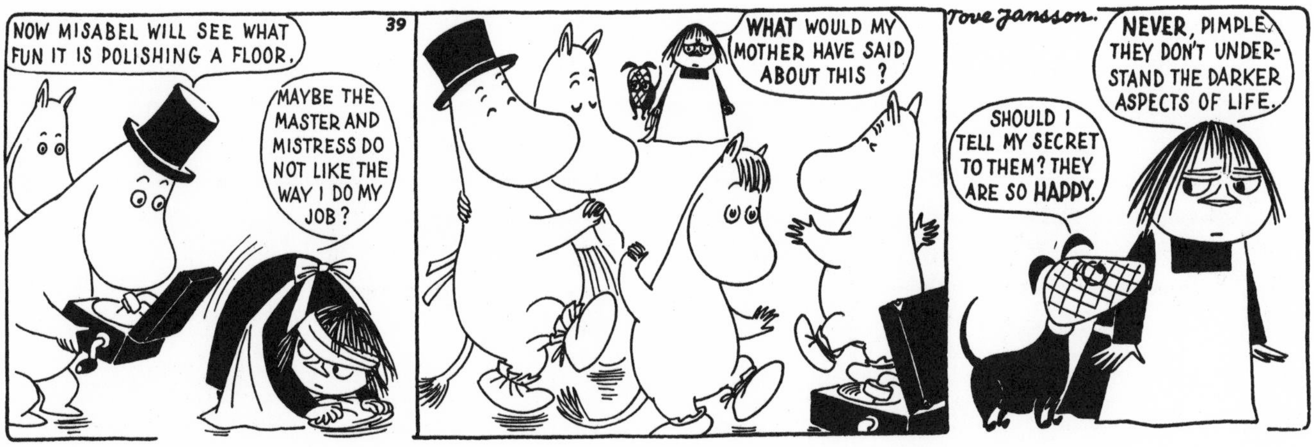
39
NOW MISABEL WILL SEE WHAT FUN IT IS POLISHING A FLOOR.
MAYBE THE MASTER AND MISTRESS DO NOT LIKE THE WAY I DO MY JOB?
WHAT WOULD MY MOTHER HAVE SAID ABOUT THIS ?
Tove Jansson.
SHOULD I TELL MY SECRET TO THEM? THEY ARE SO HAPPY.
NEVER, PIMPLE. THEY DON'T UNDERSTAND THE DARKER ASPECTS OF LIFE.

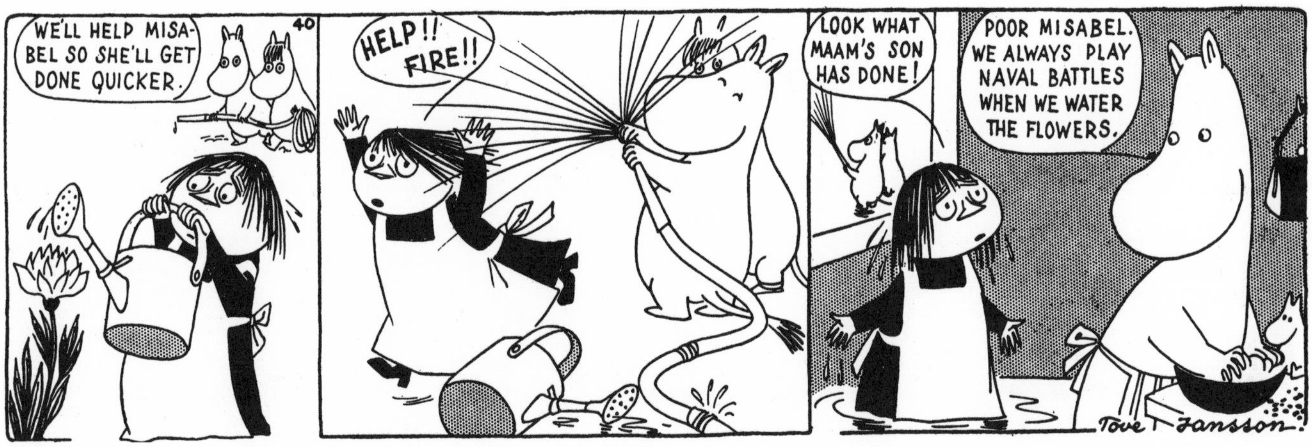
WE'LL HELP MISABEL SO SHE'LL GET DONE QUICKER.
40
HELP!! FIRE!!
LOOK WHAT MAAM'S SON HAS DONE!
POOR MISABEL. WE ALWAYS PLAY NAVAL BATTLES WHEN WE WATER THE FLOWERS.
Tove Jansson.

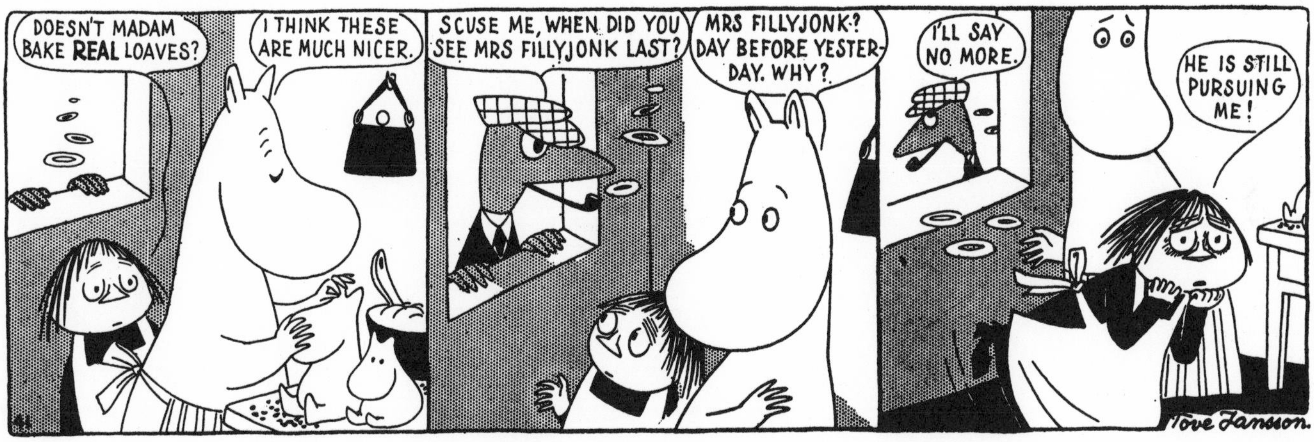
DOESN'T MADAM BAKE REAL LOAVES?
I THINK THESE ARE MUCH NICER.
SCUSE ME, WHEN DID YOU SEE MRS FILLYJONK LAST?
MRS FILLYJONK? DAY BEFORE YESTERDAY. WHY?
I'LL SAY NO MORE.
HE IS STILL PURSUING ME!
Tove Jansson.

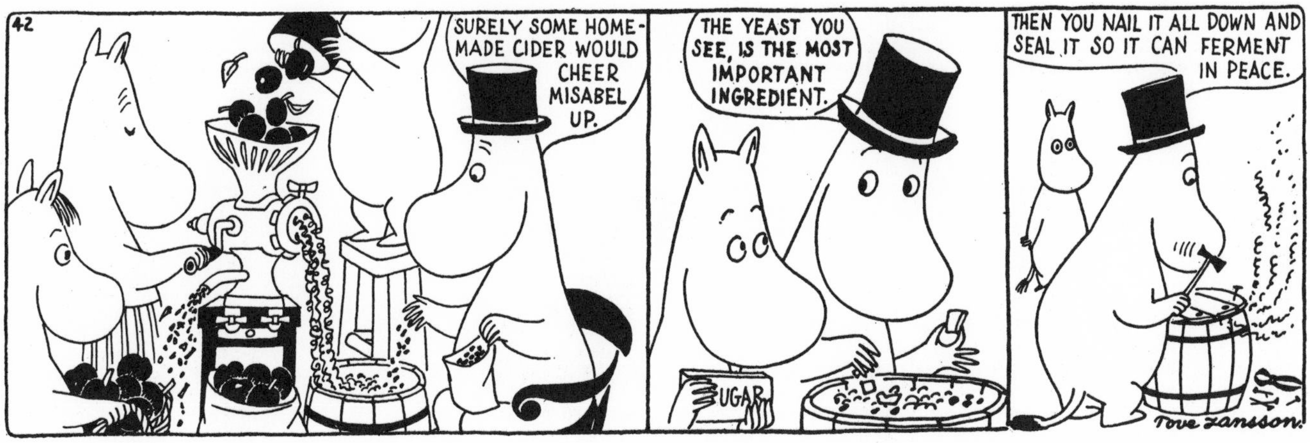
42
SURELY SOME HOME-MADE CIDER WOULD CHEER MISABEL UP.
THE YEAST YOU SEE, IS THE MOST IMPORTANT INGREDIENT.
UGAR
THEN YOU NAIL IT ALL DOWN AND SEAL IT SO IT CAN FERMENT IN PEACE.
Tove Jansson.

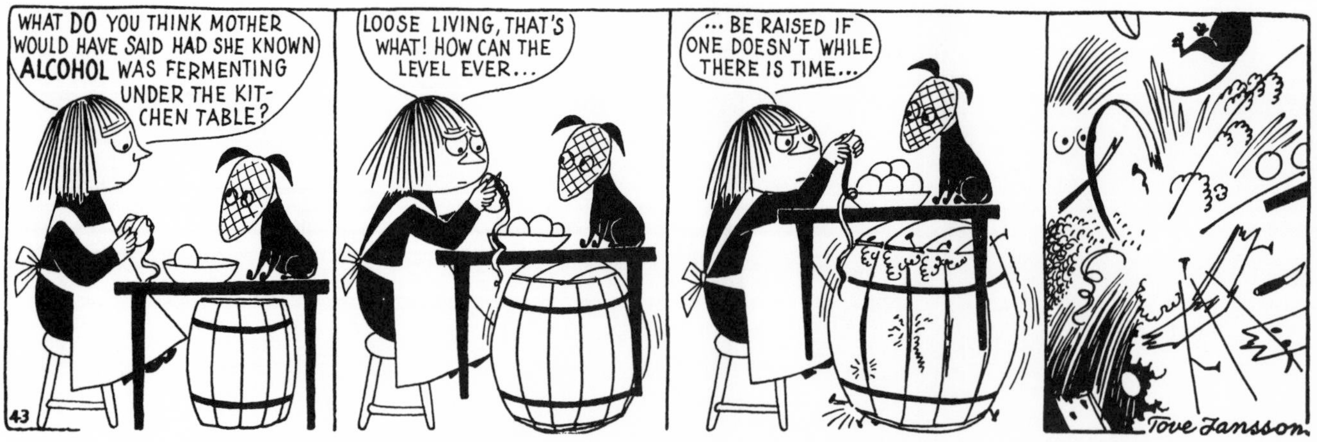
43
WHAT DO YOU THINK MOTHER WOULD HAVE SAID HAD SHE KNOWN ALCOHOL WAS FERMENTING UNDER THE KITCHEN TABLE?
LOOSE LIVING, THAT'S WHAT! HOW CAN THE LEVEL EVER...
... BE RAISED IF ONE DOESN'T WHILE THERE IS TIME...
Tove Jansson

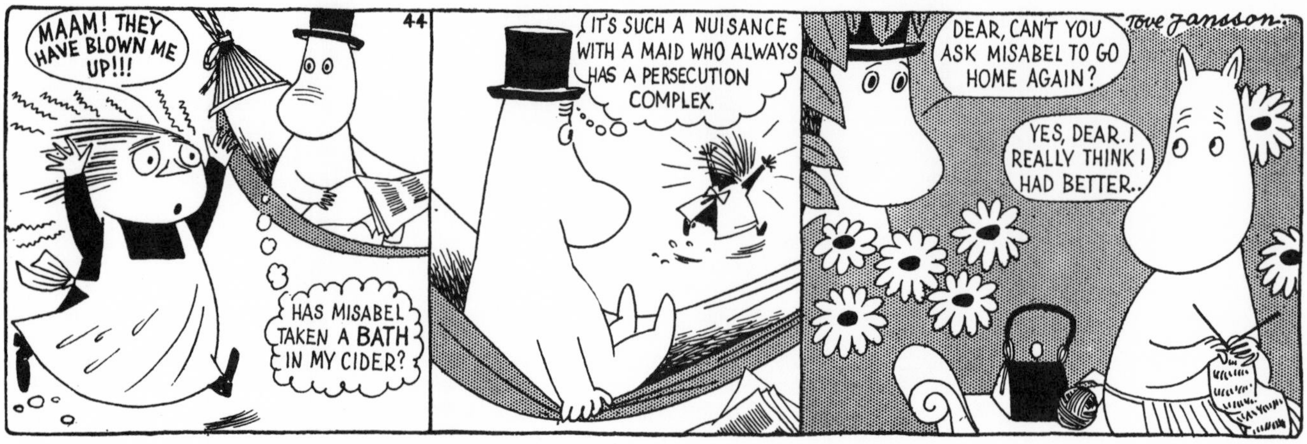
44
MAAM! THEY HAVE BLOWN ME UP!!!
HAS MISABEL TAKEN A BATH IN MY CIDER?
IT'S SUCH A NUISANCE WITH A MAID WHO ALWAYS HAS A PERSECUTION COMPLEX.
Tove Jansson
DEAR, CAN'T YOU ASK MISABEL TO GO HOME AGAIN?
YES, DEAR. I REALLY THINK I HAD BETTER..

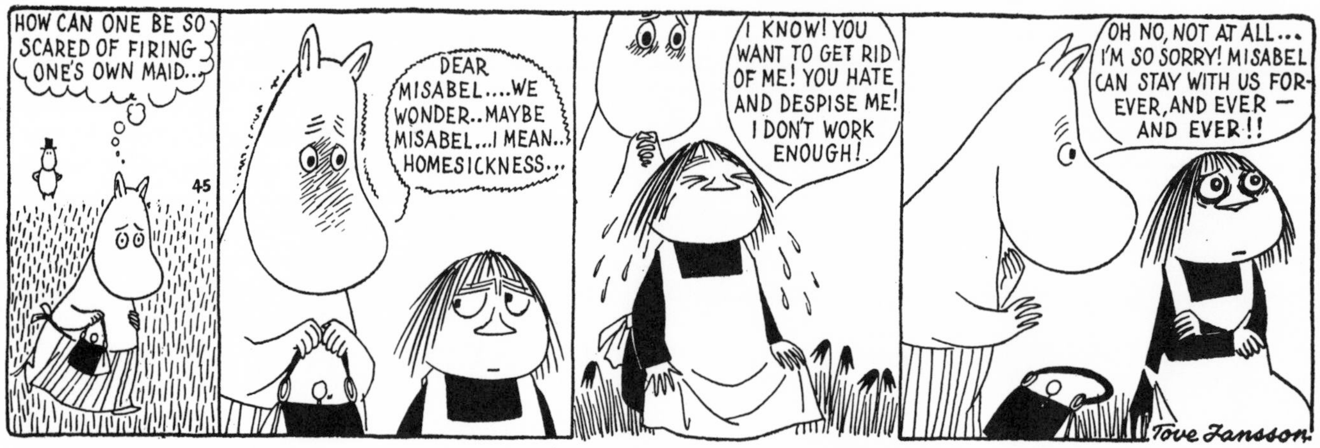
45
HOW CAN ONE BE SO SCARED OF FIRING ONE'S OWN MAID...
DEAR MISABEL....WE WONDER..MAYBE MISABEL...I MEAN.. HOMESICKNESS...
I KNOW! YOU WANT TO GET RID OF ME! YOU HATE AND DESPISE ME! I DON'T WORK ENOUGH!
OH NO, NOT AT ALL... I'M SO SORRY! MISABEL CAN STAY WITH US FOREVER, AND EVER — AND EVER!!
Tove Jansson

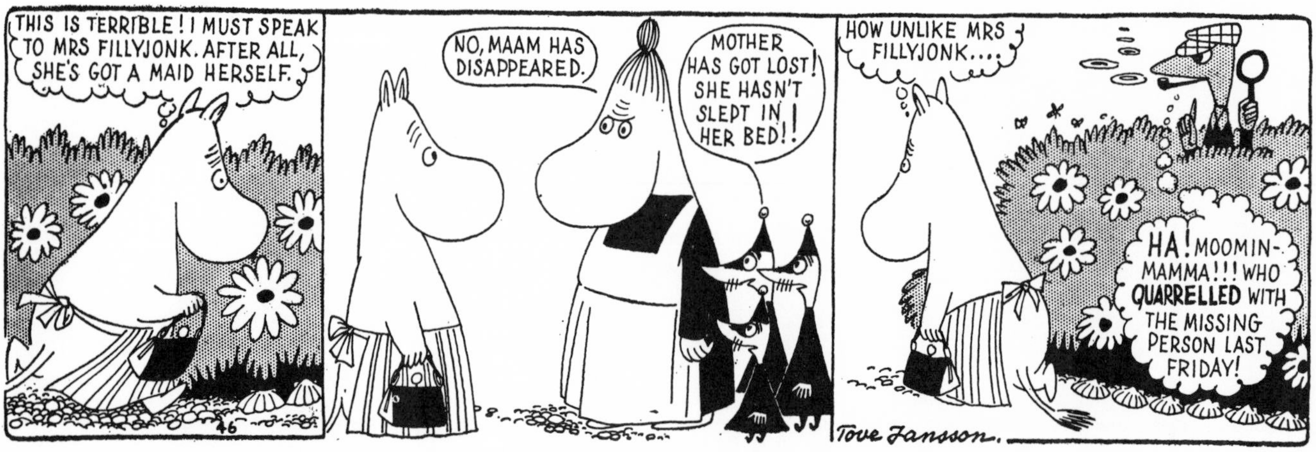
46
THIS IS TERRIBLE! I MUST SPEAK TO MRS FILLYJONK. AFTER ALL, SHE'S GOT A MAID HERSELF.
NO, MAAM HAS DISAPPEARED.
MOTHER HAS GOT LOST! SHE HASN'T SLEPT IN HER BED!!
HOW UNLIKE MRS FILLYJONK....
HA! MOOMINMAMMA!!! WHO QUARRELLED WITH THE MISSING PERSON LAST FRIDAY!
Tove Jansson

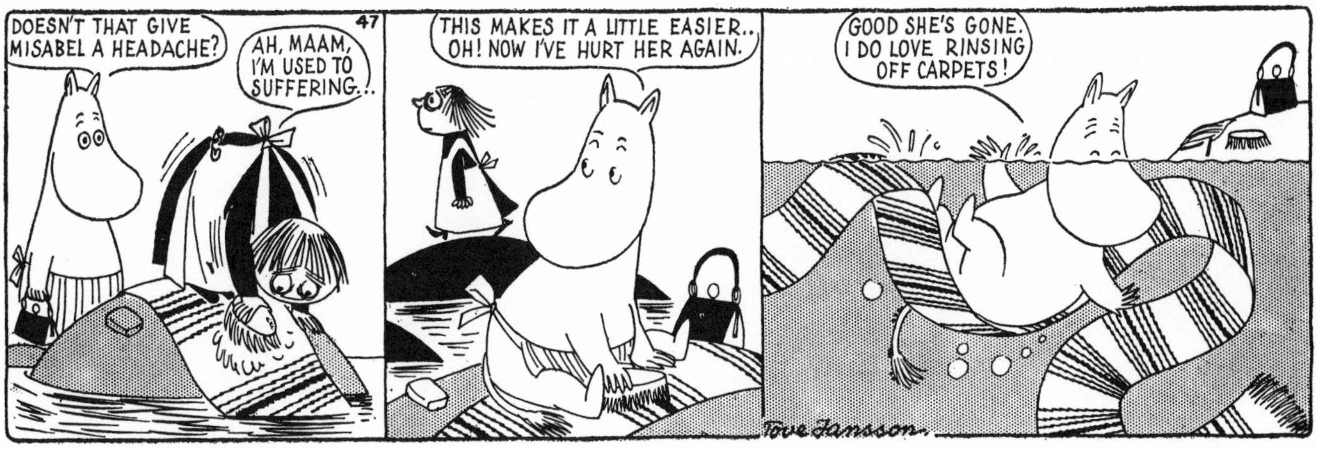
47
DOESN'T THAT GIVE MISABEL A HEADACHE?
AH, MAAM, I'M USED TO SUFFERING...
THIS MAKES IT A LITTLE EASIER.. OH! NOW I'VE HURT HER AGAIN.
GOOD SHE'S GONE. I DO LOVE RINSING OFF CARPETS!
Tove Jansson.

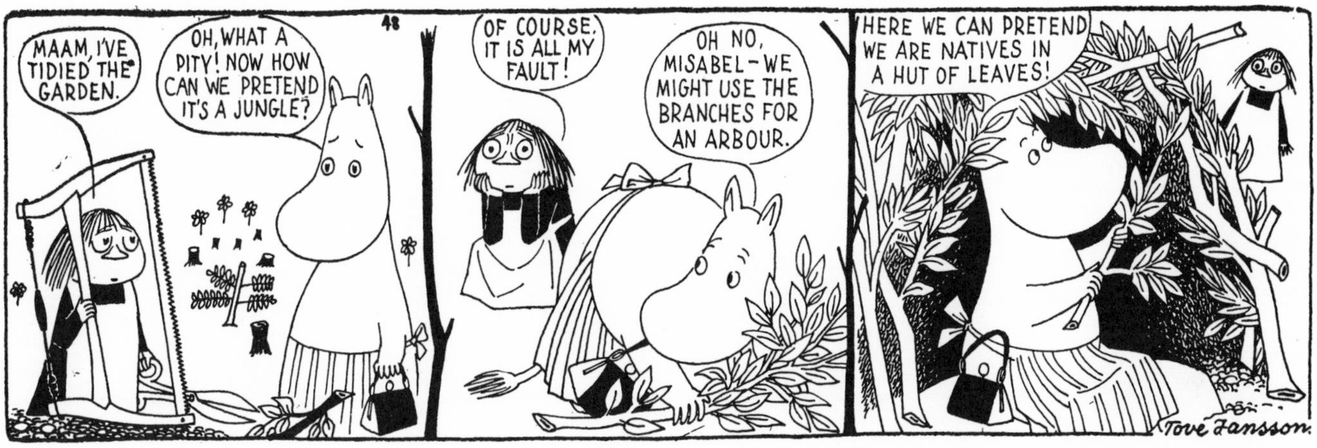
48
MAAM, I'VE TIDIED THE GARDEN.
OH, WHAT A PITY! NOW HOW CAN WE PRETEND IT'S A JUNGLE?
OF COURSE. IT IS ALL MY FAULT!
OH NO, MISABEL - WE MIGHT USE THE BRANCHES FOR AN ARBOUR.
HERE WE CAN PRETEND WE ARE NATIVES IN A HUT OF LEAVES!
Tove Jansson.

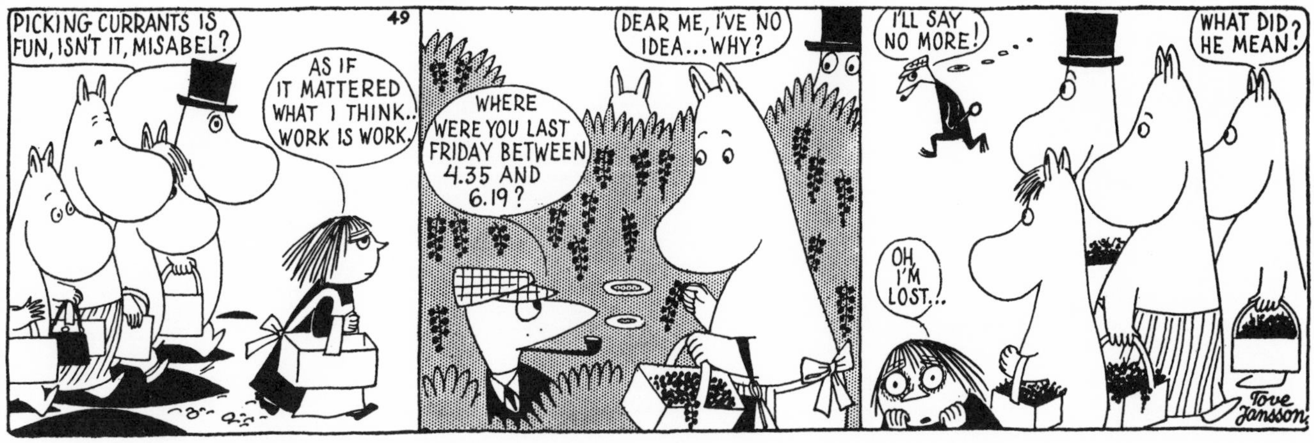
49
PICKING CURRANTS IS FUN, ISN'T IT, MISABEL?
AS IF IT MATTERED WHAT I THINK.. WORK IS WORK.
DEAR ME, I'VE NO IDEA... WHY?
WHERE WERE YOU LAST FRIDAY BETWEEN 4.35 AND 6.19?
I'LL SAY NO MORE!
WHAT DID HE MEAN?
OH, I'M LOST...
Tove Jansson.

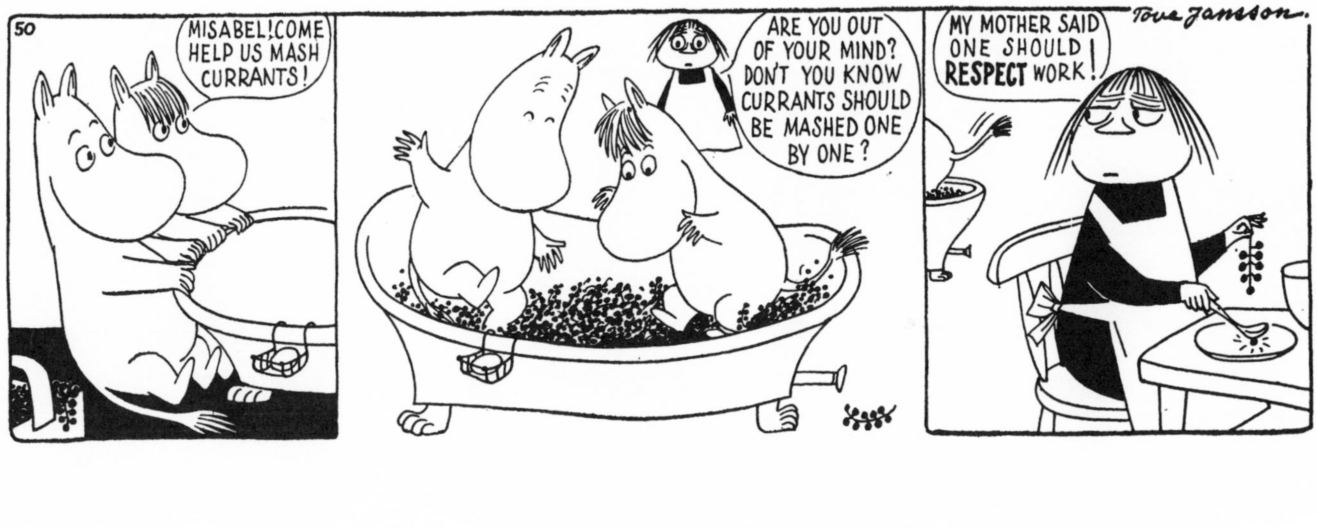
50
MISABEL! COME HELP US MASH CURRANTS!
ARE YOU OUT OF YOUR MIND? DON'T YOU KNOW CURRANTS SHOULD BE MASHED ONE BY ONE?
MY MOTHER SAID ONE SHOULD RESPECT WORK!
Tove Jansson.

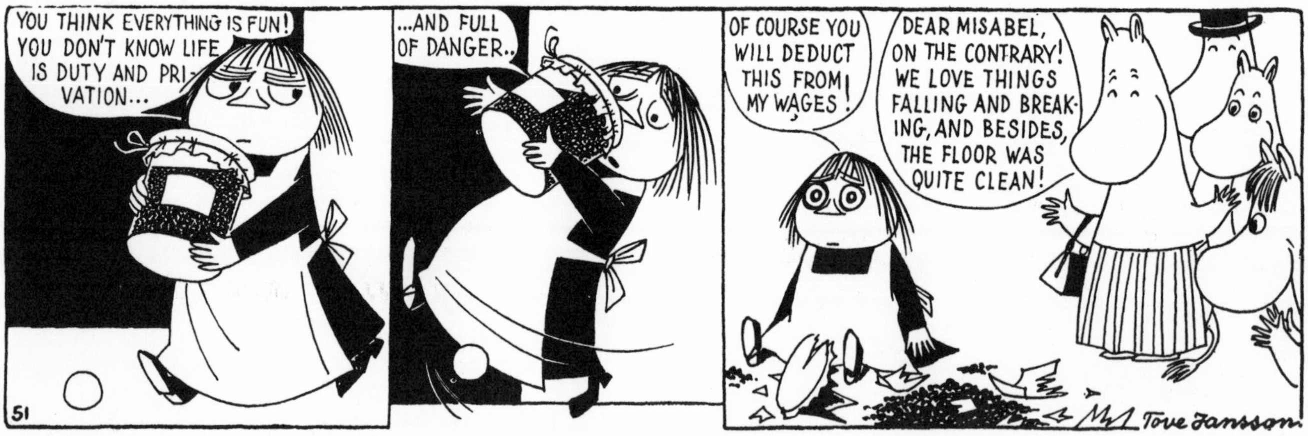
YOU THINK EVERYTHING IS FUN! YOU DON'T KNOW LIFE IS DUTY AND PRI-VATION...
51
...AND FULL OF DANGER..
OF COURSE YOU WILL DEDUCT THIS FROM MY WAGES!
DEAR MISABEL, ON THE CONTRARY! WE LOVE THINGS FALLING AND BREAK-ING, AND BESIDES, THE FLOOR WAS QUITE CLEAN!
Tove Jansson

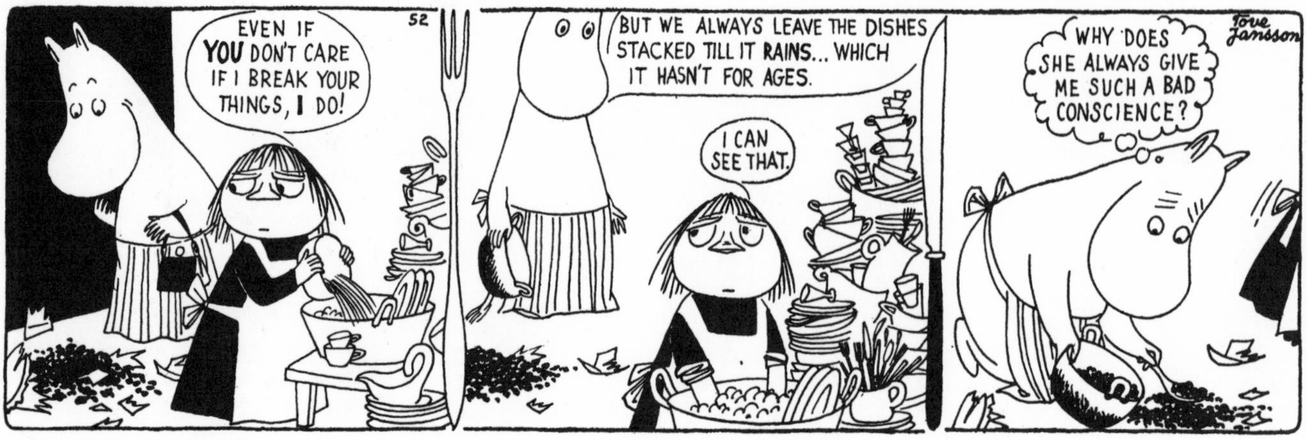
EVEN IF YOU DON'T CARE IF I BREAK YOUR THINGS, I DO!
52
BUT WE ALWAYS LEAVE THE DISHES STACKED TILL IT RAINS... WHICH IT HASN'T FOR AGES.
I CAN SEE THAT.
WHY DOES SHE ALWAYS GIVE ME SUCH A BAD CONSCIENCE?
Tove Jansson

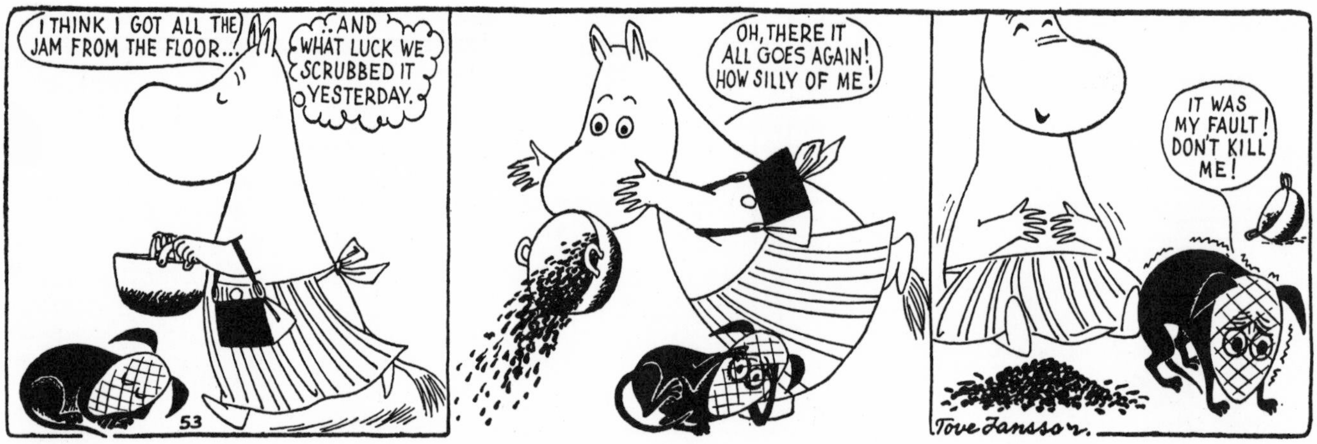
I THINK I GOT ALL THE JAM FROM THE FLOOR...
..AND WHAT LUCK WE SCRUBBED IT YESTERDAY.
53
OH, THERE IT ALL GOES AGAIN! HOW SILLY OF ME!
IT WAS MY FAULT! DON'T KILL ME!
Tove Jansson

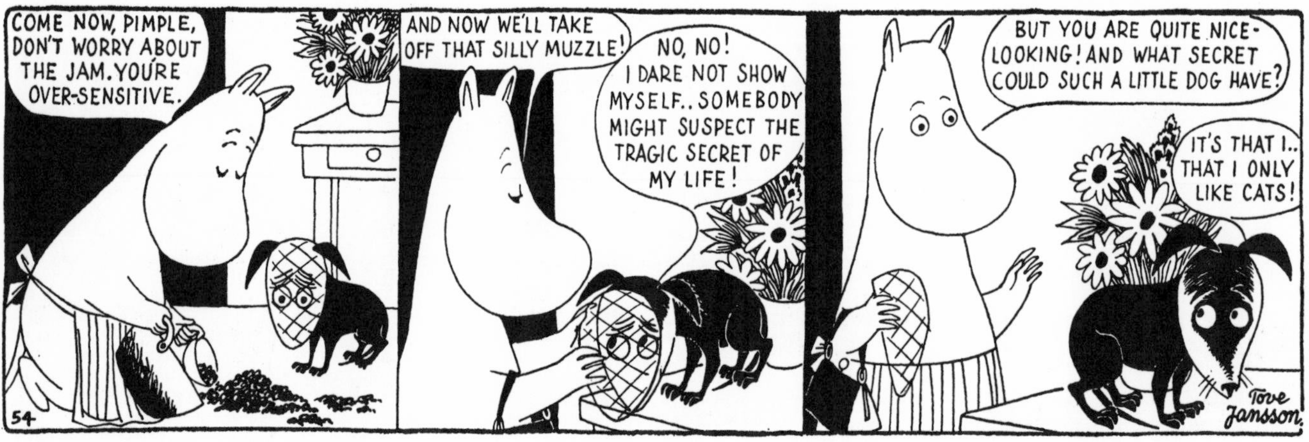
COME NOW, PIMPLE, DON'T WORRY ABOUT THE JAM. YOU'RE OVER-SENSITIVE.
54
AND NOW WE'LL TAKE OFF THAT SILLY MUZZLE!
NO, NO! I DARE NOT SHOW MYSELF.. SOMEBODY MIGHT SUSPECT THE TRAGIC SECRET OF MY LIFE!
BUT YOU ARE QUITE NICE-LOOKING! AND WHAT SECRET COULD SUCH A LITTLE DOG HAVE?
IT'S THAT I.. THAT I ONLY LIKE CATS!
Tove Jansson

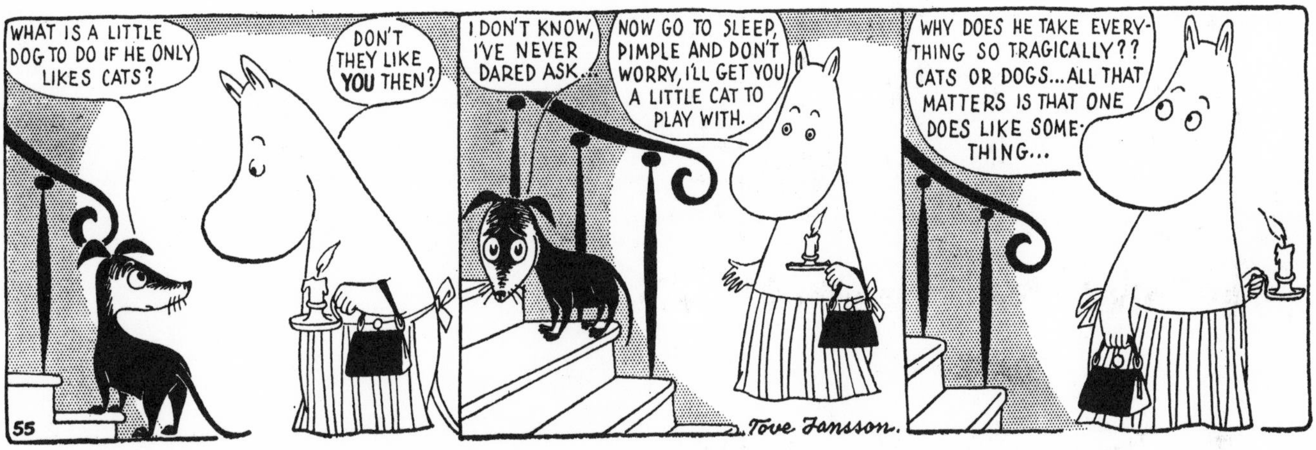
WHAT IS A LITTLE DOG TO DO IF HE ONLY LIKES CATS?
DON'T THEY LIKE YOU THEN?
55
I DON'T KNOW, I'VE NEVER DARED ASK...
NOW GO TO SLEEP, PIMPLE AND DON'T WORRY, I'LL GET YOU A LITTLE CAT TO PLAY WITH.
Tove Jansson.
WHY DOES HE TAKE EVERYTHING SO TRAGICALLY?? CATS OR DOGS...ALL THAT MATTERS IS THAT ONE DOES LIKE SOMETHING...

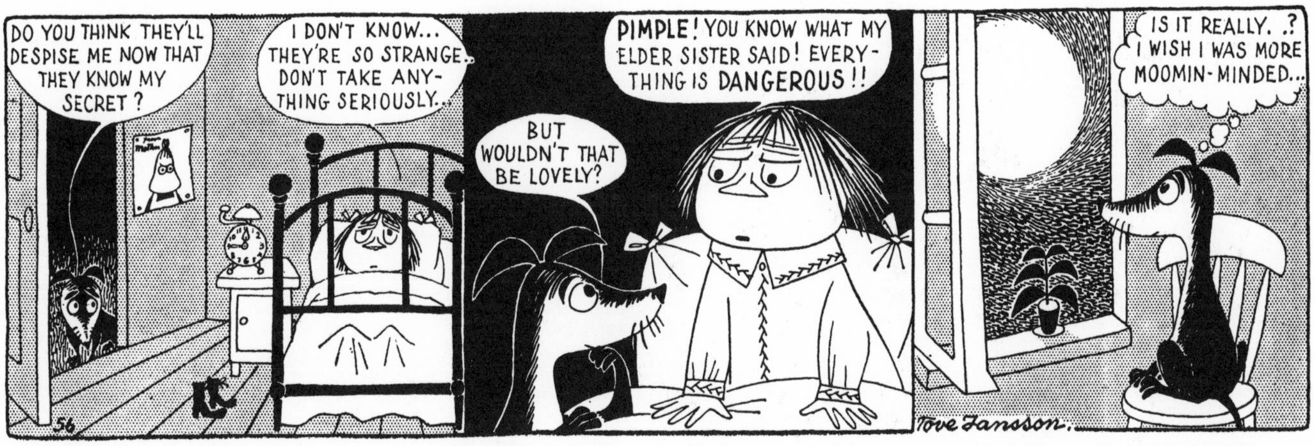
DO YOU THINK THEY'LL DESPISE ME NOW THAT THEY KNOW MY SECRET?
I DON'T KNOW... THEY'RE SO STRANGE.. DON'T TAKE ANYTHING SERIOUSLY...
56
PIMPLE! YOU KNOW WHAT MY ELDER SISTER SAID! EVERYTHING IS DANGEROUS!!
BUT WOULDN'T THAT BE LOVELY?
IS IT REALLY. .? I WISH I WAS MORE MOOMIN-MINDED...
Tove Jansson.

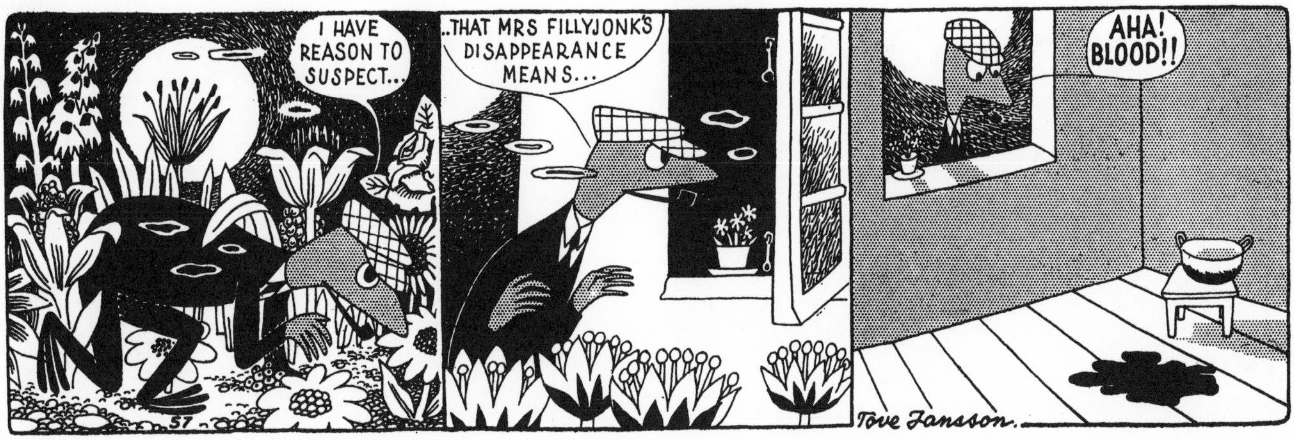
I HAVE REASON TO SUSPECT...
57
..THAT MRS FILLYJONK'S DISAPPEARANCE MEANS...
AHA! BLOOD!!
Tove Jansson.

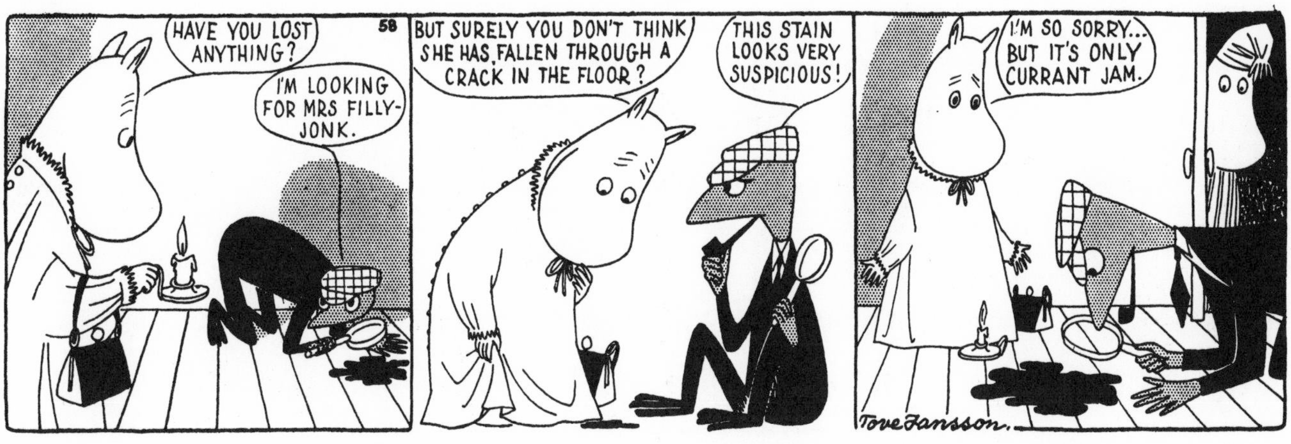
HAVE YOU LOST ANYTHING?
58
I'M LOOKING FOR MRS FILLYJONK.
BUT SURELY YOU DON'T THINK SHE HAS FALLEN THROUGH A CRACK IN THE FLOOR?
THIS STAIN LOOKS VERY SUSPICIOUS!
I'M SO SORRY... BUT IT'S ONLY CURRANT JAM.
Tove Jansson.

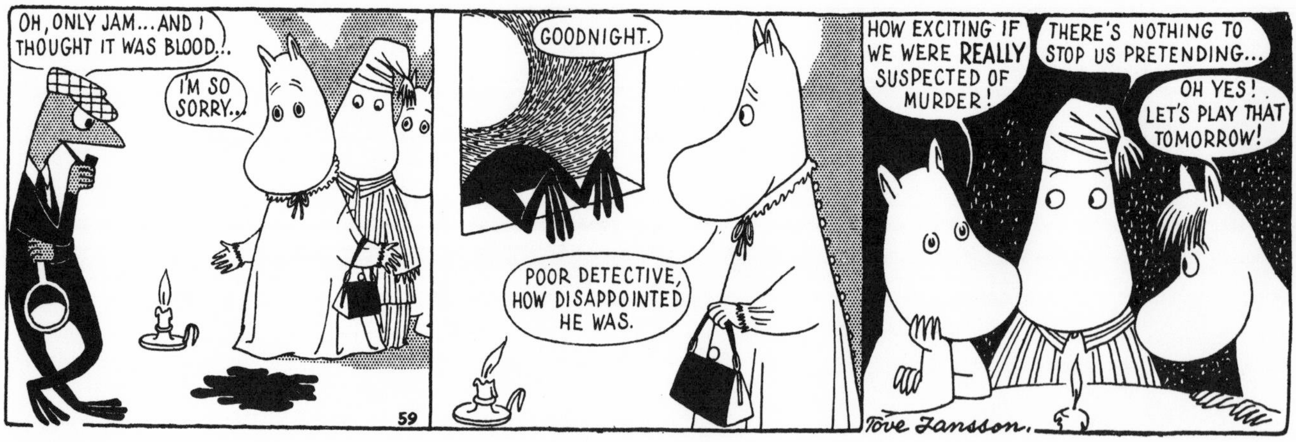
OH, ONLY JAM... AND I THOUGHT IT WAS BLOOD...
I'M SO SORRY...
59
GOODNIGHT.
POOR DETECTIVE, HOW DISAPPOINTED HE WAS.
HOW EXCITING IF WE WERE REALLY SUSPECTED OF MURDER!
THERE'S NOTHING TO STOP US PRETENDING...
OH YES! LET'S PLAY THAT TOMORROW!
Tove Jansson.

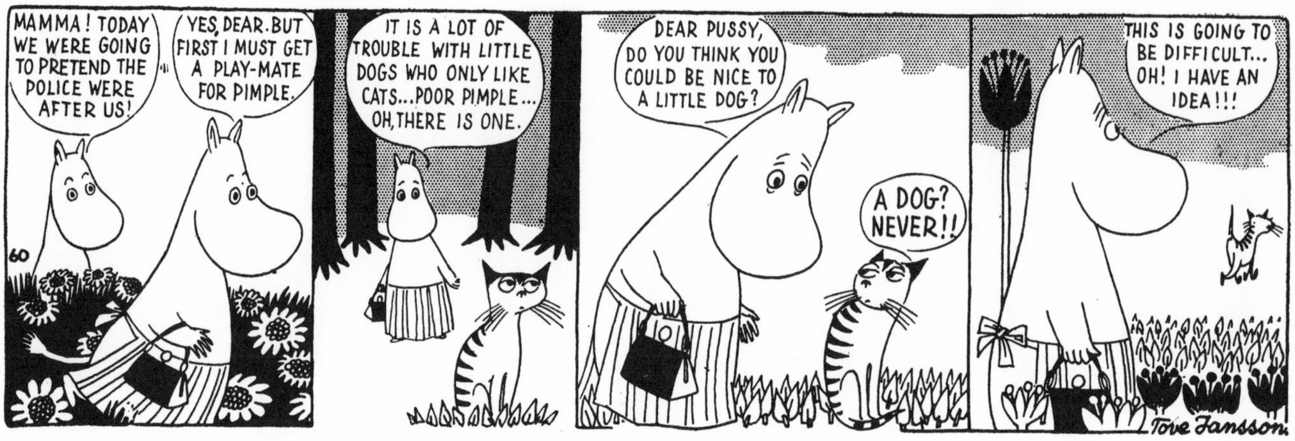
MAMMA! TODAY WE WERE GOING TO PRETEND THE POLICE WERE AFTER US!
YES, DEAR. BUT FIRST I MUST GET A PLAY-MATE FOR PIMPLE.
60
IT IS A LOT OF TROUBLE WITH LITTLE DOGS WHO ONLY LIKE CATS... POOR PIMPLE... OH, THERE IS ONE.
DEAR PUSSY, DO YOU THINK YOU COULD BE NICE TO A LITTLE DOG?
A DOG? NEVER!!
THIS IS GOING TO BE DIFFICULT... OH! I HAVE AN IDEA!!!
Tove Jansson.

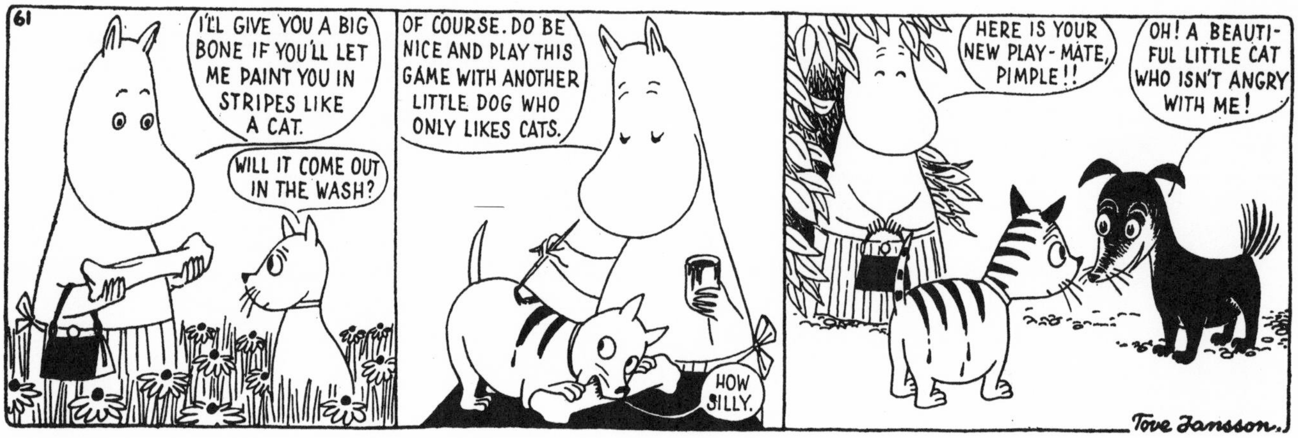
61
I'LL GIVE YOU A BIG BONE IF YOU'LL LET ME PAINT YOU IN STRIPES LIKE A CAT.
WILL IT COME OUT IN THE WASH?
OF COURSE. DO BE NICE AND PLAY THIS GAME WITH ANOTHER LITTLE DOG WHO ONLY LIKES CATS.
HOW SILLY.
HERE IS YOUR NEW PLAY-MATE, PIMPLE!!
OH! A BEAUTIFUL LITTLE CAT WHO ISN'T ANGRY WITH ME!
Tove Jansson.

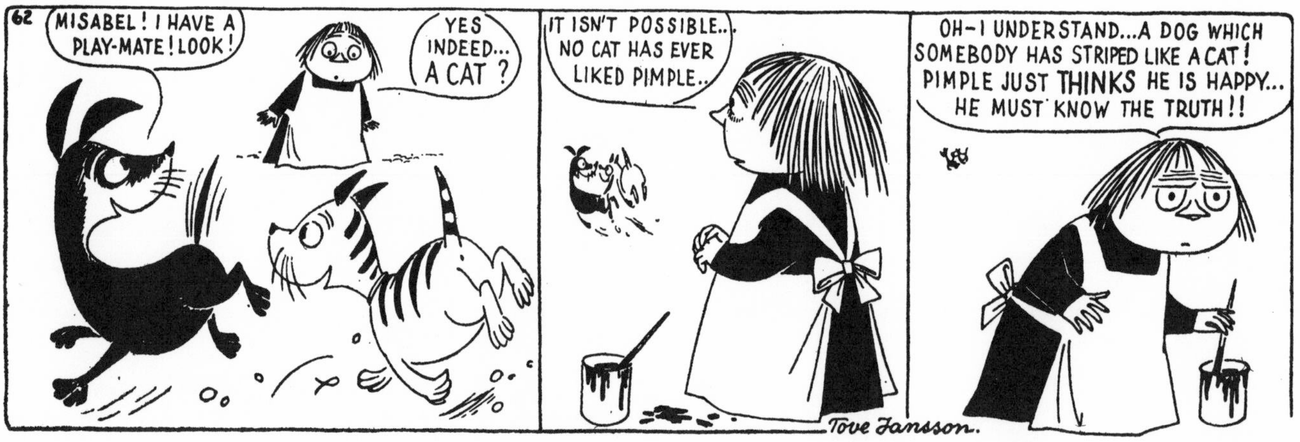
62
MISABEL! I HAVE A PLAY-MATE! LOOK!
YES INDEED... A CAT?
IT ISN'T POSSIBLE... NO CAT HAS EVER LIKED PIMPLE...
OH-I UNDERSTAND... A DOG WHICH SOMEBODY HAS STRIPED LIKE A CAT! PIMPLE JUST THINKS HE IS HAPPY... HE MUST KNOW THE TRUTH!!
Tove Jansson.

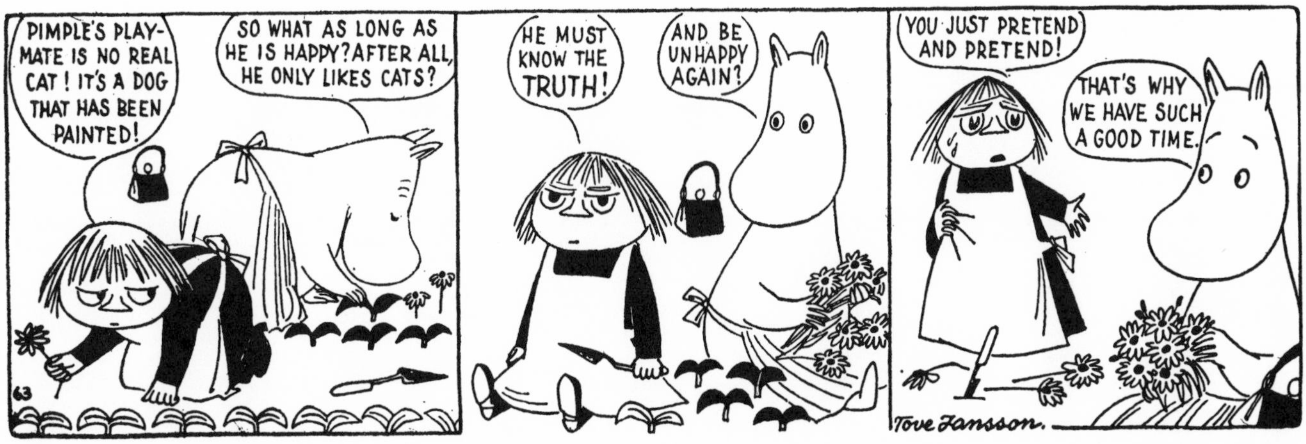
PIMPLE'S PLAY-MATE IS NO REAL CAT! IT'S A DOG THAT HAS BEEN PAINTED!
SO WHAT AS LONG AS HE IS HAPPY? AFTER ALL, HE ONLY LIKES CATS?
63
HE MUST KNOW THE TRUTH!
AND BE UNHAPPY AGAIN?
YOU JUST PRETEND AND PRETEND!
THAT'S WHY WE HAVE SUCH A GOOD TIME.
Tove Jansson.

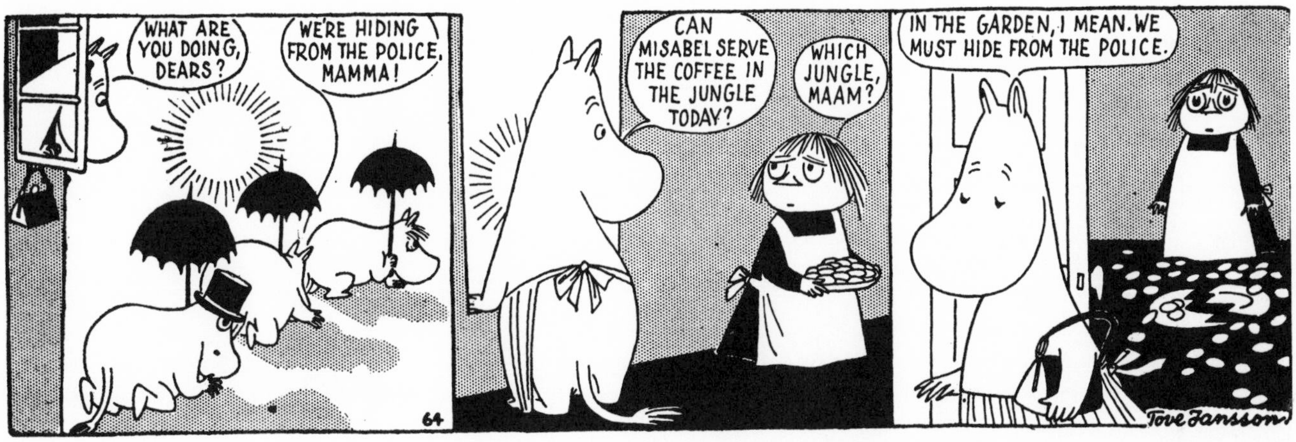
WHAT ARE YOU DOING, DEARS?
WE'RE HIDING FROM THE POLICE, MAMMA!
64
CAN MISABEL SERVE THE COFFEE IN THE JUNGLE TODAY?
WHICH JUNGLE, MAAM?
IN THE GARDEN, I MEAN. WE MUST HIDE FROM THE POLICE.
Tove Jansson.

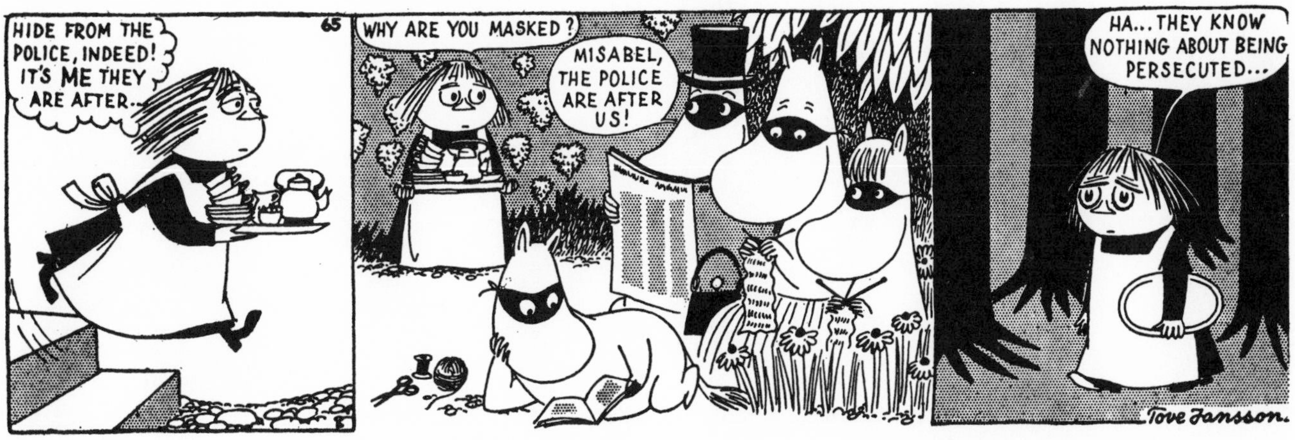
HIDE FROM THE POLICE, INDEED! IT'S ME THEY ARE AFTER..
65
WHY ARE YOU MASKED?
MISABEL, THE POLICE ARE AFTER US!
HA... THEY KNOW NOTHING ABOUT BEING PERSECUTED...
Tove Jansson.

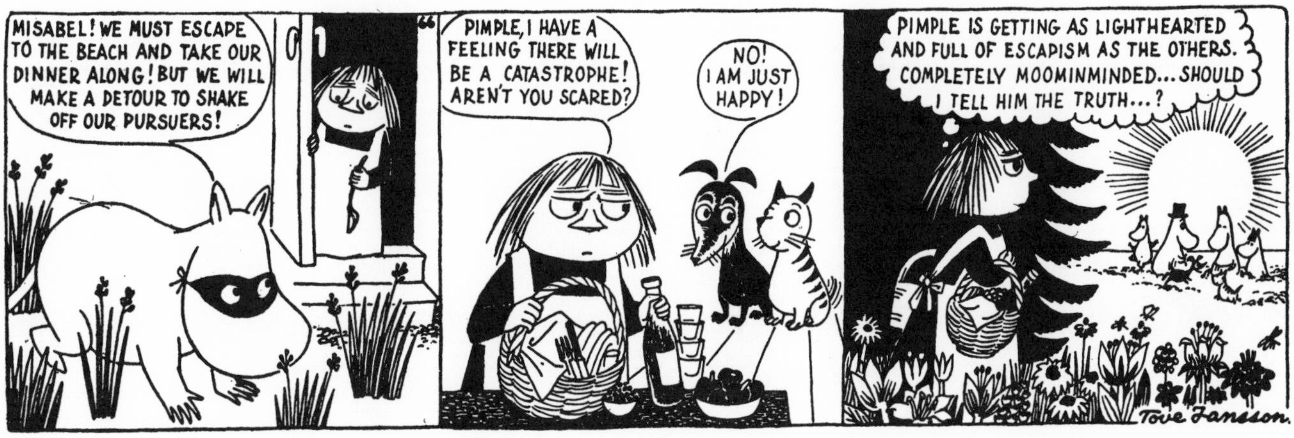
MISABEL! WE MUST ESCAPE TO THE BEACH AND TAKE OUR DINNER ALONG! BUT WE WILL MAKE A DETOUR TO SHAKE OFF OUR PURSUERS!
66
PIMPLE, I HAVE A FEELING THERE WILL BE A CATASTROPHE! AREN'T YOU SCARED?
NO! I AM JUST HAPPY!
PIMPLE IS GETTING AS LIGHTHEARTED AND FULL OF ESCAPISM AS THE OTHERS. COMPLETELY MOOMINMINDED... SHOULD I TELL HIM THE TRUTH...?
Tove Jansson.

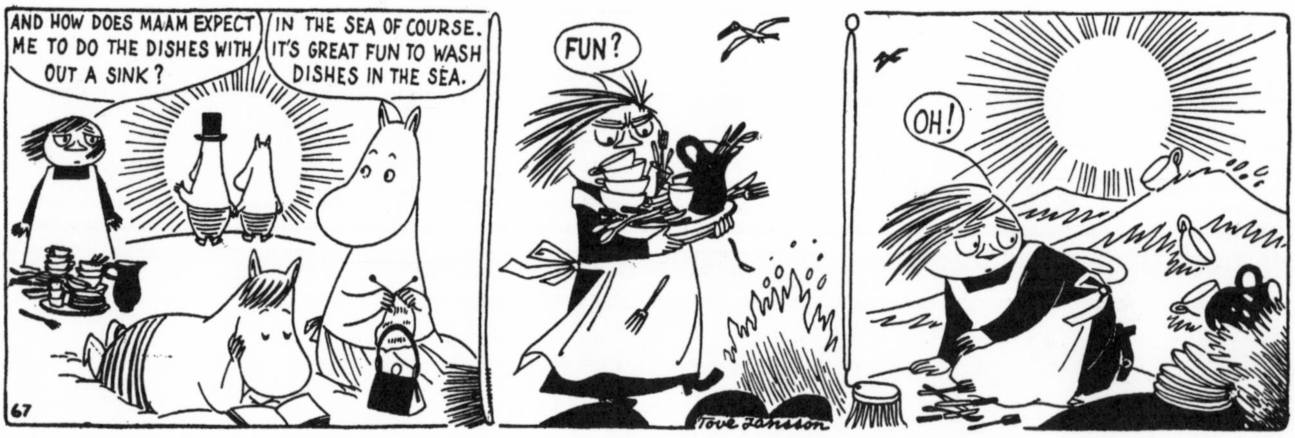
AND HOW DOES MA'AM EXPECT ME TO DO THE DISHES WITH OUT A SINK?
IN THE SEA OF COURSE. IT'S GREAT FUN TO WASH DISHES IN THE SEA.
FUN?
OH!

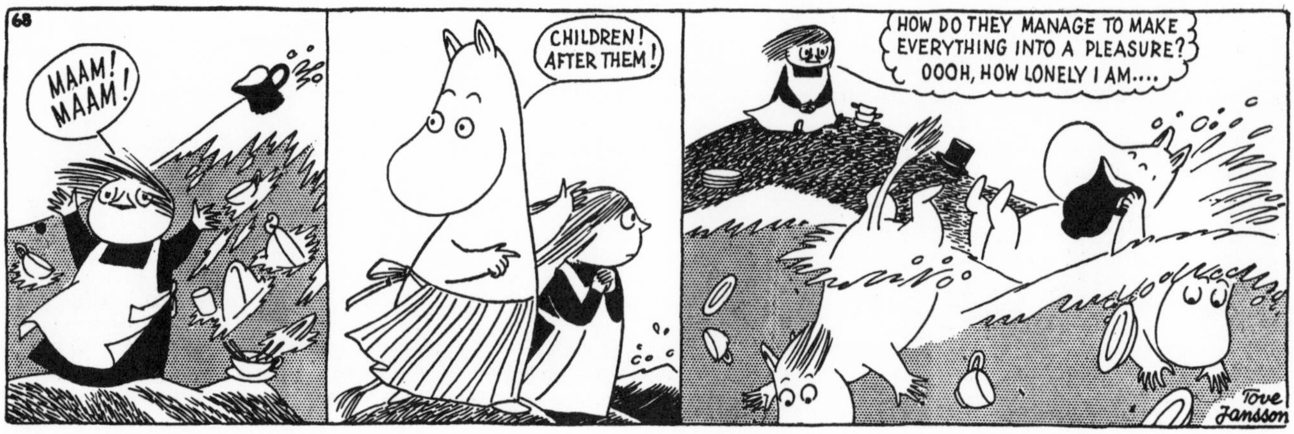
MAAM! MAAM!
CHILDREN! AFTER THEM!
HOW DO THEY MANAGE TO MAKE EVERYTHING INTO A PLEASURE? OOOH, HOW LONELY I AM....

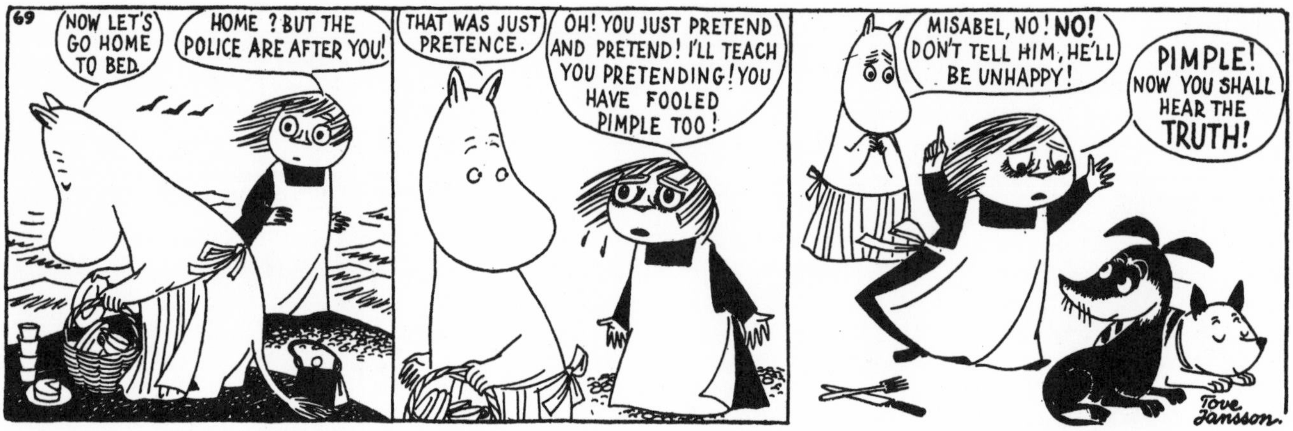
NOW LET'S GO HOME TO BED.
HOME ? BUT THE POLICE ARE AFTER YOU!
THAT WAS JUST PRETENCE.
OH! YOU JUST PRETEND AND PRETEND! I'LL TEACH YOU PRETENDING! YOU HAVE FOOLED PIMPLE TOO!
MISABEL, NO! NO! DON'T TELL HIM, HE'LL BE UNHAPPY!
PIMPLE! NOW YOU SHALL HEAR THE TRUTH!

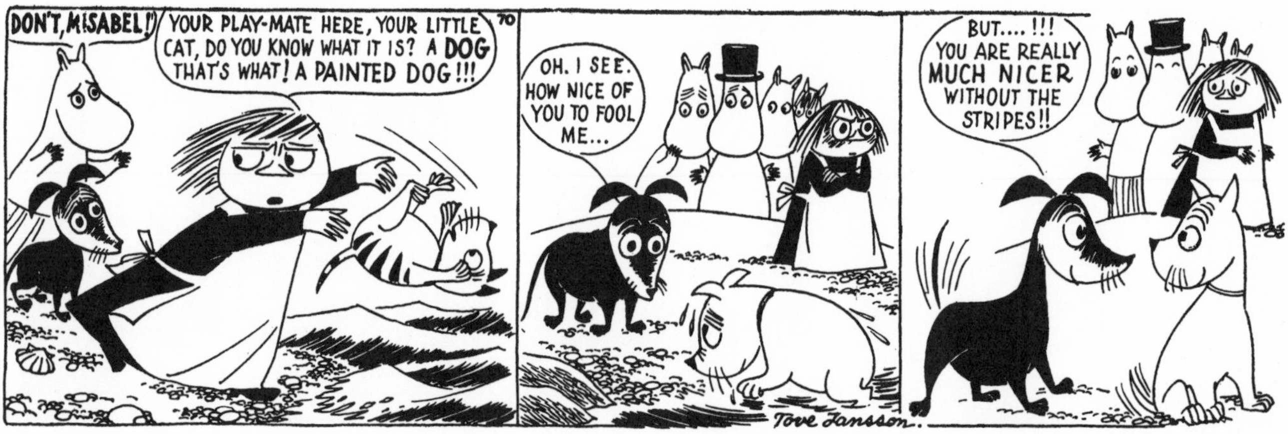
DON'T, MISABEL!
YOUR PLAY-MATE HERE, YOUR LITTLE CAT, DO YOU KNOW WHAT IT IS? A DOG THAT'S WHAT! A PAINTED DOG!!!
OH. I SEE. HOW NICE OF YOU TO FOOL ME...
BUT.... !!! YOU ARE REALLY MUCH NICER WITHOUT THE STRIPES!!

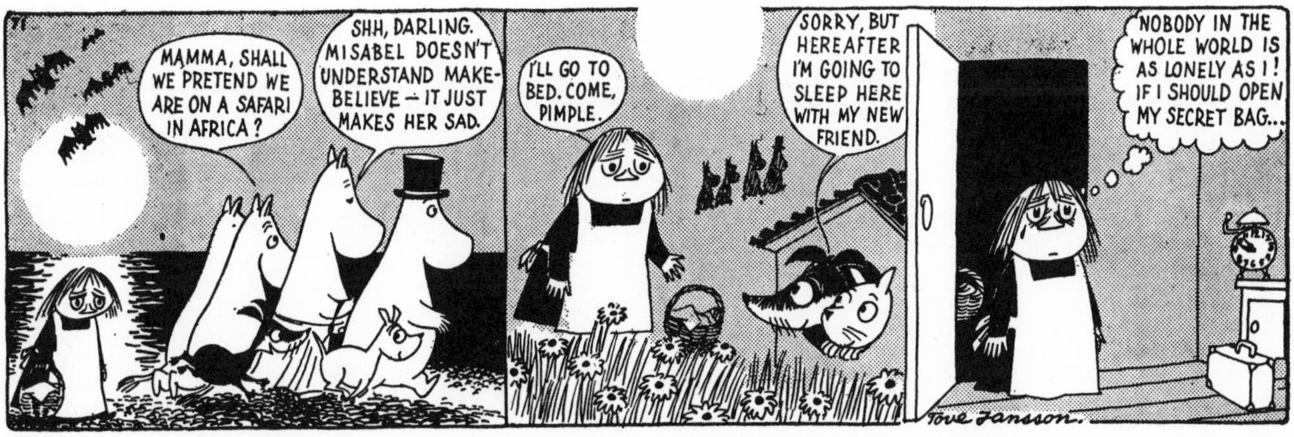
71
MAMMA, SHALL WE PRETEND WE ARE ON A SAFARI IN AFRICA?
SHH, DARLING. MISABEL DOESN'T UNDERSTAND MAKE-BELIEVE – IT JUST MAKES HER SAD.
I'LL GO TO BED. COME, PIMPLE.
SORRY, BUT HEREAFTER I'M GOING TO SLEEP HERE WITH MY NEW FRIEND.
NOBODY IN THE WHOLE WORLD IS AS LONELY AS I! IF I SHOULD OPEN MY SECRET BAG...
Tove Jansson.

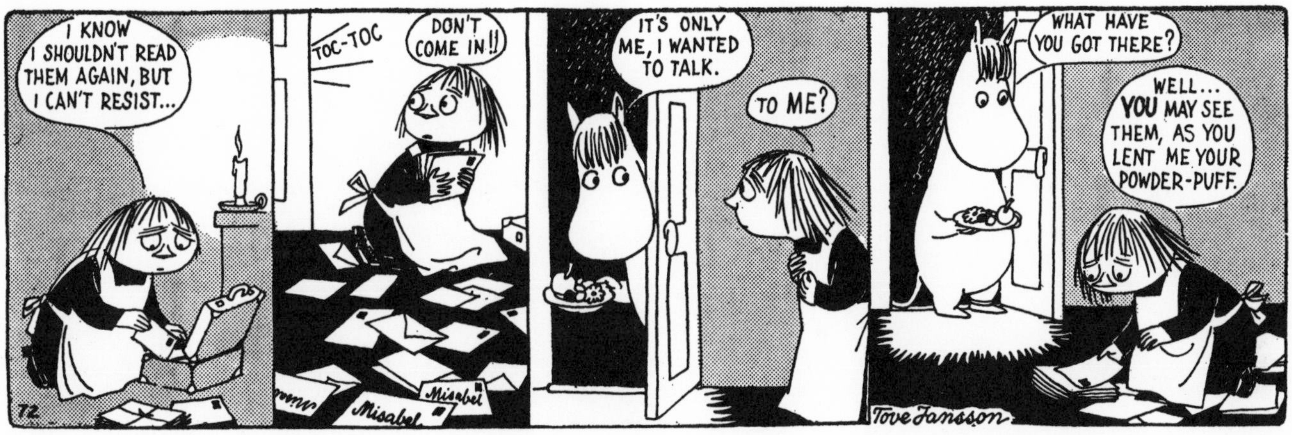
I KNOW I SHOULDN'T READ THEM AGAIN, BUT I CAN'T RESIST...
72
TOC-TOC
DON'T COME IN!!
Misabel
Misabel
IT'S ONLY ME, I WANTED TO TALK.
TO ME?
WHAT HAVE YOU GOT THERE?
WELL... YOU MAY SEE THEM, AS YOU LENT ME YOUR POWDER-PUFF.
Tove Jansson

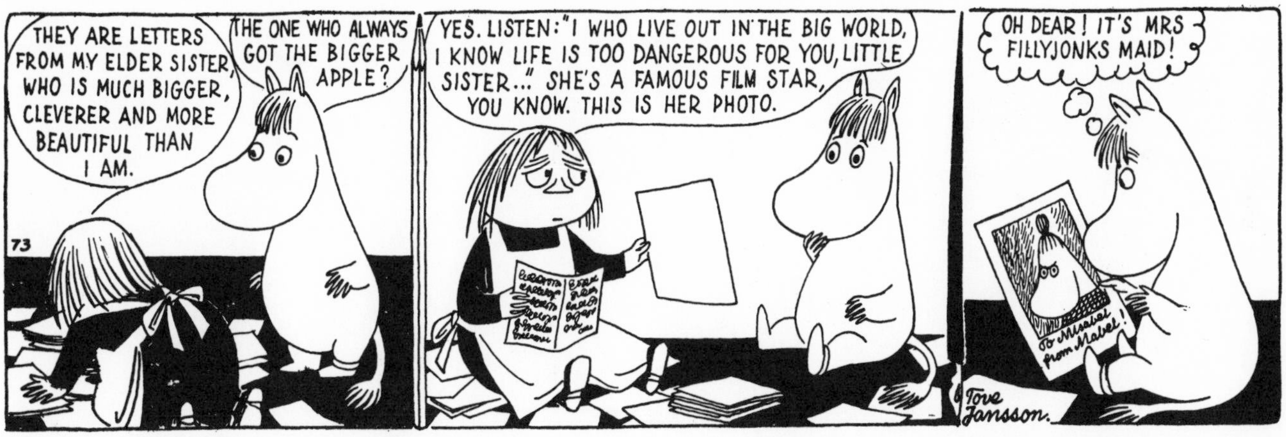
THEY ARE LETTERS FROM MY ELDER SISTER, WHO IS MUCH BIGGER, CLEVERER AND MORE BEAUTIFUL THAN I AM.
THE ONE WHO ALWAYS GOT THE BIGGER APPLE?
73
YES. LISTEN: "I WHO LIVE OUT IN THE BIG WORLD, I KNOW LIFE IS TOO DANGEROUS FOR YOU, LITTLE SISTER..." SHE'S A FAMOUS FILM STAR, YOU KNOW. THIS IS HER PHOTO.
OH DEAR! IT'S MRS FILLYJONKS MAID!
To Misabel from Mabel!
Tove Jansson.

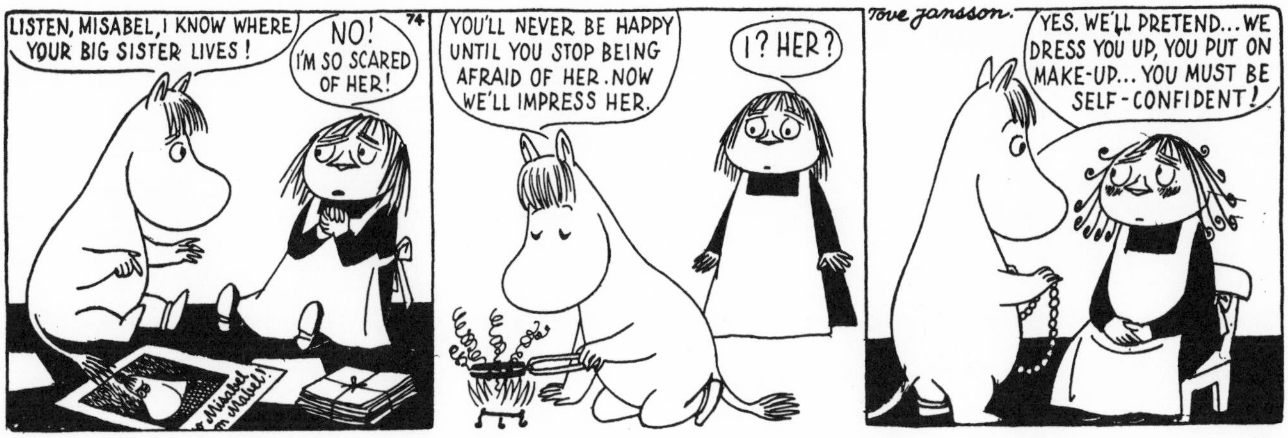
LISTEN, MISABEL, I KNOW WHERE YOUR BIG SISTER LIVES!
NO! I'M SO SCARED OF HER!
74
YOU'LL NEVER BE HAPPY UNTIL YOU STOP BEING AFRAID OF HER. NOW WE'LL IMPRESS HER.
I? HER?
Tove Jansson.
YES. WE'LL PRETEND... WE DRESS YOU UP, YOU PUT ON MAKE-UP... YOU MUST BE SELF-CONFIDENT!

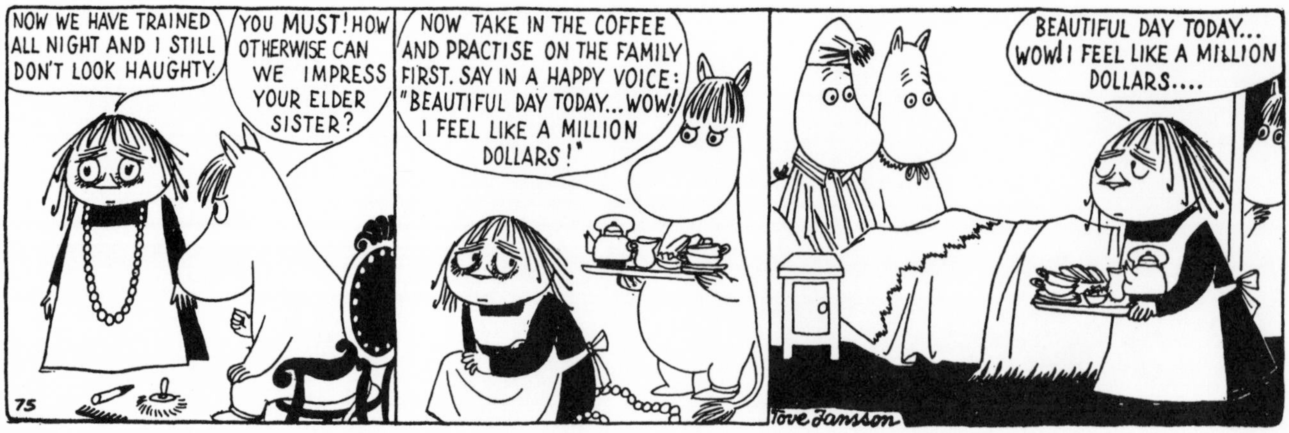
NOW WE HAVE TRAINED ALL NIGHT AND I STILL DON'T LOOK HAUGHTY.
YOU MUST! HOW OTHERWISE CAN WE IMPRESS YOUR ELDER SISTER?
75
NOW TAKE IN THE COFFEE AND PRACTISE ON THE FAMILY FIRST. SAY IN A HAPPY VOICE: "BEAUTIFUL DAY TODAY...WOW! I FEEL LIKE A MILLION DOLLARS!"
BEAUTIFUL DAY TODAY... WOW! I FEEL LIKE A MILLION DOLLARS....
Tove Jansson

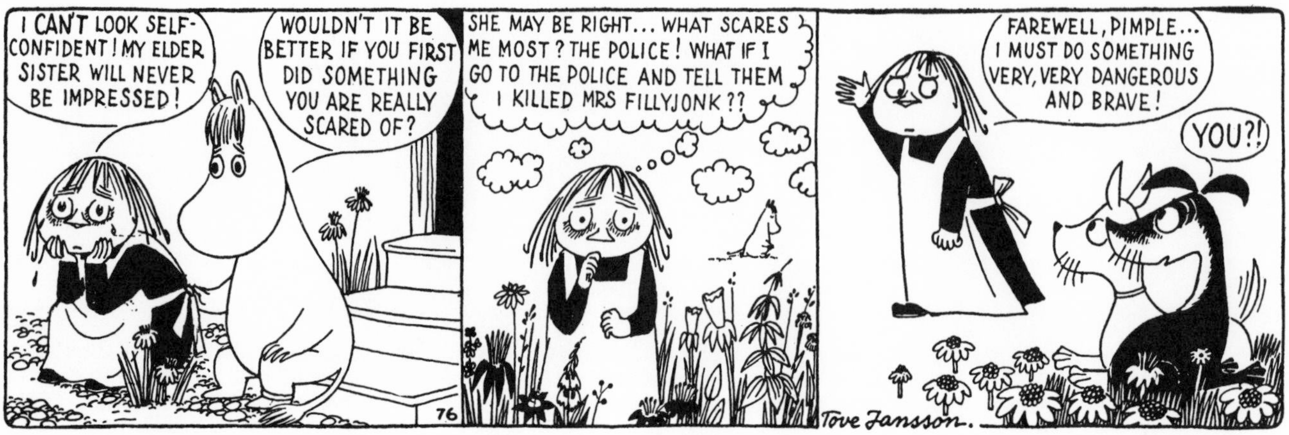
I CAN'T LOOK SELF-CONFIDENT! MY ELDER SISTER WILL NEVER BE IMPRESSED!
WOULDN'T IT BE BETTER IF YOU FIRST DID SOMETHING YOU ARE REALLY SCARED OF?
SHE MAY BE RIGHT... WHAT SCARES ME MOST? THE POLICE! WHAT IF I GO TO THE POLICE AND TELL THEM I KILLED MRS FILLYJONK??
76
FAREWELL, PIMPLE... I MUST DO SOMETHING VERY, VERY DANGEROUS AND BRAVE!
YOU?!
Tove Jansson.

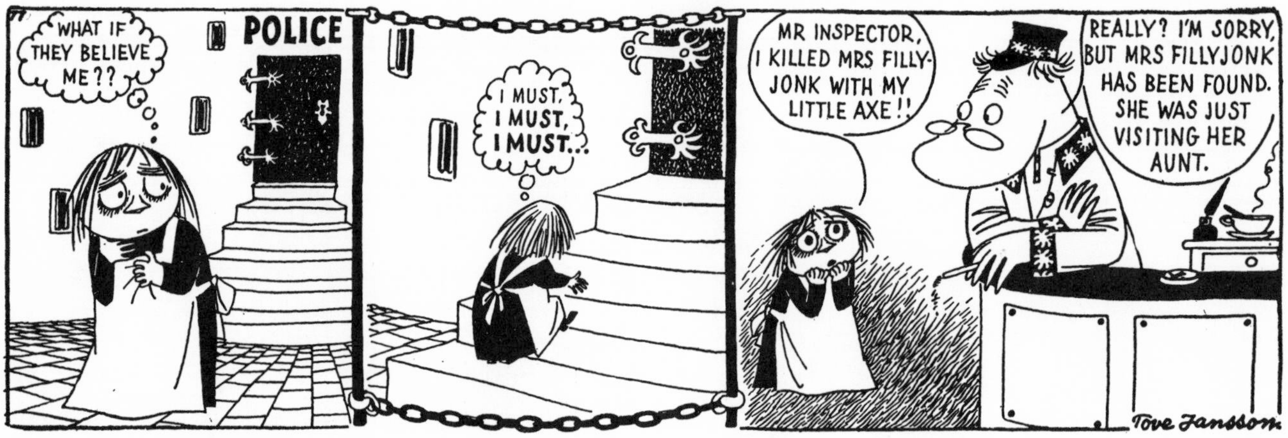
77
WHAT IF THEY BELIEVE ME??
POLICE
I MUST. I MUST, I MUST...
MR INSPECTOR, I KILLED MRS FILLYJONK WITH MY LITTLE AXE!!
REALLY? I'M SORRY, BUT MRS FILLYJONK HAS BEEN FOUND. SHE WAS JUST VISITING HER AUNT.
Tove Jansson

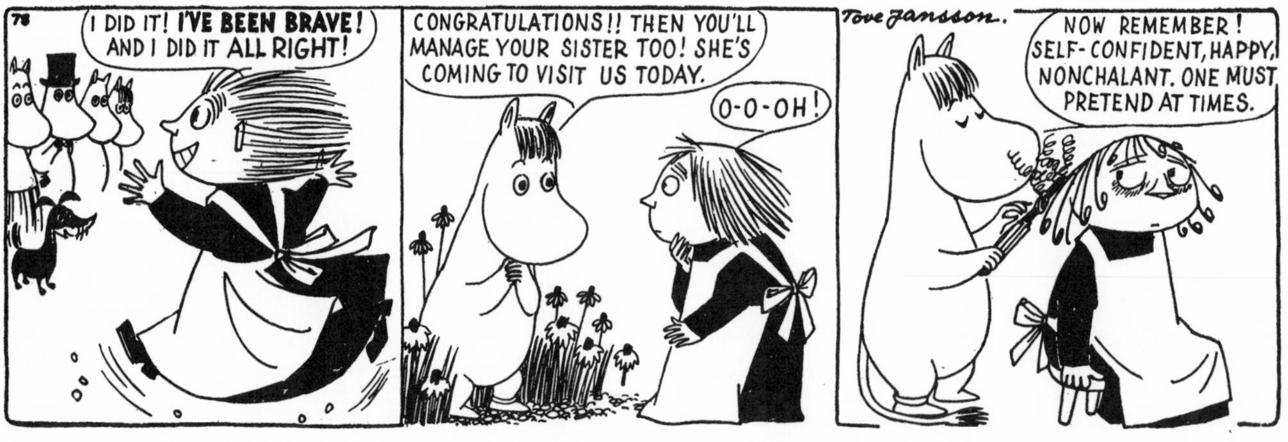
78
I DID IT! I'VE BEEN BRAVE! AND I DID IT ALL RIGHT!
CONGRATULATIONS!! THEN YOU'LL MANAGE YOUR SISTER TOO! SHE'S COMING TO VISIT US TODAY.
O-O-OH!
Tove Jansson.
NOW REMEMBER! SELF-CONFIDENT, HAPPY, NONCHALANT. ONE MUST PRETEND AT TIMES.

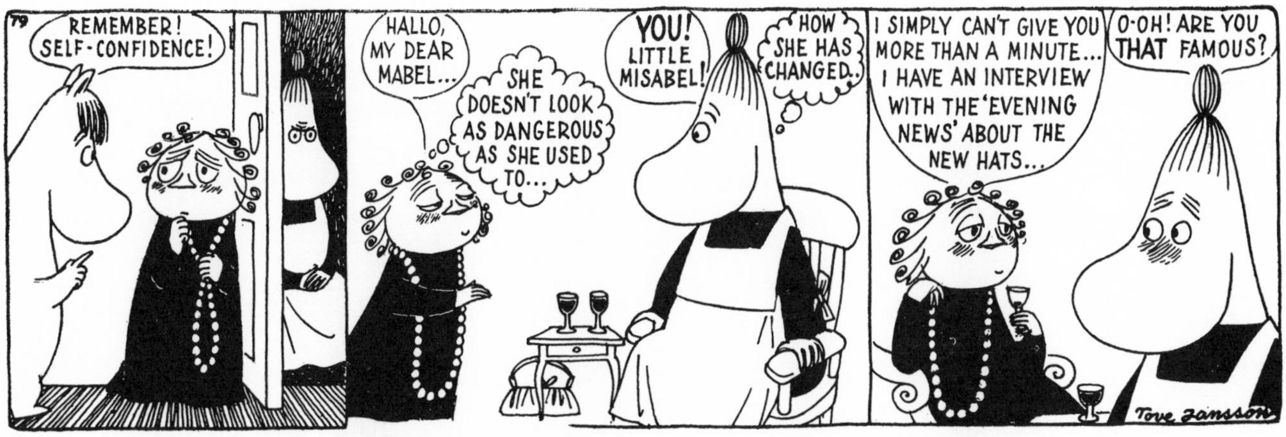
79
REMEMBER! SELF-CONFIDENCE!
HALLO, MY DEAR MABEL...
SHE DOESN'T LOOK AS DANGEROUS AS SHE USED TO...
YOU! LITTLE MISABEL!
HOW SHE HAS CHANGED..
I SIMPLY CAN'T GIVE YOU MORE THAN A MINUTE... I HAVE AN INTERVIEW WITH THE 'EVENING NEWS' ABOUT THE NEW HATS...
O-OH! ARE YOU THAT FAMOUS?
Tove Jansson

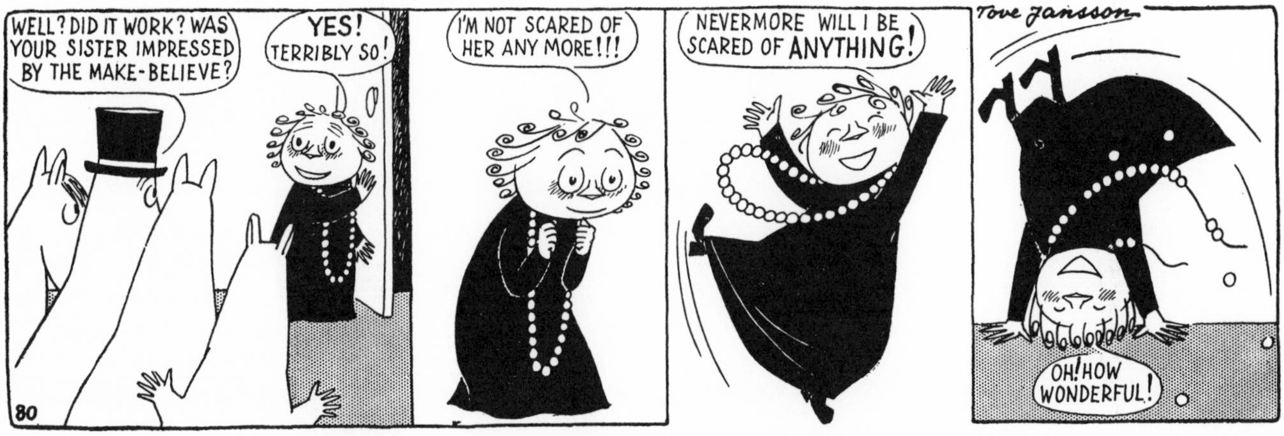
WELL? DID IT WORK? WAS YOUR SISTER IMPRESSED BY THE MAKE-BELIEVE?
YES! TERRIBLY SO!
80
I'M NOT SCARED OF HER ANY MORE!!!
NEVERMORE WILL I BE SCARED OF ANYTHING!
Tove Jansson
OH! HOW WONDERFUL!

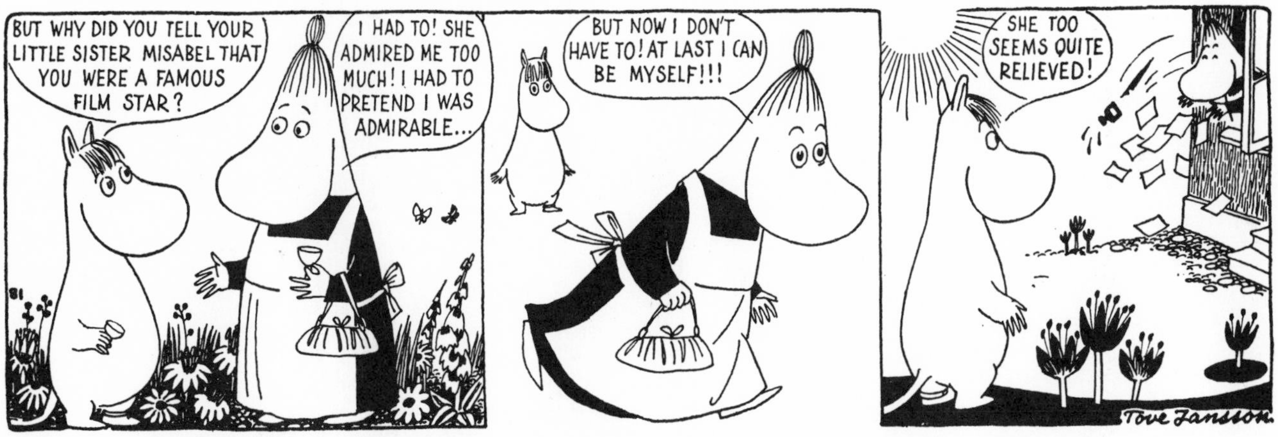
BUT WHY DID YOU TELL YOUR LITTLE SISTER MISABEL THAT YOU WERE A FAMOUS FILM STAR?
I HAD TO! SHE ADMIRED ME TOO MUCH! I HAD TO PRETEND I WAS ADMIRABLE...
81
BUT NOW I DON'T HAVE TO! AT LAST I CAN BE MYSELF!!!
SHE TOO SEEMS QUITE RELIEVED!
Tove Jansson

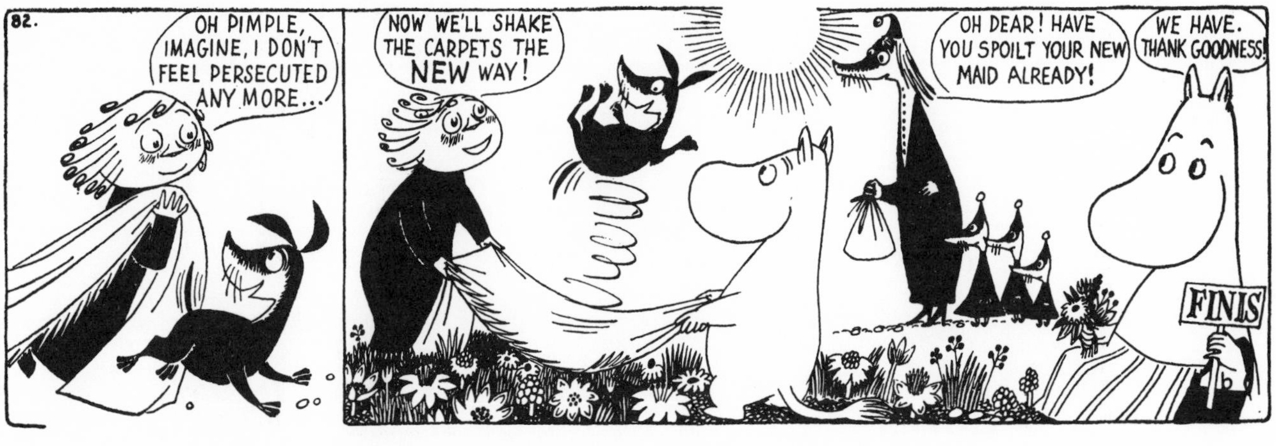
82.
OH PIMPLE, IMAGINE, I DON'T FEEL PERSECUTED ANY MORE...
NOW WE'LL SHAKE THE CARPETS THE NEW WAY!
OH DEAR! HAVE YOU SPOILT YOUR NEW MAID ALREADY!
WE HAVE. THANK GOODNESS!
FINIS

7. Moomin Builds a House

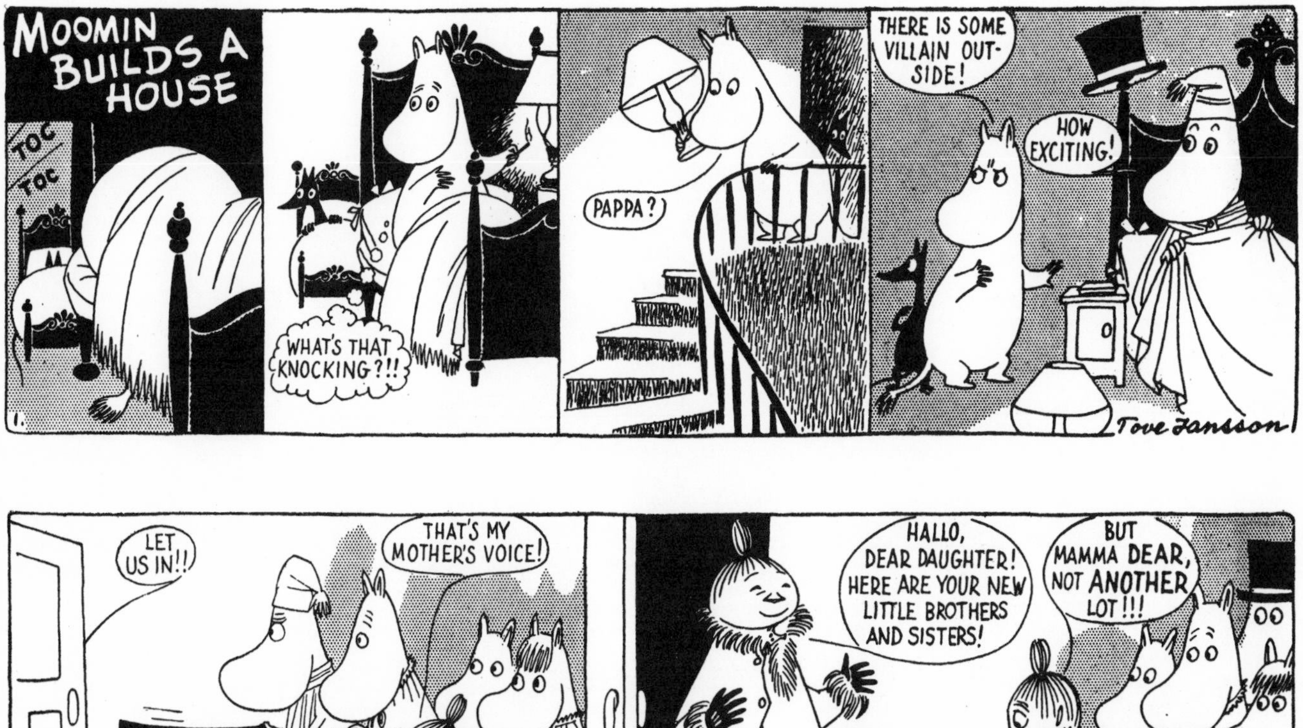

MOOMIN BUILDS A HOUSE
TOC TOC
WHAT'S THAT KNOCKING?!!
PAPPA?
THERE IS SOME VILLAIN OUT-SIDE!
HOW EXCITING!
Tove Jansson

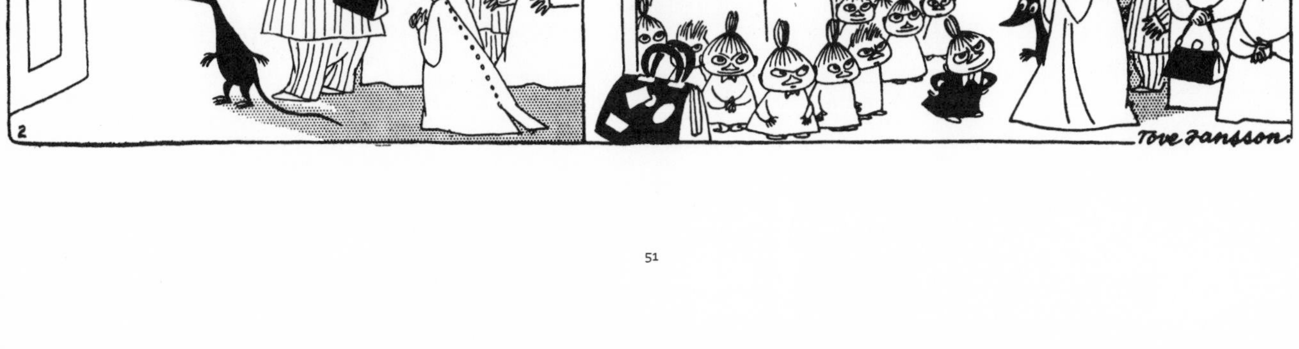

LET US IN!!
THAT'S MY MOTHER'S VOICE!
HALLO, DEAR DAUGHTER! HERE ARE YOUR NEW LITTLE BROTHERS AND SISTERS!
BUT MAMMA DEAR, NOT ANOTHER LOT!!!
Tove Jansson

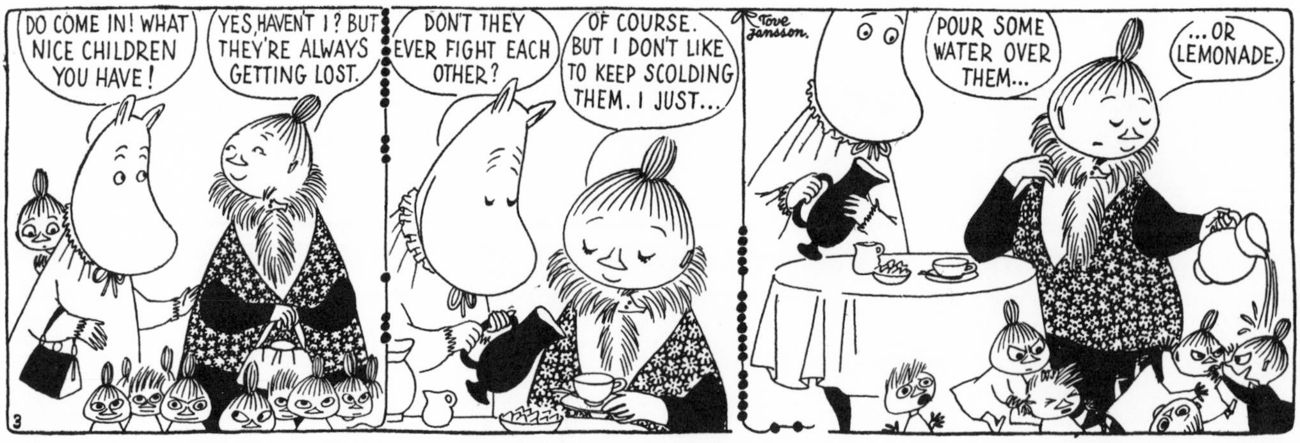
DO COME IN! WHAT NICE CHILDREN YOU HAVE!
YES, HAVEN'T I? BUT THEY'RE ALWAYS GETTING LOST.
DON'T THEY EVER FIGHT EACH OTHER?
OF COURSE. BUT I DON'T LIKE TO KEEP SCOLDING THEM. I JUST...
Tove Jansson.
POUR SOME WATER OVER THEM...
...OR LEMONADE.

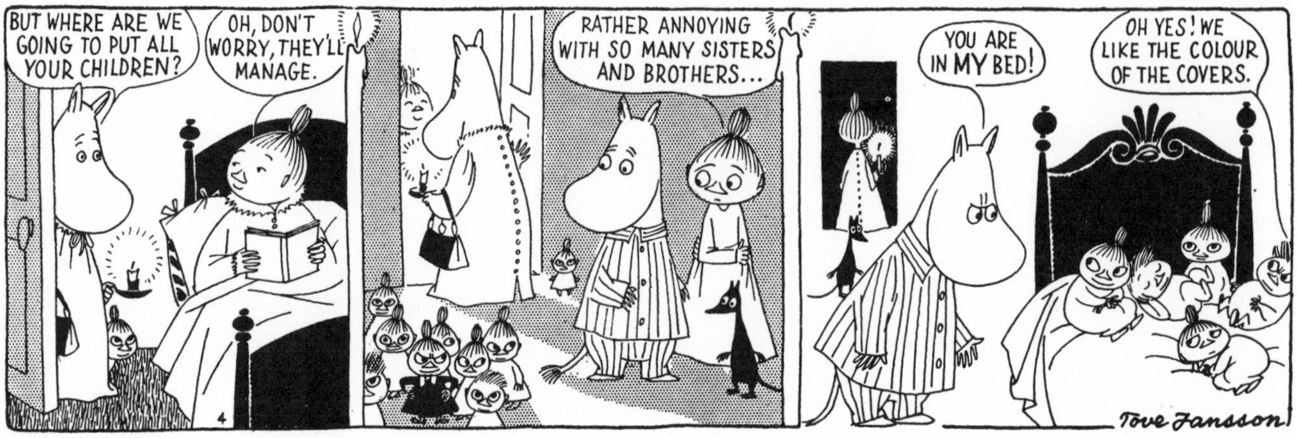
BUT WHERE ARE WE GOING TO PUT ALL YOUR CHILDREN?
OH, DON'T WORRY, THEY'LL MANAGE.
RATHER ANNOYING WITH SO MANY SISTERS AND BROTHERS...
YOU ARE IN MY BED!
OH YES! WE LIKE THE COLOUR OF THE COVERS.
Tove Jansson

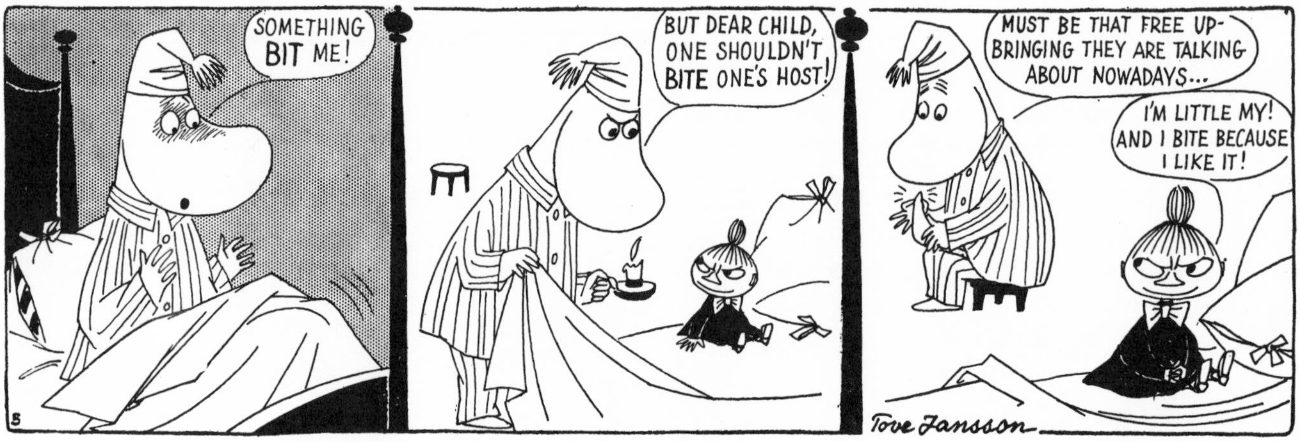
SOMETHING BIT ME!
BUT DEAR CHILD, ONE SHOULDN'T BITE ONE'S HOST!
MUST BE THAT FREE UP-BRINGING THEY ARE TALKING ABOUT NOWADAYS...
I'M LITTLE MY! AND I BITE BECAUSE I LIKE IT!
Tove Jansson

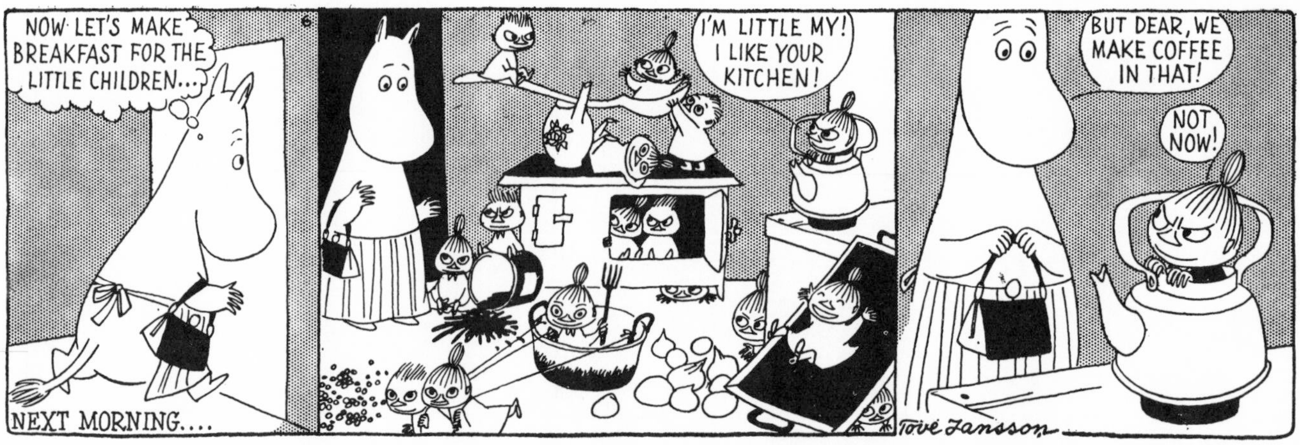
NOW LET'S MAKE BREAKFAST FOR THE LITTLE CHILDREN...
NEXT MORNING....
I'M LITTLE MY! I LIKE YOUR KITCHEN!
BUT DEAR, WE MAKE COFFEE IN THAT!
NOT NOW!
Tove Jansson

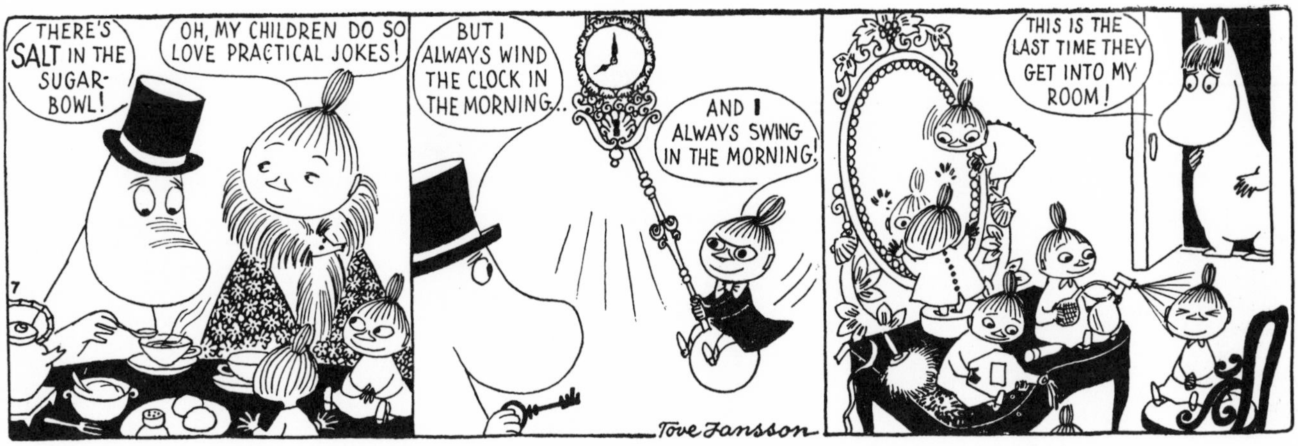
THERE'S SALT IN THE SUGAR-BOWL!
OH, MY CHILDREN DO SO LOVE PRACTICAL JOKES!
7
BUT I ALWAYS WIND THE CLOCK IN THE MORNING...
AND I ALWAYS SWING IN THE MORNING!
Tove Jansson
THIS IS THE LAST TIME THEY GET INTO MY ROOM!

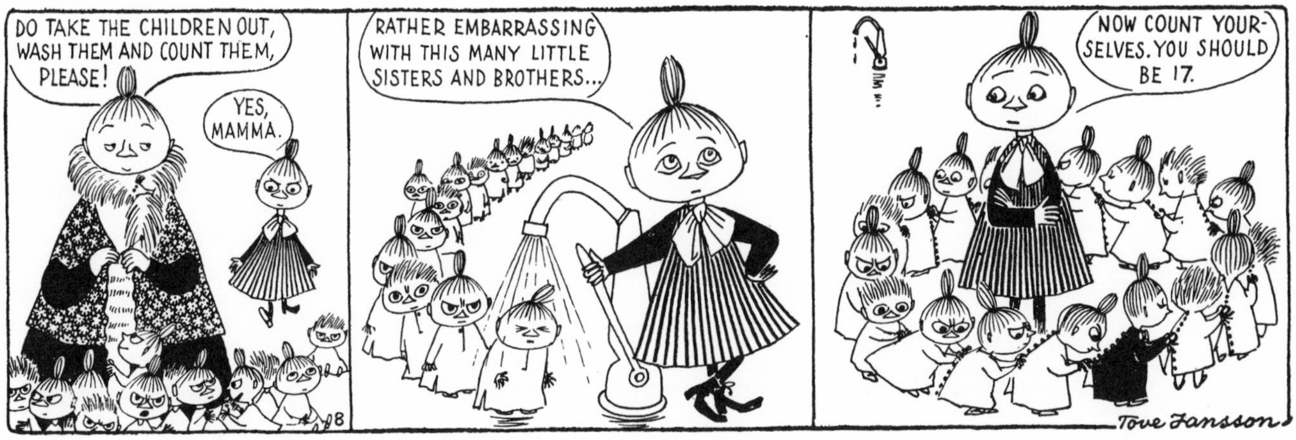
DO TAKE THE CHILDREN OUT, WASH THEM AND COUNT THEM, PLEASE!
YES, MAMMA.
8
RATHER EMBARRASSING WITH THIS MANY LITTLE SISTERS AND BROTHERS...
NOW COUNT YOURSELVES. YOU SHOULD BE 17.
Tove Jansson

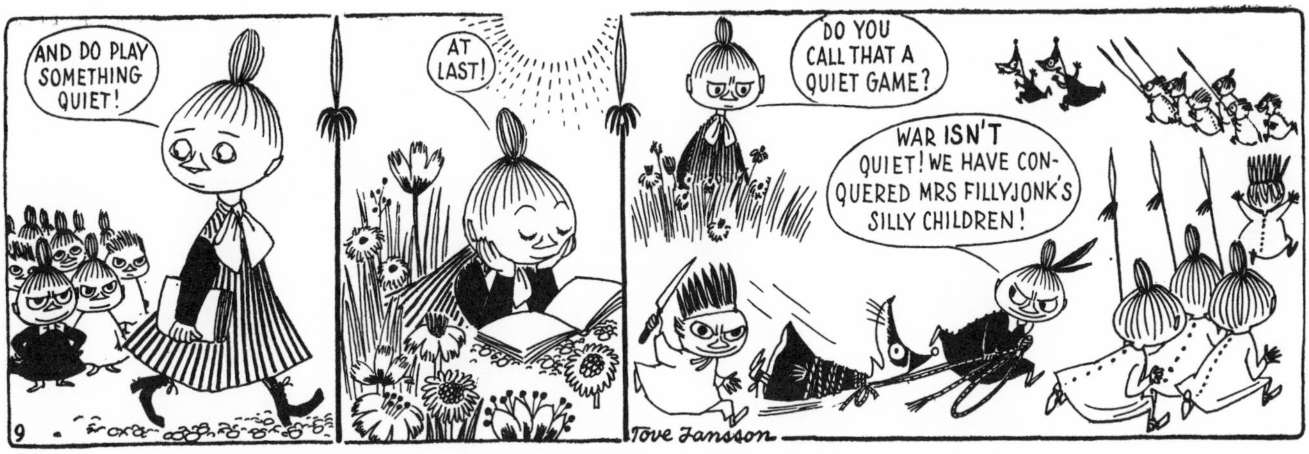
AND DO PLAY SOMETHING QUIET!
9
AT LAST!
DO YOU CALL THAT A QUIET GAME?
WAR ISN'T QUIET! WE HAVE CONQUERED MRS FILLYJONK'S SILLY CHILDREN!
Tove Jansson

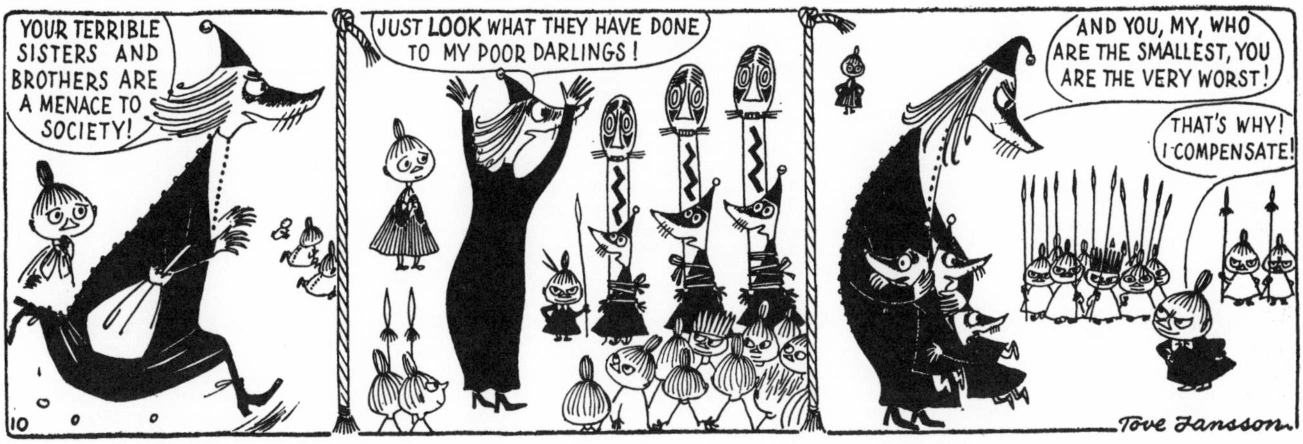
YOUR TERRIBLE SISTERS AND BROTHERS ARE A MENACE TO SOCIETY!
10
JUST LOOK WHAT THEY HAVE DONE TO MY POOR DARLINGS!
AND YOU, MY, WHO ARE THE SMALLEST, YOU ARE THE VERY WORST!
THAT'S WHY! I COMPENSATE!
Tove Jansson

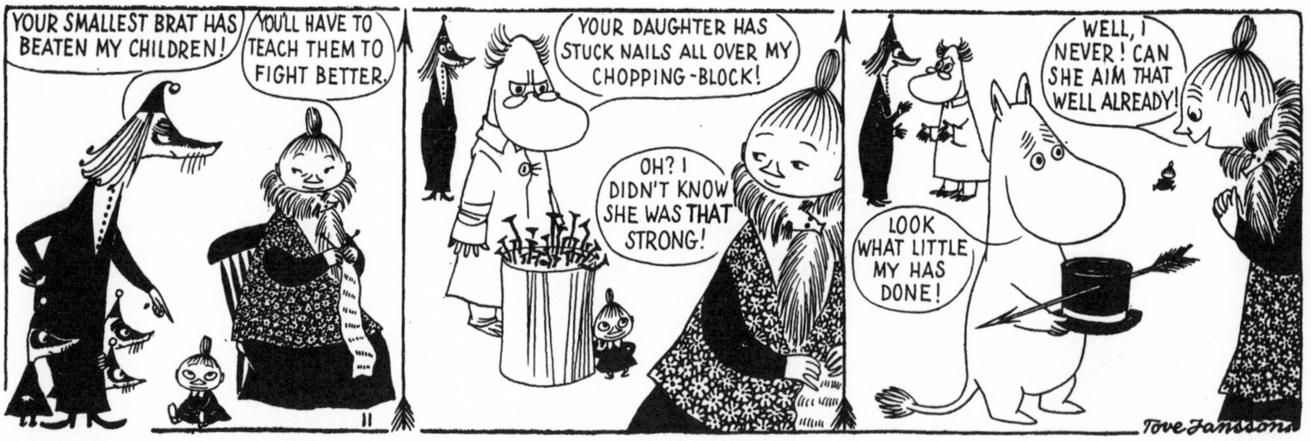
YOUR SMALLEST BRAT HAS BEATEN MY CHILDREN!
YOU'LL HAVE TO TEACH THEM TO FIGHT BETTER.
11
YOUR DAUGHTER HAS STUCK NAILS ALL OVER MY CHOPPING-BLOCK!
OH? I DIDN'T KNOW SHE WAS THAT STRONG!
WELL, I NEVER! CAN SHE AIM THAT WELL ALREADY!
LOOK WHAT LITTLE MY HAS DONE!
Tove Jansson

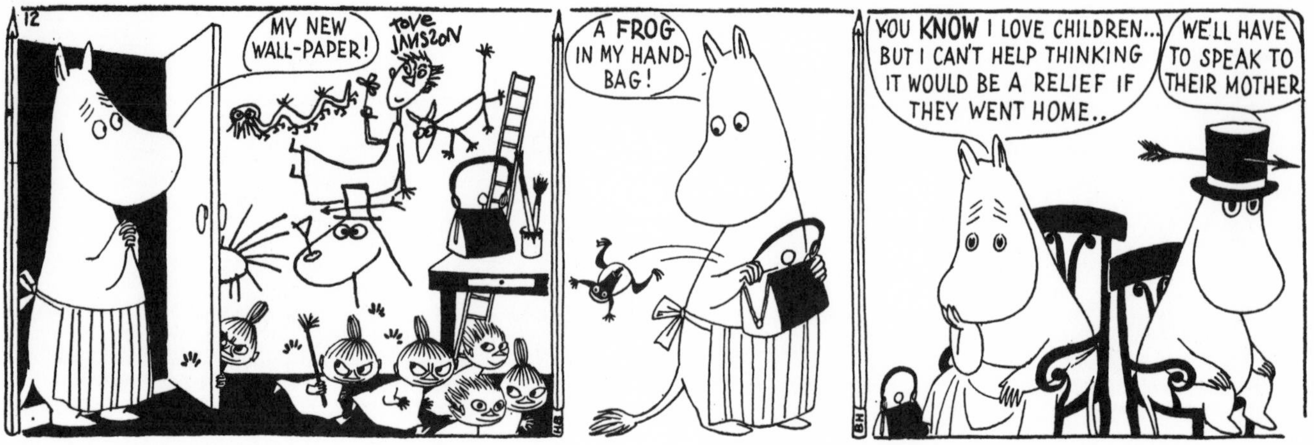
12
MY NEW WALL-PAPER!
TOVE JANSSON
A FROG IN MY HAND-BAG!
YOU KNOW I LOVE CHILDREN... BUT I CAN'T HELP THINKING IT WOULD BE A RELIEF IF THEY WENT HOME..
WE'LL HAVE TO SPEAK TO THEIR MOTHER

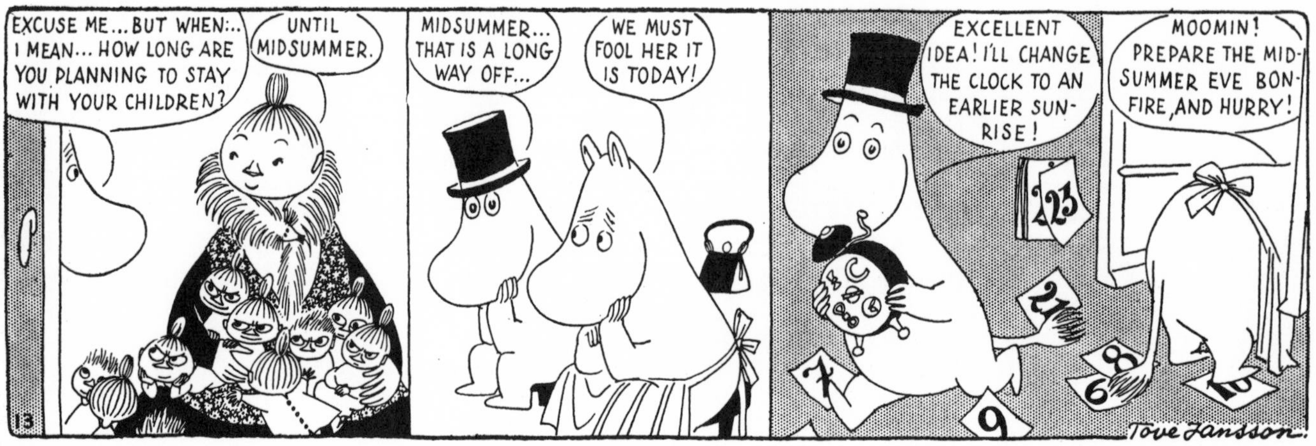
EXCUSE ME... BUT WHEN:.. I MEAN... HOW LONG ARE YOU PLANNING TO STAY WITH YOUR CHILDREN?
UNTIL MIDSUMMER.
13
MIDSUMMER... THAT IS A LONG WAY OFF...
WE MUST FOOL HER IT IS TODAY!
EXCELLENT IDEA! I'LL CHANGE THE CLOCK TO AN EARLIER SUN-RISE!
MOOMIN! PREPARE THE MID-SUMMER EVE BON-FIRE, AND HURRY!
Tove Jansson

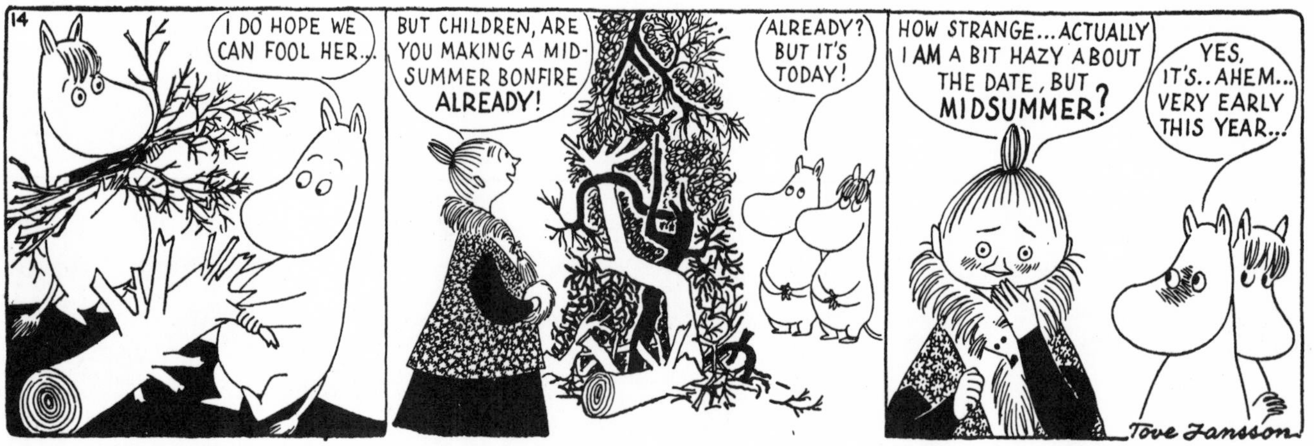
14
I DO HOPE WE CAN FOOL HER...
BUT CHILDREN, ARE YOU MAKING A MID-SUMMER BONFIRE ALREADY!
ALREADY? BUT IT'S TODAY!
HOW STRANGE... ACTUALLY I AM A BIT HAZY ABOUT THE DATE, BUT MIDSUMMER?
YES, IT'S.. AHEM... VERY EARLY THIS YEAR...
Tove Jansson

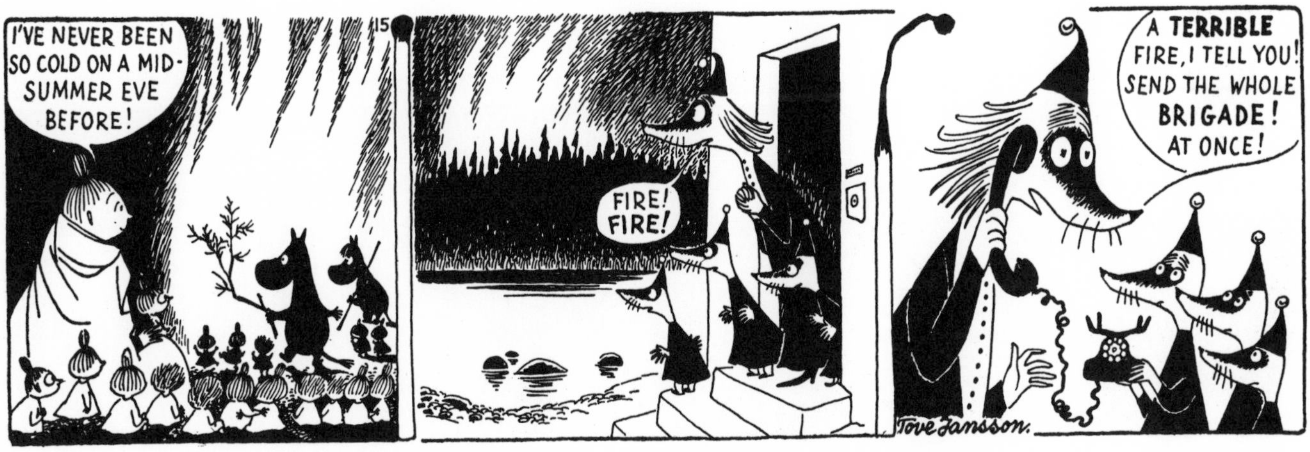
15
I'VE NEVER BEEN SO COLD ON A MID-SUMMER EVE BEFORE!
FIRE! FIRE!
A TERRIBLE FIRE, I TELL YOU! SEND THE WHOLE BRIGADE! AT ONCE!
Tove Jansson.

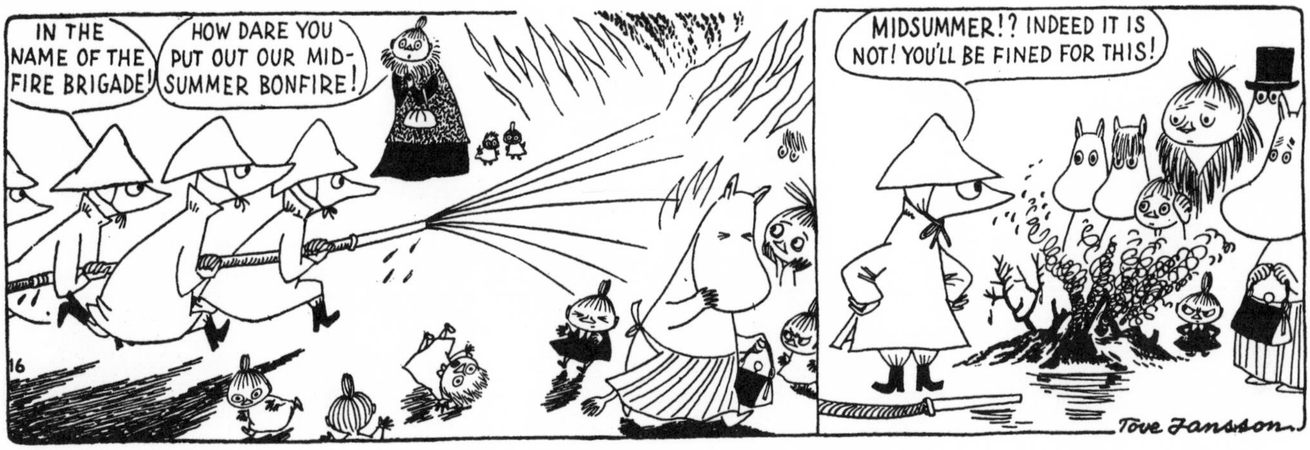
16
IN THE NAME OF THE FIRE BRIGADE!
HOW DARE YOU PUT OUT OUR MID-SUMMER BONFIRE!
MIDSUMMER!? INDEED IT IS NOT! YOU'LL BE FINED FOR THIS!
Tove Jansson.

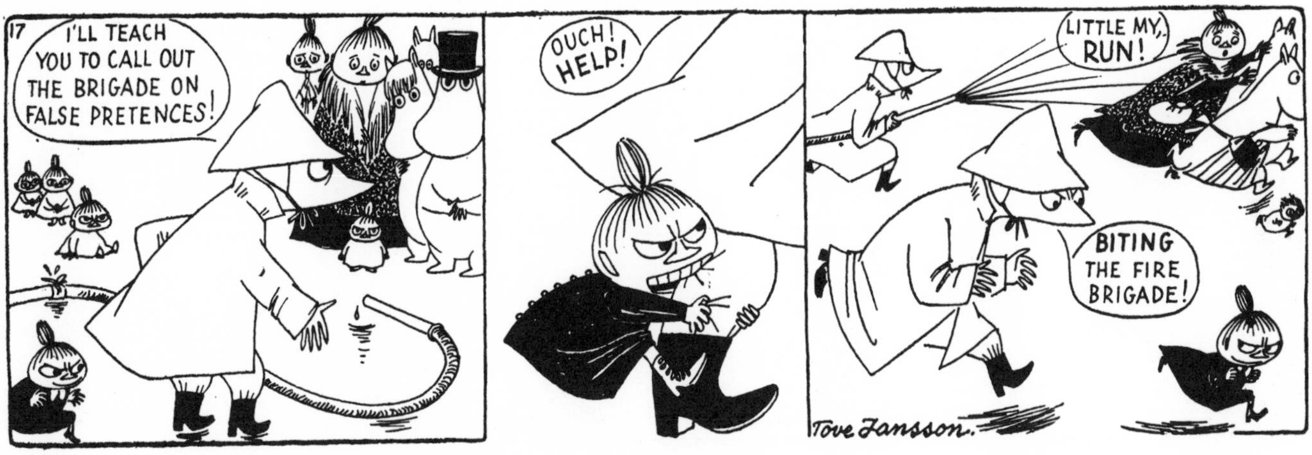
17
I'LL TEACH YOU TO CALL OUT THE BRIGADE ON FALSE PRETENCES!
OUCH! HELP!
LITTLE MY, RUN!
BITING THE FIRE BRIGADE!
Tove Jansson.

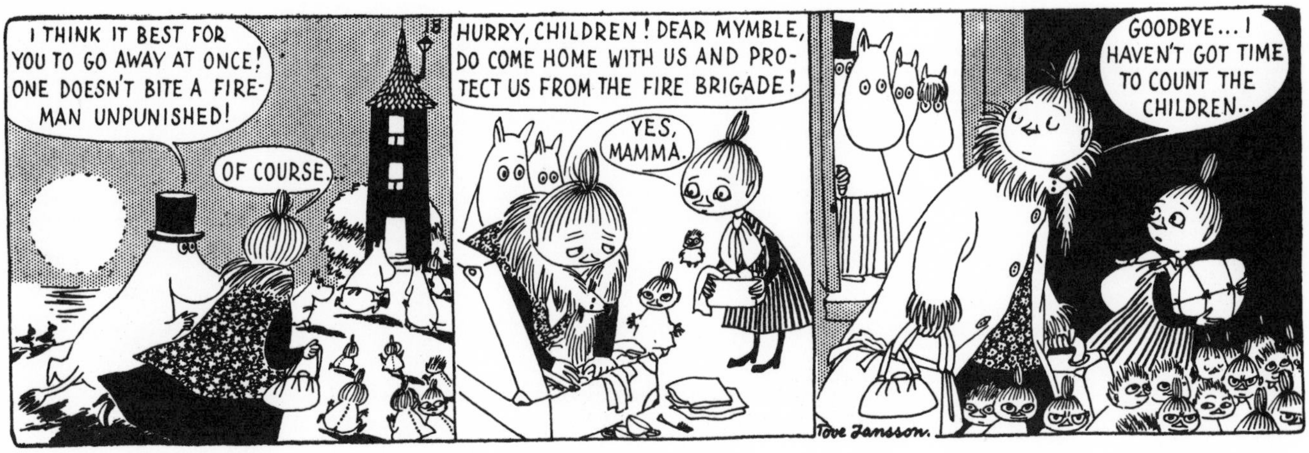
18
I THINK IT BEST FOR YOU TO GO AWAY AT ONCE! ONE DOESN'T BITE A FIRE-MAN UNPUNISHED!
OF COURSE.
HURRY, CHILDREN! DEAR MYMBLE, DO COME HOME WITH US AND PRO-TECT US FROM THE FIRE BRIGADE!
YES, MAMMA.
GOODBYE... I HAVEN'T GOT TIME TO COUNT THE CHILDREN...
Tove Jansson.

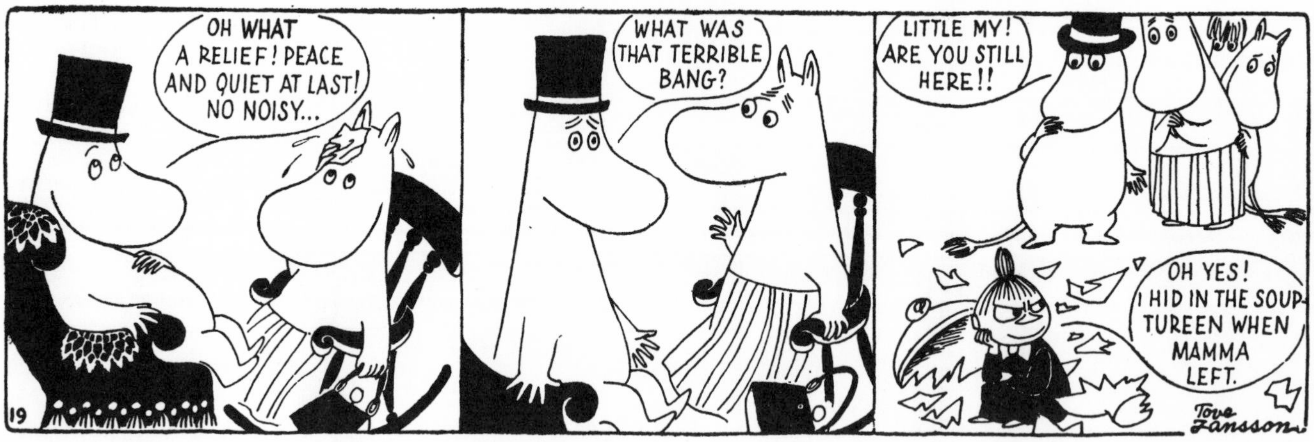
19
OH WHAT A RELIEF! PEACE AND QUIET AT LAST! NO NOISY...
WHAT WAS THAT TERRIBLE BANG?
LITTLE MY! ARE YOU STILL HERE!!
OH YES! I HID IN THE SOUP TUREEN WHEN MAMMA LEFT.
Tove Jansson

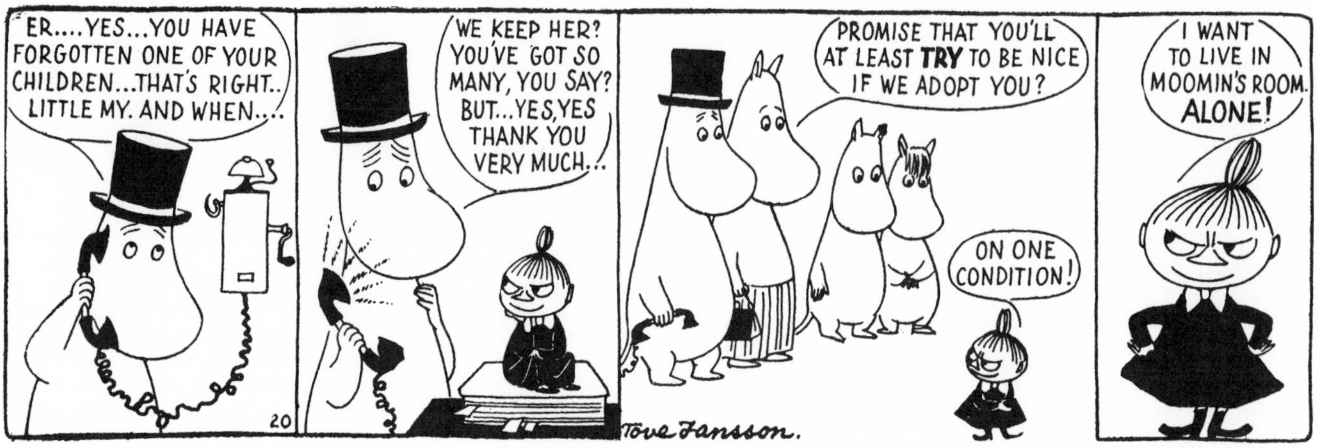
ER....YES...YOU HAVE FORGOTTEN ONE OF YOUR CHILDREN...THAT'S RIGHT.. LITTLE MY. AND WHEN....
20
WE KEEP HER? YOU'VE GOT SO MANY, YOU SAY? BUT...YES,YES THANK YOU VERY MUCH...
PROMISE THAT YOU'LL AT LEAST TRY TO BE NICE IF WE ADOPT YOU?
ON ONE CONDITION!
Tove Jansson.
I WANT TO LIVE IN MOOMIN'S ROOM. ALONE!

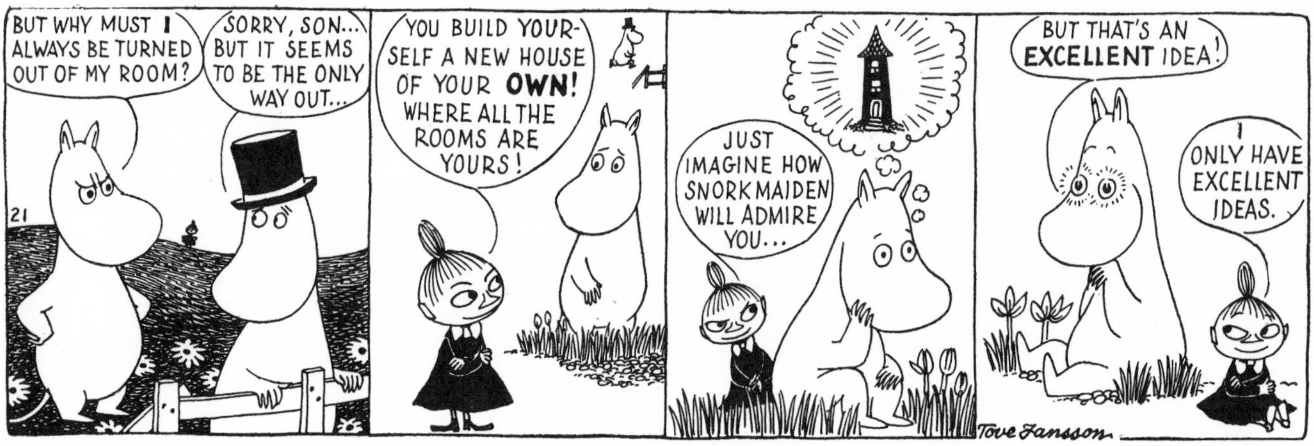
BUT WHY MUST I ALWAYS BE TURNED OUT OF MY ROOM?
SORRY, SON... BUT IT SEEMS TO BE THE ONLY WAY OUT...
21
YOU BUILD YOURSELF A NEW HOUSE OF YOUR OWN! WHERE ALL THE ROOMS ARE YOURS!
JUST IMAGINE HOW SNORKMAIDEN WILL ADMIRE YOU...
BUT THAT'S AN EXCELLENT IDEA!
I ONLY HAVE EXCELLENT IDEAS.
Tove Jansson

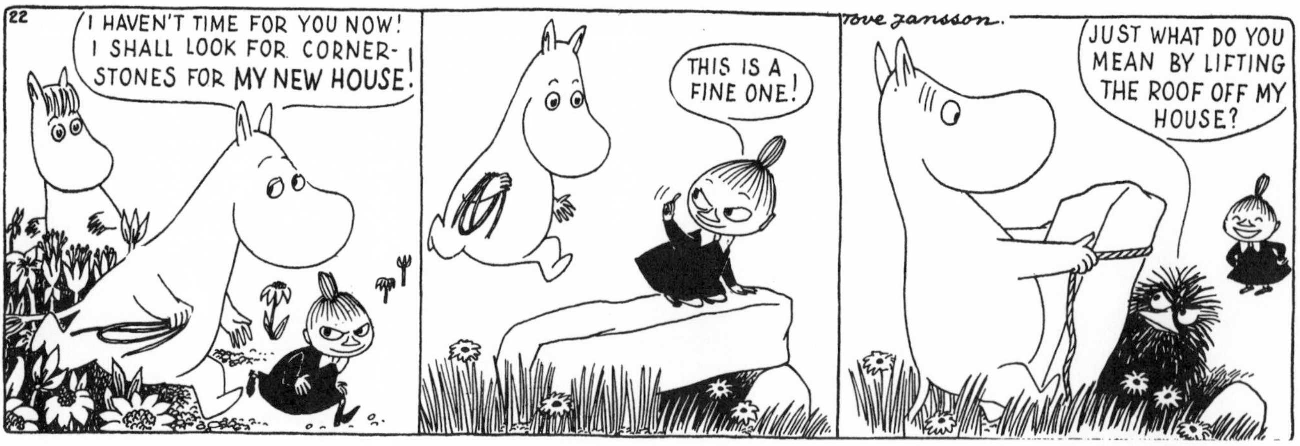
22
I HAVEN'T TIME FOR YOU NOW! I SHALL LOOK FOR CORNER-STONES FOR MY NEW HOUSE!
THIS IS A FINE ONE!
Tove Jansson.
JUST WHAT DO YOU MEAN BY LIFTING THE ROOF OFF MY HOUSE?

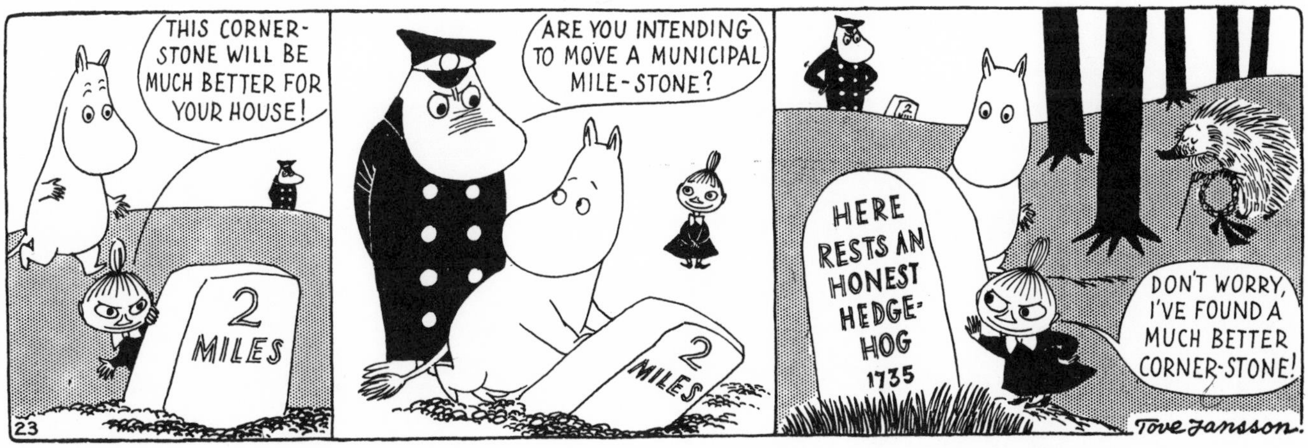

23
THIS CORNER-STONE WILL BE MUCH BETTER FOR YOUR HOUSE!
2 MILES
ARE YOU INTENDING TO MOVE A MUNICIPAL MILE-STONE?
2 MILES
HERE RESTS AN HONEST HEDGE-HOG 1735
DON'T WORRY, I'VE FOUND A MUCH BETTER CORNER-STONE!
Tove Jansson

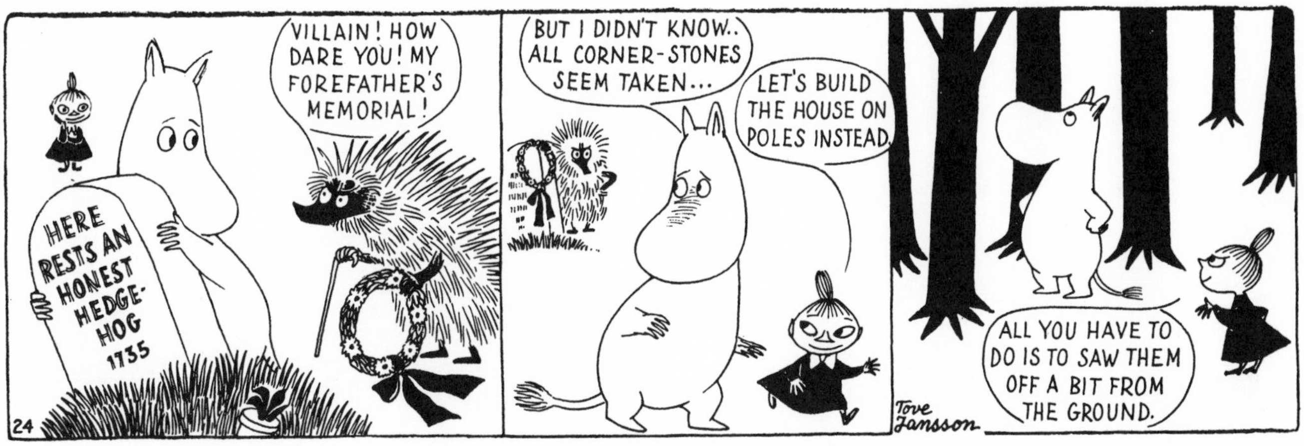

24
HERE RESTS AN HONEST HEDGE-HOG 1735
VILLAIN! HOW DARE YOU! MY FOREFATHER'S MEMORIAL!
BUT I DIDN'T KNOW.. ALL CORNER-STONES SEEM TAKEN...
LET'S BUILD THE HOUSE ON POLES INSTEAD.
ALL YOU HAVE TO DO IS TO SAW THEM OFF A BIT FROM THE GROUND.
Tove Jansson

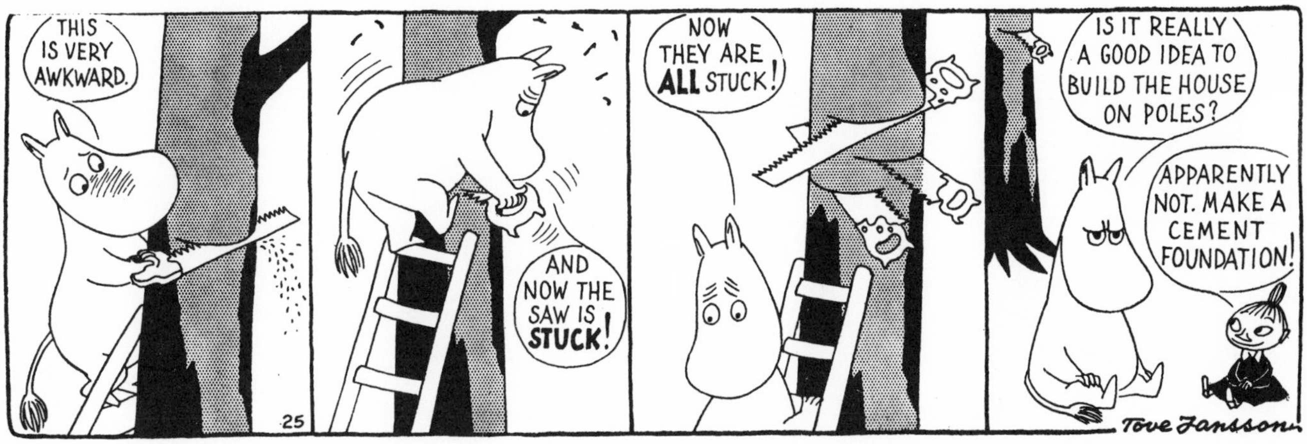

THIS IS VERY AWKWARD.
25
AND NOW THE SAW IS STUCK!
NOW THEY ARE ALL STUCK!
IS IT REALLY A GOOD IDEA TO BUILD THE HOUSE ON POLES?
APPARENTLY NOT. MAKE A CEMENT FOUNDATION!
Tove Jansson

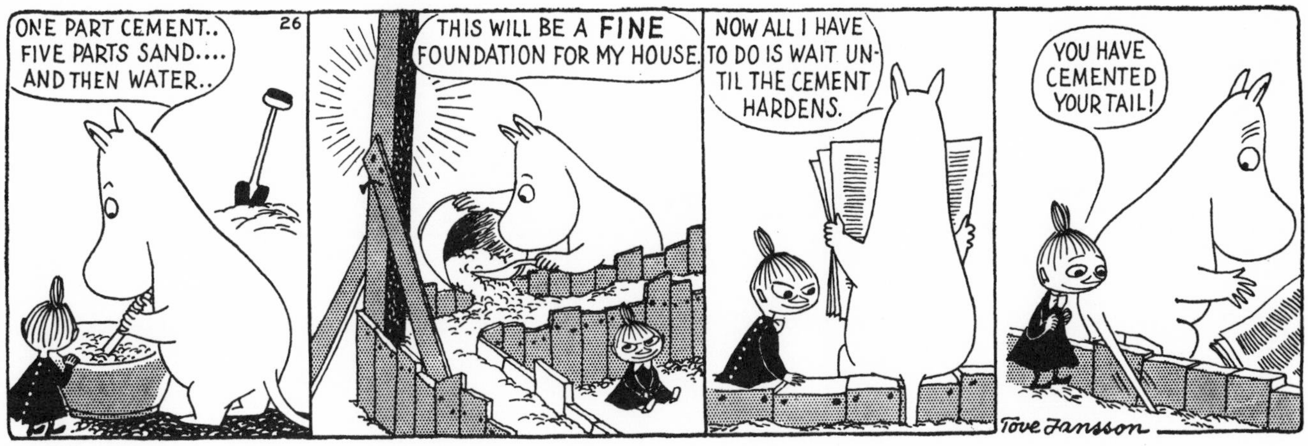

26
ONE PART CEMENT.. FIVE PARTS SAND.... AND THEN WATER..
THIS WILL BE A FINE FOUNDATION FOR MY HOUSE.
NOW ALL I HAVE TO DO IS WAIT UNTIL THE CEMENT HARDENS.
YOU HAVE CEMENTED YOUR TAIL!
Tove Jansson

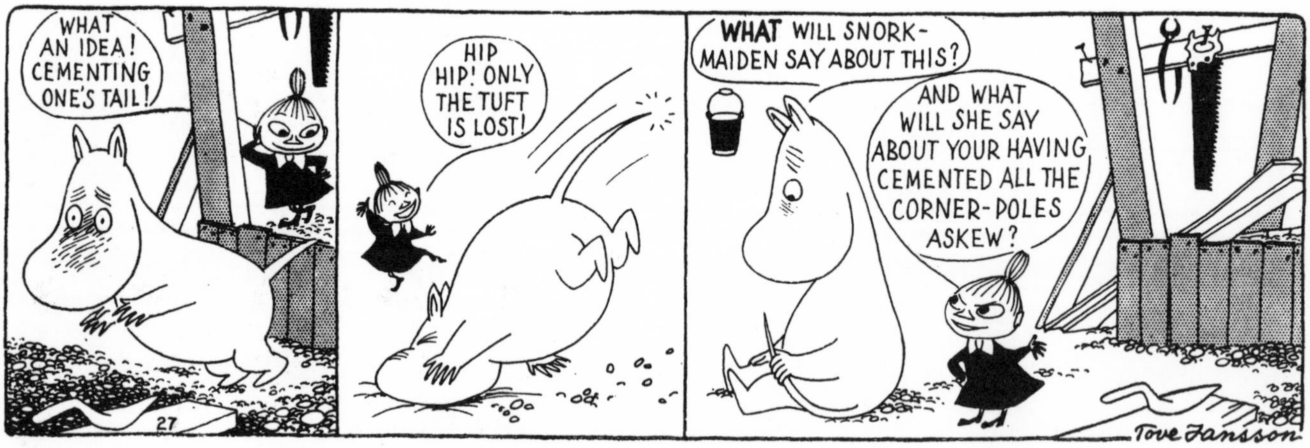
WHAT AN IDEA! CEMENTING ONE'S TAIL!
27
HIP HIP! ONLY THE TUFT IS LOST!
WHAT WILL SNORK-MAIDEN SAY ABOUT THIS?
AND WHAT WILL SHE SAY ABOUT YOUR HAVING CEMENTED ALL THE CORNER-POLES ASKEW?
Tove Jansson

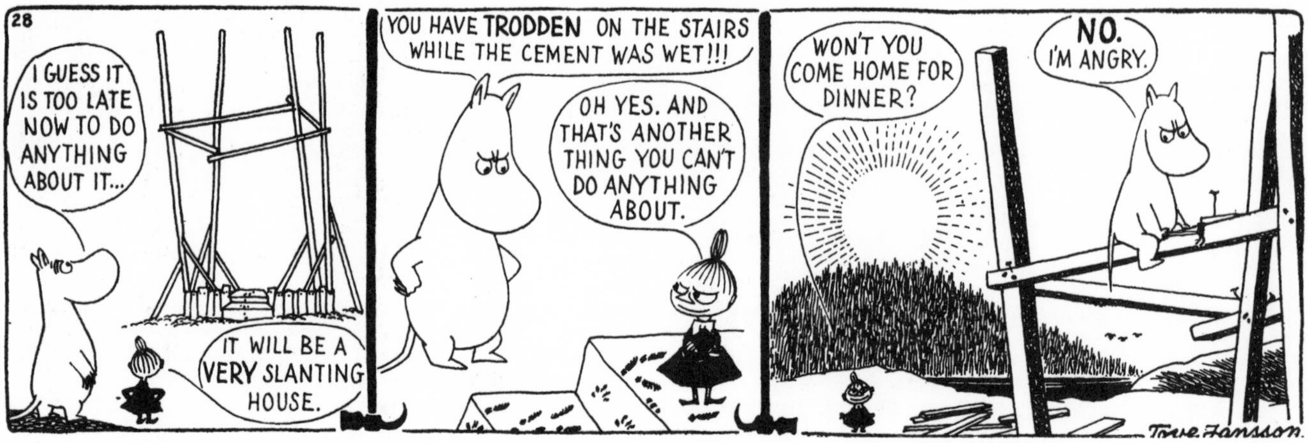
28
I GUESS IT IS TOO LATE NOW TO DO ANYTHING ABOUT IT...
IT WILL BE A VERY SLANTING HOUSE.
YOU HAVE TRODDEN ON THE STAIRS WHILE THE CEMENT WAS WET!!!
OH YES. AND THAT'S ANOTHER THING YOU CAN'T DO ANYTHING ABOUT.
WON'T YOU COME HOME FOR DINNER?
NO. I'M ANGRY.
Tove Jansson

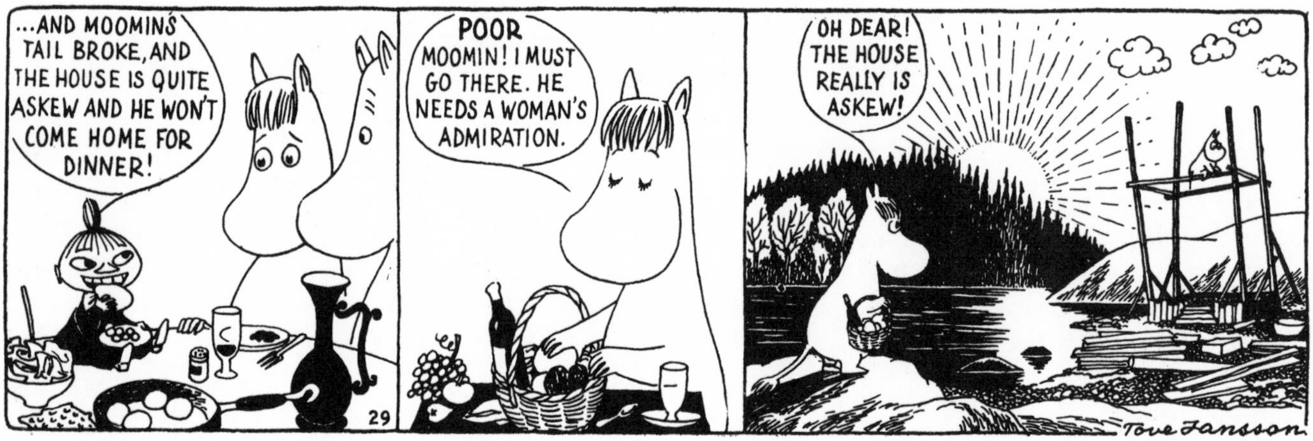
...AND MOOMINS TAIL BROKE, AND THE HOUSE IS QUITE ASKEW AND HE WON'T COME HOME FOR DINNER!
29
POOR MOOMIN! I MUST GO THERE. HE NEEDS A WOMAN'S ADMIRATION.
OH DEAR! THE HOUSE REALLY IS ASKEW!
Tove Jansson

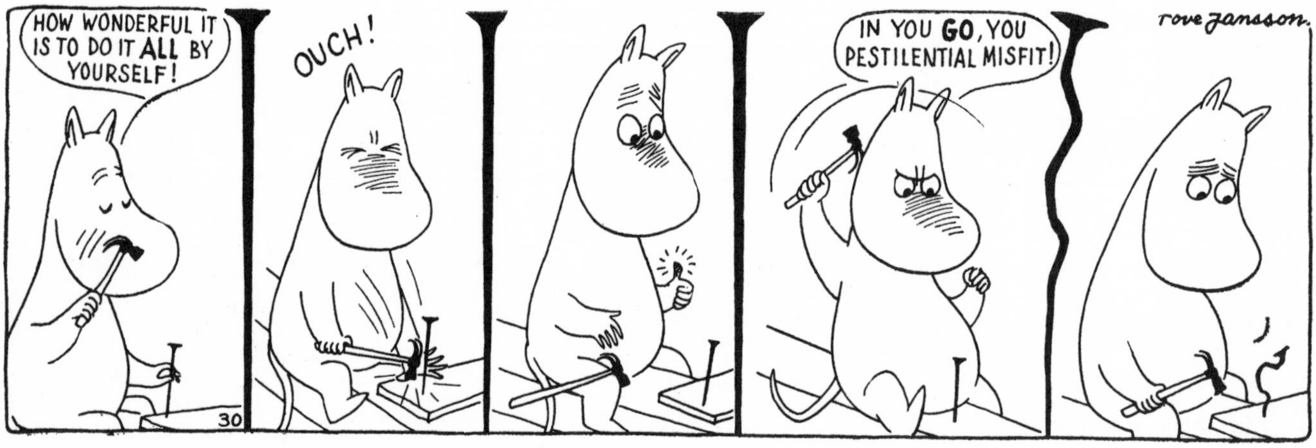
HOW WONDERFUL IT IS TO DO IT ALL BY YOURSELF!
30
OUCH!
IN YOU GO, YOU PESTILENTIAL MISFIT!
Tove Jansson

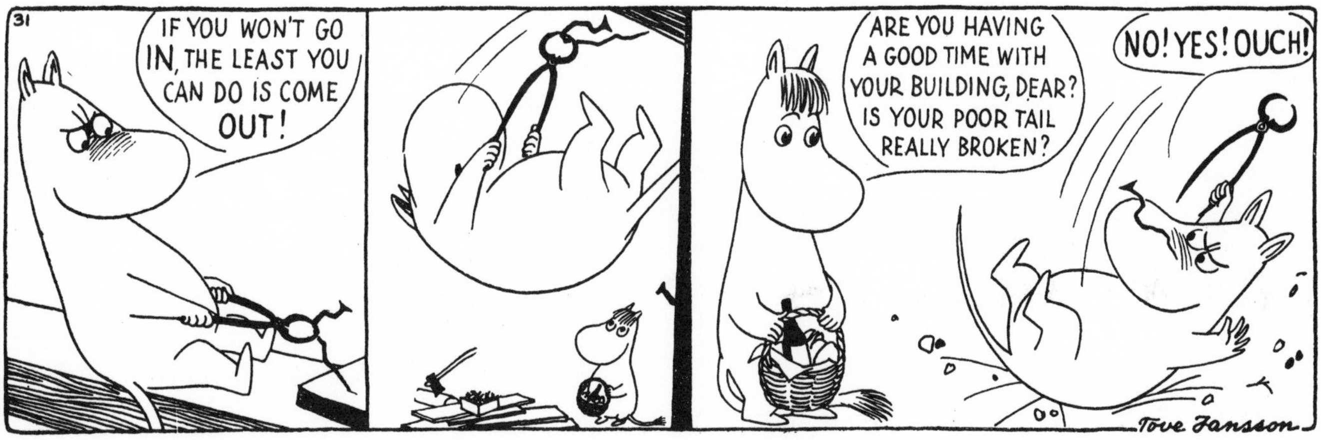
31
IF YOU WON'T GO IN, THE LEAST YOU CAN DO IS COME OUT!
ARE YOU HAVING A GOOD TIME WITH YOUR BUILDING, DEAR? IS YOUR POOR TAIL REALLY BROKEN?
NO! YES! OUCH!
Tove Jansson

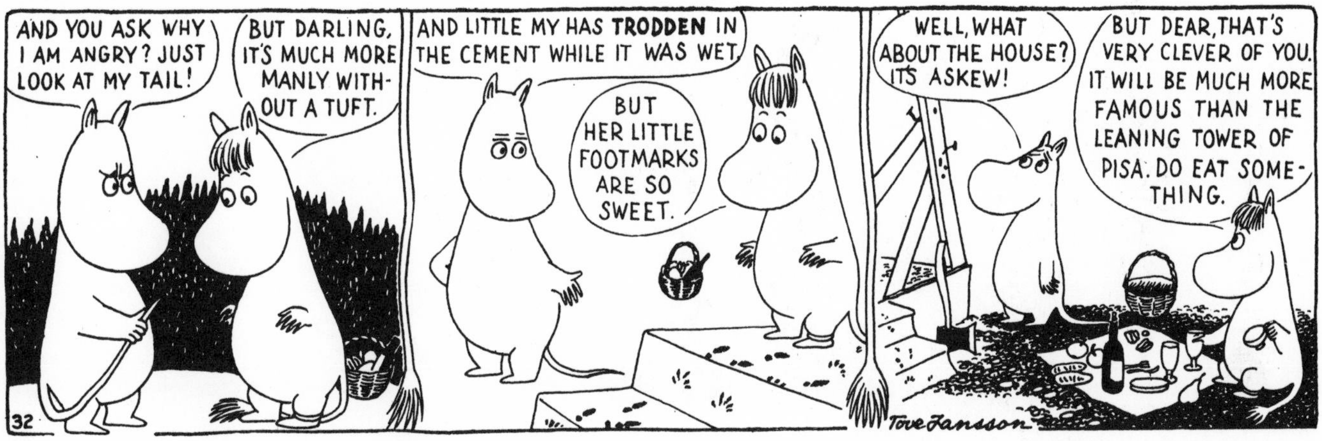
AND YOU ASK WHY I AM ANGRY? JUST LOOK AT MY TAIL!
BUT DARLING, IT'S MUCH MORE MANLY WITHOUT A TUFT.
32
AND LITTLE MY HAS TRODDEN IN THE CEMENT WHILE IT WAS WET.
BUT HER LITTLE FOOTMARKS ARE SO SWEET.
WELL, WHAT ABOUT THE HOUSE? ITS ASKEW!
BUT DEAR, THAT'S VERY CLEVER OF YOU. IT WILL BE MUCH MORE FAMOUS THAN THE LEANING TOWER OF PISA. DO EAT SOMETHING.
Tove Jansson

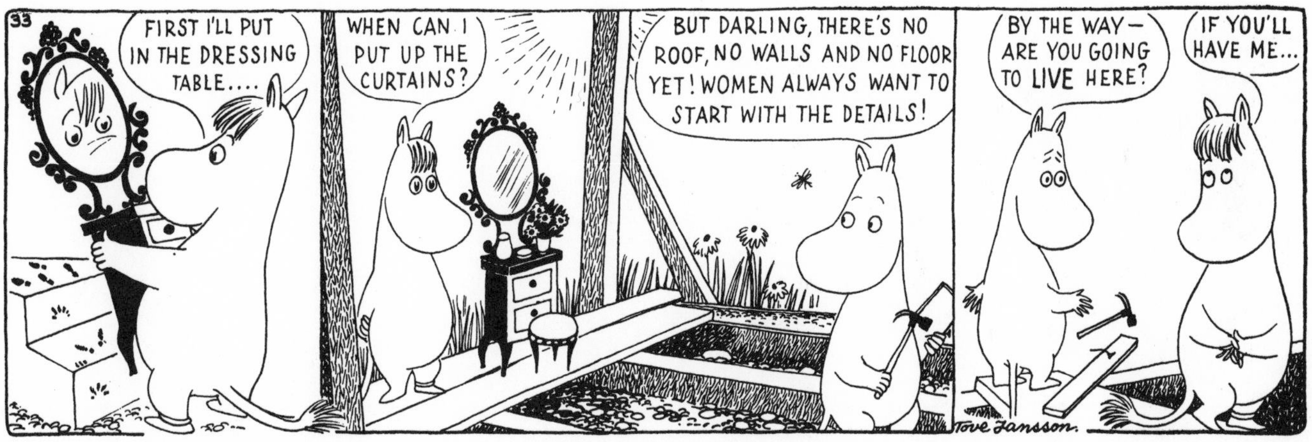
33
FIRST I'LL PUT IN THE DRESSING TABLE....
WHEN CAN I PUT UP THE CURTAINS?
BUT DARLING, THERE'S NO ROOF, NO WALLS AND NO FLOOR YET! WOMEN ALWAYS WANT TO START WITH THE DETAILS!
BY THE WAY – ARE YOU GOING TO LIVE HERE?
IF YOU'LL HAVE ME...
Tove Jansson

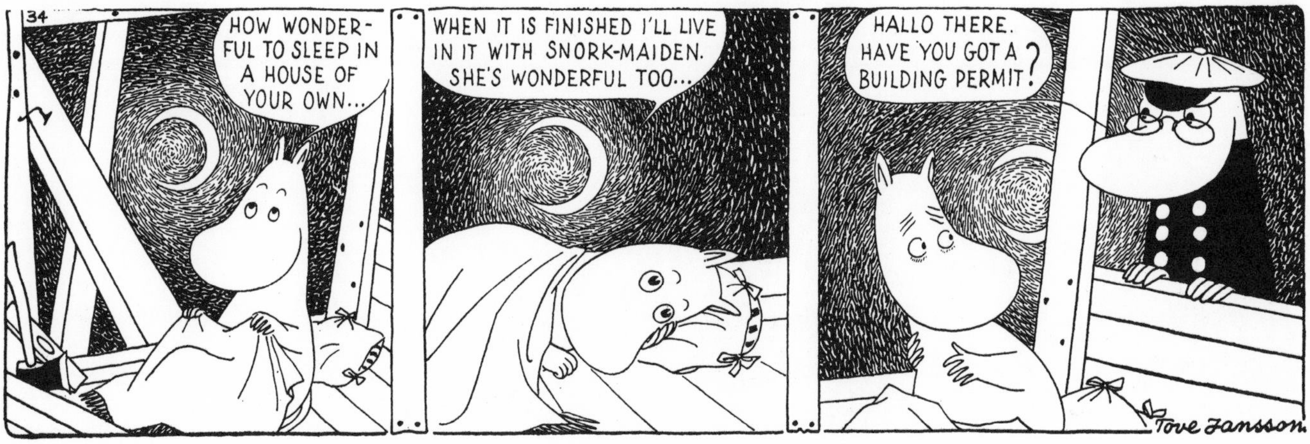
34
HOW WONDERFUL TO SLEEP IN A HOUSE OF YOUR OWN...
WHEN IT IS FINISHED I'LL LIVE IN IT WITH SNORK-MAIDEN. SHE'S WONDERFUL TOO...
HALLO THERE. HAVE YOU GOT A BUILDING PERMIT?
Tove Jansson

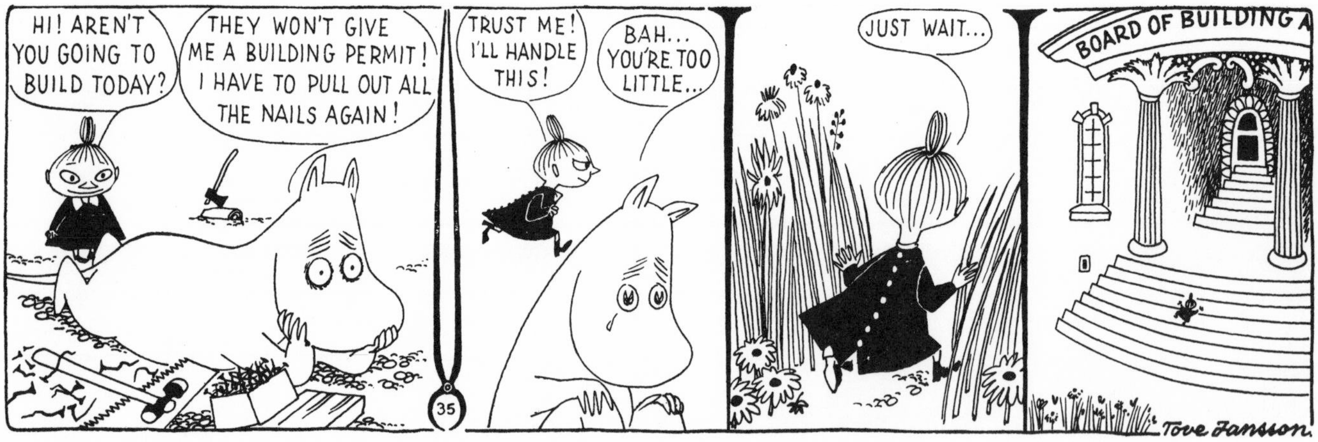
HI! AREN'T YOU GOING TO BUILD TODAY?
THEY WON'T GIVE ME A BUILDING PERMIT! I HAVE TO PULL OUT ALL THE NAILS AGAIN!
35
TRUST ME! I'LL HANDLE THIS!
BAH... YOU'RE TOO LITTLE...
JUST WAIT...
BOARD OF BUILDING A
Tove Jansson.

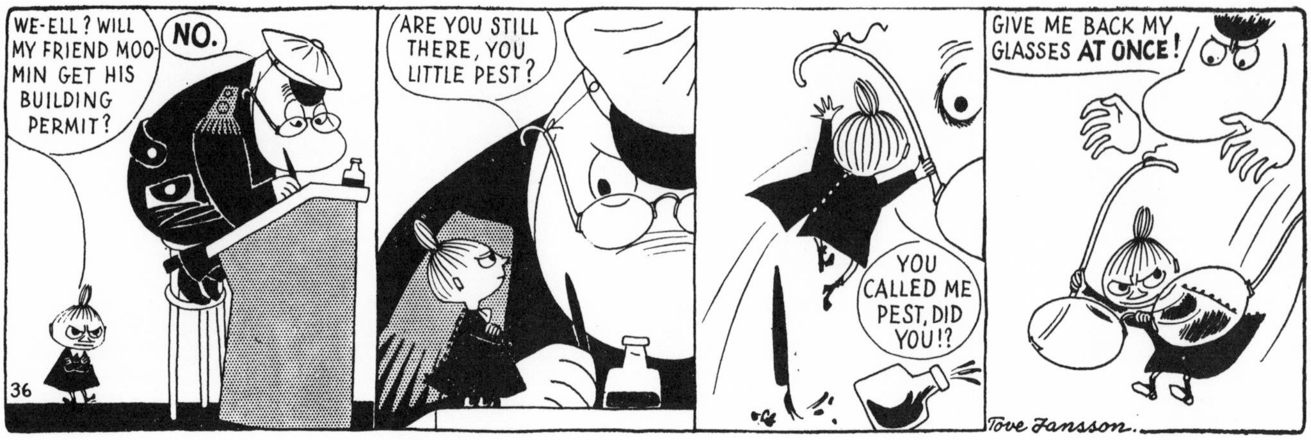
WE-ELL? WILL MY FRIEND MOOMIN GET HIS BUILDING PERMIT?
NO.
36
ARE YOU STILL THERE, YOU LITTLE PEST?
YOU CALLED ME PEST, DID YOU!?
GIVE ME BACK MY GLASSES AT ONCE!
Tove Jansson.

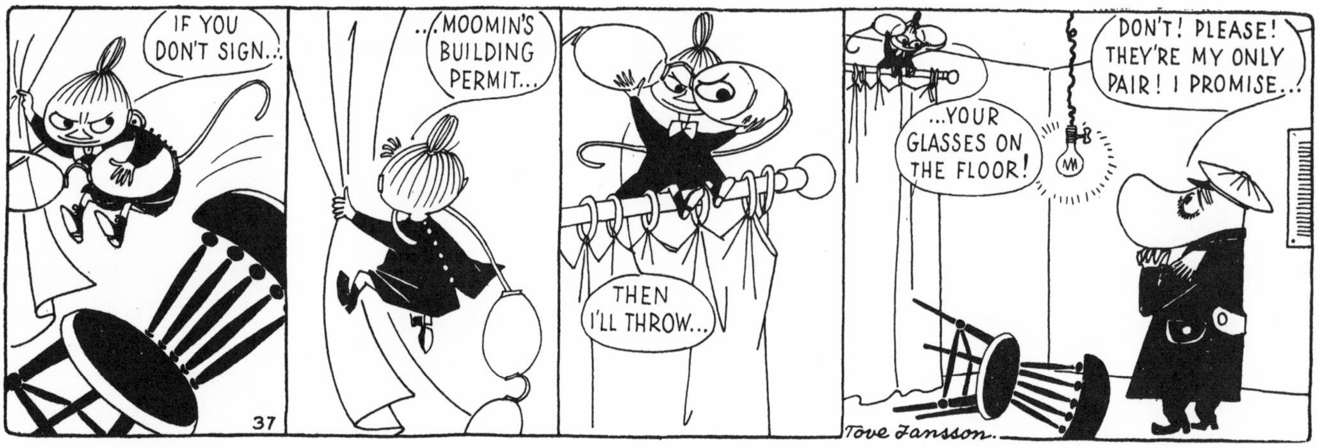
IF YOU DON'T SIGN...
37
...MOOMIN'S BUILDING PERMIT...
THEN I'LL THROW...
...YOUR GLASSES ON THE FLOOR!
DON'T! PLEASE! THEY'RE MY ONLY PAIR! I PROMISE...
Tove Jansson.

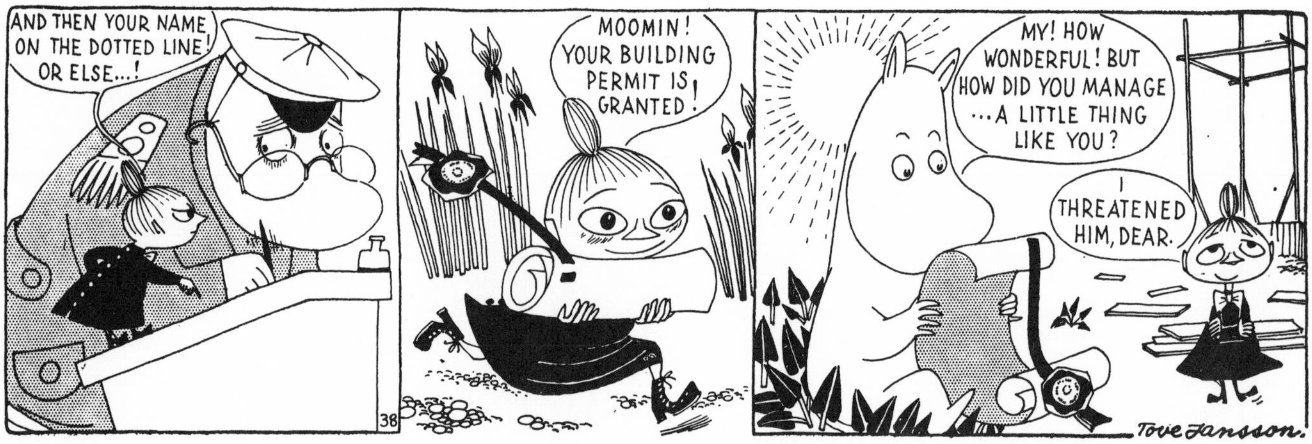
AND THEN YOUR NAME ON THE DOTTED LINE! OR ELSE...!
38
MOOMIN! YOUR BUILDING PERMIT IS GRANTED!
MY! HOW WONDERFUL! BUT HOW DID YOU MANAGE ...A LITTLE THING LIKE YOU?
I THREATENED HIM, DEAR.
Tove Jansson.

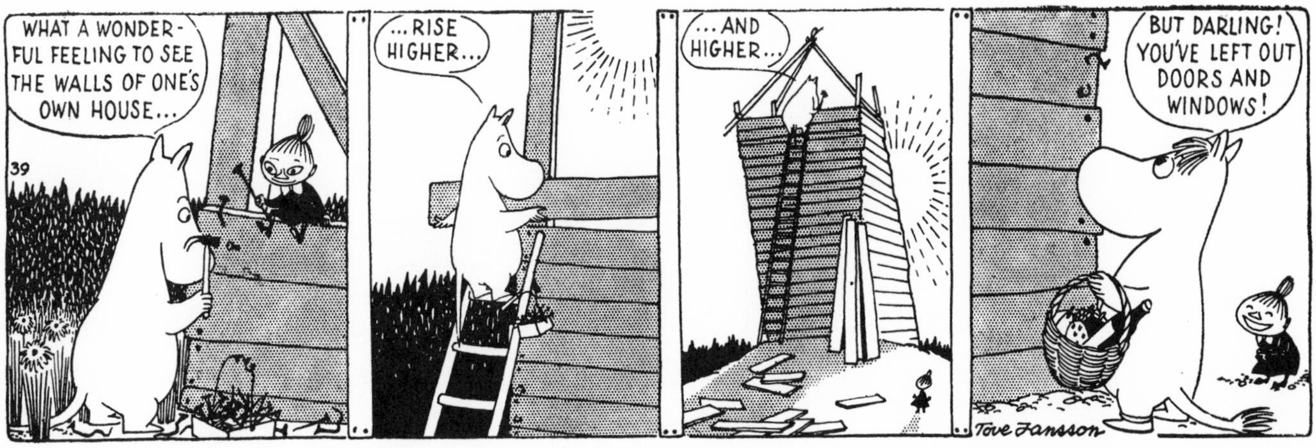
WHAT A WONDERFUL FEELING TO SEE THE WALLS OF ONE'S OWN HOUSE...
39
...RISE HIGHER...
...AND HIGHER...
BUT DARLING! YOU'VE LEFT OUT DOORS AND WINDOWS!
Tove Jansson

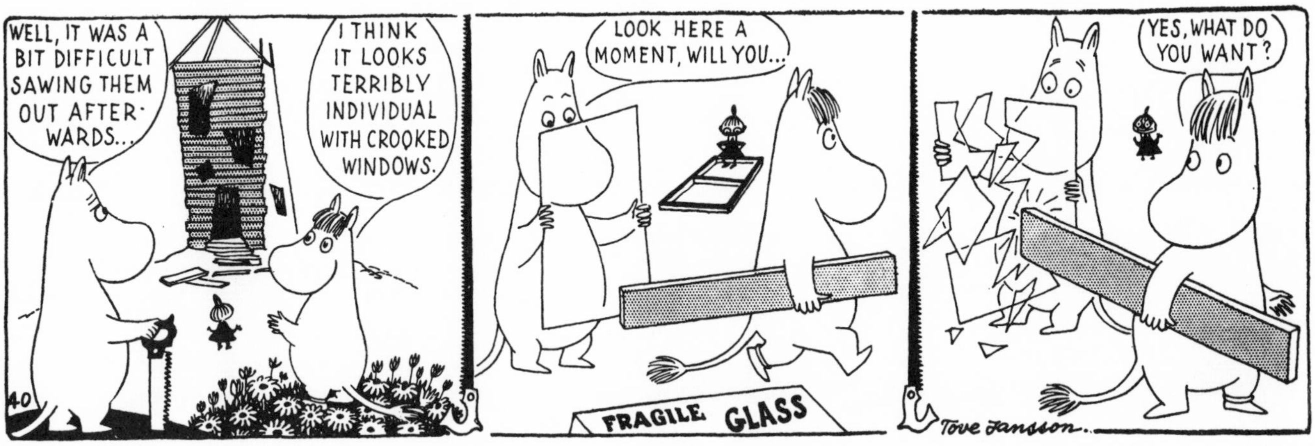
WELL, IT WAS A BIT DIFFICULT SAWING THEM OUT AFTERWARDS...
I THINK IT LOOKS TERRIBLY INDIVIDUAL WITH CROOKED WINDOWS.
40
LOOK HERE A MOMENT, WILL YOU...
FRAGILE GLASS
YES, WHAT DO YOU WANT?
Tove Jansson

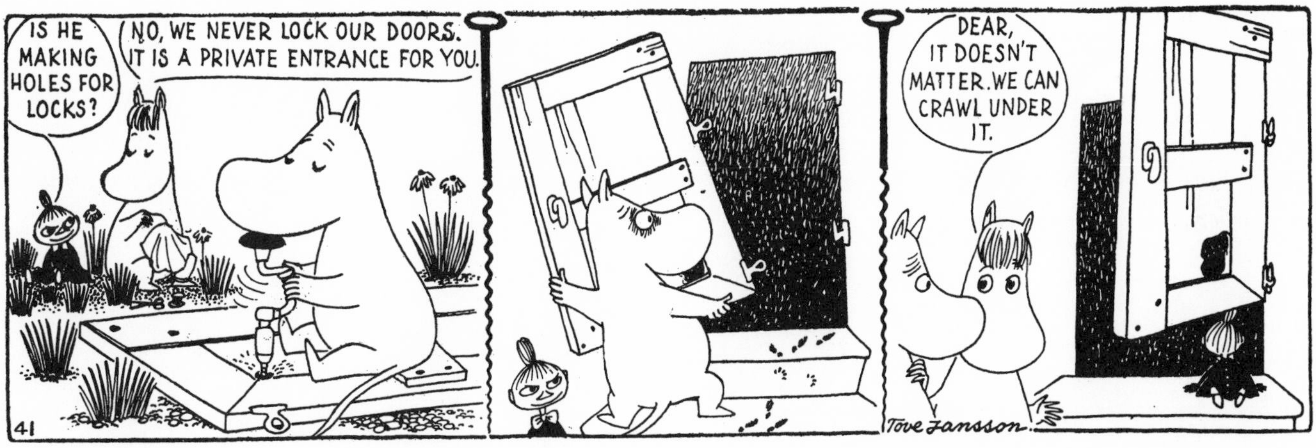
IS HE MAKING HOLES FOR LOCKS?
NO, WE NEVER LOCK OUR DOORS. IT IS A PRIVATE ENTRANCE FOR YOU.
41
DEAR, IT DOESN'T MATTER. WE CAN CRAWL UNDER IT.
Tove Jansson

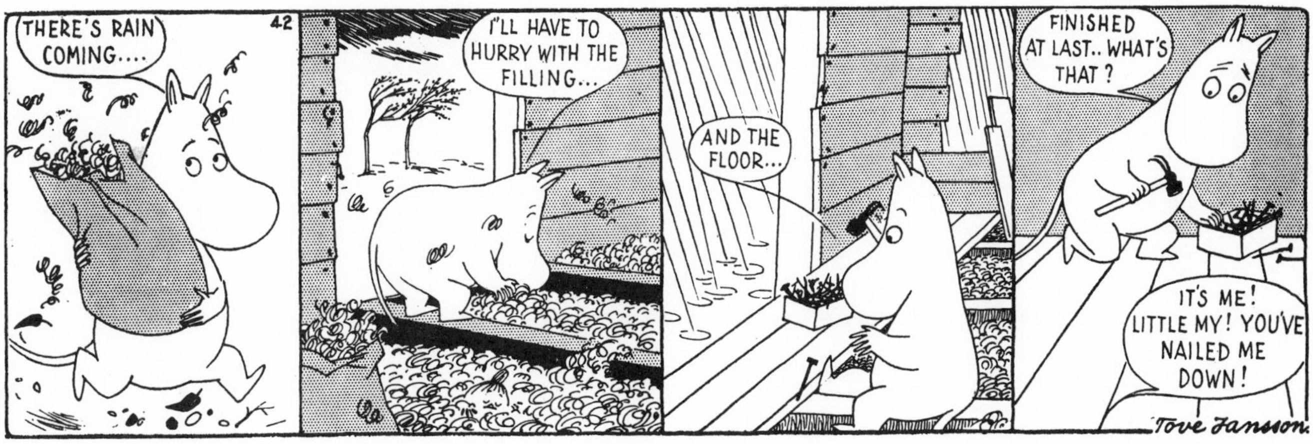
THERE'S RAIN COMING....
42
I'LL HAVE TO HURRY WITH THE FILLING...
AND THE FLOOR...
FINISHED AT LAST.. WHAT'S THAT?
IT'S ME! LITTLE MY! YOU'VE NAILED ME DOWN!
Tove Jansson

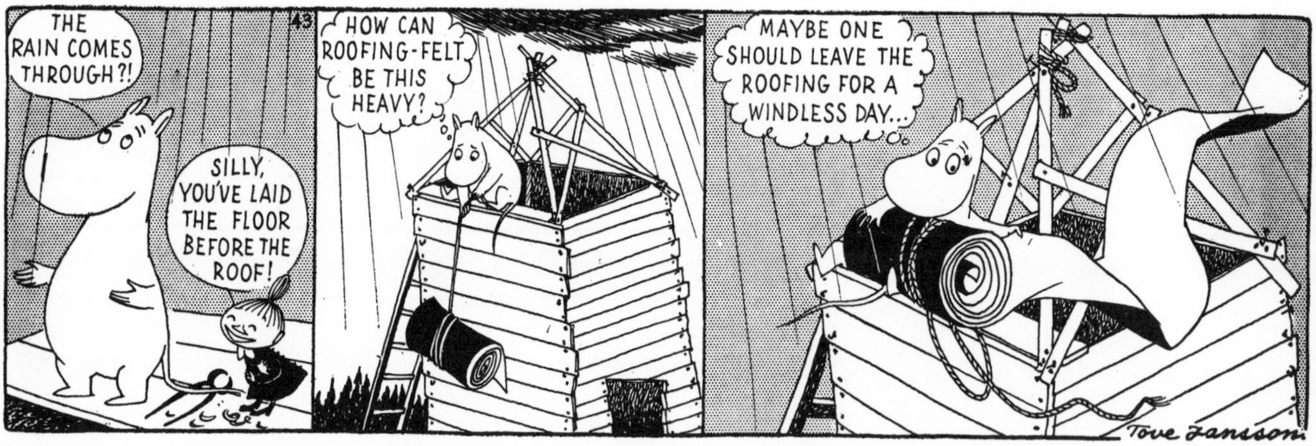
THE RAIN COMES THROUGH?!
HOW CAN ROOFING-FELT BE THIS HEAVY?
SILLY, YOU'VE LAID THE FLOOR BEFORE THE ROOF!
MAYBE ONE SHOULD LEAVE THE ROOFING FOR A WINDLESS DAY...
Tove Jansson

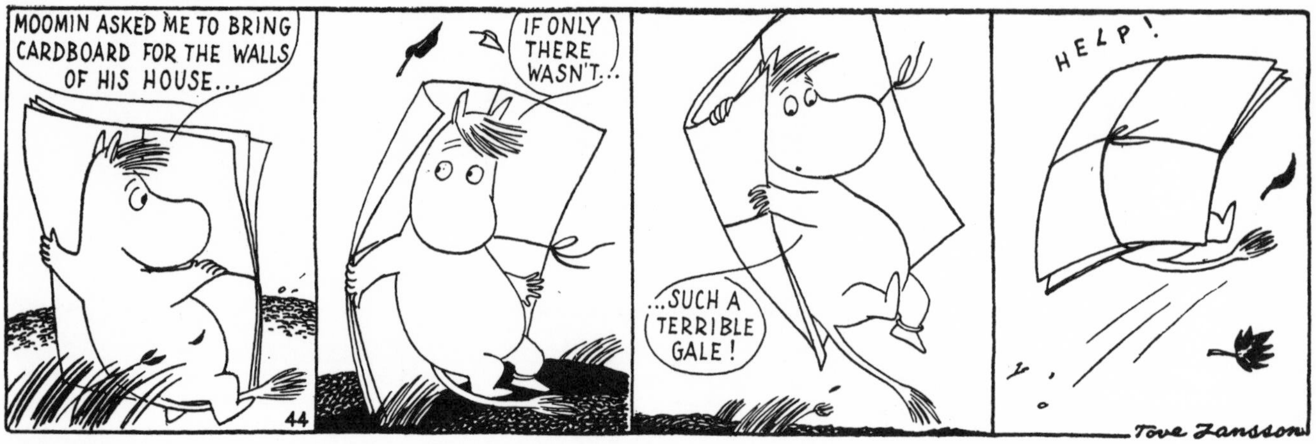
MOOMIN ASKED ME TO BRING CARDBOARD FOR THE WALLS OF HIS HOUSE...
IF ONLY THERE WASN'T...
...SUCH A TERRIBLE GALE!
HELP!
Tove Jansson

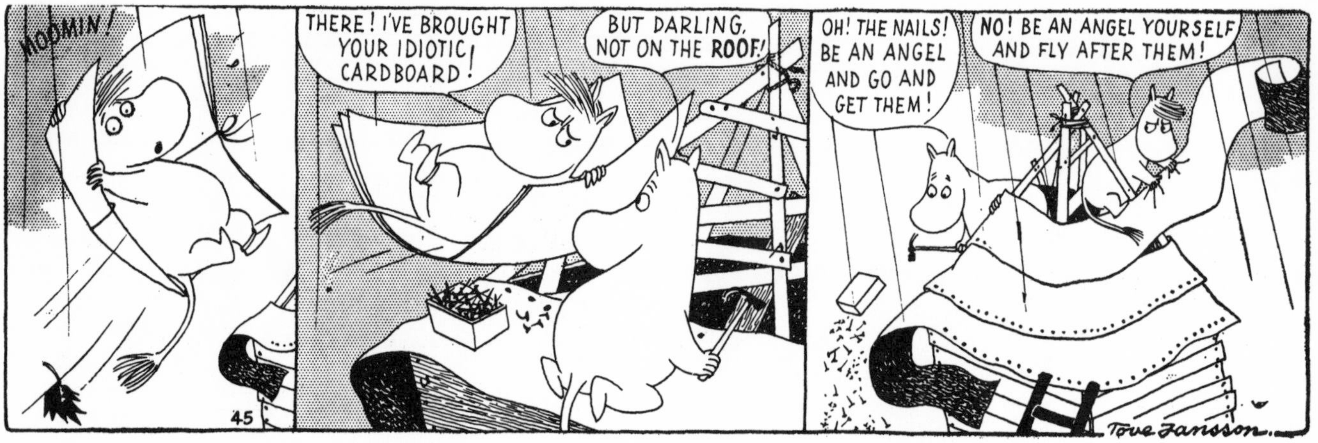
MOOMIN!
THERE! I'VE BROUGHT YOUR IDIOTIC CARDBOARD!
BUT DARLING, NOT ON THE ROOF!
OH! THE NAILS! BE AN ANGEL AND GO AND GET THEM!
NO! BE AN ANGEL YOURSELF AND FLY AFTER THEM!
Tove Jansson

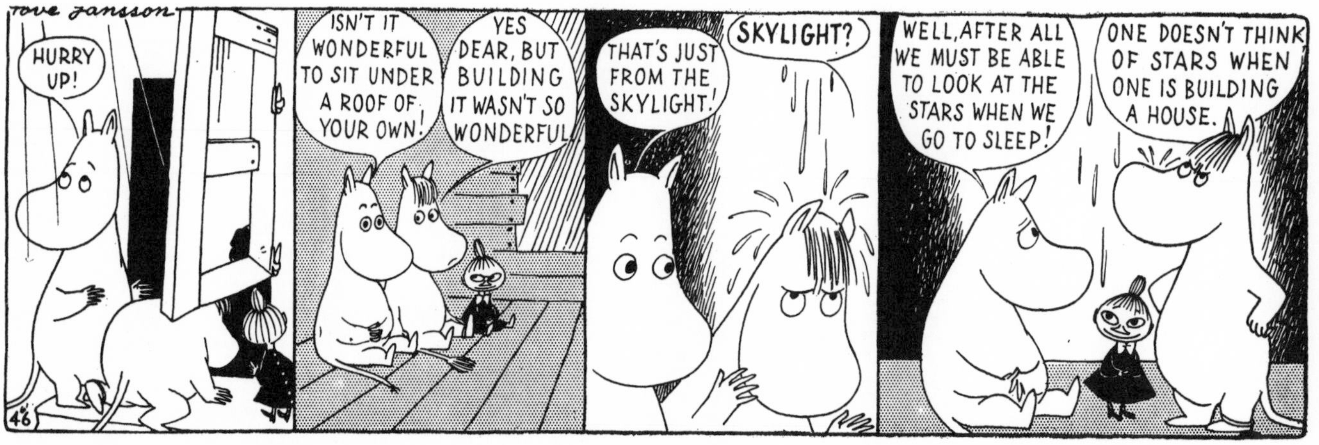
Tove Jansson
HURRY UP!
ISN'T IT WONDERFUL TO SIT UNDER A ROOF OF YOUR OWN!
YES DEAR, BUT BUILDING IT WASN'T SO WONDERFUL
THAT'S JUST FROM THE SKYLIGHT!
SKYLIGHT?
WELL, AFTER ALL WE MUST BE ABLE TO LOOK AT THE STARS WHEN WE GO TO SLEEP!
ONE DOESN'T THINK OF STARS WHEN ONE IS BUILDING A HOUSE.

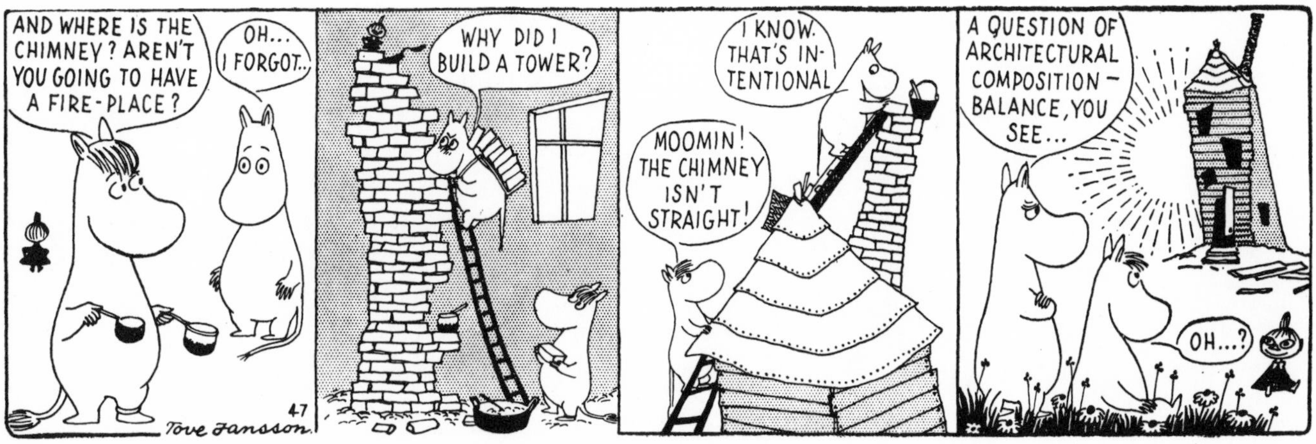
AND WHERE IS THE CHIMNEY? AREN'T YOU GOING TO HAVE A FIRE-PLACE?
OH... I FORGOT...
47
Tove Jansson
WHY DID I BUILD A TOWER?
MOOMIN! THE CHIMNEY ISN'T STRAIGHT!
I KNOW. THAT'S INTENTIONAL
A QUESTION OF ARCHITECTURAL COMPOSITION – BALANCE, YOU SEE...
OH...?

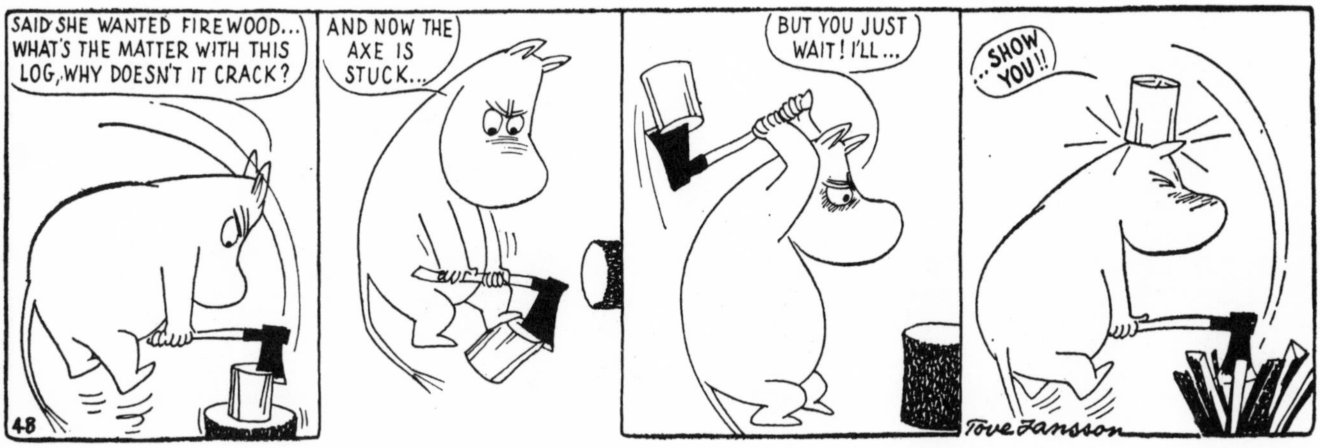
SAID SHE WANTED FIREWOOD... WHAT'S THE MATTER WITH THIS LOG, WHY DOESN'T IT CRACK?
48
AND NOW THE AXE IS STUCK...
BUT YOU JUST WAIT! I'LL...
...SHOW YOU!!
Tove Jansson

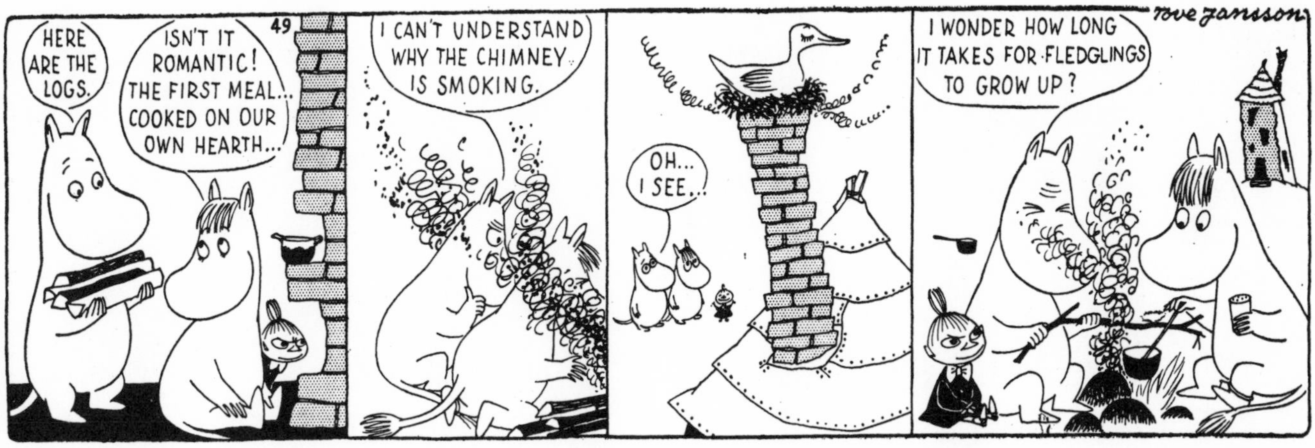
HERE ARE THE LOGS.
ISN'T IT ROMANTIC! THE FIRST MEAL... COOKED ON OUR OWN HEARTH...
49
I CAN'T UNDERSTAND WHY THE CHIMNEY IS SMOKING.
OH... I SEE...
Tove Jansson
I WONDER HOW LONG IT TAKES FOR FLEDGLINGS TO GROW UP?

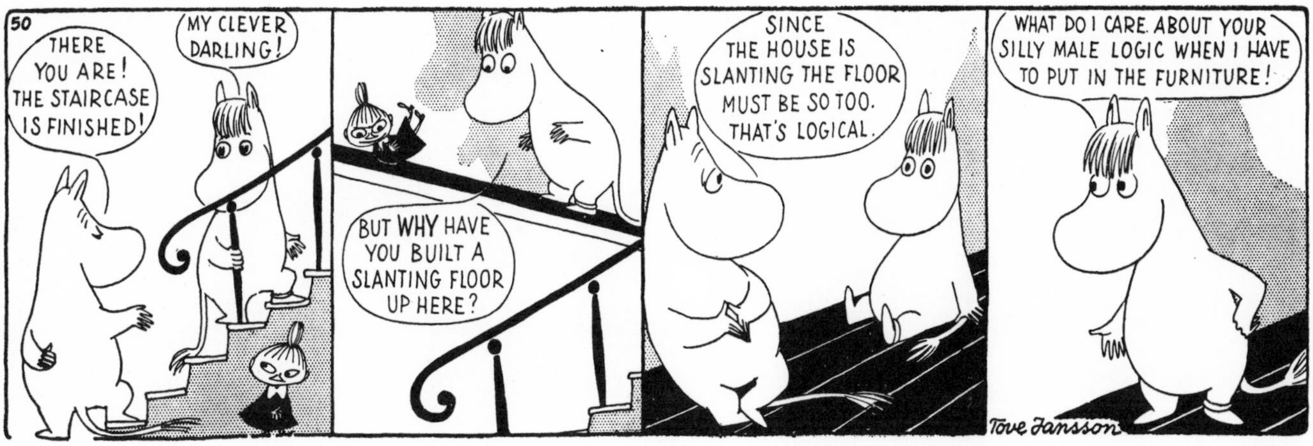
50
THERE YOU ARE! THE STAIRCASE IS FINISHED!
MY CLEVER DARLING!
BUT WHY HAVE YOU BUILT A SLANTING FLOOR UP HERE?
SINCE THE HOUSE IS SLANTING THE FLOOR MUST BE SO TOO. THAT'S LOGICAL.
WHAT DO I CARE ABOUT YOUR SILLY MALE LOGIC WHEN I HAVE TO PUT IN THE FURNITURE!
Tove Jansson

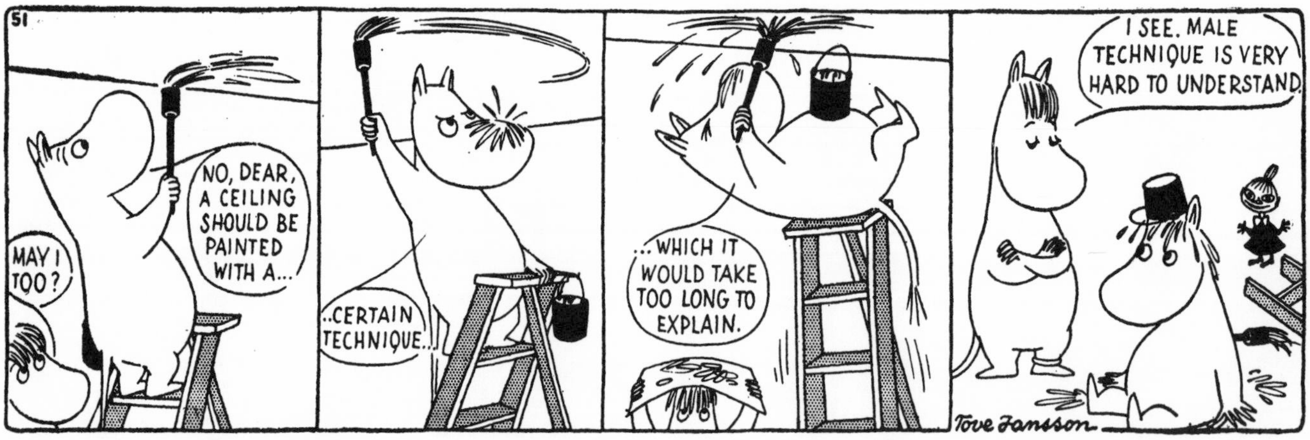
51
MAY I TOO?
NO, DEAR, A CEILING SHOULD BE PAINTED WITH A...
..CERTAIN TECHNIQUE..
...WHICH IT WOULD TAKE TOO LONG TO EXPLAIN.
I SEE. MALE TECHNIQUE IS VERY HARD TO UNDERSTAND.
Tove Jansson

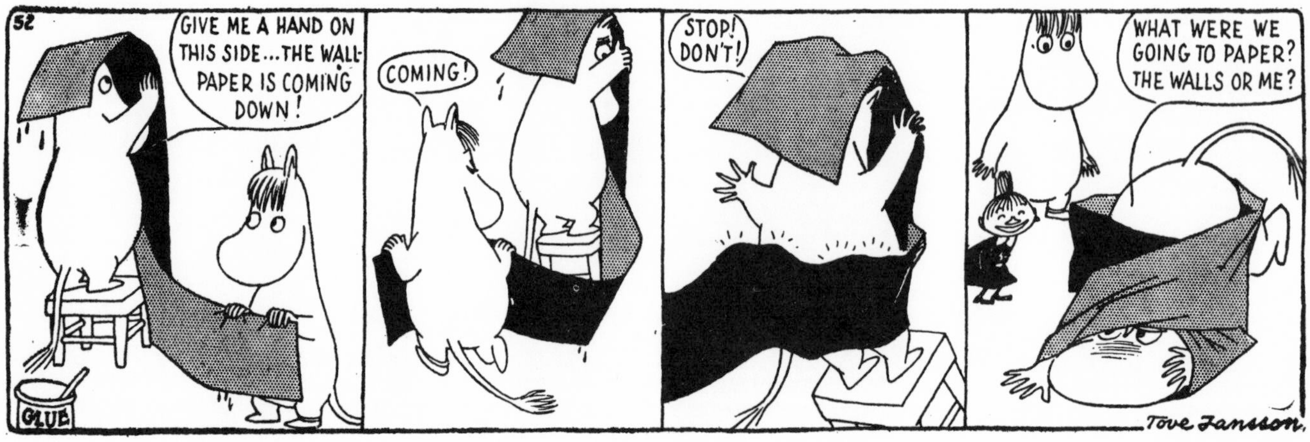
52
GIVE ME A HAND ON THIS SIDE...THE WALL-PAPER IS COMING DOWN!
GLUE
COMING!
STOP! DON'T!
WHAT WERE WE GOING TO PAPER? THE WALLS OR ME?
Tove Jansson

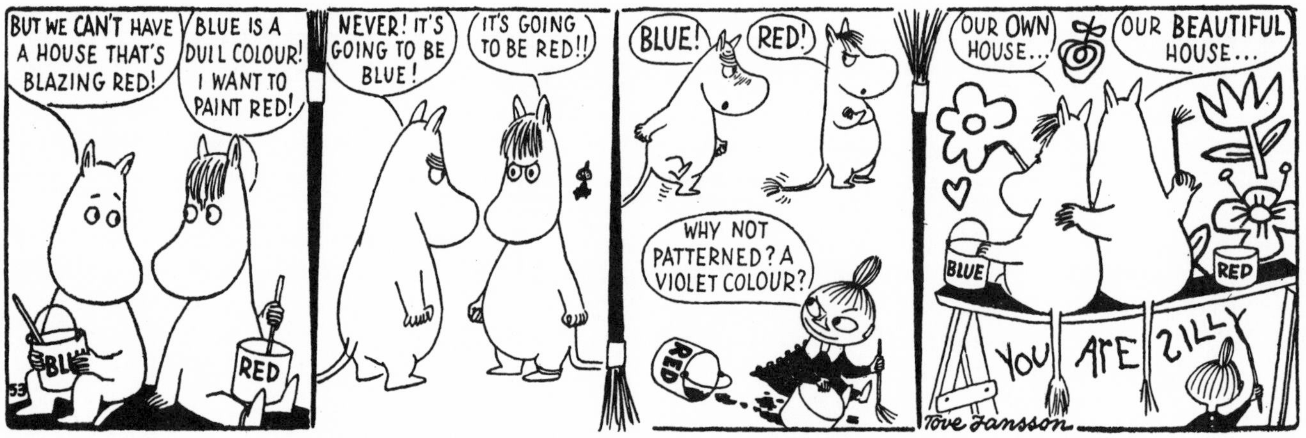
BUT WE CAN'T HAVE A HOUSE THAT'S BLAZING RED!
BLUE IS A DULL COLOUR! I WANT TO PAINT RED!
BLU
RED
53
NEVER! IT'S GOING TO BE BLUE!
IT'S GOING TO BE RED!!
BLUE!
RED!
WHY NOT PATTERNED? A VIOLET COLOUR?
RED
OUR OWN HOUSE...
OUR BEAUTIFUL HOUSE...
BLUE
RED
YOU ARE SILLY
Tove Jansson

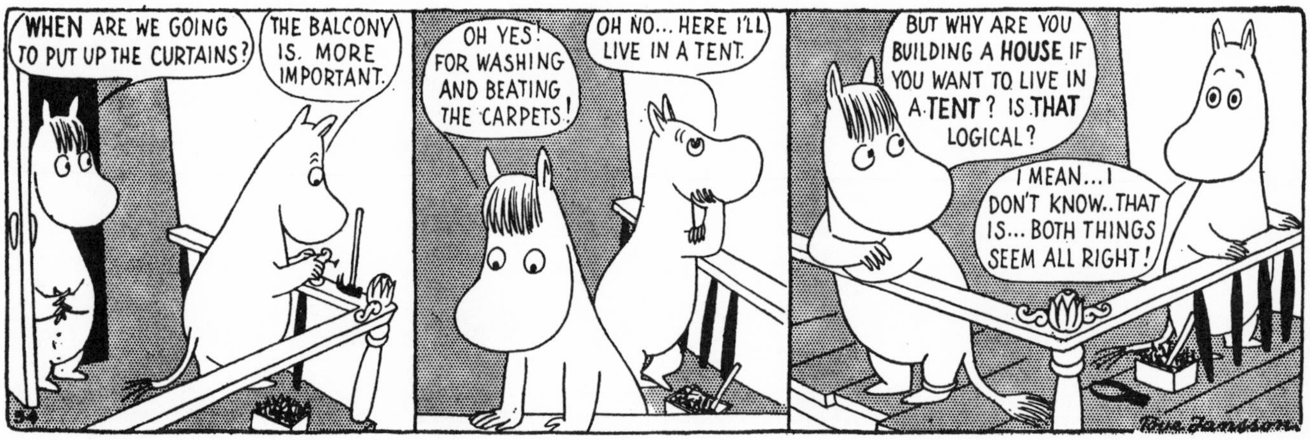
WHEN ARE WE GOING TO PUT UP THE CURTAINS?
THE BALCONY IS. MORE IMPORTANT.
54
OH YES! FOR WASHING AND BEATING THE CARPETS!
OH NO... HERE I'LL LIVE IN A TENT.
BUT WHY ARE YOU BUILDING A HOUSE IF YOU WANT TO LIVE IN A TENT? IS THAT LOGICAL?
I MEAN...I DON'T KNOW..THAT IS... BOTH THINGS SEEM ALL RIGHT!
Tove Jansson

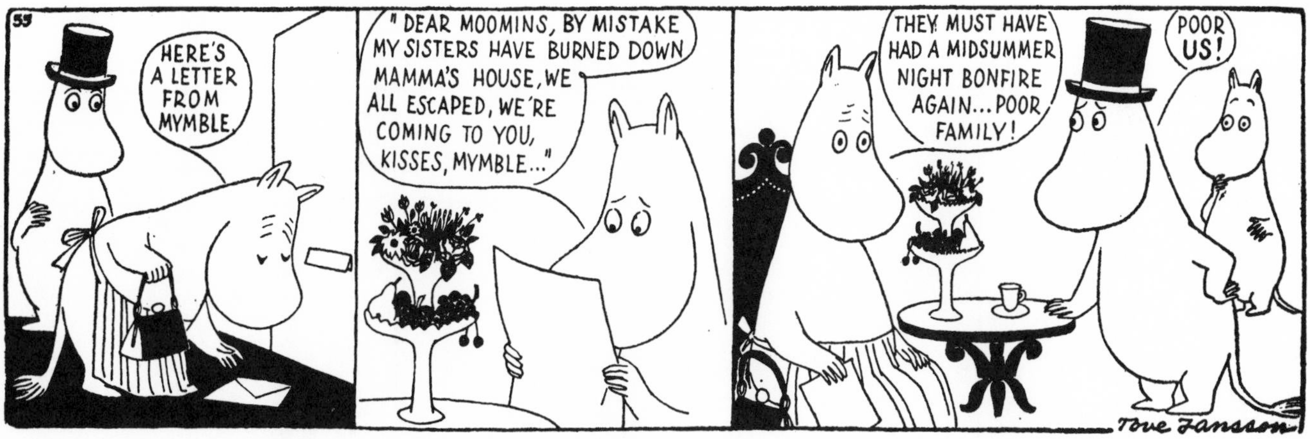
55
HERE'S A LETTER FROM MYMBLE.
" DEAR MOOMINS, BY MISTAKE MY SISTERS HAVE BURNED DOWN MAMMA'S HOUSE, WE ALL ESCAPED, WE'RE COMING TO YOU, KISSES, MYMBLE ..."
THEY MUST HAVE HAD A MIDSUMMER NIGHT BONFIRE AGAIN... POOR FAMILY!
POOR US!
Tove Jansson

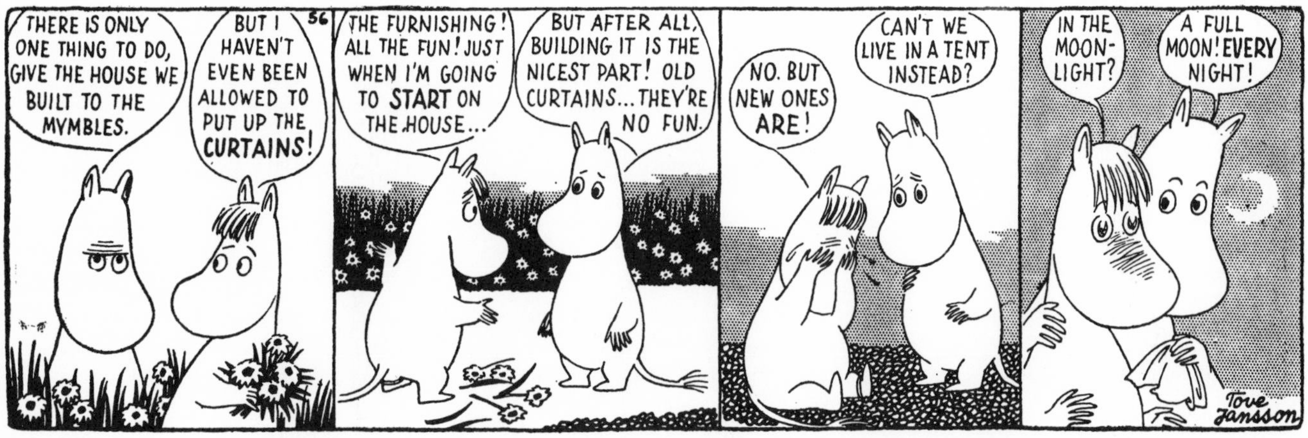
THERE IS ONLY ONE THING TO DO, GIVE THE HOUSE WE BUILT TO THE MYMBLES.
BUT I HAVEN'T EVEN BEEN ALLOWED TO PUT UP THE CURTAINS!
56
THE FURNISHING! ALL THE FUN! JUST WHEN I'M GOING TO START ON THE HOUSE...
BUT AFTER ALL, BUILDING IT IS THE NICEST PART! OLD CURTAINS... THEY'RE NO FUN.
NO. BUT NEW ONES ARE!
CAN'T WE LIVE IN A TENT INSTEAD?
IN THE MOON-LIGHT?
A FULL MOON! EVERY NIGHT!
Tove Jansson

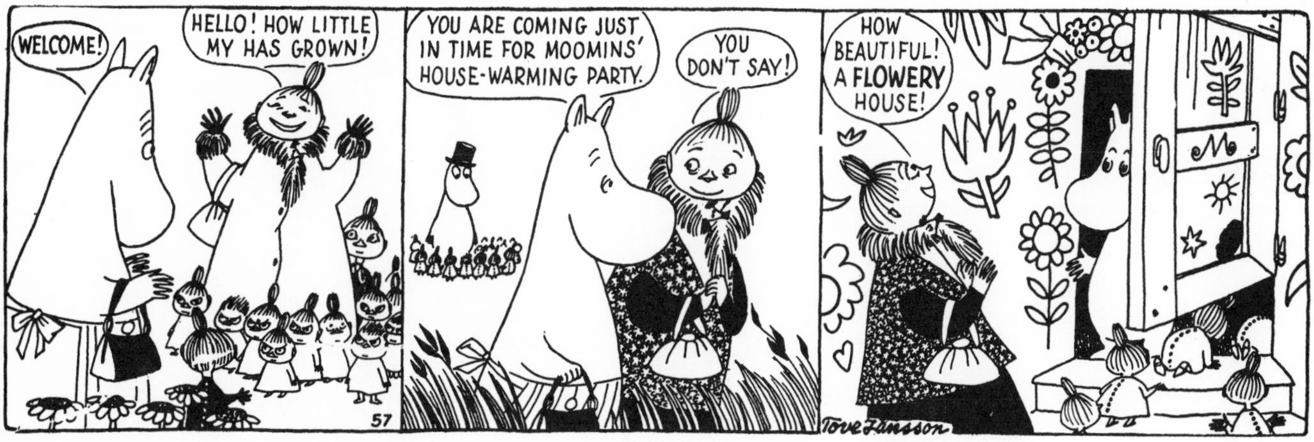
WELCOME!
HELLO! HOW LITTLE MY HAS GROWN!
57
YOU ARE COMING JUST IN TIME FOR MOOMINS' HOUSE-WARMING PARTY.
YOU DON'T SAY!
HOW BEAUTIFUL! A FLOWERY HOUSE!
Tove Jansson

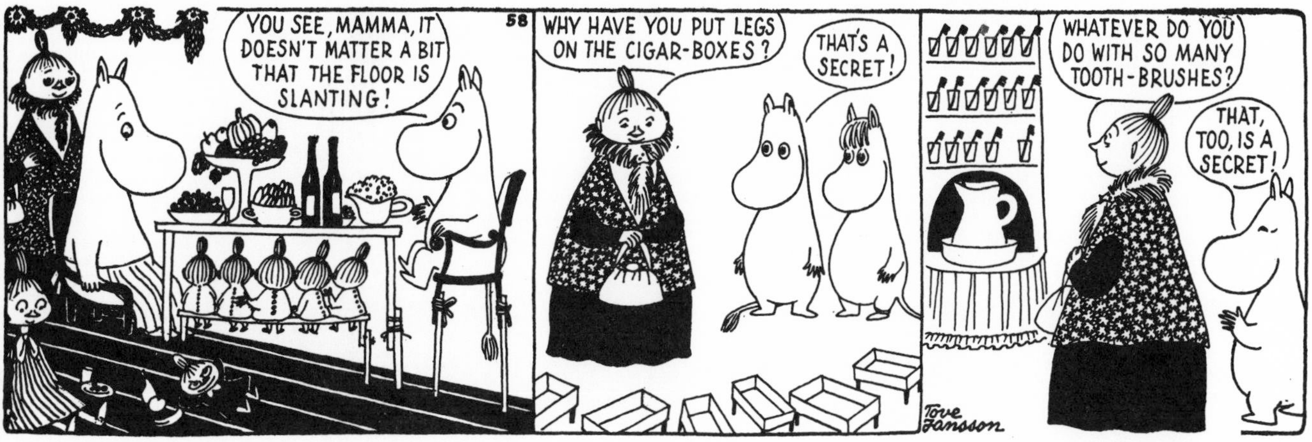
YOU SEE, MAMMA, IT DOESN'T MATTER A BIT THAT THE FLOOR IS SLANTING!
58
WHY HAVE YOU PUT LEGS ON THE CIGAR-BOXES?
THAT'S A SECRET!
WHATEVER DO YOU DO WITH SO MANY TOOTH-BRUSHES?
THAT, TOO, IS A SECRET!
Tove Jansson

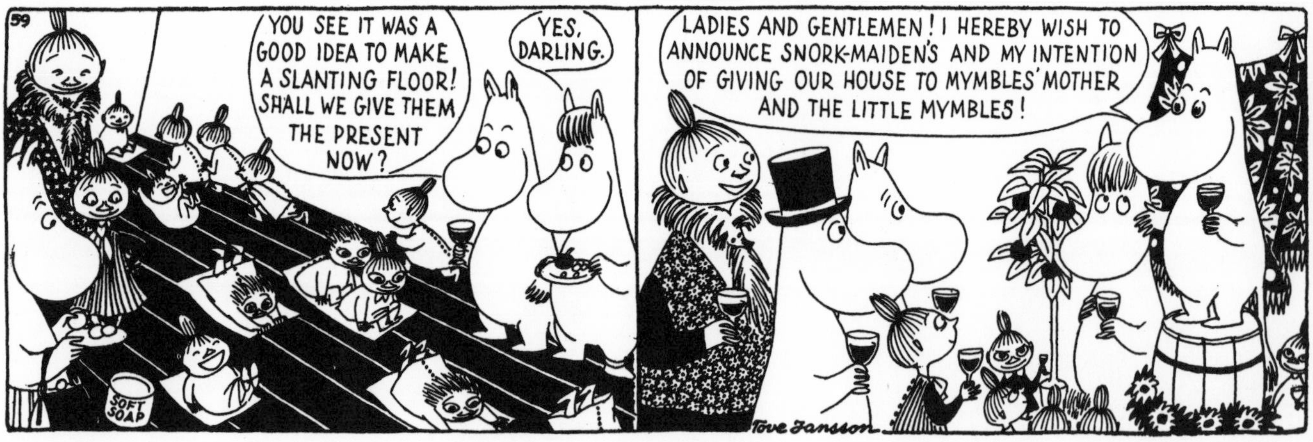
59
YOU SEE IT WAS A GOOD IDEA TO MAKE A SLANTING FLOOR! SHALL WE GIVE THEM THE PRESENT NOW?
YES, DARLING.
SOFT SOAP
LADIES AND GENTLEMEN! I HEREBY WISH TO ANNOUNCE SNORK-MAIDEN'S AND MY INTENTION OF GIVING OUR HOUSE TO MYMBLES' MOTHER AND THE LITTLE MYMBLES!
Tove Jansson

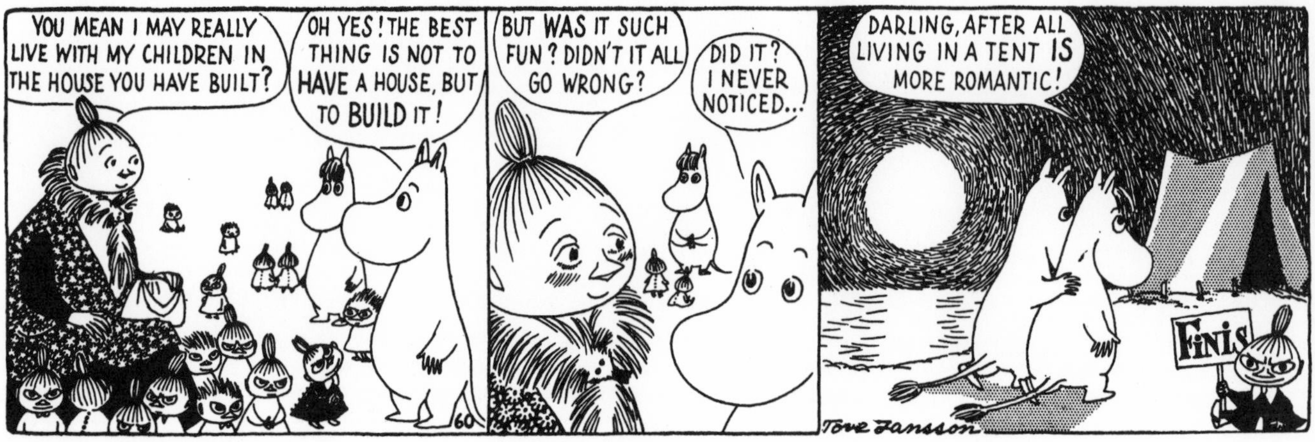
YOU MEAN I MAY REALLY LIVE WITH MY CHILDREN IN THE HOUSE YOU HAVE BUILT?
OH YES! THE BEST THING IS NOT TO HAVE A HOUSE, BUT TO BUILD IT!
60
BUT WAS IT SUCH FUN? DIDN'T IT ALL GO WRONG?
DID IT? I NEVER NOTICED...
DARLING, AFTER ALL LIVING IN A TENT IS MORE ROMANTIC!
FINIS
Tove Jansson

8. Moomin Begins a New Life

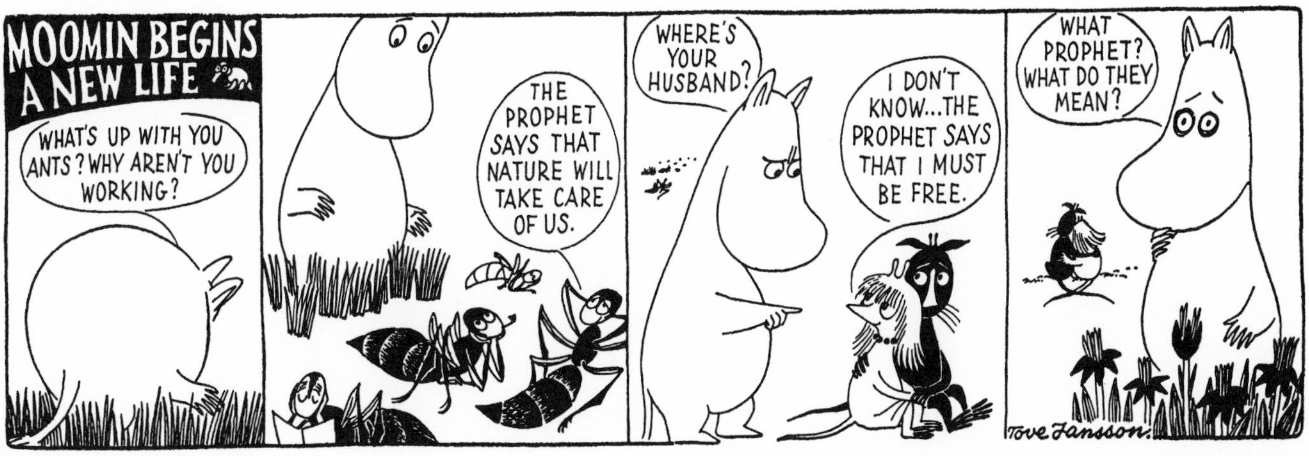
MOOMIN BEGINS A NEW LIFE
WHAT'S UP WITH YOU ANTS? WHY AREN'T YOU WORKING?
THE PROPHET SAYS THAT NATURE WILL TAKE CARE OF US.
WHERE'S YOUR HUSBAND?
I DON'T KNOW...THE PROPHET SAYS THAT I MUST BE FREE.
WHAT PROPHET? WHAT DO THEY MEAN?
Tove Jansson.

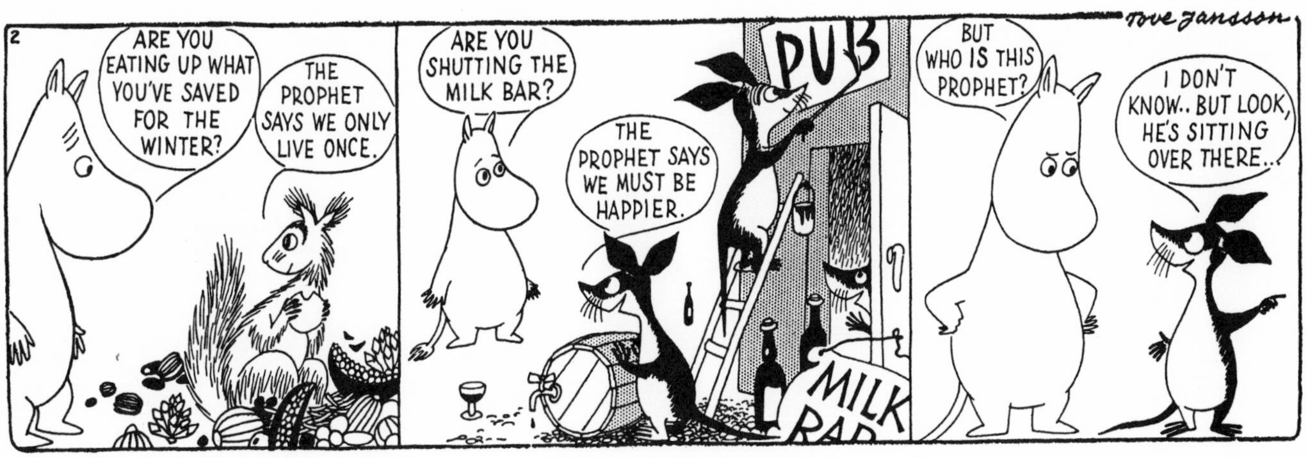
Tove Jansson
2
ARE YOU EATING UP WHAT YOU'VE SAVED FOR THE WINTER?
THE PROPHET SAYS WE ONLY LIVE ONCE.
ARE YOU SHUTTING THE MILK BAR?
THE PROPHET SAYS WE MUST BE HAPPIER.
PUB
MILK BAR
BUT WHO IS THIS PROPHET?
I DON'T KNOW.. BUT LOOK, HE'S SITTING OVER THERE...

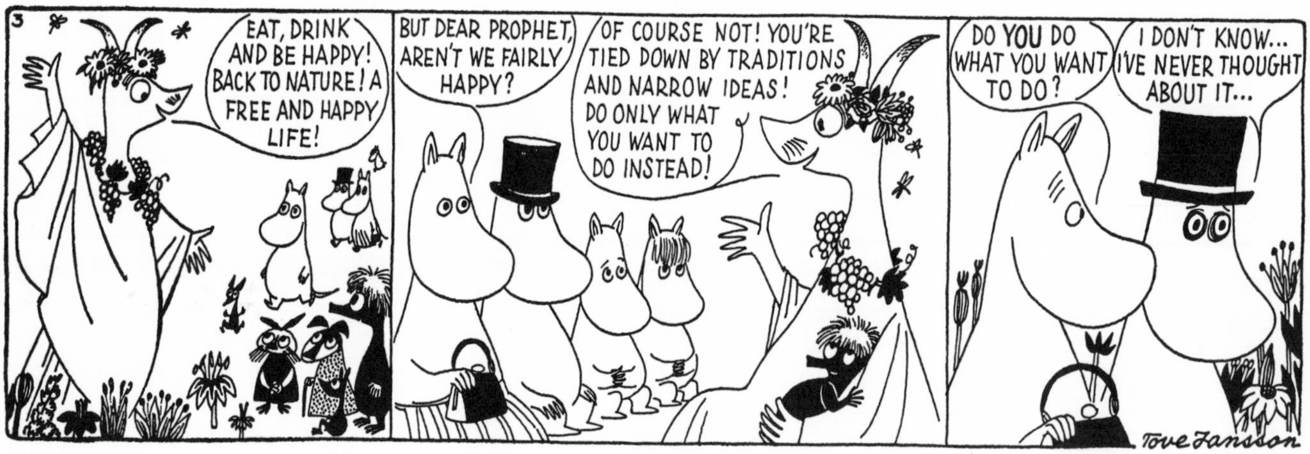
3
EAT, DRINK AND BE HAPPY! BACK TO NATURE! A FREE AND HAPPY LIFE!
BUT DEAR PROPHET, AREN'T WE FAIRLY HAPPY?
OF COURSE NOT! YOU'RE TIED DOWN BY TRADITIONS AND NARROW IDEAS! DO ONLY WHAT YOU WANT TO DO INSTEAD!
DO YOU DO WHAT YOU WANT TO DO?
I DON'T KNOW... I'VE NEVER THOUGHT ABOUT IT...
Tove Jansson

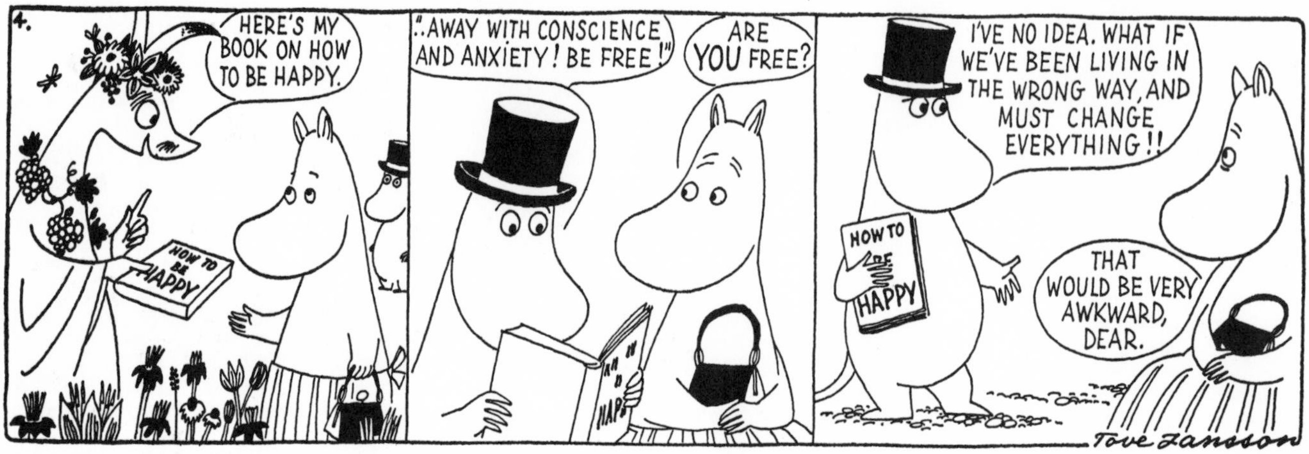
4.
HERE'S MY BOOK ON HOW TO BE HAPPY.
HOW TO BE HAPPY
"..AWAY WITH CONSCIENCE AND ANXIETY! BE FREE!"
ARE YOU FREE?
I'VE NO IDEA. WHAT IF WE'VE BEEN LIVING IN THE WRONG WAY, AND MUST CHANGE EVERYTHING!!
HOW TO BE HAPPY
THAT WOULD BE VERY AWKWARD, DEAR.
Tove Jansson

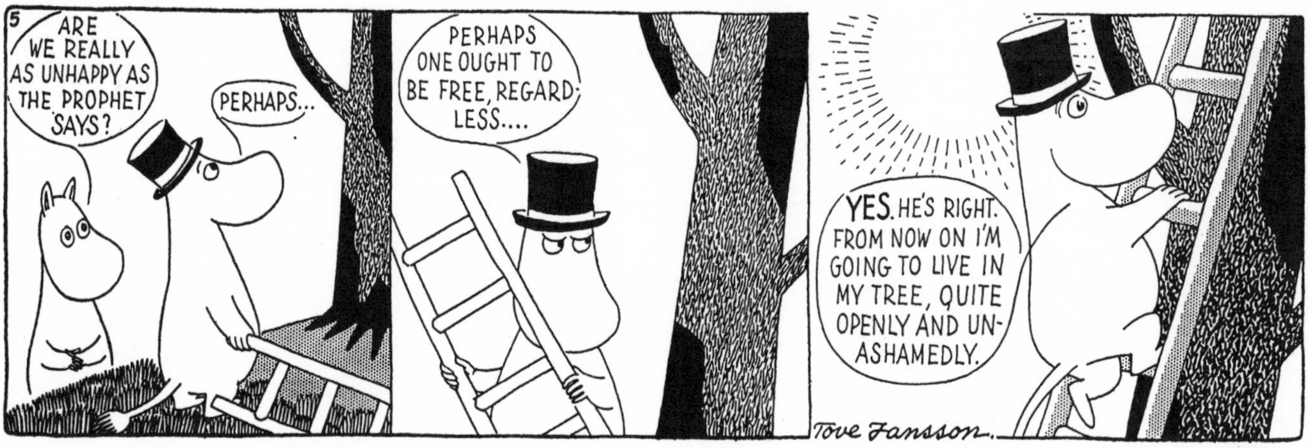
5
ARE WE REALLY AS UNHAPPY AS THE PROPHET SAYS?
PERHAPS...
PERHAPS ONE OUGHT TO BE FREE, REGARDLESS....
YES. HE'S RIGHT. FROM NOW ON I'M GOING TO LIVE IN MY TREE, QUITE OPENLY AND UNASHAMEDLY.
Tove Jansson.

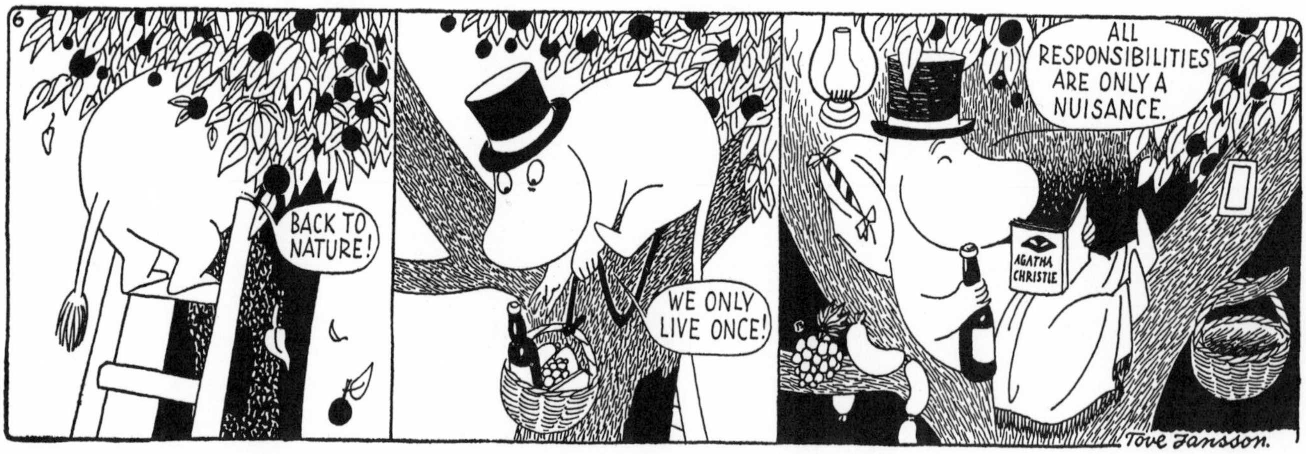
6
BACK TO NATURE!
WE ONLY LIVE ONCE!
ALL RESPONSIBILITIES ARE ONLY A NUISANCE.
AGATHA CHRISTIE
Tove Jansson.

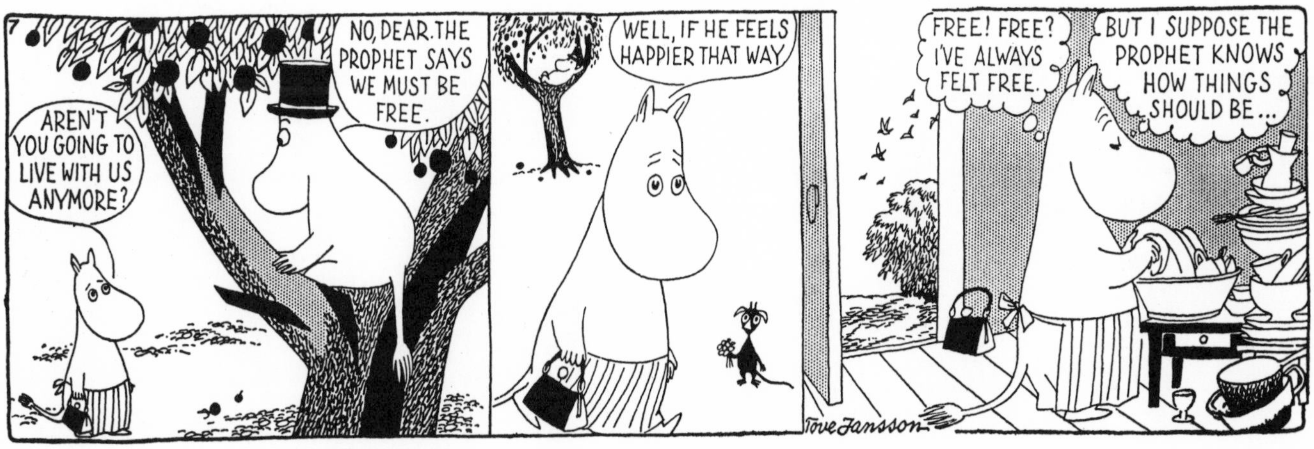
7
AREN'T YOU GOING TO LIVE WITH US ANYMORE?
NO, DEAR. THE PROPHET SAYS WE MUST BE FREE.
WELL, IF HE FEELS HAPPIER THAT WAY
FREE! FREE? I'VE ALWAYS FELT FREE.
BUT I SUPPOSE THE PROPHET KNOWS HOW THINGS SHOULD BE...
Tove Jansson

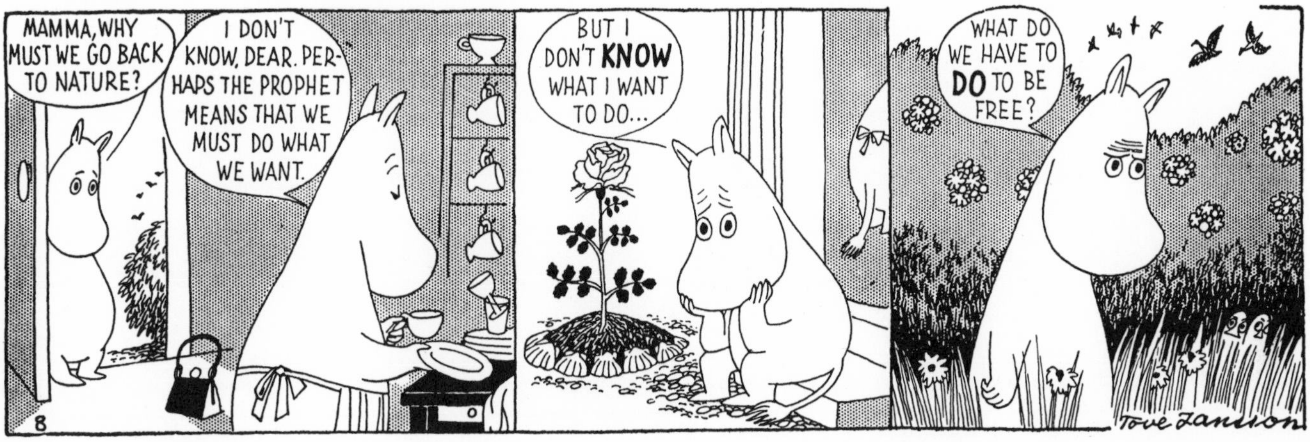
MAMMA, WHY MUST WE GO BACK TO NATURE?
I DON'T KNOW, DEAR. PERHAPS THE PROPHET MEANS THAT WE MUST DO WHAT WE WANT.
8
BUT I DON'T KNOW WHAT I WANT TO DO...
WHAT DO WE HAVE TO DO TO BE FREE?
Tove Jansson

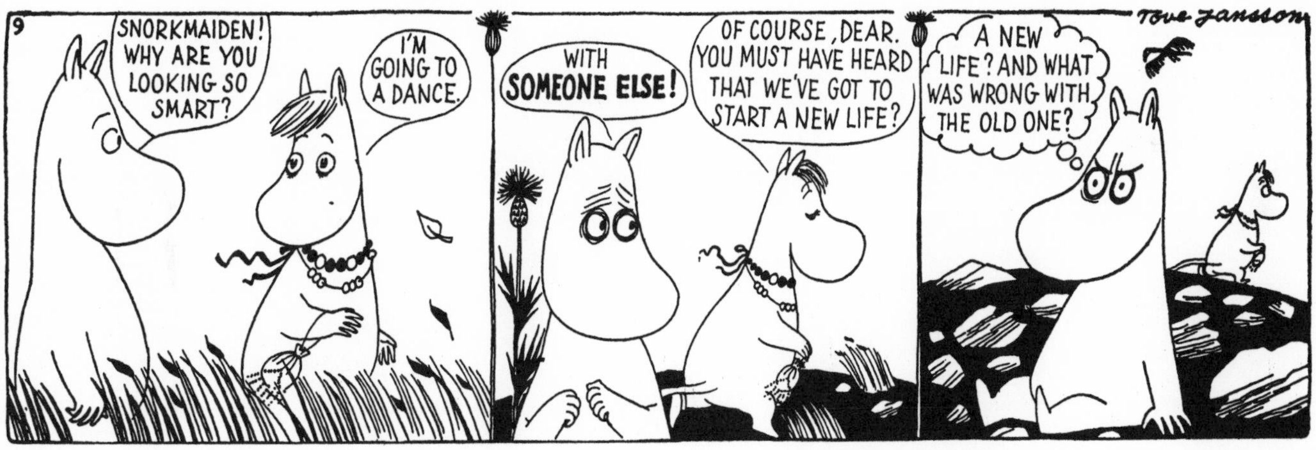
9
SNORKMAIDEN! WHY ARE YOU LOOKING SO SMART?
I'M GOING TO A DANCE.
WITH SOMEONE ELSE!
OF COURSE, DEAR. YOU MUST HAVE HEARD THAT WE'VE GOT TO START A NEW LIFE?
A NEW LIFE? AND WHAT WAS WRONG WITH THE OLD ONE?
Tove Jansson

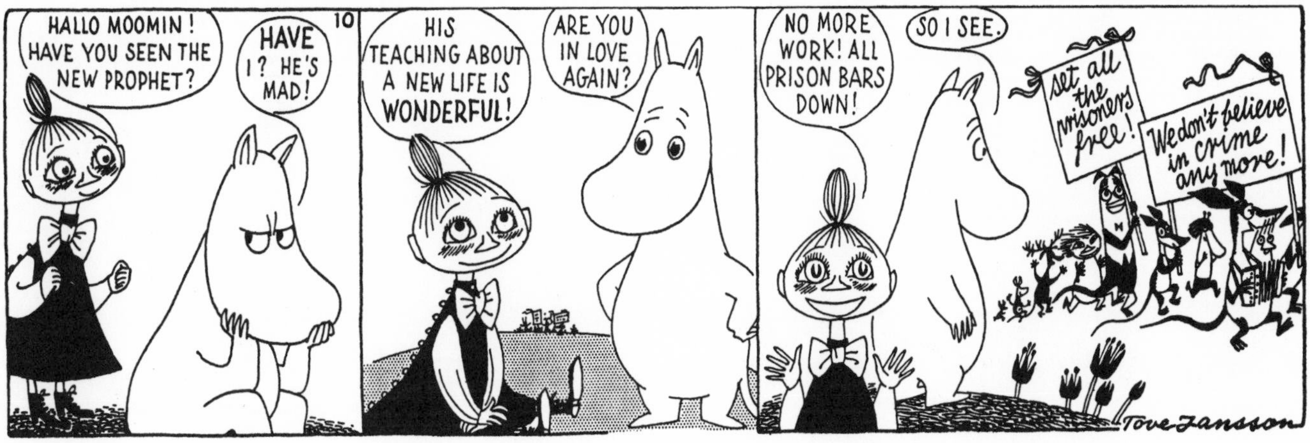
HALLO MOOMIN! HAVE YOU SEEN THE NEW PROPHET?
HAVE I? HE'S MAD!
10
HIS TEACHING ABOUT A NEW LIFE IS WONDERFUL!
ARE YOU IN LOVE AGAIN?
NO MORE WORK! ALL PRISON BARS DOWN!
SO I SEE.
set all the prisoners free!
We don't believe in crime any more!
Tove Jansson

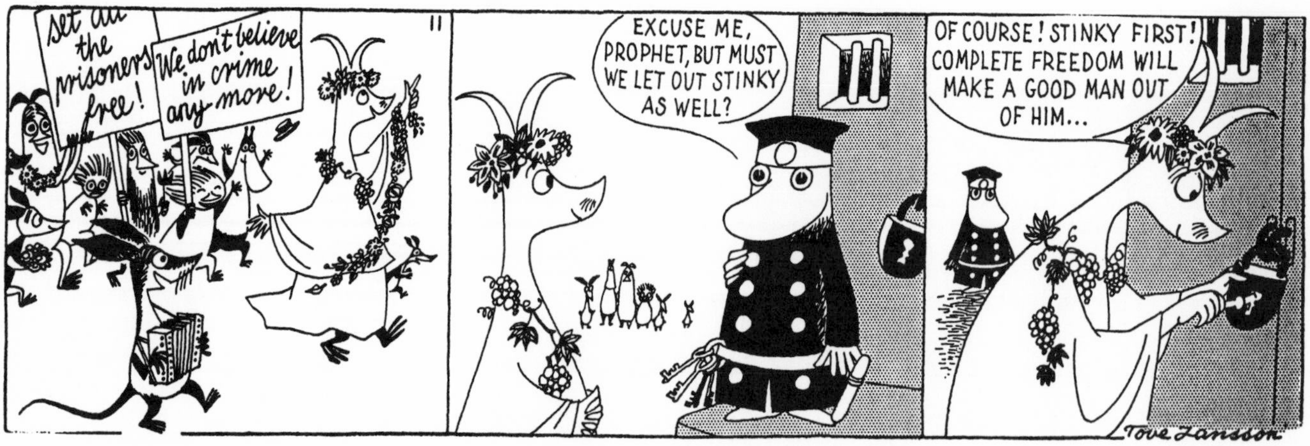
Set all the prisoners free!
We don't believe in crime any more!
EXCUSE ME, PROPHET, BUT MUST WE LET OUT STINKY AS WELL?
OF COURSE! STINKY FIRST! COMPLETE FREEDOM WILL MAKE A GOOD MAN OUT OF HIM...
Tove Jansson

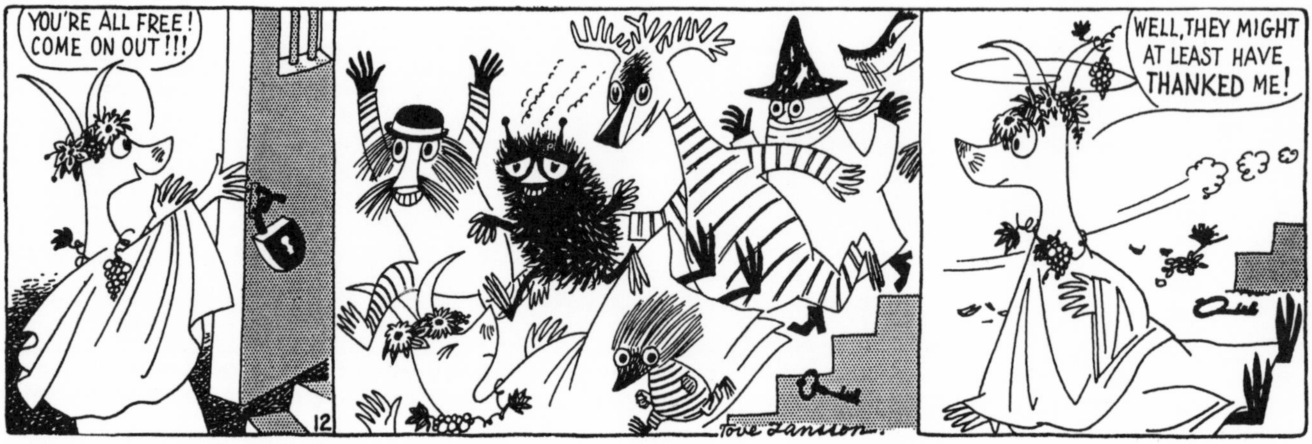
YOU'RE ALL FREE! COME ON OUT!!!
WELL, THEY MIGHT AT LEAST HAVE THANKED ME!
Tove Jansson

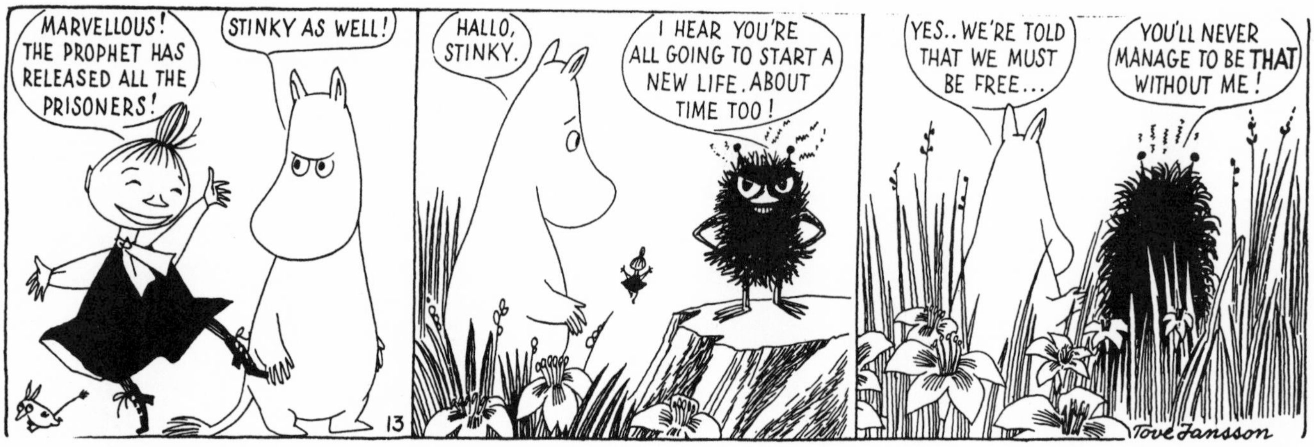
MARVELLOUS! THE PROPHET HAS RELEASED ALL THE PRISONERS!
STINKY AS WELL!
HALLO, STINKY.
I HEAR YOU'RE ALL GOING TO START A NEW LIFE. ABOUT TIME TOO!
YES.. WE'RE TOLD THAT WE MUST BE FREE...
YOU'LL NEVER MANAGE TO BE THAT WITHOUT ME!
Tove Jansson

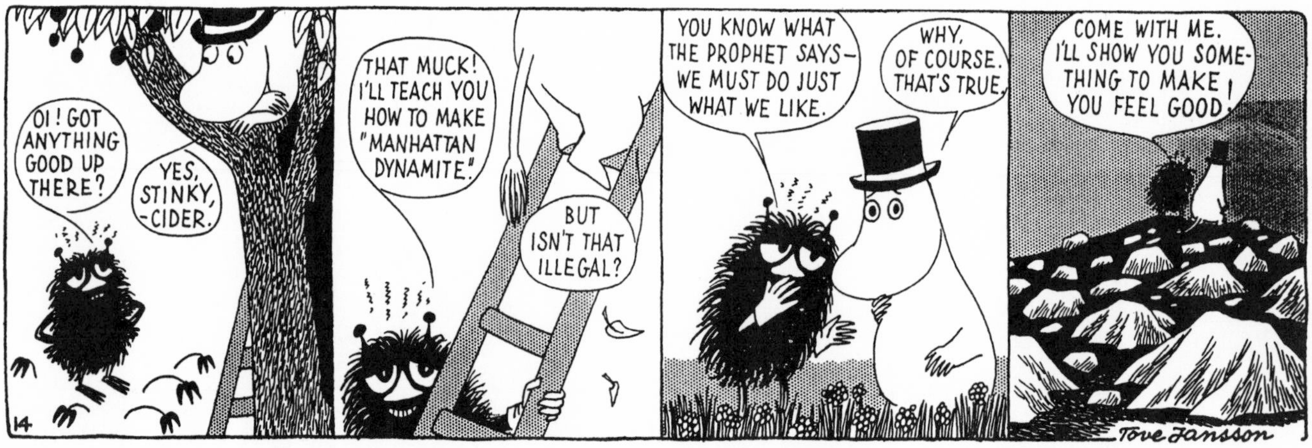
OI! GOT ANYTHING GOOD UP THERE?
YES, STINKY, -CIDER.
THAT MUCK! I'LL TEACH YOU HOW TO MAKE "MANHATTAN DYNAMITE."
BUT ISN'T THAT ILLEGAL?
YOU KNOW WHAT THE PROPHET SAYS— WE MUST DO JUST WHAT WE LIKE.
WHY, OF COURSE. THAT'S TRUE.
COME WITH ME. I'LL SHOW YOU SOMETHING TO MAKE YOU FEEL GOOD!
Tove Jansson

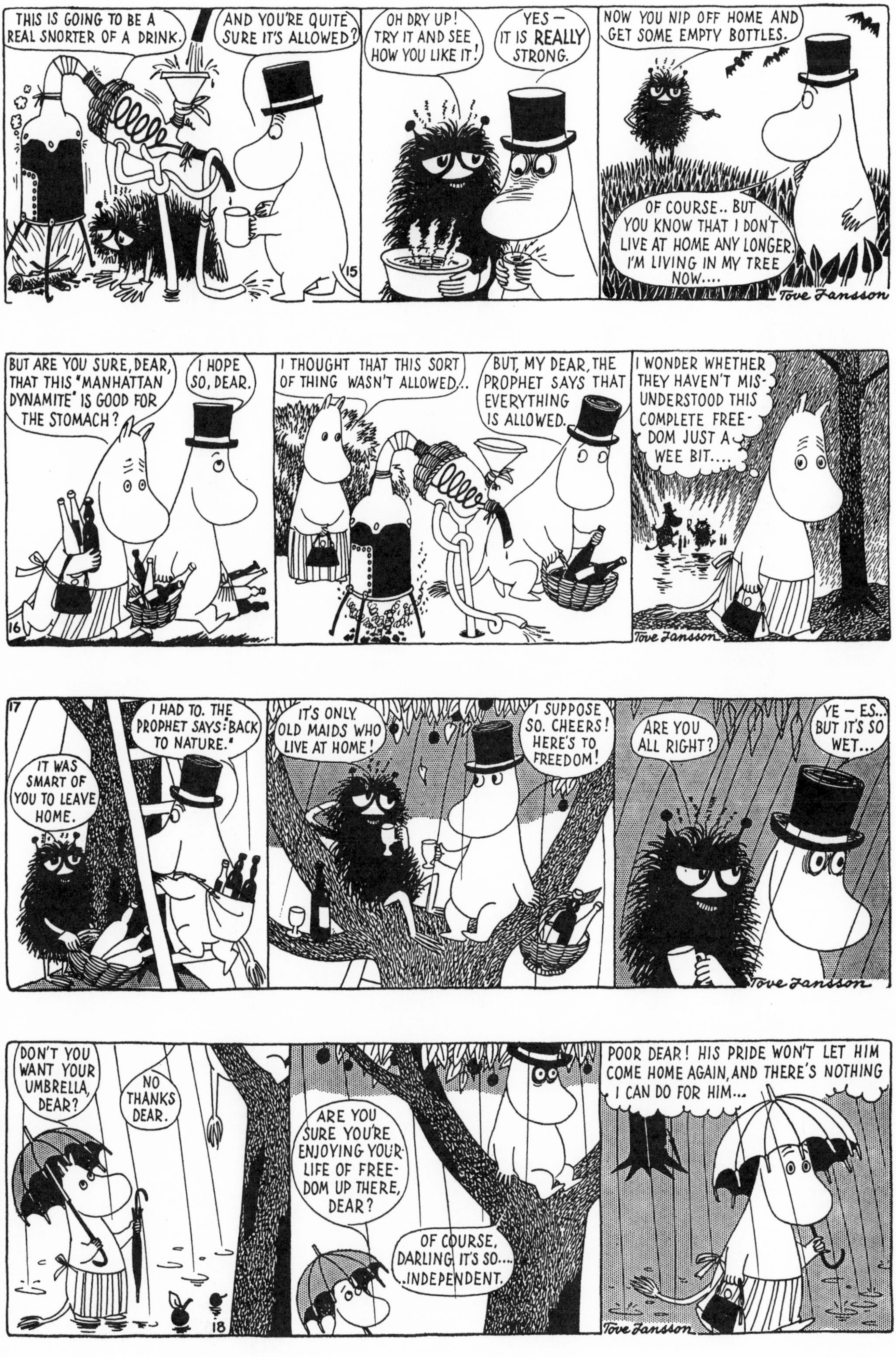
THIS IS GOING TO BE A REAL SNORTER OF A DRINK.
AND YOU'RE QUITE SURE IT'S ALLOWED?
15
OH DRY UP! TRY IT AND SEE HOW YOU LIKE IT!
YES — IT IS REALLY STRONG.
NOW YOU NIP OFF HOME AND GET SOME EMPTY BOTTLES.
OF COURSE.. BUT YOU KNOW THAT I DON'T LIVE AT HOME ANY LONGER. I'M LIVING IN MY TREE NOW....
Tove Jansson
BUT ARE YOU SURE, DEAR, THAT THIS "MANHATTAN DYNAMITE" IS GOOD FOR THE STOMACH?
I HOPE SO, DEAR.
16
I THOUGHT THAT THIS SORT OF THING WASN'T ALLOWED...
BUT, MY DEAR, THE PROPHET SAYS THAT EVERYTHING IS ALLOWED.
I WONDER WHETHER THEY HAVEN'T MISUNDERSTOOD THIS COMPLETE FREEDOM JUST A WEE BIT....
Tove Jansson
17
IT WAS SMART OF YOU TO LEAVE HOME.
I HAD TO. THE PROPHET SAYS: "BACK TO NATURE."
IT'S ONLY OLD MAIDS WHO LIVE AT HOME!
I SUPPOSE SO. CHEERS! HERE'S TO FREEDOM!
ARE YOU ALL RIGHT?
YE — ES... BUT IT'S SO WET...
Tove Jansson
DON'T YOU WANT YOUR UMBRELLA, DEAR?
NO THANKS DEAR.
18
ARE YOU SURE YOU'RE ENJOYING YOUR LIFE OF FREEDOM UP THERE, DEAR?
OF COURSE, DARLING IT'S SO.... ..INDEPENDENT.
POOR DEAR! HIS PRIDE WON'T LET HIM COME HOME AGAIN, AND THERE'S NOTHING I CAN DO FOR HIM...
Tove Jansson

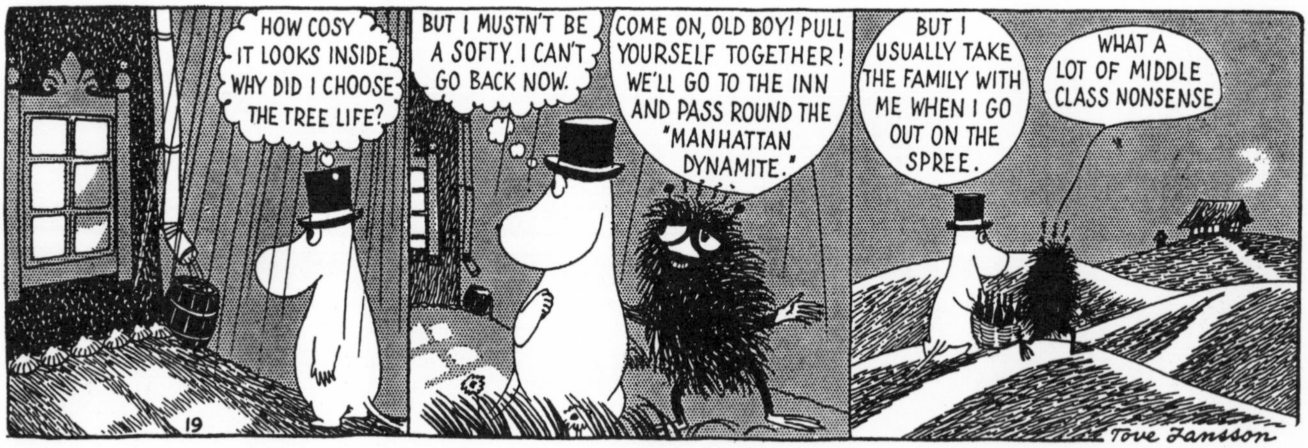
HOW COSY IT LOOKS INSIDE. WHY DID I CHOOSE THE TREE LIFE?
19
BUT I MUSTN'T BE A SOFTY. I CAN'T GO BACK NOW.
COME ON, OLD BOY! PULL YOURSELF TOGETHER! WE'LL GO TO THE INN AND PASS ROUND THE "MANHATTAN DYNAMITE."
BUT I USUALLY TAKE THE FAMILY WITH ME WHEN I GO OUT ON THE SPREE.
WHAT A LOT OF MIDDLE CLASS NONSENSE.
Tove Jansson

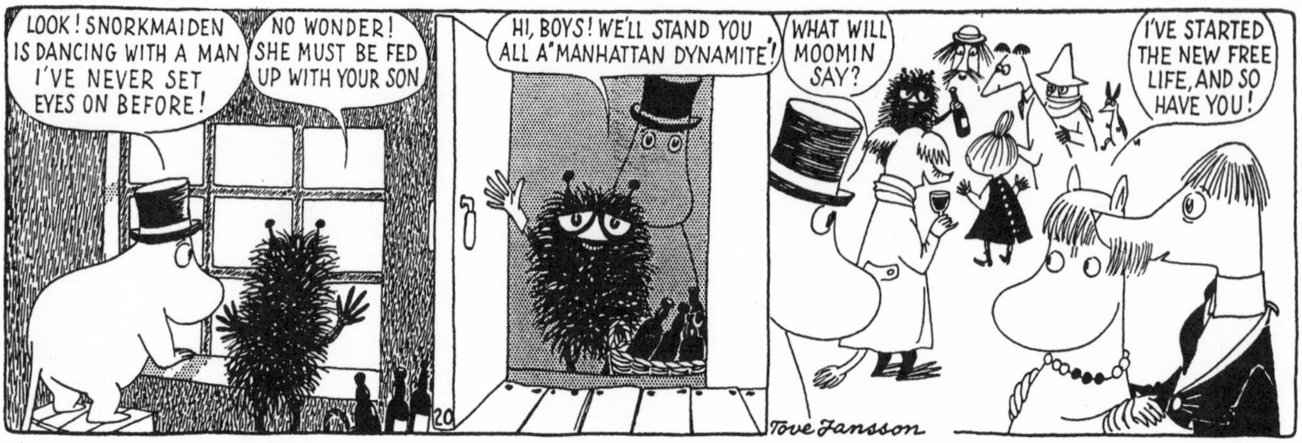
LOOK! SNORKMAIDEN IS DANCING WITH A MAN I'VE NEVER SET EYES ON BEFORE!
NO WONDER! SHE MUST BE FED UP WITH YOUR SON.
20
HI, BOYS! WE'LL STAND YOU ALL A "MANHATTAN DYNAMITE"!
WHAT WILL MOOMIN SAY?
I'VE STARTED THE NEW FREE LIFE, AND SO HAVE YOU!
Tove Jansson

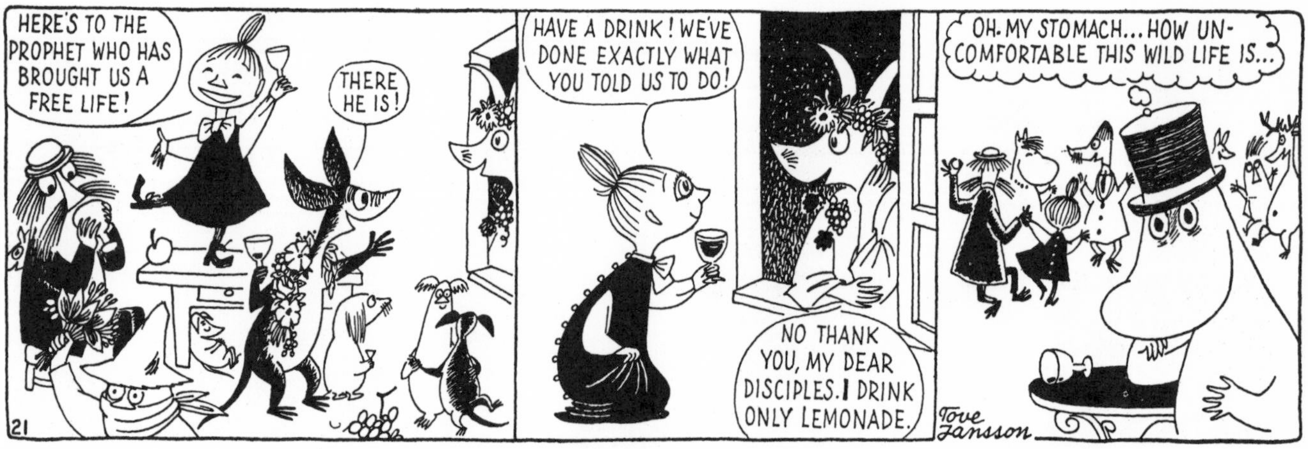
HERE'S TO THE PROPHET WHO HAS BROUGHT US A FREE LIFE!
THERE HE IS!
21
HAVE A DRINK! WE'VE DONE EXACTLY WHAT YOU TOLD US TO DO!
NO THANK YOU, MY DEAR DISCIPLES. I DRINK ONLY LEMONADE.
OH. MY STOMACH... HOW UNCOMFORTABLE THIS WILD LIFE IS...
Tove Jansson

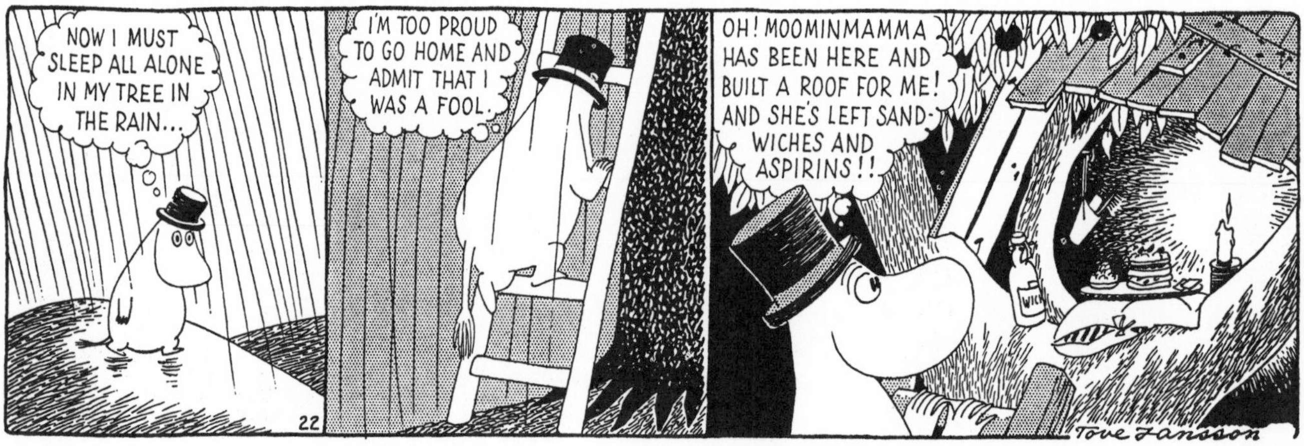
NOW I MUST SLEEP ALL ALONE IN MY TREE IN THE RAIN...
22
I'M TOO PROUD TO GO HOME AND ADMIT THAT I WAS A FOOL.
OH! MOOMINMAMMA HAS BEEN HERE AND BUILT A ROOF FOR ME! AND SHE'S LEFT SANDWICHES AND ASPIRINS!!
Tove Jansson

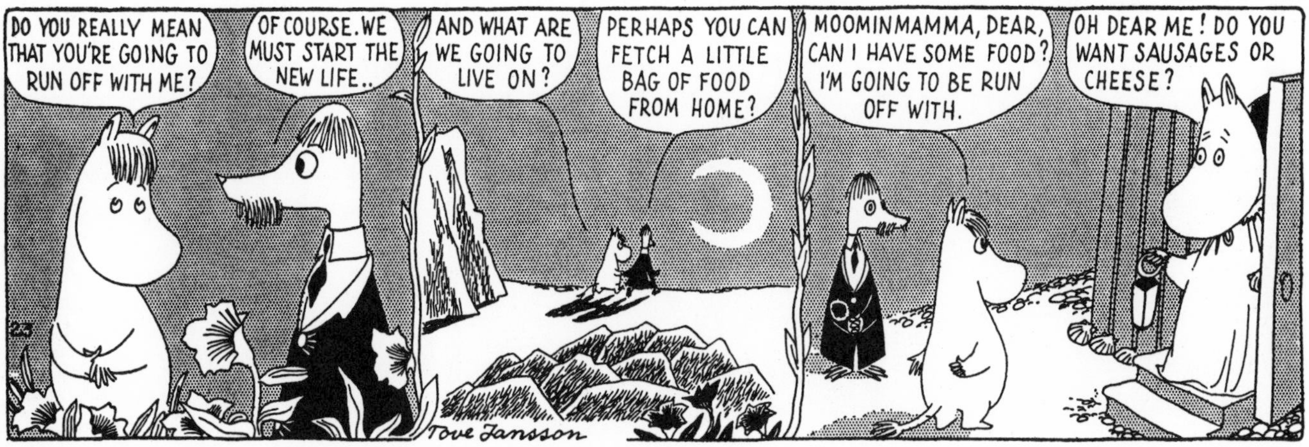
DO YOU REALLY MEAN THAT YOU'RE GOING TO RUN OFF WITH ME?
OF COURSE. WE MUST START THE NEW LIFE..
AND WHAT ARE WE GOING TO LIVE ON?
PERHAPS YOU CAN FETCH A LITTLE BAG OF FOOD FROM HOME?
MOOMINMAMMA, DEAR, CAN I HAVE SOME FOOD? I'M GOING TO BE RUN OFF WITH.
OH DEAR ME! DO YOU WANT SAUSAGES OR CHEESE?
23
Tove Jansson

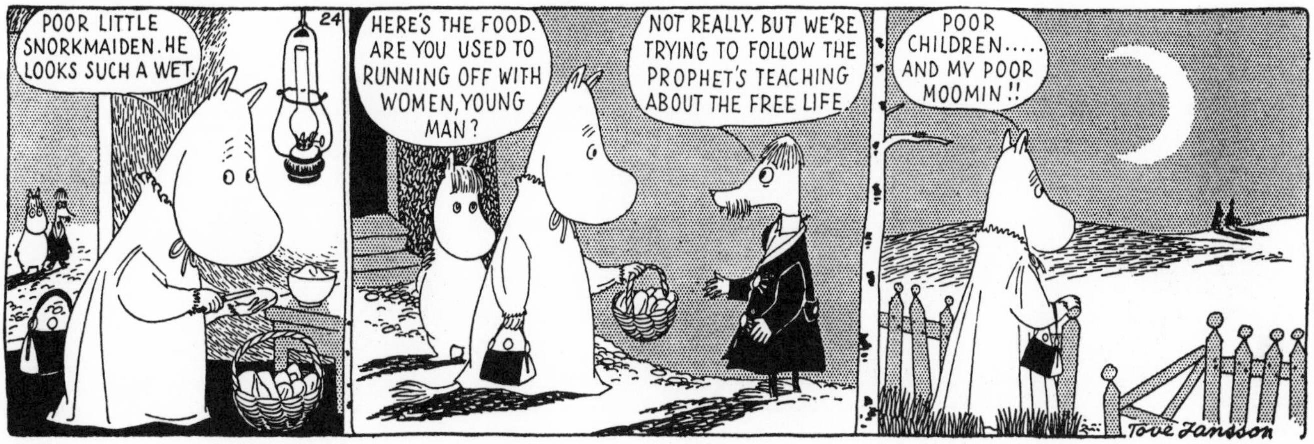
POOR LITTLE SNORKMAIDEN. HE LOOKS SUCH A WET.
24
HERE'S THE FOOD. ARE YOU USED TO RUNNING OFF WITH WOMEN, YOUNG MAN?
NOT REALLY. BUT WE'RE TRYING TO FOLLOW THE PROPHET'S TEACHING ABOUT THE FREE LIFE.
POOR CHILDREN..... AND MY POOR MOOMIN!!
Tove Jansson

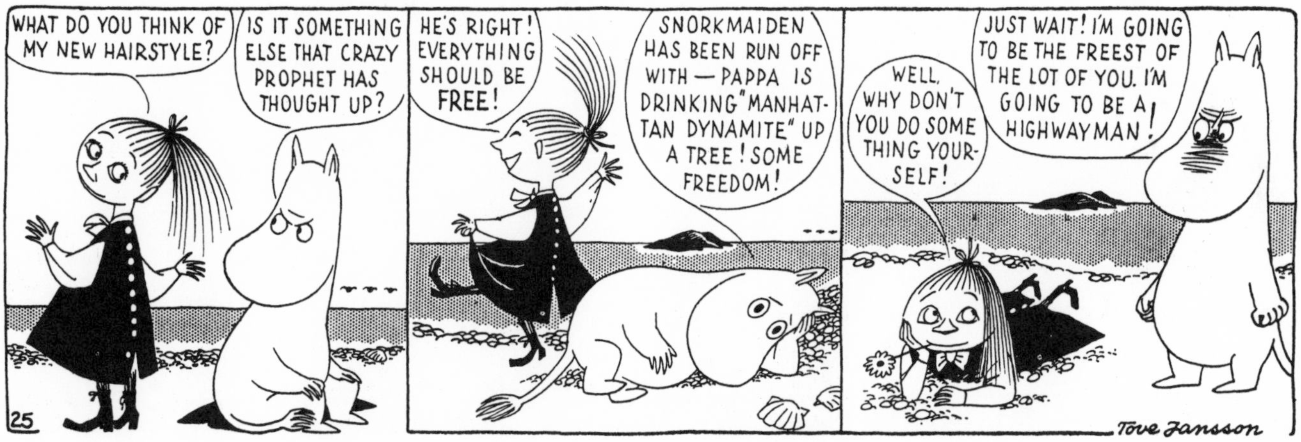
WHAT DO YOU THINK OF MY NEW HAIRSTYLE?
IS IT SOMETHING ELSE THAT CRAZY PROPHET HAS THOUGHT UP?
25
HE'S RIGHT! EVERYTHING SHOULD BE FREE!
SNORKMAIDEN HAS BEEN RUN OFF WITH — PAPPA IS DRINKING "MANHATTAN DYNAMITE" UP A TREE! SOME FREEDOM!
WELL, WHY DON'T YOU DO SOME THING YOURSELF!
JUST WAIT! I'M GOING TO BE THE FREEST OF THE LOT OF YOU. I'M GOING TO BE A HIGHWAYMAN!
Tove Jansson

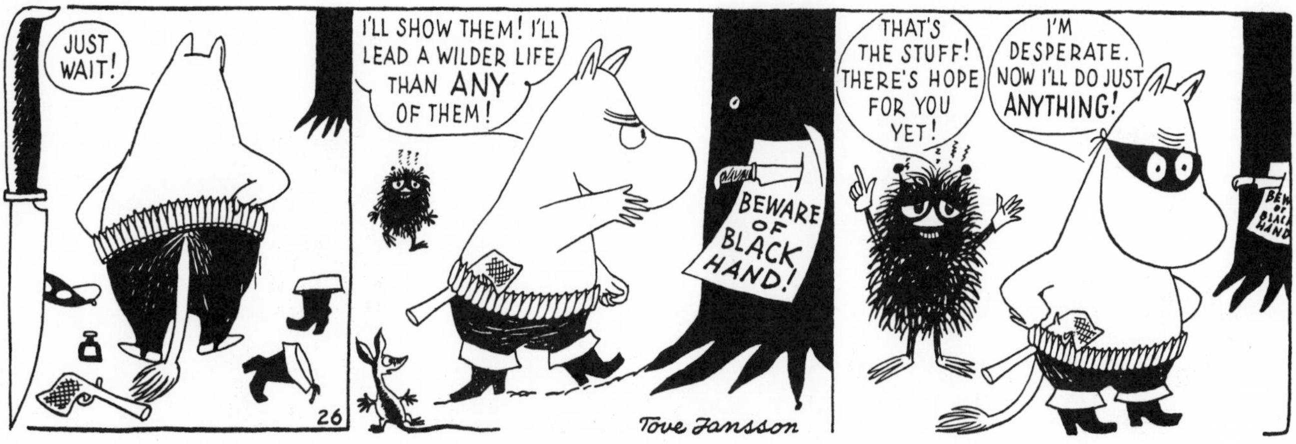
JUST WAIT!
26
I'LL SHOW THEM! I'LL LEAD A WILDER LIFE THAN ANY OF THEM!
BEWARE OF BLACK HAND!
THAT'S THE STUFF! THERE'S HOPE FOR YOU YET!
I'M DESPERATE. NOW I'LL DO JUST ANYTHING!
Tove Jansson

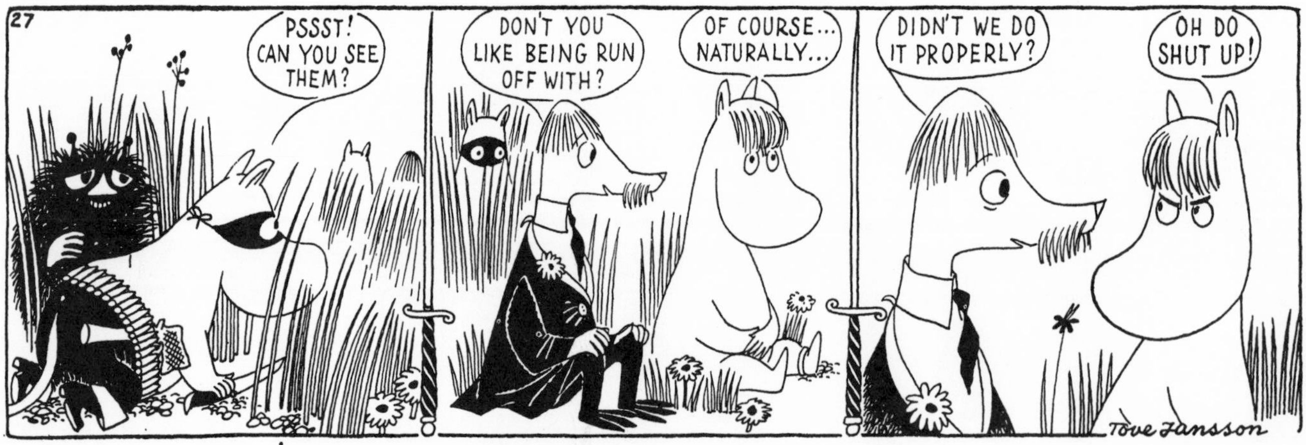
27
PSSST! CAN YOU SEE THEM?
DON'T YOU LIKE BEING RUN OFF WITH?
OF COURSE... NATURALLY...
DIDN'T WE DO IT PROPERLY?
OH DO SHUT UP!
Tove Jansson

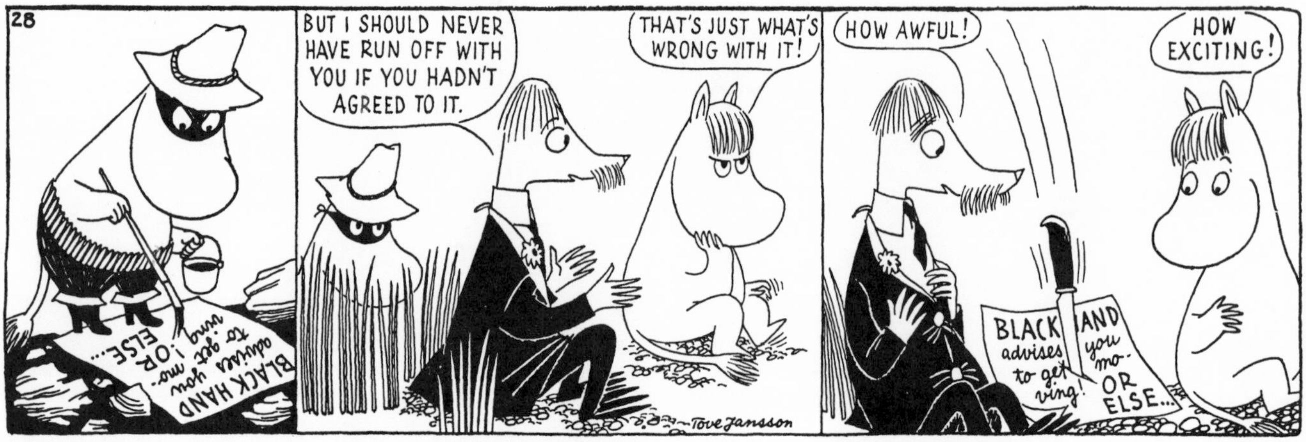
28
BUT I SHOULD NEVER HAVE RUN OFF WITH YOU IF YOU HADN'T AGREED TO IT.
THAT'S JUST WHAT'S WRONG WITH IT!
Tove Jansson
HOW AWFUL!
HOW EXCITING!
BLACK HAND advises you to get mo- ving! OR ELSE...

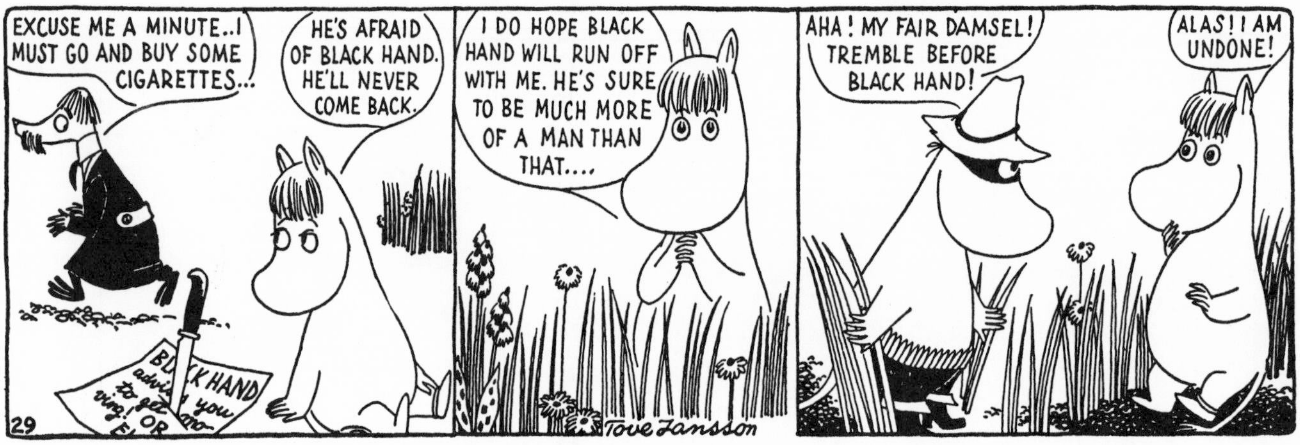
EXCUSE ME A MINUTE..I MUST GO AND BUY SOME CIGARETTES...
HE'S AFRAID OF BLACK HAND. HE'LL NEVER COME BACK.
29
I DO HOPE BLACK HAND WILL RUN OFF WITH ME. HE'S SURE TO BE MUCH MORE OF A MAN THAN THAT....
Tove Jansson
AHA! MY FAIR DAMSEL! TREMBLE BEFORE BLACK HAND!
ALAS!! I AM UNDONE!

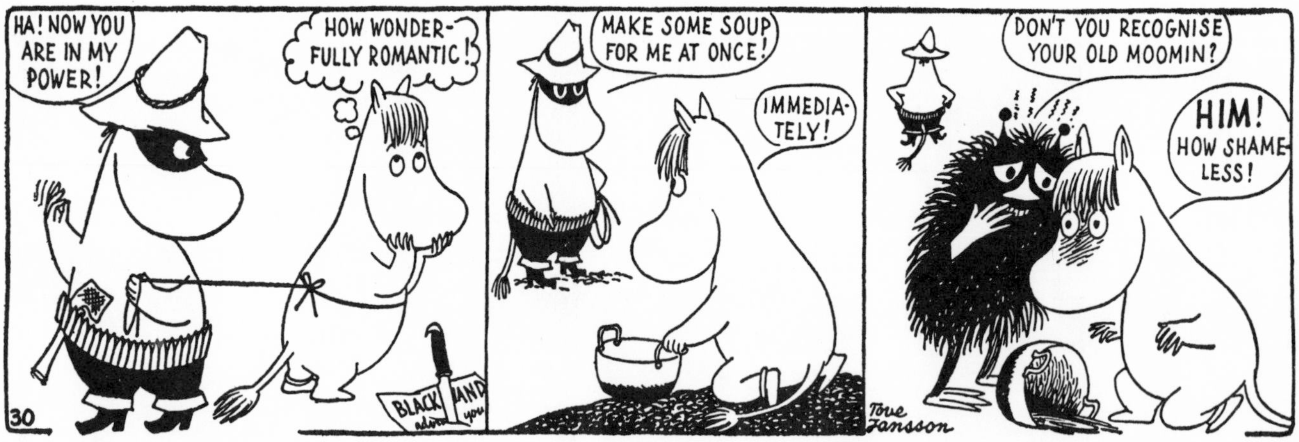
HA! NOW YOU ARE IN MY POWER!
HOW WONDER-FULLY ROMANTIC!
30
MAKE SOME SOUP FOR ME AT ONCE!
IMMEDIA-TELY!
DON'T YOU RECOGNISE YOUR OLD MOOMIN?
HIM! HOW SHAME-LESS!
Tove Jansson

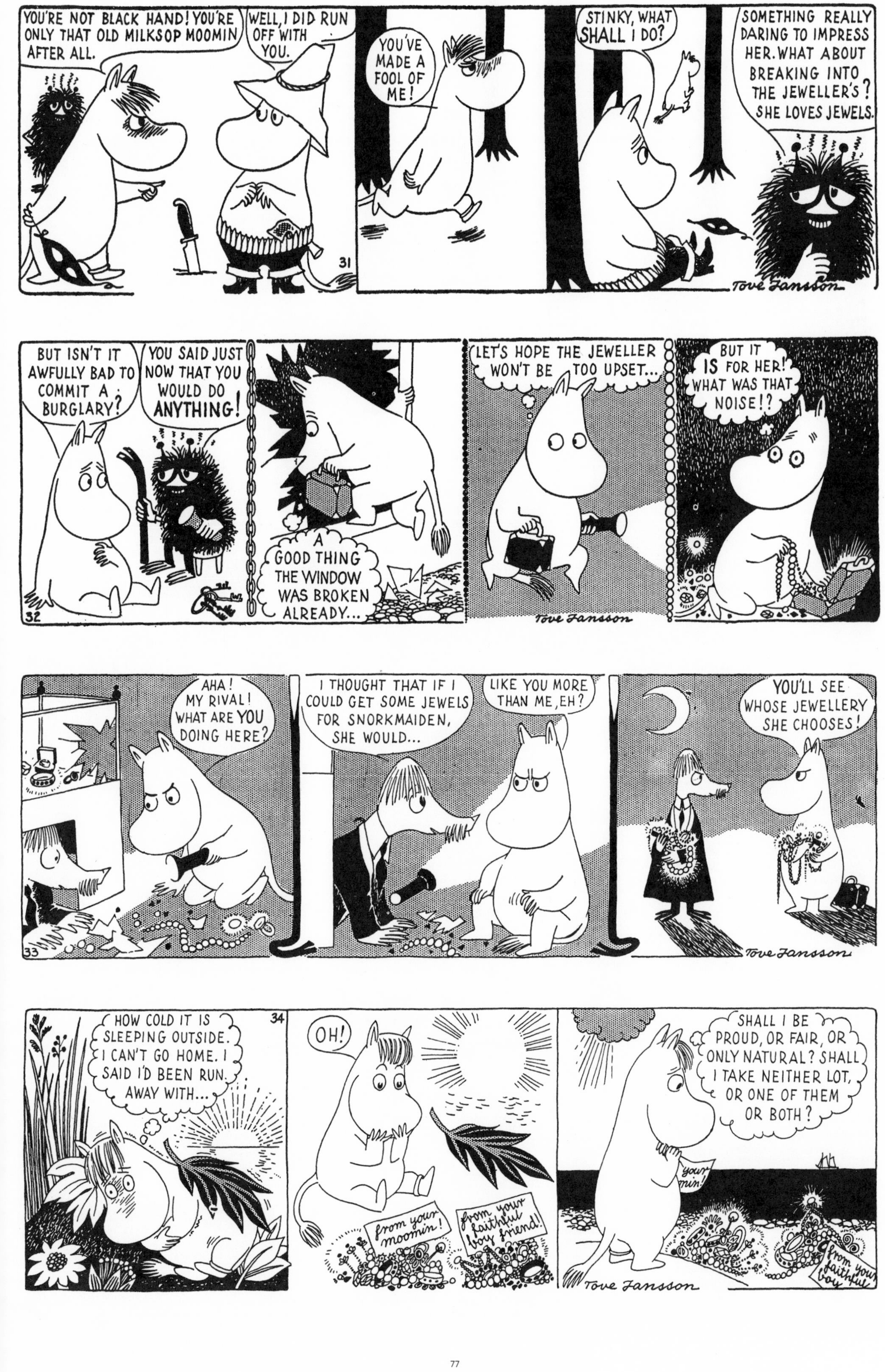
YOU'RE NOT BLACK HAND! YOU'RE ONLY THAT OLD MILKSOP MOOMIN AFTER ALL.
WELL, I DID RUN OFF WITH YOU.
31
YOU'VE MADE A FOOL OF ME!
STINKY, WHAT SHALL I DO?
SOMETHING REALLY DARING TO IMPRESS HER. WHAT ABOUT BREAKING INTO THE JEWELLER'S? SHE LOVES JEWELS.
Tove Jansson
BUT ISN'T IT AWFULLY BAD TO COMMIT A BURGLARY?
YOU SAID JUST NOW THAT YOU WOULD DO ANYTHING!
32
A GOOD THING THE WINDOW WAS BROKEN ALREADY...
LET'S HOPE THE JEWELLER WON'T BE TOO UPSET...
Tove Jansson
BUT IT IS FOR HER! WHAT WAS THAT NOISE!?
AHA! MY RIVAL! WHAT ARE YOU DOING HERE?
33
I THOUGHT THAT IF I COULD GET SOME JEWELS FOR SNORKMAIDEN, SHE WOULD...
LIKE YOU MORE THAN ME, EH?
YOU'LL SEE WHOSE JEWELLERY SHE CHOOSES!
Tove Jansson
HOW COLD IT IS SLEEPING OUTSIDE. I CAN'T GO HOME. I SAID I'D BEEN RUN AWAY WITH...
34
OH!
from your moomin!
from your faithful boy friend!
SHALL I BE PROUD, OR FAIR, OR ONLY NATURAL? SHALL I TAKE NEITHER LOT, OR ONE OF THEM OR BOTH?
your min!
from your faithful boy
Tove Jansson

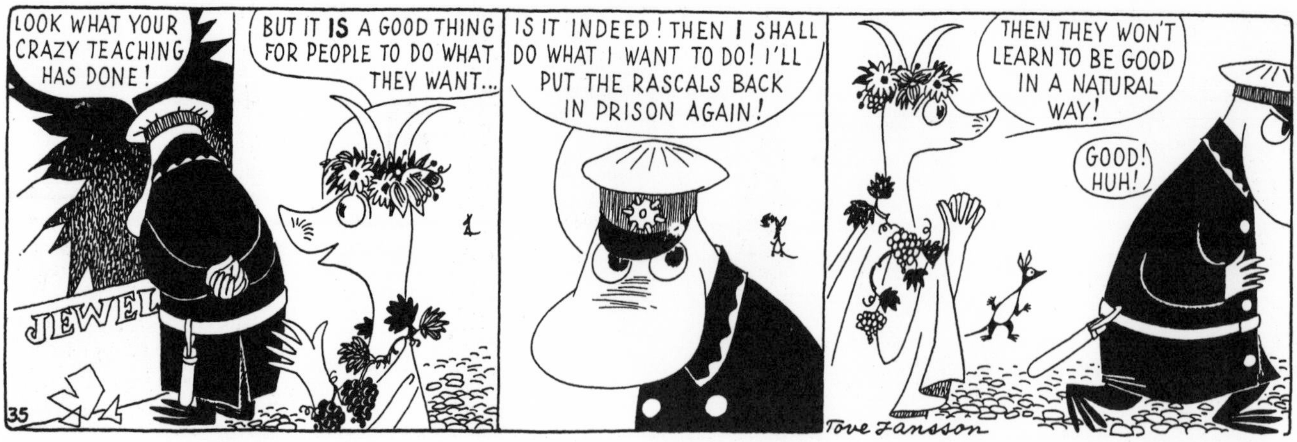
LOOK WHAT YOUR CRAZY TEACHING HAS DONE!
JEWEL
BUT IT IS A GOOD THING FOR PEOPLE TO DO WHAT THEY WANT...
IS IT INDEED! THEN I SHALL DO WHAT I WANT TO DO! I'LL PUT THE RASCALS BACK IN PRISON AGAIN!
THEN THEY WON'T LEARN TO BE GOOD IN A NATURAL WAY!
GOOD! HUH!
Tove Jansson

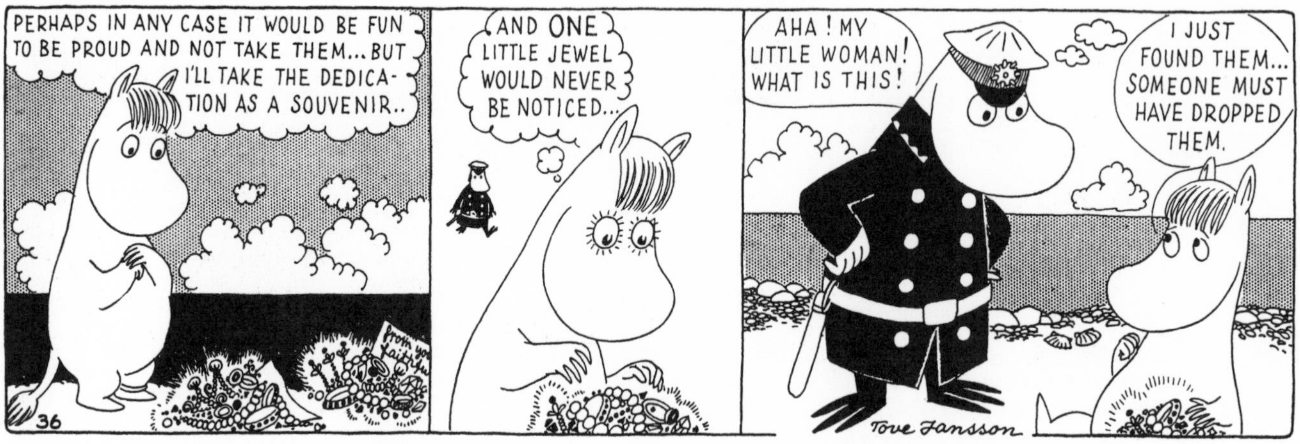
PERHAPS IN ANY CASE IT WOULD BE FUN TO BE PROUD AND NOT TAKE THEM... BUT I'LL TAKE THE DEDICATION AS A SOUVENIR..
AND ONE LITTLE JEWEL WOULD NEVER BE NOTICED...
AHA! MY LITTLE WOMAN! WHAT IS THIS!
I JUST FOUND THEM... SOMEONE MUST HAVE DROPPED THEM.
Tove Jansson

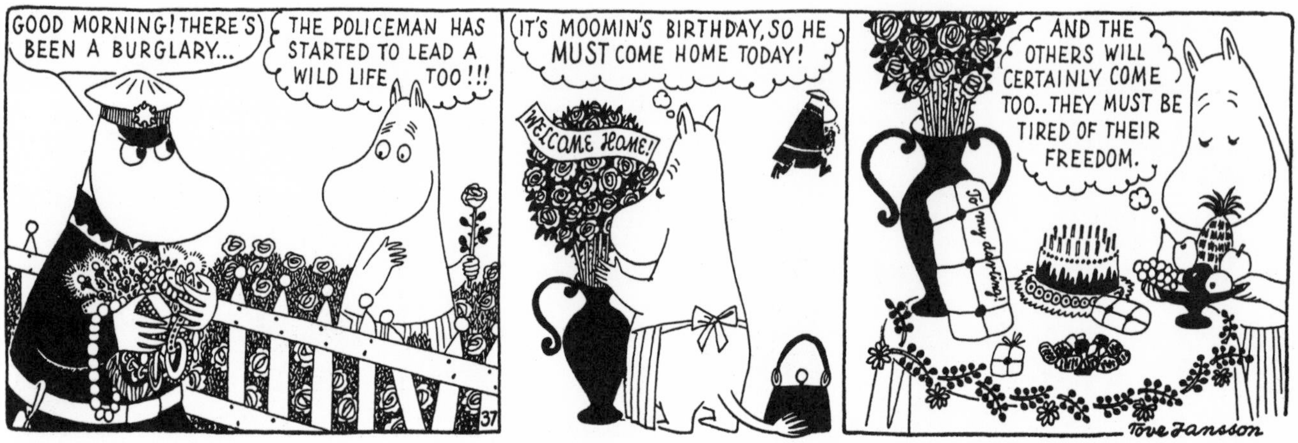
GOOD MORNING! THERE'S BEEN A BURGLARY...
THE POLICEMAN HAS STARTED TO LEAD A WILD LIFE TOO!!!
IT'S MOOMIN'S BIRTHDAY, SO HE MUST COME HOME TODAY!
WELCOME HOME!
AND THE OTHERS WILL CERTAINLY COME TOO.. THEY MUST BE TIRED OF THEIR FREEDOM.
To my darling!
Tove Jansson

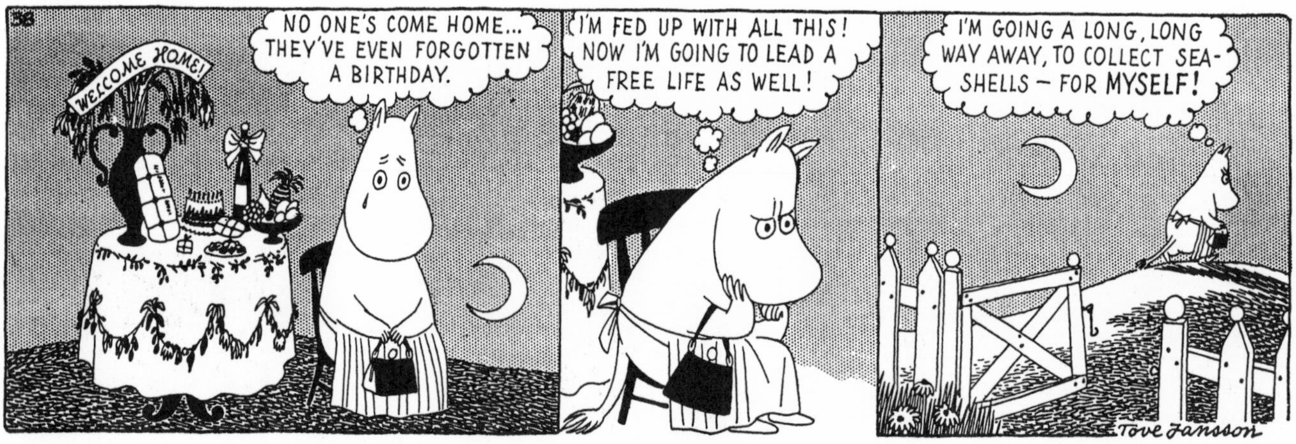
WELCOME HOME!
NO ONE'S COME HOME... THEY'VE EVEN FORGOTTEN A BIRTHDAY.
I'M FED UP WITH ALL THIS! NOW I'M GOING TO LEAD A FREE LIFE AS WELL!
I'M GOING A LONG, LONG WAY AWAY, TO COLLECT SEA-SHELLS — FOR MYSELF!
Tove Jansson

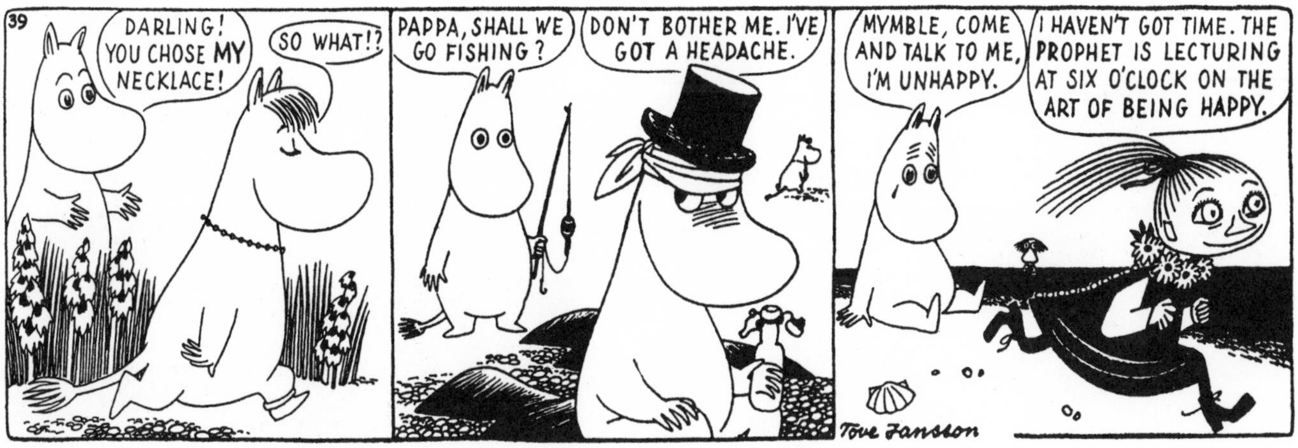
39
DARLING! YOU CHOSE MY NECKLACE!
SO WHAT!?
PAPPA, SHALL WE GO FISHING?
DON'T BOTHER ME. I'VE GOT A HEADACHE.
MYMBLE, COME AND TALK TO ME, I'M UNHAPPY.
I HAVEN'T GOT TIME. THE PROPHET IS LECTURING AT SIX O'CLOCK ON THE ART OF BEING HAPPY.
Tove Jansson

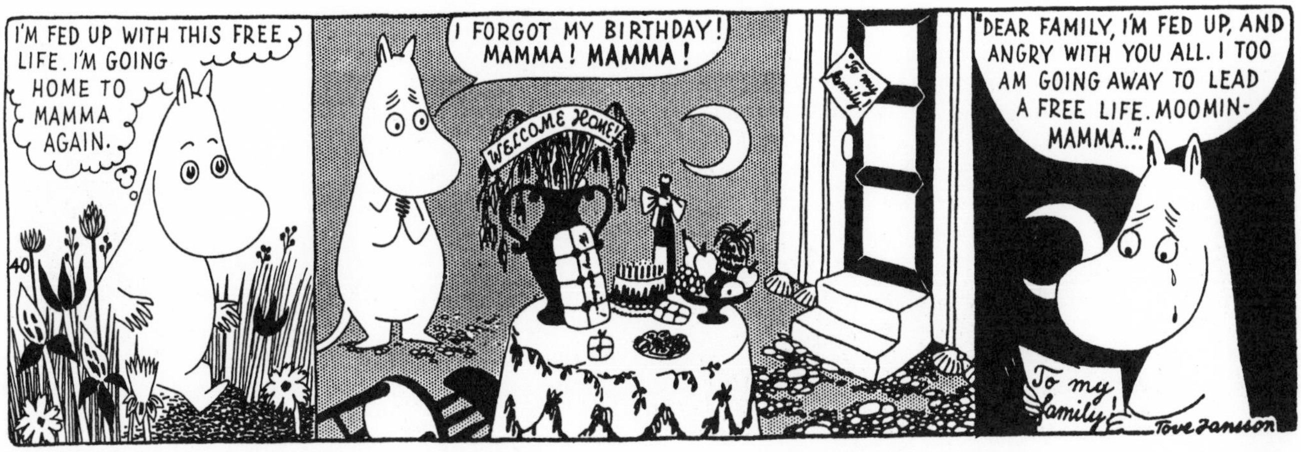
40
I'M FED UP WITH THIS FREE LIFE. I'M GOING HOME TO MAMMA AGAIN.
I FORGOT MY BIRTHDAY! MAMMA! MAMMA!
WELCOME HOME!
To my family
"DEAR FAMILY, I'M FED UP, AND ANGRY WITH YOU ALL. I TOO AM GOING AWAY TO LEAD A FREE LIFE. MOOMIN-MAMMA.."
To my family!
Tove Jansson

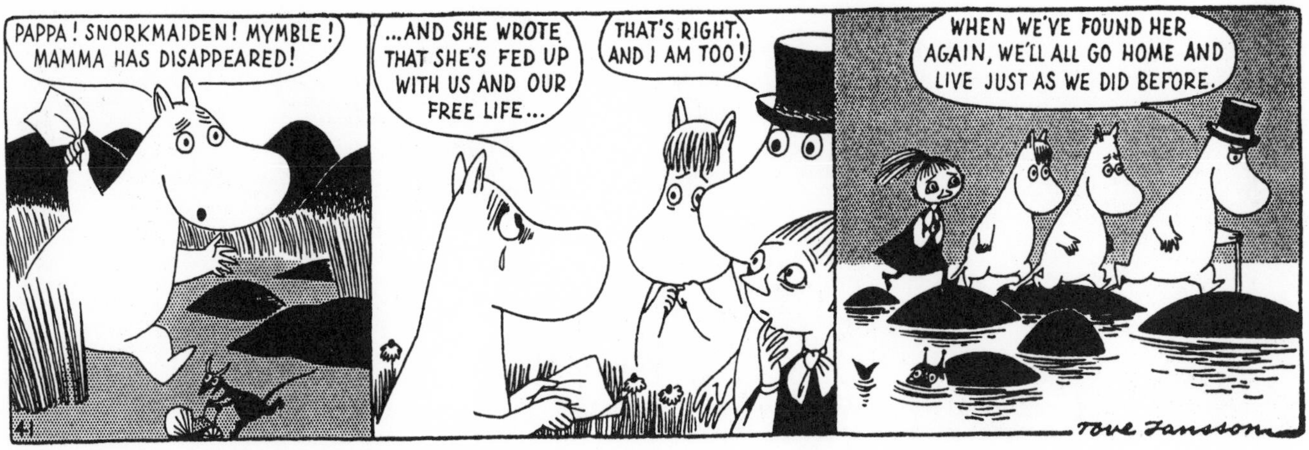
41
PAPPA! SNORKMAIDEN! MYMBLE! MAMMA HAS DISAPPEARED!
...AND SHE WROTE THAT SHE'S FED UP WITH US AND OUR FREE LIFE...
THAT'S RIGHT, AND I AM TOO!
WHEN WE'VE FOUND HER AGAIN, WE'LL ALL GO HOME AND LIVE JUST AS WE DID BEFORE.
Tove Jansson

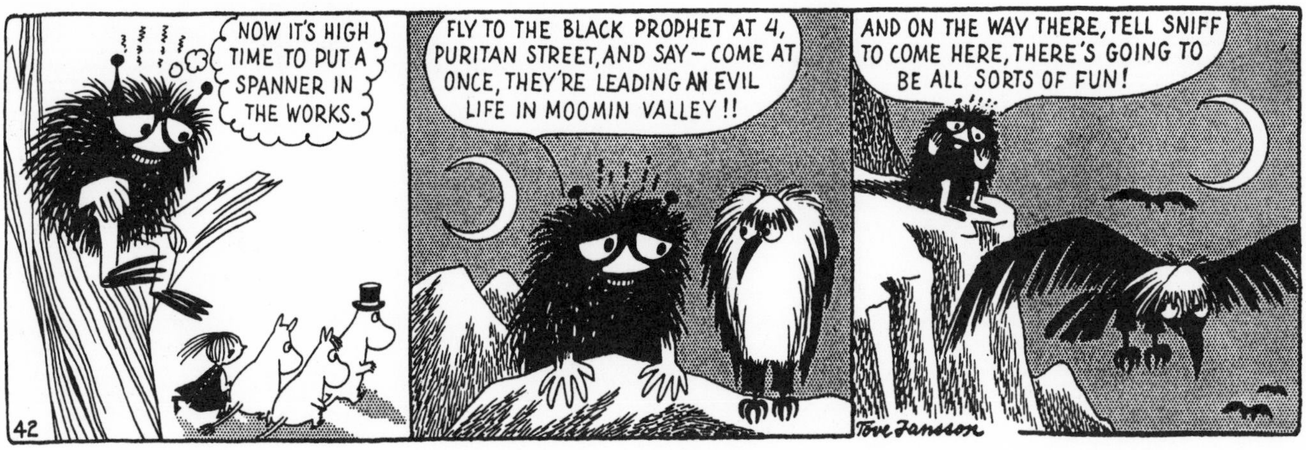
42
NOW IT'S HIGH TIME TO PUT A SPANNER IN THE WORKS.
FLY TO THE BLACK PROPHET AT 4, PURITAN STREET, AND SAY – COME AT ONCE, THEY'RE LEADING AN EVIL LIFE IN MOOMIN VALLEY!!
AND ON THE WAY THERE, TELL SNIFF TO COME HERE, THERE'S GOING TO BE ALL SORTS OF FUN!
Tove Jansson

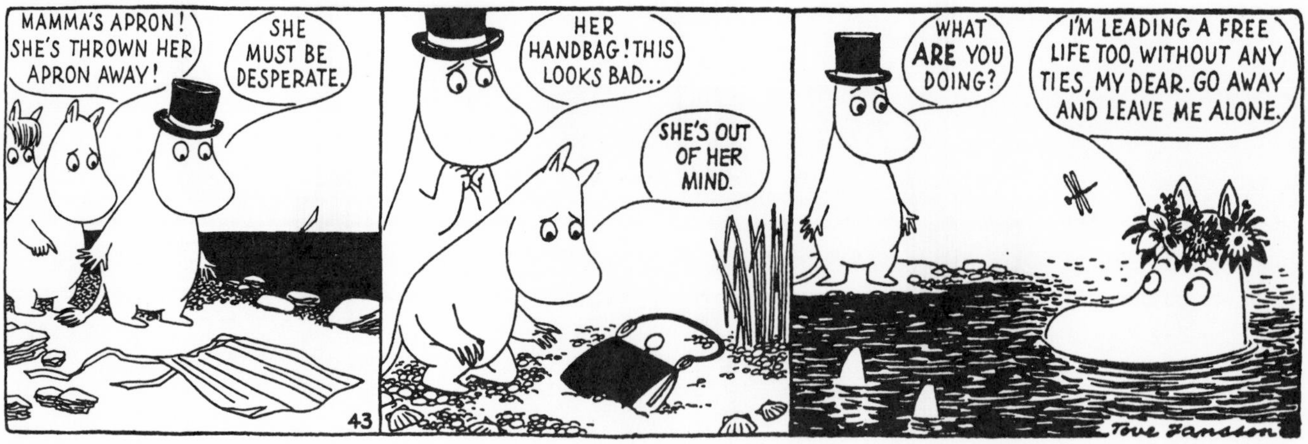
MAMMA'S APRON! SHE'S THROWN HER APRON AWAY!
SHE MUST BE DESPERATE.
43
HER HANDBAG! THIS LOOKS BAD...
SHE'S OUT OF HER MIND.
WHAT ARE YOU DOING?
I'M LEADING A FREE LIFE TOO, WITHOUT ANY TIES, MY DEAR. GO AWAY AND LEAVE ME ALONE.
Tove Jansson

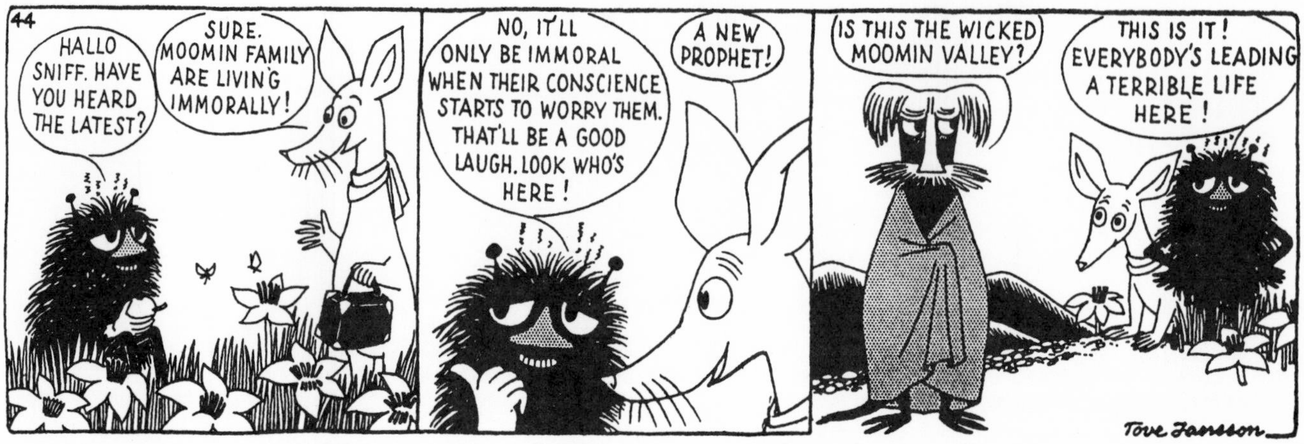
44
HALLO SNIFF. HAVE YOU HEARD THE LATEST?
SURE. MOOMIN FAMILY ARE LIVING IMMORALLY!
NO, IT'LL ONLY BE IMMORAL WHEN THEIR CONSCIENCE STARTS TO WORRY THEM. THAT'LL BE A GOOD LAUGH. LOOK WHO'S HERE!
A NEW PROPHET!
IS THIS THE WICKED MOOMIN VALLEY?
THIS IS IT! EVERYBODY'S LEADING A TERRIBLE LIFE HERE!
Tove Jansson

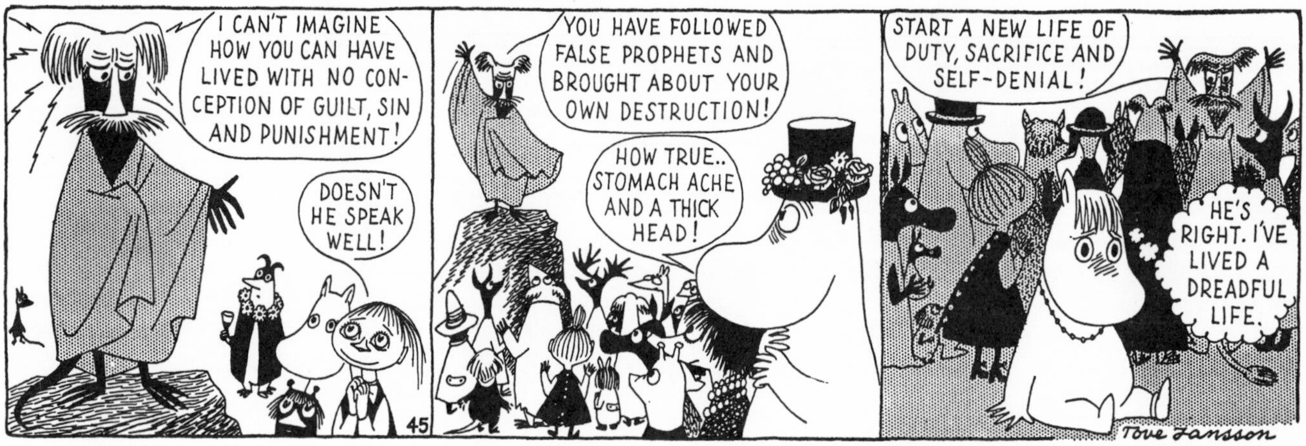
I CAN'T IMAGINE HOW YOU CAN HAVE LIVED WITH NO CONCEPTION OF GUILT, SIN AND PUNISHMENT!
DOESN'T HE SPEAK WELL!
45
YOU HAVE FOLLOWED FALSE PROPHETS AND BROUGHT ABOUT YOUR OWN DESTRUCTION!
HOW TRUE.. STOMACH ACHE AND A THICK HEAD!
START A NEW LIFE OF DUTY, SACRIFICE AND SELF-DENIAL!
HE'S RIGHT. I'VE LIVED A DREADFUL LIFE.
Tove Jansson

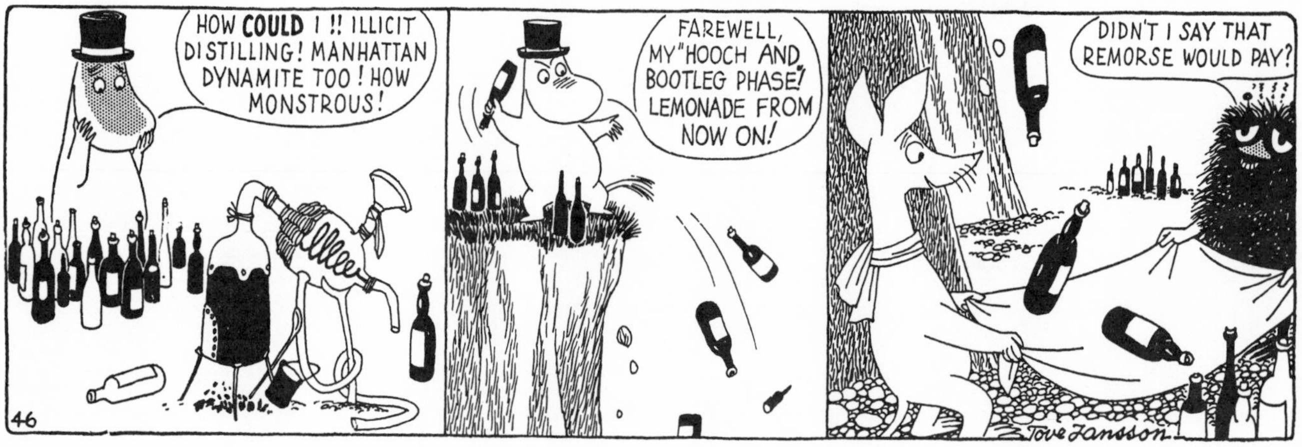
HOW COULD I !! ILLICIT DISTILLING! MANHATTAN DYNAMITE TOO! HOW MONSTROUS!
46
FAREWELL, MY "HOOCH AND BOOTLEG PHASE"! LEMONADE FROM NOW ON!
DIDN'T I SAY THAT REMORSE WOULD PAY?
Tove Jansson

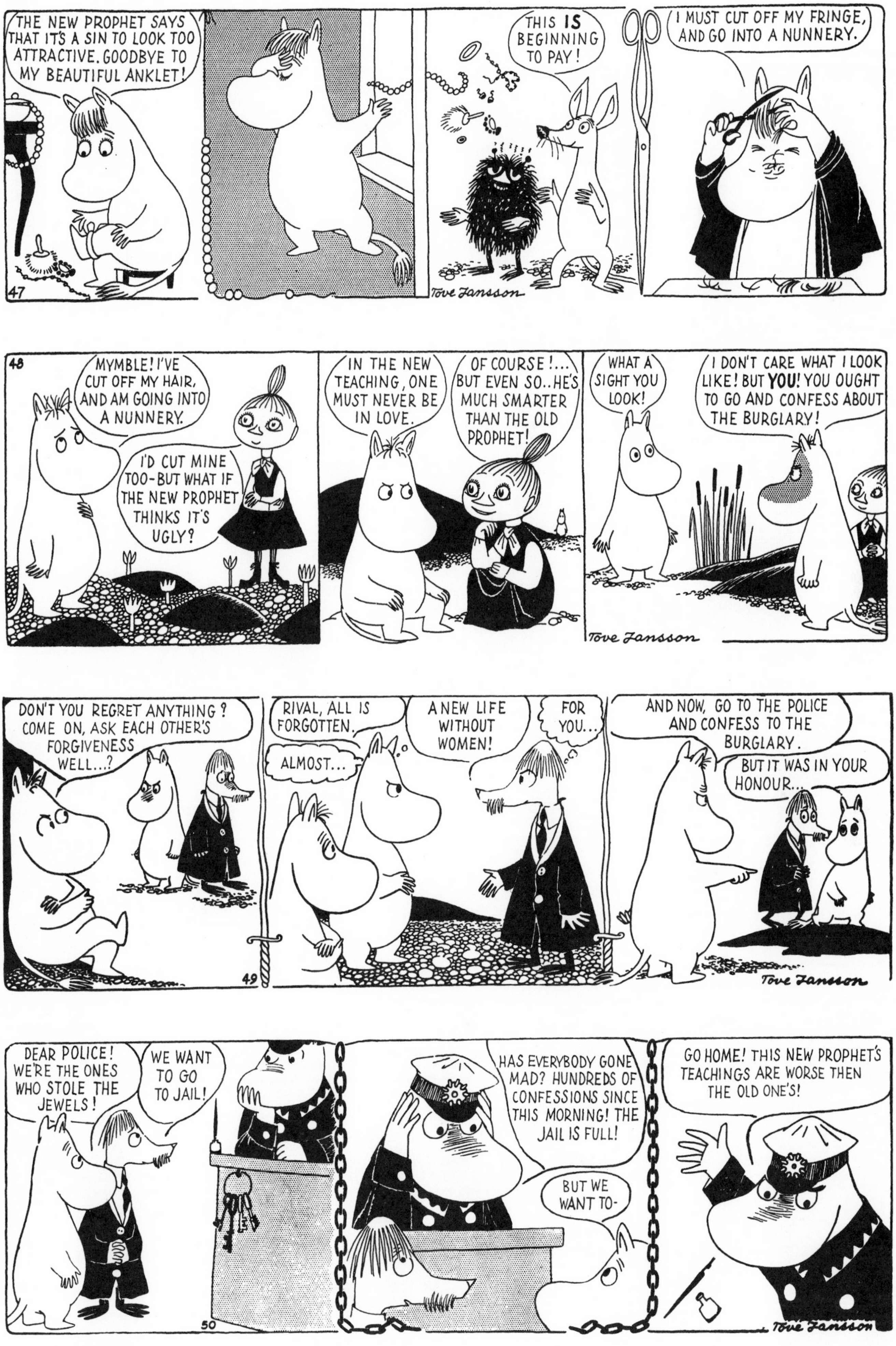
47
THE NEW PROPHET SAYS THAT IT'S A SIN TO LOOK TOO ATTRACTIVE. GOODBYE TO MY BEAUTIFUL ANKLET!
THIS IS BEGINNING TO PAY!
Tove Jansson
I MUST CUT OFF MY FRINGE, AND GO INTO A NUNNERY.
48
MYMBLE! I'VE CUT OFF MY HAIR, AND AM GOING INTO A NUNNERY.
I'D CUT MINE TOO-BUT WHAT IF THE NEW PROPHET THINKS IT'S UGLY?
IN THE NEW TEACHING, ONE MUST NEVER BE IN LOVE.
OF COURSE!... BUT EVEN SO..HE'S MUCH SMARTER THAN THE OLD PROPHET!
WHAT A SIGHT YOU LOOK!
I DON'T CARE WHAT I LOOK LIKE! BUT YOU! YOU OUGHT TO GO AND CONFESS ABOUT THE BURGLARY!
Tove Jansson
DON'T YOU REGRET ANYTHING? COME ON, ASK EACH OTHER'S FORGIVENESS
WELL...?
49
RIVAL, ALL IS FORGOTTEN.
ALMOST...
A NEW LIFE WITHOUT WOMEN!
FOR YOU...
AND NOW, GO TO THE POLICE AND CONFESS TO THE BURGLARY.
BUT IT WAS IN YOUR HONOUR...
Tove Jansson
DEAR POLICE! WE'RE THE ONES WHO STOLE THE JEWELS!
WE WANT TO GO TO JAIL!
50
HAS EVERYBODY GONE MAD? HUNDREDS OF CONFESSIONS SINCE THIS MORNING! THE JAIL IS FULL!
BUT WE WANT TO-
GO HOME! THIS NEW PROPHET'S TEACHINGS ARE WORSE THEN THE OLD ONE'S!
Tove Jansson

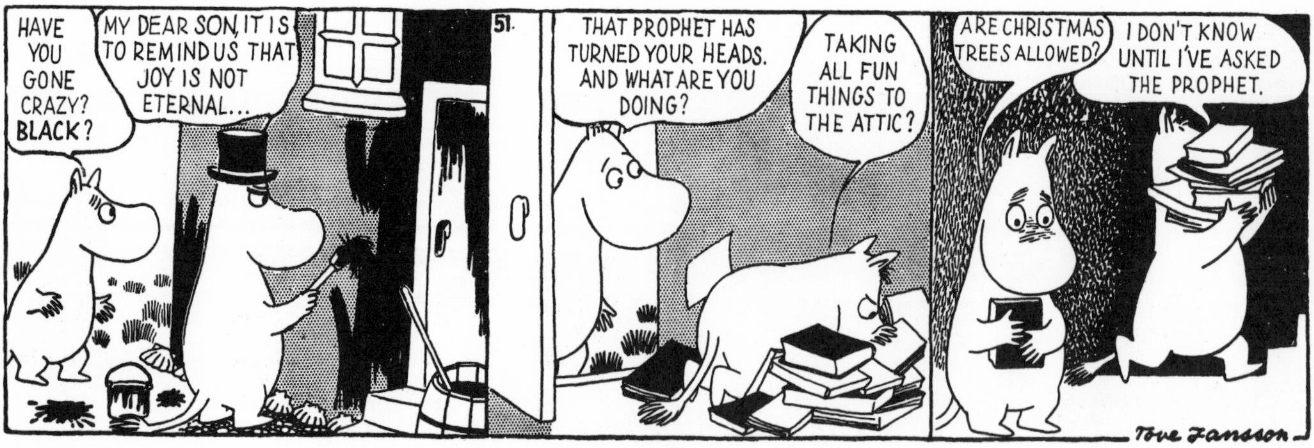
HAVE YOU GONE CRAZY? BLACK?
MY DEAR SON, IT IS TO REMIND US THAT JOY IS NOT ETERNAL...
51.
THAT PROPHET HAS TURNED YOUR HEADS. AND WHAT ARE YOU DOING?
TAKING ALL FUN THINGS TO THE ATTIC?
ARE CHRISTMAS TREES ALLOWED?
I DON'T KNOW UNTIL I'VE ASKED THE PROPHET.
Tove Jansson

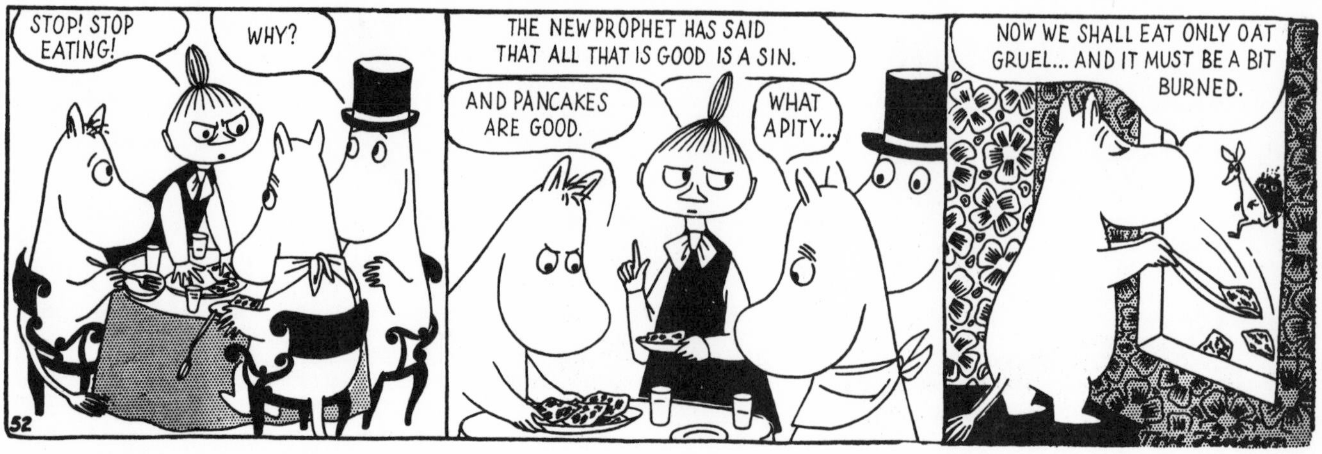
STOP! STOP EATING!
WHY?
52
THE NEW PROPHET HAS SAID THAT ALL THAT IS GOOD IS A SIN.
AND PANCAKES ARE GOOD.
WHAT A PITY...
NOW WE SHALL EAT ONLY OAT GRUEL... AND IT MUST BE A BIT BURNED.

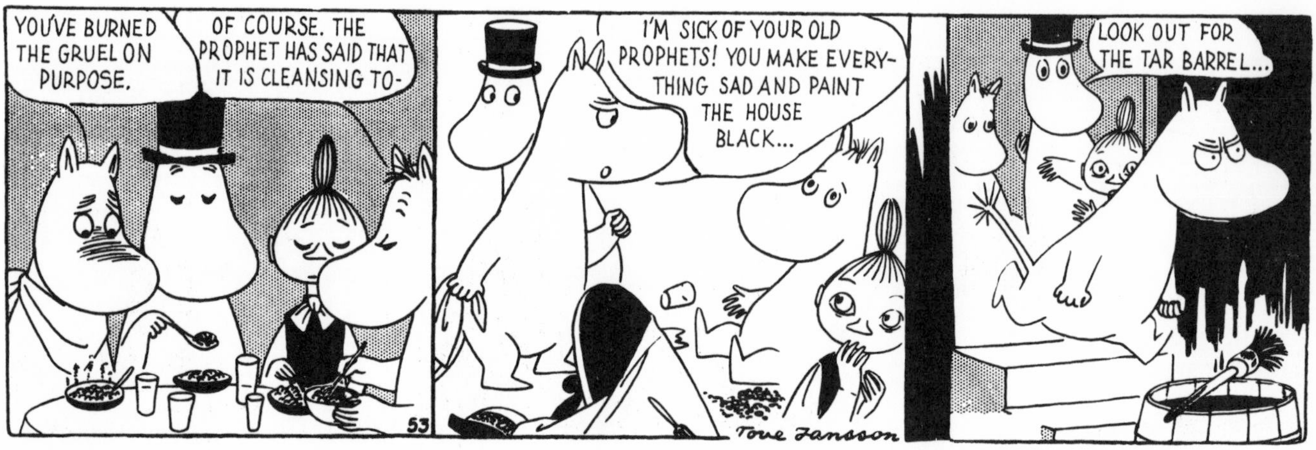
YOU'VE BURNED THE GRUEL ON PURPOSE.
OF COURSE. THE PROPHET HAS SAID THAT IT IS CLEANSING TO-
53
I'M SICK OF YOUR OLD PROPHETS! YOU MAKE EVERYTHING SAD AND PAINT THE HOUSE BLACK...
Tove Jansson
LOOK OUT FOR THE TAR BARREL...

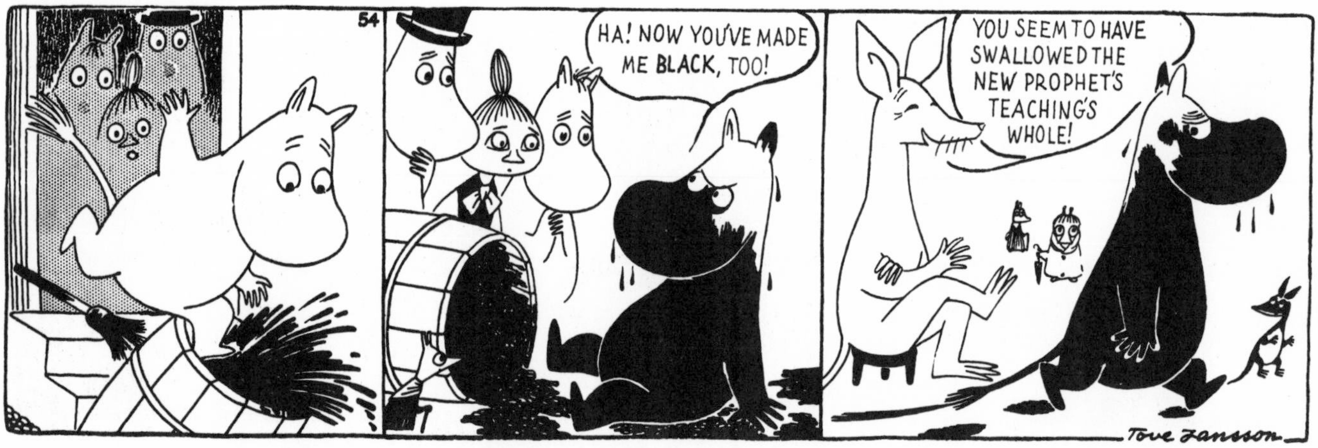
54
HA! NOW YOU'VE MADE ME BLACK, TOO!
YOU SEEM TO HAVE SWALLOWED THE NEW PROPHET'S TEACHINGS WHOLE!
Tove Jansson

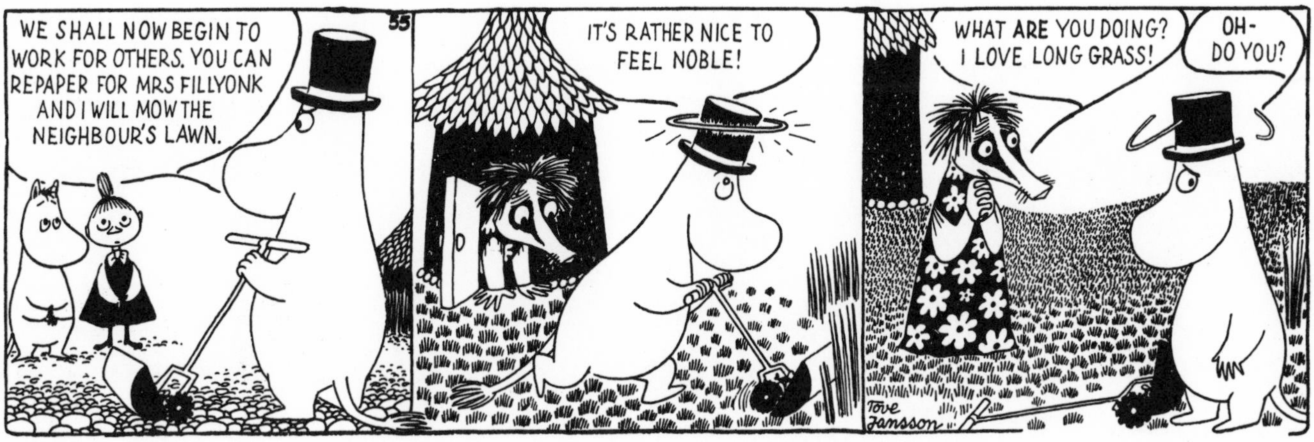
55
WE SHALL NOW BEGIN TO WORK FOR OTHERS. YOU CAN REPAPER FOR MRS FILLYONK AND I WILL MOW THE NEIGHBOUR'S LAWN.
IT'S RATHER NICE TO FEEL NOBLE!
WHAT **ARE** YOU DOING? I LOVE LONG GRASS!
OH- DO YOU?
Tove Jansson

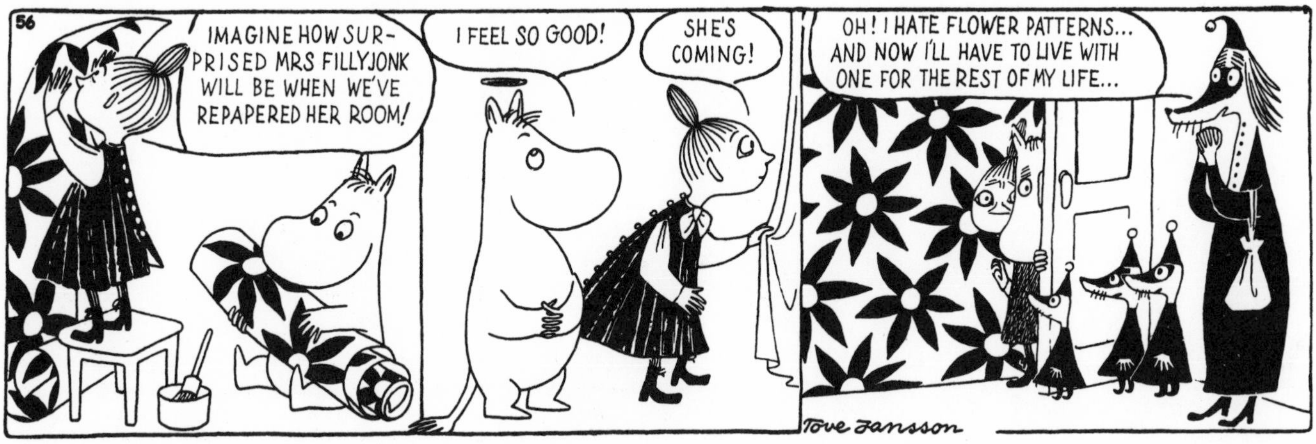
56
IMAGINE HOW SURPRISED MRS FILLYJONK WILL BE WHEN WE'VE REPAPERED HER ROOM!
I FEEL SO GOOD!
SHE'S COMING!
OH! I HATE FLOWER PATTERNS... AND NOW I'LL HAVE TO LIVE WITH ONE FOR THE REST OF MY LIFE...
Tove Jansson

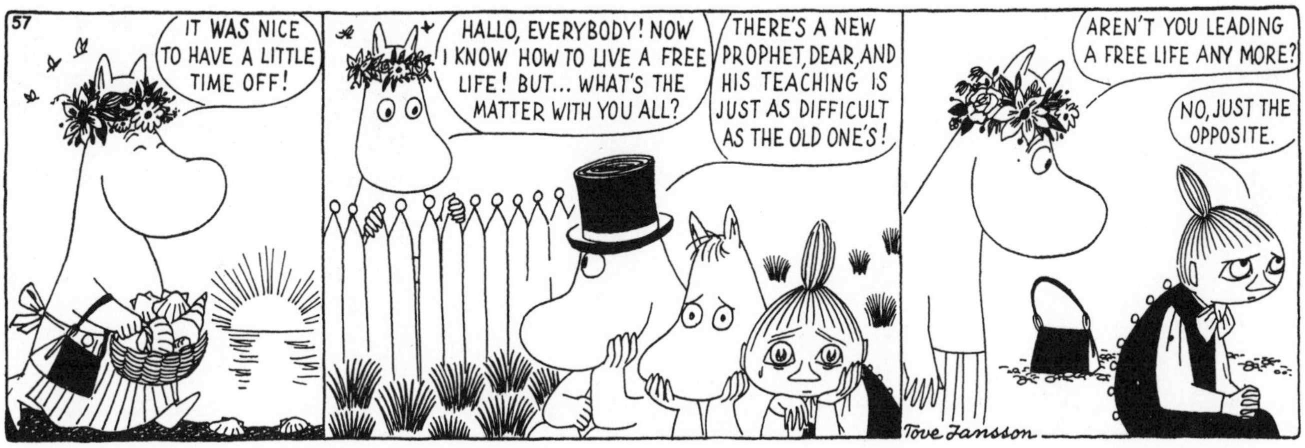
57
IT **WAS** NICE TO HAVE A LITTLE TIME OFF!
HALLO, EVERYBODY! NOW I KNOW HOW TO LIVE A FREE LIFE! BUT... WHAT'S THE MATTER WITH YOU ALL?
THERE'S A NEW PROPHET, DEAR, AND HIS TEACHING IS JUST AS DIFFICULT AS THE OLD ONE'S!
AREN'T YOU LEADING A FREE LIFE ANY MORE?
NO, JUST THE OPPOSITE.
Tove Jansson

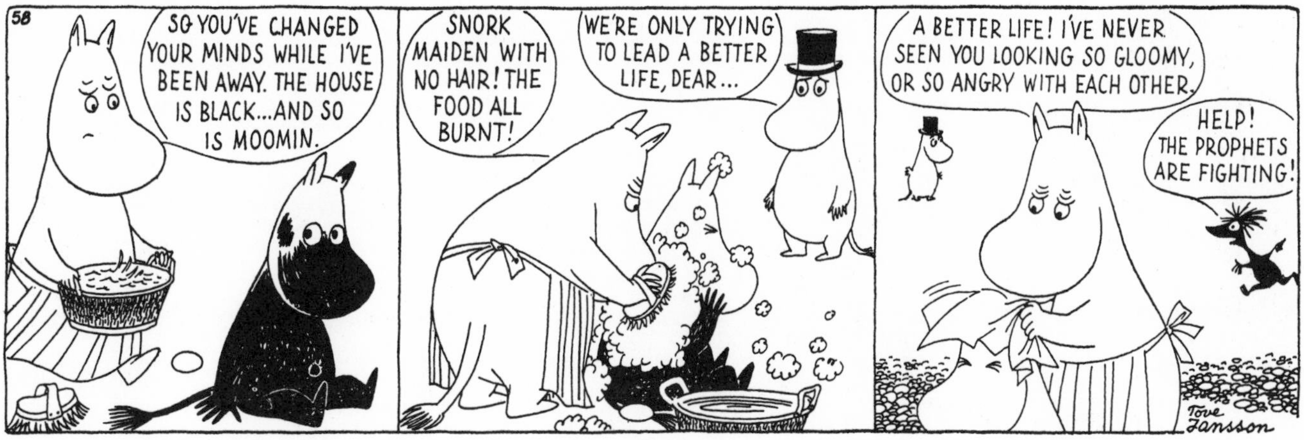
58
SO YOU'VE CHANGED YOUR MINDS WHILE I'VE BEEN AWAY. THE HOUSE IS BLACK...AND SO IS MOOMIN.
SNORK MAIDEN WITH NO HAIR! THE FOOD ALL BURNT!
WE'RE ONLY TRYING TO LEAD A BETTER LIFE, DEAR...
A BETTER LIFE! I'VE NEVER SEEN YOU LOOKING SO GLOOMY, OR SO ANGRY WITH EACH OTHER.
HELP! THE PROPHETS ARE FIGHTING!
Tove Jansson

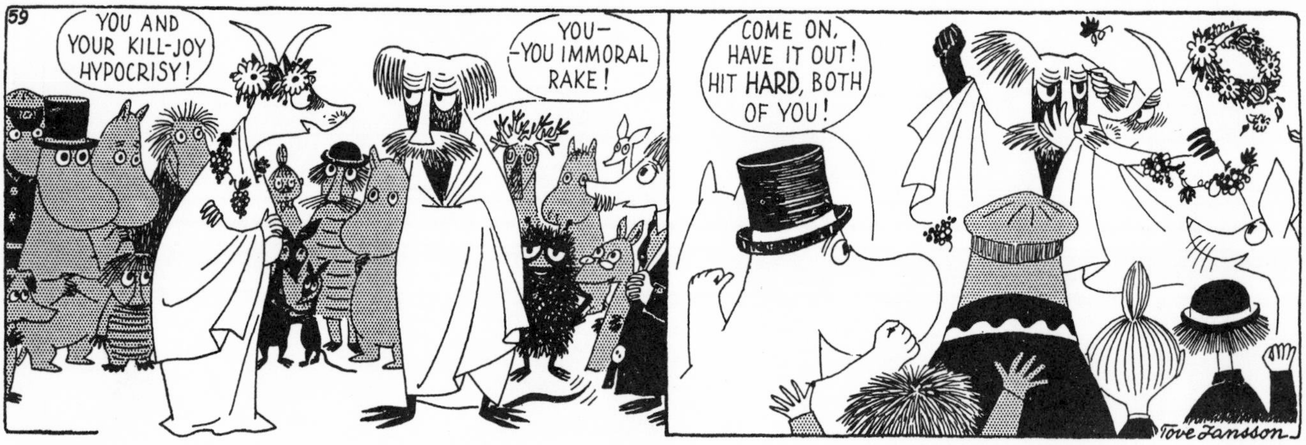
59
YOU AND YOUR KILL-JOY HYPOCRISY!
YOU— -YOU IMMORAL RAKE!
COME ON, HAVE IT OUT! HIT HARD, BOTH OF YOU!
Tove Jansson

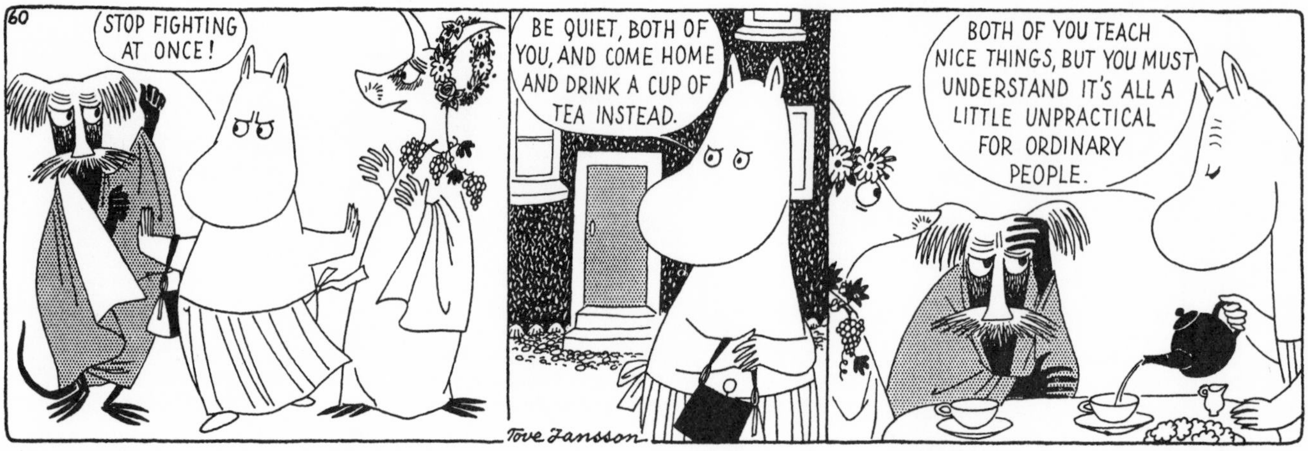
60
STOP FIGHTING AT ONCE!
Tove Jansson
BE QUIET, BOTH OF YOU, AND COME HOME AND DRINK A CUP OF TEA INSTEAD.
BOTH OF YOU TEACH NICE THINGS, BUT YOU MUST UNDERSTAND IT'S ALL A LITTLE UNPRACTICAL FOR ORDINARY PEOPLE.

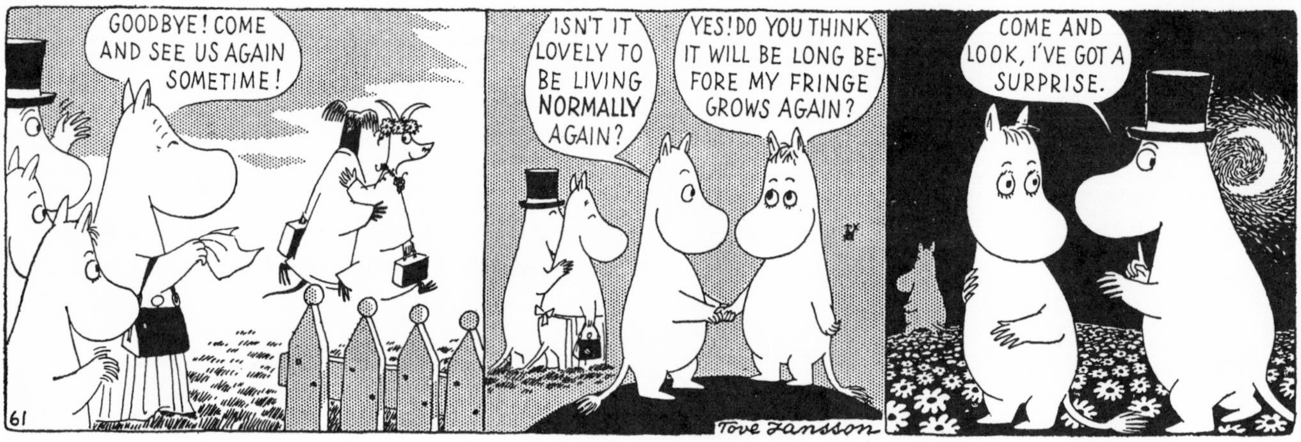
GOODBYE! COME AND SEE US AGAIN SOMETIME!
61
ISN'T IT LOVELY TO BE LIVING NORMALLY AGAIN?
YES! DO YOU THINK IT WILL BE LONG BEFORE MY FRINGE GROWS AGAIN?
Tove Jansson
COME AND LOOK, I'VE GOT A SURPRISE.

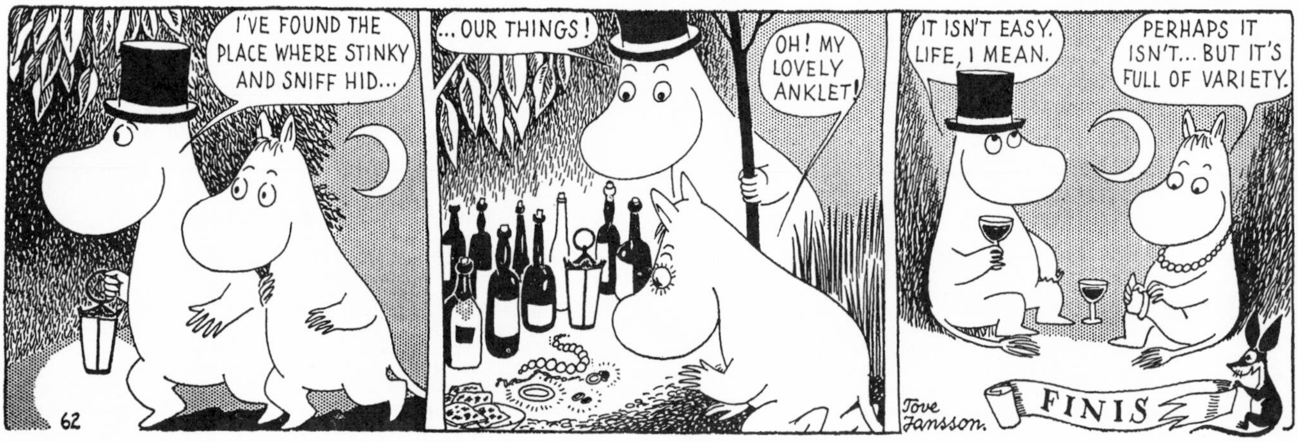
I'VE FOUND THE PLACE WHERE STINKY AND SNIFF HID...
62
...OUR THINGS!
OH! MY LOVELY ANKLET!
IT ISN'T EASY. LIFE, I MEAN.
PERHAPS IT ISN'T... BUT IT'S FULL OF VARIETY.
Tove Jansson.
FINIS

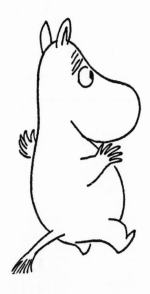

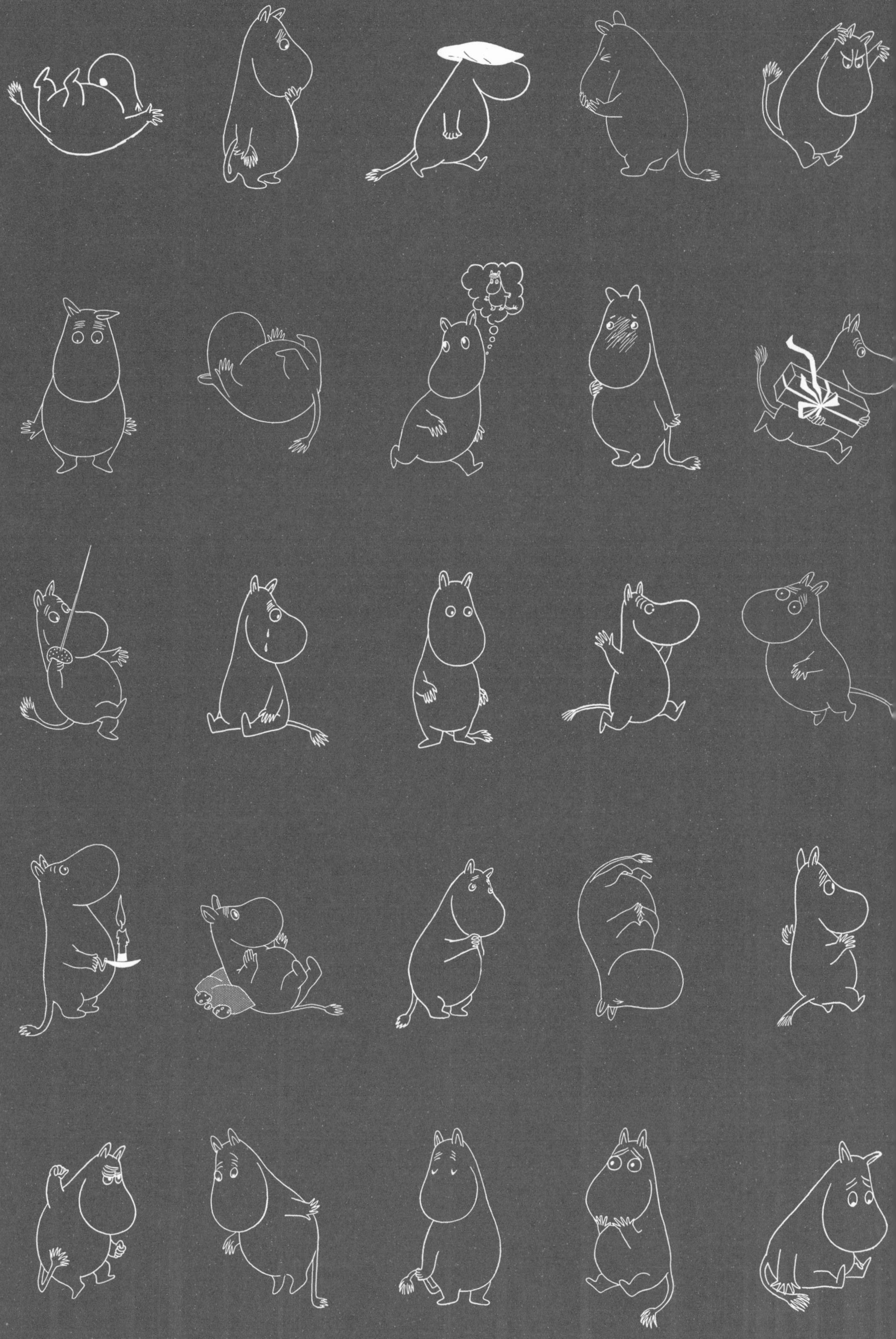